Antike und Abendland

Antike und Abendland

Beiträge zum Verständnis der Griechen und Römer
und ihres Nachlebens

herausgegeben von

Werner von Koppenfels · Helmut Krasser
Wilhelm Kühlmann · Christoph Riedweg · Ernst A. Schmidt
Wolfgang Schuller · Rainer Stillers

Band LII

2006

Walter de Gruyter · Berlin · New York

Manuskripteinsendungen werden an die folgenden Herausgeber erbeten: Prof. Dr. Werner von Koppenfels, Boberweg 18, 81929 München – Prof. Dr. Helmut Krasser, Institut für Altertumswissenschaften, Universität, Otto-Behaghel-Str. 10, Haus G, 35394 Gießen – Prof. Dr. Wilhelm Kühlmann, Universität Heidelberg, Germanistisches Seminar, Hauptstr. 207–209, 69117 Heidelberg – Prof. Dr. Christoph Riedweg, Kluseggstr. 18, CH-8032 Zürich – Prof. Dr. Ernst A. Schmidt, Philologisches Seminar, Universität, Wilhelmstr. 36, 72074 Tübingen – Prof. Dr. Wolfgang Schuller, Philosophische Fakultät, Universität, Postfach 5560, 78434 Konstanz – Prof. Dr. Rainer Stillers, Institut für Romanische Philologie der Philipps-Universität Marburg, Wilhelm-Köpke-Str. 6D, 35032 Marburg. *Korrekturen und Korrespondenz, die das Manuskript und den Druck betrifft*, sind an den Schriftleiter Prof. Dr. Helmut Krasser zu richten.

Buchbesprechungen werden nicht aufgenommen; zugesandte Rezensionsexemplare können nicht zurückgeschickt werden.

ISBN-13 (Print): 978-3-11-018634-5
ISBN-10 (Print): 3-11-018634-9
ISBN-13 (Online): 978-3-11-018635-2
ISBN-10 (Online): 3-11-018635-7
ISBN-13 (Print + Online): 978-3-11-018636-9
ISBN-10 (Print + Online): 3-11-018636-5

ISSN 0003-5696

Bibliografische Information der Deutschen Nationalbibliothek

Die Deutsche Nationalbibliothek verzeichnet diese Publikation in der Deutschen Nationalbibliografie; detaillierte bibliografische Daten sind im Internet über http://dnb.d-nb.de abrufbar.

© Copyright 2006 by Walter de Gruyter GmbH & Co. KG, D-10785 Berlin

Dieses Werk einschließlich aller seiner Teile ist urheberrechtlich geschützt. Jede Verwertung außerhalb der engen Grenzen des Urheberrechtsgesetzes ist ohne Zustimmung des Verlages unzulässig und strafbar. Das gilt insbesondere für Vervielfältigungen, Übersetzungen, Mikroverfilmungen und die Einspeicherung und Verarbeitung in elektronischen Systemen.

Printed in Germany
Satz: Dörlemann Satz, 49448 Lemförde

Inhaltsverzeichnis

Michael Lurje, Göttingen
   Misreading Sophocles: or Why Does the History of Interpretation Matter? . . .   1

Ivana Petrovic, Durham
   Delusions of Grandeur: Homer, Zeus and the Telchines in
   Callimachus' Reply (Aitia Fr. 1) and Iambus 6   16

Alexander Hardie, London
   The Aloades on Helicon: Music, Territory and Cosmic Order   42

Peter Habermehl, Berlin
   Quod crimen praeter amasse? Dido und das Hohelied der Liebe (Ovid *her. vii*)   72

Beate Czapla, Bonn
   Die Wandlung der Nereide Galatea von einer Kokotte zur Heiligen oder
   die Usurpation eines griechischen Mythos durch den Petrarkismus   95

Paul Barone, Offenburg
   Herakles in der Moderne. Zu Schillers Rezeption des antiken Mythos   126

Gunnar Hindrichs, Heidelberg
   Ein Wort des Äsop bei Hegel und bei Marx   142

Eugen Braun, Potsdam
   «Kultur-» und «Fachmenschentum». Altertumswissenschaftliche
   Marginalien zu Max Weber als Erzieher   147

Jan Cölln, Rostock
   Alexander der Große in Europa und Asien. Mythisierung von
   Geschichte und ihre Präsenz nach dem Ersten Weltkrieg   183

Mitarbeiter des Bandes

Dr. Paul Barone, Goldgasse 12, 77652 Offenburg

Dr. Eugen Braun, Universität Potsdam, Klassische Philologie, Am Neuen Palais 10, 14469 Potsdam

Dr. Jan Cölln, Institut für Germanistik, August-Bebel-Str. 28, 18055 Rostock

Dr. Beate Czapla, Institut für griechische und lateinische Philologie, Romanistik und Altamerikatistik, Abteilung für griechische und lateinische Philologie, Am Hof 1 e, 53113 Bonn

PD Dr. Peter Habermehl, Berlin-Brandenburgische-Akademie der Wissenschaften, Jägerstraße 22/23, 10117 Berlin

Dr. Alexander Hardie, Flat 561, Imperial Court, 225 Kennington Lane, London SE15QN

Dr. Gunnar Hindrichs, Philosophisches Seminar der Universität Heidelberg, Schulgasse 6, 69117 Heidelberg

Dr. Michael Lurje, Classics, School of History and Classics, The University of Edinburgh, David Hume Tower, George Square, Edinburgh EH8 9JX, Scotland

Dr. Ivana Petrovic, Department of Classics and Ancient History, Durham University, 38 North Bailey, Durham DH2 3EU, England

MICHAEL LURJE

Misreading Sophocles: or Why Does the History of Interpretation Matter?[1]

1. What do we know about the history of interpretation of Greek tragedy?

Ever since literary criticism has been invaded by a literary theory that declares the author dead while turning the reader into the proper subject of interpretation of the text he is reading, the flood of studies examining the reception of Greek tragedy in modern times has never ceased. Scholars have not grown tired of dealing with the different forms of the so called ‹productive› reception. In the 1960s, 1970s and 1980s, poetical imitation, adaptation and transformation of ancient models was at the centre of interest. Then in the 1990s, scholars started to look for different material and discovered forms of reception such as translation, film, and most of all, stage production of Greek tragedy. Greatly promoted by Oxford's ‹Archive of Performances of Greek and Roman Drama›, the performance history of Greek tragedy has become the central and most dominant topic in reception studies.

Amidst all the excitement about the ‹performative Turn› in the studies of Greek tragedy it is worthwhile to pause and wonder why we have always shied away from the history of interpretation. The history of interpretation is in fact the only broad subject in the reception history of Greek tragedy that has – oddly enough – been totally neglected. We know almost everything about the various Oedipus- and Electra-dramas of modern times. It is increasingly easy today to find out about practically every *Medea-* or *Electra*-production that ever took place in Rome, Paris, Berlin, or New York, regardless of its importance or success. Yet, we know little or nothing about how the tragedies by Sophocles were understood, interpreted and judged in the 16th, 17th or 18th centuries.

Very often scholars do not even seem to be aware of the fact that in the 16th, 17th or 18th centuries Aeschylus, Sophocles and Euripides had not only been philologically edited and translated, had not only been poetically transformed and experimentally staged, but had also been controversially interpreted and discussed.[2] From those few studies in which the

---

[1] This article is a revised and slightly expanded version of a lecture read at the magnificent European Cultural Centre of Delphi in June 2004. The lecture form has been retained. I should like to thank Carl Joachim Classen, Irene Polinskaya and Marc Witkin for their valuable comments and suggestions.
[2] This impression is conveyed at least by the most recent guides, as e. g. in *The Cambridge Companion to Greek Tragedy* (1997), which offers only two large and overlapping contributions on the history of performance (228–283 and 284–323). The introductory volume *Reception Studies* by Hardwick (2003) regards the reception history of Greek tragedy almost exclusively as the history of performance, film-making and translation. The overview of the history of reception of Greek tragedy in Europe by Zimmermann (2000) deals also almost exclusively with the performance history. Garland (2004) 117f. 147–185, too, has a lot to say about translations and productions of Greek tragedy between 1500 and 2001 and little or nothing about the history of interpretation between 1500 and 1800. A similar picture emerges from the new Blackwell *Companion to Greek Tragedy* (Gregory 2005).

history of interpretation is touched upon, one gets the impression that the history of serious modern interpretation of Greek tragedy only began in the 19th century with F. W. J. Schelling and the Schlegel brothers.[3]

The Schlegel brothers and Schelling, however, were not the first to think about the meaning of ancient tragedy. Greek tragedy, in general, and Sophocles, in particular, had already been the subject of a very intense critical debate in the middle of the 16th century throughout Europe.[4] Already in the first half of the 16th century two very significant developments in the interpretation of Greek tragedy emerged. These two strands continuously grew closer and have in their interconnection not only moulded the whole ‹productive› reception and dramatic theory of modern times, but also had a major influence on all variations of modern understanding of Greek tragedy. They still retain their influence today.

2. Aristotelisation and Christianisation of Greek tragedy in the 16th century

2.1. Aristotelisation: Joachim Camerarius 1534

The first development, which could be called ‹Aristotelisation›, depended, of course, on the rediscovery of Aristotle's *Poetics*. The fact that Aristotle's normative theory was misunderstood to be a descriptive analysis and, therefore, to present a key to the reading of ancient drama, was the reason why scholars believed – and some still do – that they always had to refer to the Aristotelian theory of tragedy when interpreting Greek tragedies. At least, they always tried to confirm the rightness of their own interpretations by demonstrating that this was how Aristotle, too, saw the matter – even if this sometimes required a little re-interpretation of his *Poetics* to suit the argument.

---

[3] See Michelini (1987) 3–51; cf. e.g. Mills (2002) 84: «Modern Euripidean criticism begins in the nineteenth century in Germany ... For critics such as F. and A.W. Schlegel ...»; a separate chapter is then dedicated to the history of ‹productive› reception since 1500 (pp. 109–129). Steiner's (1984) history of interpretation of *Antigone* was also centred on ‹philosophical› interpretations of the 19th century. The title of Schmidt's book *On Germans and other Greeks* (2001) speaks for itself; cf. also Pöggeler (2004). The overview by Niefanger (2003) shows once again, if only involuntarily, how little is known about the history of understanding of Greek tragedy in 16th, 17th and 18th centuries.

[4] So far scholars have been mostly concerned with the history of the printing tradition, textual criticism and translation of Greek tragedy in the 16th century: for Aeschylus see Lachmann/Cranz (1971); Gruys (1981) and Mund-Dopchie (1984), cf. now also Mund-Dopchie (2001), Kallegris (1994/95) and Avezzù (2001); for Sophocles see Borza (2002), (2003a), (2001) and (2003b); for Euripides see Kannicht (1969) Bd. 1, 109–119; Pertusi (1960) and (1963); Porro (1981) and (1992); Petrina (1999); for the *Aldinae* s. Sicherl (1997); for editions produced in Bâle, see Hieronymus (1992) 279–287. For recent studies on the history of translation of Greek tragedy in the 16th century as a history of re-interpretation, see Garnier (1999); Loehr (2001); Mastroianni (2004). On some aspects of the history of interpretation of Euripides' *Hecuba*, see Heath (1987). Daskarolis (2000) attempted to combine the history of ‹productive› reception with the history of Sophoclean criticism in Germany in the 16th century, but unfortunately failed to evaluate the most important sources. On the value of the study of the history of interpretation for today's classicists in general, see Heath (1987) 68, the thoughtful remarks by Reeve (2001), and the *plaidoyer* by De Smet (2001). The present article is not concerned with the history of Classical scholarship but rather with the history of one of the central intellectual contests in the cultural history of Europe.

This tendency towards Aristotelisation can be already seen in the text that constitutes the very beginning of modern Sophoclean criticism: the nowadays completely forgotten *Argumentum Fabulae* by Joachim Camerarius (1500–1574), published in his commentary on Sophocles' Theban plays of 1534 and reprinted several times in different editions and translations of Sophocles during the 16th century.[5] This remarkable text deserves to be quoted at length:

> «Sciendum cum Tragicae fabulae complectantur imitationem rerum grandium & non levium aut vulgarium, vel ut Graeci aiunt τῶν δεινῶν potiss. laudari, quae magnam afferat expectationem exitus *miserabilis*, inopinati, *terribilis*, ut in ipsa expositione auditores, quamquam extra pericula, tamen *horrescant* representatione eorum quae diximus. Quapropter omnium consensu huic fabulae [sc. *OT*] & alteri Oedipo | Coloneo, primae datae sunt: Et ex Euripideis in admiratione est Orestes, Hippolytus, Phoenissae. At Rhesum & Cyclopem, sunt qui negent Euripidis esse. Quis enim percellatur aut *timore aut misericordia*, cum Polyphemo strui malum & interitum, qui humanis carnibus pasceretur, intellexerit? Quis autem non ferat aequo animo, malo interitu occidere illum gloriantem Thraca, deumque & hominum contemptorem? Quin potius talibus eventibus patefieri *divinam ultionem & vindictam* existimant. At ubi *vir bonus & honestatis virtutisque amans, indignum in malum* impellitur quasi *fatali vi*, aut peccata *vel non voluntate, vel ignoratione* quoque comissa, poenas extremas sustinent, tum & *metus* & *misericordia* talibus ab exemplis homines invadit, & *lamenta horroresque* excitantur. Haec igitur fabula [sc. *OT*] merito laudem prae omnium alijs habet.»[6]

Camerarius's interpretation of *Oedipus Rex* is intricately connected with an understanding of tragedy that is based on some of the central categories of Aristotle's theory of tragedy:[7] firstly, an Aristotelian definition of tragedy as an imitation of major pitiful and fearful events entailing an unexpected and undeserved change of the tragic hero's fortune from good to bad that is meant to arouse fear and pity – a definition that does not try to link the specific tragic emotions to any moral purpose.[8] Secondly, being grounded in Aristotle's notion of the emotional effect of tragedy that should result from its plot-structure, this definition involves categorical rejection of tragedies in which divine justice is simply presented, and the evildoers get what they deserve, because in such cases the theatregoer or reader can neither feel fear nor have pity. Thirdly and closely connected to this, is Camerarius' interpretation of Aristotle's concept of tragic *hamartia* as an involuntary crime committed out of ignorance or against one's own will. This Aristotelian understanding of tragedy proposed by Camerarius already integrates an interpretation of *Oedipus Rex* as the best tragedy, that is to say, one that serves best to evoke fear and pity in the audience – because Oedipus, a morally good, honourable and virtuous human being, forced by some dark power of fate into misery he does not deserve, commits crimes unknowingly and against his own will, that lead to the hardest punishments.

---

[5] Camerarius (1534) 9[r]–11[v]. The text was reprinted at least in the following editions: Winshemius (1546); ²1549; ³1551) 118–123; Camerarius (1556) 313–316; Camerarius/Stephanus (1568) [462+] 148 f.; Camerarius/Stephanus (1603) [788+[32]+52+] 105–107; see further Lurje (2004) 94–97. Already on December 5th 1534 Melanchthon could write to Camerarius (MBW T6, Nr. 1510, 35 f.): «[sc. Georg] Sabinus narrat tuas commentationes in Sophocles *Romae* in admiratione esse.»

[6] Camerarius (1534) 10[v]–11[r].

[7] Camerarius (1534) refers twice to Aristotle's *Poetics* explicitly (fol. 6[v] and 11[r] f.).

[8] This definition also consciously and cautiously avoids any explicit interpretation of tragic *katharsis*. On the difficulties the humanists encountered with the interpretation of *katharsis* in the first half of the 16th century, see Lurje (2004) 66–74, cf. also 16–25.

That was in 1534. The first reliable Latin translation of the *Poetics* by Alessandro Pazzi would only be published two years later (1536). And only 14 years later (1548) would Francesco Robortello publish the first commentary on Aristotle's *Poetics*. But even at this early stage interpretations of Greek tragedy and of Aristotle's theory already seem inextricably intertwined. That, unfortunately, was only the beginning of a rather sad story. Within a few years Pietro Vettori attempted to analyse and interpret not just *Oedipus Rex*, but *all* of the surviving plays by Sophocles *and* Euripides with the help of the central categories of what he believed to be Aristotle's theory of tragedy.[9] Many others would follow in his footsteps. The resulting interdependence between interpretations of ancient tragedy and of Aristotle's *Poetics* proved to be a hermeneutical disaster.

2.2. Christianisation, or the Denial of Tragedy: Philipp Melanchthon 1545

While the Aristotelisation of tragedy after Camerarius took place mainly in Italy, in the second most influential development – the process which could be called Christianisation of Greek tragedy – Protestant humanists played a major role, first of all Philipp Melanchthon (1497–1560). His manifesto entitled *Cohortatio ad legendas tragoedias et comoedias*, written in 1545 and published by Joachim Camerarius as a preface to his edition of Terence in 1546, marks a decisive turn in the history of understanding of Greek tragedy.

The first half of the 16th century was dominated by the idea that tragedy was a warning depiction of the changeability of unpredictable *Fortuna* and, as such, of the frailty of human happiness as well as of the misery of human life. Jodocus Badius Ascensius (1462–1535), for example, defined tragedy in his *Praenotamenta in Comoedias Terentii* of the year 1502 – one of the most influential tractates in dramatic theory in the first half of the 16th century – as «ludus metrice compositus in quo principaliter ostenditur *fragilitas humanarum rerum*».[10] The tragic poet's principal duty was to demonstrate the «*infelicitas & miseria humane vite*».[11] In the dedicatory epistle to his voluminous edition of Seneca's tragedies published in 1514, Badius declared tragedies particularly beneficial to kings and rulers, who are to be reminded of misfortunes of humanity «as they see so many people fallen down from such a high throne into such a low dust».[12] Guillaume Bouchetel claimed in the preface to his translation of Euripides' *Hekabe* of 1544 that tragedy had been invented by the Ancients «pour remonstrer aux roys et grans seigneurs *l'incertitude et lubrique instabilité des choses temporelles.*»[13]

---

[9] Vettori's *argumenta* were published by Pratesi (1985); see further Lurje (2004) 111–113.
[10] Badius (1502) V[r]: «Sciendum, quod tragedia est quidam ludus metrice compositus in quo principaliter ostenditur fragilitas humanarum rerum. Nam reges et principes qui se primum perbeatos & precipue felices arbitrabantur, in fine tragediarum in extremam miseriam redacti exclamationibus & dedignationibus celum & terram confundunt omniaque & celestia & terrestria incusant ...»
[11] Badius (1502) V[v]: «proprium officium tragici scriptoris est ostendere *infelicitatem & miseriam humane vite*, ex eo quoque etiam reges & principes qui a multis beati reputantur sepe miserabilem atque infelicem exitum sortiuntur usque adeo ut multi omnibus privati in exilio constituti mortem sepe precentur atque exoptent.» For a more detailed discussion of Badius' understanding of tragedy in his *Praenotamenta*, see Lurje (2004) 45–48.
[12] Badius (1514): «Ut vero sileam *fructum legendae tragoediae* omnibus perspicuum ac evidentem, qui est summos quosque et reges, et principes *humanorum casuum admoneri, cum videant e tam sublimi solio in tam demissum quam plurimos decidisse pulverem.*»
[13] Bouchetel (1544) 108.

Melanchthon opposed this predominant understanding of tragedy in his manifesto of 1545. He claimed with religious fervour that the Greek tragedians had not written their plays for kings and rulers to be warned of unpredictable misfortunes at all, but with the intention of forcing the souls of their fellow-citizens to keep their pernicious passions in check out of fear of God's punitive justice. This was so, he argued, because in all their tragedies Aeschylus, Sophocles and Euripides had tried to show to the audience that just deeds would be rewarded in the end, and crimes would always be punished.[14] In depicting the tragic end of a great hero as the just – though terrible – punishment of crimes ensuing from his own vice and pernicious passion,[15] they tried to make people believe that it was not unpredictable fate but divine providence that ruled the world, that there was an eternal spirit that always punished crime and protected the just, if not always, at least most of the time. In this way, Melanchthon interpreted *all* of the Greek tragedies as a uniform theodicy that warned of God's punitive justice, a theodicy that was perfectly in agreement with the doctrines of the Christian church:

> «Et sicut Pindarus [*Pyth.* 2, 40 ff.] inquit, Ixionem implicitum rotae apud inferos clamitare hanc vocem, quam Virgilius reddidit, *Discite Iustitiam moniti et non spernere Divos* [*Aen.* 6,620][16]: *Ita Tragoediarum omnium hoc praecipuum est argumentum*. Hanc sententiam volunt omnium animis infingere, *esse aliquam mentem aeternam, quae semper atrocia scelera insignibus exemplis punit*, moderatis vero et iustis plerumque dat tranquilliorem cursum. Et quanquam hos etiam interdum fortuiti casus opprimunt, sunt enim multae arcanae causae, tamen illa manifesta regula non propterea aboletur, videlicet semper Erinnyas et saevas calamitates comites esse atrocium delictorum. Haec sententia multos ad moderationem flectebat, quae nos quidem magis movere debet, qui scimus eam et Ecclesiae clara Dei voce saepe traditam esse.»[17]

Melanchthon's *Cohortatio*, which was reprinted at least 11 times during the second half of the 16th century,[18] was a powerful and compelling appeal not just to read Greek tragedies, but to interpret them and, in doing so, help others to understand them in the manner he himself had postulated. It had to be shown by the analysis of each of the dramas that

---

[14] Melanchthon (1545a) 567: «Saepe de hominum moribus et de disciplina cogitans, Graecorum consilium valde admiror, qui initio Tragoedias populo proposuerunt, nequaquam ut vulgo existimatur, tantum oblectationis causa, sed multo magis, ut rudes ac feros animos consideratione atrocium exemplorum et casuum *flecterent ad moderationem, et frenandas cupiditates*, quod in illis Regum et urbium eventibus imbecillitatem naturae hominum, fortunae inconstantiam, et *exitus placidos iuste factorum, et contra vero tristissimas scelerum poenas* ostendebant.»

[15] Melanchthon (1545a) 567: «Qua in re et hoc singularis prudentiae fuit, eligere argumenta non vulgarium casuum, sed insignium et atrocium, quorum commemoratione *cohorrescerent* tota theatra. Non enim movetur populus levium aut mediocrium miseriarum cogitatione, sed *terribilis species* obiicienda est oculis, quae penetret in animos et diu haereat, et moveat illa ipsa commiseratione, *ut de causis humanarum calamitatum cogitent & singuli se ad illas imagines conferant*. Ego ipse saepe toto corpore cohorresco legens tantum, non etiam intuens ut in theatro agentes, Sophoclis aut Euripidis Tragoedias.» Cf. 568: «Haec igitur agebantur, spectabantur, legebantur, audiebantur a sapientibus & a populo, non ut erotica [sic], sed ut doctrina de gubernatione vitae. Eventus isti commonefaciebant homines *de causis humanarum calamitatum, quas accersi & cumulari pravis cupiditatibus, in his exemplis cernebant*.»

[16] Cf. Servius *Aen.* 6,660 and Claud. Don. *Aen.* 6,624.

[17] Melanchthon (1545a) 568. For a more detailed discussion of Melanchthon's *Cohortatio* (1545a), see Lurje (2004) 49–56. Garland (2004) 114 misdates the text he knows only from the English (and incorrect) translation by Stone (1974) 41 f. to 1518.

[18] Wetzel (1997) 102 n. 8.

Aeschylus, Sophocles and Euripides had, indeed, written their tragedies as highly effective missionary texts, in which the tragic fortune of a great hero had always been described as the consequence of a depraved action he himself was to blame for and, therefore, as God's just punishment. Thus philology was given its missionary purpose, and the interpretation of Greek tragedy became a tool in the service of theodicy.

And indeed, Melanchthon did not want to content himself with pronouncing general, ungrounded statements, but was prepared to search in the text of Greek tragedies for the meaning he claimed was intended by all of the Greek tragedians. The same year (1545) he was giving lectures on Sophocles at Wittenberg that were published one year later by his student Veit Winshemius (1501–1570).[19] In his general introduction, which is very close to Melanchthon's *Cohortatio*, Winshemius ardently proclaimed the true meaning of Greek tragedy that he had been taught by his master at Wittenberg.[20] More importantly, he prefaced each of the translations with an interpretative essay written by Melanchthon for his own lectures.[21] These were new, detailed interpretations of Sophocles' tragedies, in which Melanchthon tried to apply to Sophocles the understanding of Greek tragedy he himself believed in, and, in doing so, to confirm it exegetically.

Melanchthon understood *Ajax* as a conflict between Ulysses as a modest and self-restrained politician and Ajax as a heavily built soldier who was driven by ambition, spite and an inability to tolerate an offence (*impatientia repulsae*) and who brought about his own downfall as a result of these vices.[22] In *The Women of Trachis* it was – according to Melanchthon and Winshemius – Heracles's own adulterous lust (*vaga libido*) that was responsible for his ruin.[23] In his search for the divine justice in *Electra*, Melanchthon had to focus on the idea of inherited guilt and family curse, and to explain the events on stage as mere links in a long chain of catastrophes with which God had the family of Pelops pay for the murder of Myrtilos.[24]

---

[19] That the translation published by Winshemius (1546) was in fact Melanchthon's work was pointed out by Rhein (1997) 153f. and (1999) 56, who rediscovered a script of Melanchthon's lectures on Sophocles made by his student Paul Obermeier (RSB Zwickau, Sign. XLIX, fol. 1–128ᵛ). The script contains Melanchthon's translations of *Ai., El., OT, Ant.* and *OC* and his prefaces (*argumenta*) to *Ai., El., Ant.* and *OC*, which are exactly the same as those published by Winshemius (1546).

[20] Winshemius (1546) A2ʳ-[A7ʳ]. The script of Melanchthon's lectures (1545b) does not contain any general introduction. It is clear, however, that Melanchthon's *Cohortatio*, dated from January 1545, was written in connection with his lectures on Sophocles. Cf. also Melanchthon's announcement of a lecture on Sophocles' *Electra* of the 18ᵗʰ January 1545, which was recently reprinted by Ritoók-Szalay (2001) 325f.

[21] On *Ajax*: Melanchthon (1545b) 1ᵛf. = Winshemius (1546) 1–3; on *Electra*: Melanchthon (1545b) 31ʳ–32ᵛ = Winshemius (1546) 57–60; on *Antigone*: Melanchthon (1545b) 71ᵛf. = Winshemius (1546) 180–183; on *Oedipus at Colonus*: Melanchthon (1545b) 95ʳ–96ʳ = Winshemius (1546) 232–235; on *The Women of Trachis*: Winshemius (1546) 305–308; on *Philoctetes*: Winshemius (1546) 356–361.

[22] Melanchthon (1545b) 3ʳ = Winshemius (1546) 2: «In Aiace, hoc est, homine militari, describitur immensa gloriae cupiditas sive ambitio, & contumacia ac impatientia repulsae, quibus vitiis plerumque obnoxii sunt homines magnanimi. In Senatore vero, hoc est in Ulyse, modestia in rebus secundis describitur & compatientia in calamitate inimici, ac moderatio in cupiditate vindictae.»

[23] Winshemius (1546) 305: «Operae precium vero est videre, qualem Catastrophen & exitum vitae sortitus sit vir tantus … Praebuit vero huic tam tristi calamitati causam *vaga libido* ipsius …»; cf. 307: «Est vero in hoc exemplo praecipue observandum, quod tam miserabiliter & tam levi momento evertitur vir tantus, cui libido & causa est & occasio poenae … Libido vero illi, quae & multis aliis, exitio fuit.»

[24] Melanchthon (1545b) 31ʳf. = Winshemius (1546) 57f.: «Haec fabula hanc doctrinam praecipue tractat, contra Epicureos, *Quod Deus res humanas curet, innocentes ac indigne oppressos respiciat, ac tandem liberet, atrocia scelera Tragicis atque horribilibus poenis vindicet.* Ad quem locum communem de providentia divina & si omnes fere Tragoediae communiter referri possunt, tamen in quibusdam magis illustria exempla & testimonia

In *Antigone*, Melanchthon did not – unlike some modern critics – blame Antigone, but Creon. Although he neither meant to praise Antigone's disobedient behaviour towards authority nor to condemn Creon as a ruler who enforced his authority by every means possible, Melanchthon did acknowledge that the tyrant Creon went too far in his immoderate cruelty and stubbornness and had to pay for it.[25]

In *Oedipus Rex*, however, Melanchthon apparently could not discern God's justice at all, nor could he prove Camerarius's interpretation wrong. As a result, he chose instead discretely to ignore the tragedy completely.[26] The Sophoclean Oedipus was made to wait for divine justice once again. This, however, did not in any way alter the lasting success of Melanchthon's understanding of tragedy or his interpretation of Sophocles. After the volume published by Winshemius in 1546 (and reprinted in 1549 and 1551), a whole range of translations and bilingual editions of Sophocles followed, produced and distributed throughout Europe, in which Sophocles was constantly, though not always convincingly, subjected to the Christianisation initiated by Melanchthon and denied the tragic sense of life he once seemed to have.[27]

---

  huius sententiae proponuntur: Sicut & in hac, quae tristissima quaedam imago est irae divinae adversus atrocia scelera … Et ostendit nobis, quantam saevissimarum calamitatum & malorum Lernam unum aliquod atrox factum secum trahit: Et quam ex uno delicto Satanas longam atque horribilem telam scelerum & poenarum texere atque accumulare soleat. Interficit Pelops Myrtilum. At filii ipsius alternis caedibus, sanguine & incestis libidinibus domum ac civitatem re-|plent, haerent in poenis non ipsi tantum, sed & horum liberi, qui ijsdem a furiis agitati, partim in suum sanguinem saeviunt, partim a proximis ipsi quoque trucidantur. Neque adhuc finis est scelerum ac poenarum, sed ad nepotes ac pronepotes usque usque tristissimae calamitates propagant. Hoc est quod verba legis divinae minantur, Deum visitare iniquitatem Patrum in tertiam & quartam generationem.» Cf. also Melanchthon (1545c).

[25] Melanchthon (1545b) 71ᵛ f. = Winshemius (1546) 182 f.: «Debent enim magistratus authoritatem suam defendere ac stabilire. Sed tamen modus quidam eius rei esse debet, eum non observant Tyranni. Plectitur vero in Catastrophe fabulae tyrannus horribiliter: amittit enim filium atque uxorem … Additur ergo in fine confessio tyranni, quantum mali illi pertinacia & saevitia attulerint. Continet igitur haec fabula illustres imagines ac descriptio-|nes officiorum iusticiae & religionis.» Winshemius' interpretation of *Philoctetes* already displays signs of boring moralising triviality: «Deinde tota series atque oeconomia fabulae nos docet, ut consilio & viribus homines instructi sint, cum res magnas aggrediuntur, nihil tamen effici, nisi adhuc tertium ac praecipuum momentum accedat, nempe successus et auxilium a Deo … | … Sapienter igitur Sophocles docet, tria requiri ad res magnas perficiendas: primum, consilium ac sapientiam: deinde, vires & efficiendi facultatem: postremo, quod praecipuum est, successum atque fortunam a Deo …» (1546, 359 f.).

[26] *Oedipus Rex* is the only Sophoclean tragedy that remained without any preface in Melanchthon (1545b) and without any new preface in Winshemius (1546), who decided, surprisingly enough, to reprint the *argumentum* by Camerarius (1534) discussed above, although it strongly contradicted the understanding of Greek tragedy articulated by Melanchthon in 1545. Melanchthon's interpretation of *Oedipus at Colonus* was rather political and biographical, cf. Melanchthon (1545b) 95ʳ f. = Winshemius (1546) 233 f.: «Non vero dubium est, quin Sophocles in his fabulis praecipuarum rerum suae aetatis quasi exempla & imagines expresserit. Et hac fabula videtur suae domus & senectutis suae fortunam deplorare. Introducit enim Oedipum caecum iam & afflictissimum senem, a liberis & Creonte in exilium pulsum, varieque vexatum, praedicentem filijs exitum ob impietatem erga parentem, & defensum ab alienis adversus suorum iniurias. Idem sibi quoque evenire Sophocles significat. Pertinet igitur haec fabula ad hanc partem legis divinae, Honora parentes, &c. Sed quemadmodum ubique solet, ita hic quoque multa politica admiscet. Monet enim hic Oedipus Thesea gravissimis verbis, ne foederi aut societati cum Boeotijs nimium confidat … | … Quasi dicat, non mirum vobis videri debet, quod Boeotij, qui olim coniunctissimi amici Atheniensibus fuerunt, nunc infestissimo odio hanc urbem prosequuntur: videtis enim quid contra me immerentem ac placidissimum senem filij mei moliantur.»

[27] See Rataller (1550) 3–10 (important general introduction as dedicatory epistle to «Ludovico a Flandria …»); Naogeorg (1552); Camerarius (1556) 8–18: «In Sophoclem Prolegomena» (very important introduction,

3. Synthesis of Aristotelisation and Christianisation: Doctrine classique

Very different developments though they originally were, Aristotelisation and Christianisation grew ever closer over time and finally, in the beginning of the 17th century, came together in the French dramatic theory to become the most important foundation stones of the *Doctrine classique*. In the meantime, Aristotle's *Poetics* also underwent a Christianising and moralising interpretation – due to the flood of learned commentaries written in Italy in the second half of the *Cinquecento*. This twofold development meant that the understanding of tragedy postulated by Melanchthon appeared to agree with what was largely declared to be Aristotle's theory of tragedy. It was, consequently, no coincidence that the Christianising interpretation of *Oedipus Rex*, which Melanchthon himself had failed to accomplish, was finally completed by – of all people – André Dacier (1651–1722) in his commentary on Aristotle's *Poetics* published in Paris in 1692.[28] With the help of a rather sophisticated moralising interpretation of Aristotle's concept of *hamartia*, which was now supposed to be not just a mistake committed out of ignorance, but a moral fault resulting from one's own character flaws and vicious passions, Dacier saw divine justice in *Oedipus Rex* after all. He argued, and with some power, that the Sophoclean Oedipus – in accordance with Aristotle's *Poetics* – did not suffer innocently at all, but due to his own weaknesses in character and because of his own vices. He insisted that Oedipus's own outbursts of anger, his pride, his curiosity, his imprudence and intemperance, so pervasively exposed by Sophocles during the action on stage, had led to patricide in the past and would now lead to his terrible but deserved ruin. For by exposing Oedipus's vices as the true causes of his misfortune, Sophocles – according to what Dacier believed to be Aristotle's theory of tragedy – had wanted the spectators and readers to ‹purge› these very vices from their wretched souls in order that they would avoid such catastrophes in their own lives:

> «Pour la faute [i.e. ἁμαρτία] d'Edipe, c'est la faute d'un homme qui emporté de colère pour l'insolence d'un Cocher tuë quatre hommes deux jours après que l'oracle l'a averty qu'il tueroit son propre père. Il conte luy-même son action dans Sophocle fort naturellement. Cette seule action marqueroit assez *son caractére*, mais Sophocle luy a donné par tout des mœurs conformes à cette action, & *qui répondent si parfaitement aux Regles d'Aristote*, qu'on voit par tout un homme qui n'est ny bon ny méchant, & qui est mêlé de

---

see especially 8–11: «De consilio autoris»), 20 (on *Ai.*), 176 (on *El.*); Bornemisza (1558); Naogeorg (1558) 3–12 (general introduction as *Epistola Nuncupatoria*); Rataller (1570; reprinted in 1576 and 1584), *2r–*5r (general introduction as dedicatory epistle to «D. Frederico Perenotto …» ~ Rataller 1550, 3–10); [A VIIvf.] (on *Ai.*, = Rataller 1550, 8f.), 64 (on *Ant.*, ~ Rataller 1550, 8), 127 (on *El.*), 272 (on *OC*), 359–361 (on *Trach.*), 420 (on *Phil.*). Cf. also the more independent and inconsistent but nonetheless strongly Christianising approach by Lalamantius (1557), 3r–5v (general introduction as *Epistola Nuncupatoria* to «Petro Marsilio Cipierro …»); 8v–9r: «In Sophoclis Tragoedias Praefatiuncula»; 9v–16r (on *Ai.*); 55v–59r (on *El.*); 101v–106v (on *OT*); 150r–151v (on *Ant.*); 189rf. (on *OC*); 238v–241v (on *Trach.*); 276v–280v (on *Phil.*). The general definition of ancient tragedy by Riccius (1566) 3v–4r, as well as Stiblin's *Praefationes* to Euripides' plays (1562) are also strongly influenced by Melanchthon; see further Lurje (2004) 52–56, 102–108. On the linguistic «christianizzazione» of Sophocles' *Antigone* in French translations of the 16th century, see Mastroianni (2004) 33–75, who unfortunately, but symptomatically, discusses only translations without even mentioning the prefaces and *argumenta* by Melanchthon, Winshemius, Rataller, Camerarius and Lalamantius mentioned above.

[28] For previous attempts of this kind made by Vettori (1560) and La Mesnardière (1640), see Lurje (2004) 111–116 and 118–122.

vertus & de vices; *ses vices d'Edipe sont l'orgüeil, la violence et l'emportement, la témérité & l'imprudence*; ce n'est proprement ny son inceste ny son parricide qui le rendent malheureux, cette punition auroit été en quelque maniére injuste, puisque ces crimes étoient entièrement involontaires et qu'il les avoit commis sans le sçavoir; il ne tombe dans ces affreuses calamitez que par sa curiosité par sa témérité & par ses violences … *voilà les vices dont Sophocle veut que nous nous corrigions* …»[29]

Thus the Christianisation of Sophocles was completed at last, and Camerarius was defeated by means of his own weapons: with another interpretation of Aristotle's *Poetics*.

4. ‹De-Christianisation› and Alienation: Querelle des Anciens et des Modernes

Greek tragedy remained the subject of a fierce intellectual debate in Europe throughout the 18th century. The *Querelle des Anciens et des Modernes* brought with it a consistent alienation and ‹de-Christianisation› of the Sophoclean tragedy. Saint-Évremond, James Drake, Jean Terrasson, Fontenelle, and later on Marmontel and others consistently tried to expose the interpretation that had been developed by Melanchthon, Dacier and others during the 16th and 17th centuries as an unfounded distortion and a serious misunderstanding.[30] They argued over and over again that in Sophocles' tragedies – absolutely alien to us, amoral and anti-Christian – there was no divine justice at all, that the individual was only a blind toy in the hands of cruel and unjust gods and an innocent victim of inevitable fate.

The starting point of this systematic assault on Greek tragedy was once again Sophocles' *Oedipus Rex*. James Drake (1666–1707), in his remarkable and highly provocative book *The Antient and Modern Stage Survey'd* of 1699, was determined to prove that there was not a word of truth in the whole interpretation by Dacier and other critics who tried in vain to «raise a *Christian* Moral upon a *Pagan* bottom».[31] For the only moral one could draw from this acclaimed ancient tragedy – and from many other Greek tragedies as well – was the irresistible power of fate and the injustice and villainy of the divine providence:

> «*Oedipus* is made [sc. by Sophocles] Virtuous, Just, and Wise, but *unhappy thro a Fatality, against which his Virtue is no security*; Justice requires that he shou'd be rewarded and encouraged, but Providence will have him afflicted, and punish with extremity of Rigour. Can anything be more disserviceable to Probity and Religion, than these Examples of Injustice, Oppression and Cowardice in their Gods?»[32]

Jean Terrasson (1670–1750), too, vehemently disagreed with Dacier in his extremely influential *Dissertation critique sur l'Iliade d'Homère* of 1715, which dealt at length not only

---

[29] Dacier (1692a) 192f. (‹remarque› 11 to Chap. XIII); cf. already p. 82 (‹remarque› 8 to Ch. VI). Cf. also Dacier's «Preface» in: Dacier (1692b) aij[r]-[aviii[r]], here [a v[v]]. See further Lurje (2004) 128–136; 147–149.

[30] On the central role of Greek tragedy in the *Querelle des Anciens et des Modernes* and for the history of understanding of Greek tragedy in general and Sophocles in particular in the 18th century, see Lurje (2004) 138–225.

[31] Drake (1699) 147.

[32] Drake (1699) 199. Drake discusses not only *Oedipus Rex* (pp. 126–147) but also Sophocles' *Ajax* (pp. 150–155), *Electra* (pp. 155f.), *Antigone* (pp. 156f.), *Oedipus at Colonus* (pp. 157–159), *The Women of Trachis* (pp. 159–61), *Philoctetes* (pp. 161–163) and Euripides' *Orestes, Electra, Medea, Hippolytos, Ion* and *Hercules Furens* (pp. 164–178). See further Lurje (2004) 151–160.

with the *Iliad* but also with Greek tragedy and theory of tragedy.³³ Terrasson insisted that *Oedipus Rex* was extremely impious and harmful to modern Christian readers, because Sophocles' dramatic intention was simply to make people believe that if a man is destined by the Gods to commit a crime, virtuous though he may be, he will be inevitably led to commit it against his own will:

> Mais je suis d'un avis bien different de M*ʳ* D.[acier] sur le sujet d'Edipe; car je tiens que dans *l'intention de Sophocle même*, c'est un des plus vertueux personnages que les Anciens aient jamais mis sur le Theâtre. *Le Poëte a voulu insinuer que quand un homme a été destiné par les Dieux à quelque crime il y est conduit malgré lui, & par les voies mêmes qu'il prend pour éviter.* La plûpart des Auteurs payens & sur tout les Poëtes tragiques sont remplis de cette idée impie: dans la vûe de l'établir, Sophocle a choisi un trés-bon Prince plein d'horreur pour le crime & d'amour pour la vertu, & il auroit regardé comme l'ennemi & le destructeur de sa Trage-|die un homme qui auroit dit de son temps qu'Edipe étoit vitieux de son propre fond, ou qu'il ne tenoit qu'à lui de se sauver des crimes & des malheurs qui lui avoient été annoncez par un Oracle.»³⁴

After having unmasked the shockingly amoral and anti-Christian character of Greek tragedy, the *Modernes* demanded from modern poets to produce new, modern Oedipus- and Antigone-tragedies that would *truly* incorporate those characteristics Melanchthon and Dacier had *erroneously* read into Sophocles' tragedies.³⁵ It was these demands for a new, modern, undeniably guilty and thus deservedly punished Oedipus that Fr. Melchiord de Folard's *Œdipe* of 1722 and Houdar de la Motte's *Œdipe* of 1726 were designed to satisfy.³⁶

This de-Christianising, alienating understanding of Greek tragedy that had developed during the French Enlightenment was to be taken over and radically re-evaluated at the end of the 18ᵗʰ century by Schelling and the Schlegel brothers and to become the basis of the

---

³³ See Terrasson (1715) P. III, Sect. I, Ch. I (T. 1, pp. 144–262): «*Digression préliminaire sur la Morale qui convient à la Poësie en general. Examen de quelques genres particulieres de Poësie, & de la Tragedie, ancienne & moderne.*» Terrasson's understanding of Greek tragedy as well as his theory of tragedy, extremely influential in the first half of the 18ᵗʰ century, have been almost completely ignored by modern scholarship; for a more detailed discussion see now Lurje (2004) 161–167. On Terrasson's defense of modern opera against Dacier, see Thomas (2002) 40–52.

³⁴ Terrasson (1715) T. 1, 188. Cf. Marmontel (1763) T. 2, 110: «Quels sont les crimes d'Œdipe? De s'être battu en homme de courage. Il est trop curieux, dit-on, parce qu'il tâche de découvrir la source des maux qui désolent Thébes. La digne cause pour ce trouver incestueux & parricide! C'est une chose étrange que le soin qu'on a pris de chercher des vices à ce bon Roi. Mais quand on aura tout épuisé pour noircir Œdipe, je demanderai par quelle faute, volontaire ou non, Jocaste a mérité de se trouver la femme de son fils parricide, destinée qui fait frémir?»; cf. T. 2, 102: «D'ailleurs ces mêmes héros, *victimes aveugles des dieux & du sort, annonçoient aux hommes leur dépendance,* & leur imprimoient une sainte terreur, ce qui donnoit au spectacle une majesté religieuse & sombre. *C'est à quoi se termine l'action de presque toutes les Tragédies Grecques,* & rien ne s'accorde mieux avec l'intérêt théâtral. *Mais comme tout s'y conduit par la fatalité, ou par la volonté des dieux, souvent bisarre, injuste & cruelle, c'est communément l'innocence & la bonté qui succombent, & le crime qui sort triomphant*: de-là vient que Socrate & Platon reprochoient à la Tragédie d'aller contre la loi, qui veut que les bons soient récompensés, & que les méchans soient punis.» For Marmontel's understanding of Greek tragedy, see Lurje (2004) 187–193 and 218–220.

³⁵ Cf. e.g. Terrasson (1714) T. 1, 193 f.

³⁶ For the reaction of the *Anciens*, who offered some fierce resistance but in the end could not but to accept, and to deal with, this new understanding of Greek tragedy, see Brumoy (1730), T. I, j–xxviij («Discours sur le Théâtre des Grecs»), 87–98 («Réflexions sur l'Œdipe»), 195–198 («Réflexions sur l'Electre de Sophocle»), and, most importantly, Batteux (1753) T. II, 202–269: «De la Tragédie». For a detailed discussion of Brumoy's and Batteux's positions, see Lurje (2004) 172–179, 198–215, 220–222.

new philosophy of tragedy that regarded Sophocles as the father of the truly tragic ‹Tragedy of Fate› (*Schicksalstragödie*). This is how we got at the *end* to the place where one usually *starts* the history of interpretation of Greek tragedy.

5. Misreading Sophocles: Why does the history of interpretation matter?

Why, then, does the history of interpretation matter? After all, the developments and interpretations I have been tracing turn out to be nothing but misreadings. And why on earth should we care about a daunting history of miserable misreadings?

It should not be forgotten that *these* misreadings have determined the understanding of Sophocles and Greek tragedy for centuries throughout Europe. Dealing with the history of interpretation of Greek tragedy is, therefore, of crucial importance to the understanding both of the whole theory of tragedy (which always depended on a certain interpretation of ancient drama), as well as of all ‹productive› reception of Greek tragedy in Europe (including the history of performance).

Moreover, the history of interpretation of Greek tragedy is not just about some remarkable theoretic and exegetic struggles of the past. It is a constant debate we all are participating in – now. The history of this self-implicating process we all engage in when reading Sophocles is, therefore, also a mirror in which we can not only recognize our *own* misreadings, but also their causes and, therefore, ourselves. The human mind – as Fontenelle once said – is less prone to go astray when it realizes to what extent, and in how many ways it itself is capable of error, and we can never therefore devote too much time to the study of the history of our aberrations.

The history of interpretation of Sophocles and Greek tragedy is after all an important part of the history of European thought. It mirrors our perennial attempts to come to terms with the inscrutability of the gods and the tragic limits of the human condition, which Sophocles exposes without providing us with an explanation.

References

1. Primary Sources 1500–1800

BADIUS 1502	J. Badius Ascensius, «Praenotamenta in Comoedias Terentii», in: *P. Terentii aphri comicorum elegantissimi Comedie: a Guidone Juvenale viro perquam litterato familiariter explanate: et ab Jodoco Badio Ascensio una cum explanationibus rursum annotate atque recognite: cumque eiusdem Ascensii praenotamentis atque annotamentis suis locis adhibitis* (Lyon '11502; edition used: ... in fine: *impensa non levi per d. Jo. Jacobum et fratres de Lignano characteribus mandate, Mediolani per Jo. Ang. Scinzenzeler*, 1513; SUB Göttingen 4 Auct. lat. I, 3657) I^r-X^v
BADIUS 1514	J. Badius Ascensius, «Domino Joanni Landano», in: *L. Annaei Senecae Tragoediae pristinae integritati restitutae ... Explanatae tribus commentariis G. Bernardino Marmita Parmensi, Daniele Gaietano Cremonensi, Iodoco Badio Ascensio* ([Paris]: Venundantur ab eodem Ascensio, 1514; UB Leipzig Poet. Lat. 72); reprinted in

	Ph. Renouard, *Bibliographie des impressions et des œuvres de Josse Badius Ascensius, imprimeur et humaniste, 1462–1535*, vol. 1–3 (Paris ¹1908; repr. New York 1967) vol. 3, 252 f.
BATTEUX 1753	Ch. Batteux, *Principes de la Littérature*, T. 1–4 (Paris 1753; here used: Göttingue & Leide: E. Luzac 1755; SUB Göttingen 8 Aesth. 3013)
BORNEMISZA 1558	P. Bornemisza, «Lectori candido», in: *Tragoedia magiar nevlenn, az Sophocles Electraiabol … Pesti Bornemizza Peter … altal* (Viennae 1558) H 6ʳ–13ʳ; reprinted in Ritoók-Szalay (2001) 333–336
BOUCHETEL 1544	[G. Bouchetel], «Préface Au Roy mon Souverain Seigneur», in: *La Tragédie d'Euripide, nommée Hecuba: traduicte de Grec en rhythme Françoise* (Paris: Robert Estienne, ¹1544; ²1550); reprinted by B. Weinberg (ed.), *Critical Prefaces of the French Renaissance* (Evanston 1950) 105–109
BRUMOY 1730	*Le Théâtre des Grecs par le R. P. Brumoy, de la Compagnie de Jesus*, T. 1–3 (Paris ¹1730; SUB Göttingen 4 Auct. gr. I, 1570)
CAMERARIUS 1534	*Commentarii interpretationum argumenti Thebaidos fabularum Sophoclis Authore Ioachimo Camerario Quaestore* (Hagenoae: Ex officina Seceriana, Anno 1534, III. Idus Martii; UB Leipzig Poet.gr.363)
CAMERARIUS 1556	*Commentatio explicationum omnium tragoediarum Sophoclis, cum exemplo duplicis conversionis, Ioachimi Camerarii Pabepergensis …* (Basileae: Oporinus, in fine: 1556, mense Augusto; SUB Göttingen 8 Auct. gr. II, 7000)
CAMERARIUS/ STEPHANUS 1568	*Sophoclis tragoediae septem. Una cum omnibus Graecis scholiis, & cum Latinis Ioach. Camerarii. Annotationes Henrici Stephani in Sophoclem & Euripidem, seorsum excusae, simul prodeunt* ([Genevae]: Stephanus, 1568; HAAB Weimar 4° XXXVIII, 13)
CAMERARIUS/ STEPHANUS 1603	*Sophoclis Tragoediae septem una cum omnibus Graecis scholiis, et latina Viti Winshemii ad verbum interpretatione. Quibus acc. Joachimi Camerarii, nec non Henrici Stephani annotationes* (Genevae: Stephanus, 1603; SUB Göttingen 8 Auct. gr. II, 6146)
DACIER 1692a	*La Poëtique d'Aristote, Contenant Les Regles les plus exactes pour juger du Poëme Heroique, & des Pieces de Theatre, la Tragedie & la Comedie. Traduite en françois, Avec Des Remarques Critiques Par Mr. Dacier* (Paris: Chez Claude Barbin, ¹1692; repr. Hildesheim 1976)
DACIER 1692b	*L'Œdipe et L'Electre de Sophocle. Tragedies Grecques. Traduites en François avec des Remarques* (Paris: chez Claude Barbin, 1692; SUB Göttingen, 8 Auct. gr. II, 6606)
DRAKE 1699	[J. Drake], *The Antient and Modern Stage Survey'd or Mr Collier's View of the Immorality and Profanes of the English Stage set in a True Light* (London 1699; repr. London/Tokyo 1996)
LALAMANTIUS 1557	*Sophoclis tragicorum veterum facile principis Tragoediae, quotquot extant, septem … Nunc primum Latinae factae, et in lucem emissae per Ioannem Lalamantium apud Agustudum Heduorum Medicum* (Lutetiae ¹1557; edition used: Lutetiae: Apud Michaelem Vascosanum … 1558; SUB Göttingen 8 Auct. gr. II, 6302)
LA MESNARDIÈRE 1640	H.-J. Pilet de la Mesnardière, *La Poëtique* (Paris 1640; repr. Genève 1972)
MARMONTEL 1763	J.-Fr. Marmontel, *La Poëtique Françoise*, t. 1–2 (Paris 1763; repr. New York 1972)
MELANCHTHON 1545a	*Cohortatio Philippi Melanchthonis ad legendas tragoedias et comoedias* («Calend. Ianuarij 1545»); first published in: *P. Terentii Comoediae*

	sex, cvm prioribvs ferme castigationibvs et plerisque explicationibus ... editae stvdio et cvra Ioachimi Camerarii Pabergensis (Lipsiae: Papa, 1546; ULB Halle Pon Vg 3942) = MBW Nr. 3782; reprinted in: CR 5, Nr. 3108, 567–572
MELANCHTHON 1545b	Ph. Melanchthon, Lectures on Sophocles at the University of Wittenberg in 1545 (script by P. Obermeier, RSB Zwickau Sign. XLIX, fol. 1–128^v)
MELANCHTHON 1545c	Ph. Melanchthon, «In Electram Sophoclis» (announcement of a lecture, 18 January 1545); reprinted in: Ritoók-Szalay (2001) 325f.
NAOGEORG 1552	Th. Naogeorgus, «Epistola Nuncupatoria», in: *Ivdas Iscariotes, Tragoedia Nova Et Sacra ... Thoma Naogeorgo autore. Adivnctae Svnt quoq[ue] duæ Sophoclis Tragœdiæ, Aiax flagellifer & Philoctetes, ab eodem autore carmine uersæ* ... (12. Sept. 1552); reprinted in: Th. Naogeorg, *Sämtliche Werke*, hrsg. von H.-G. Roloff, Bd. 4, Teil 1: Dramen 5/6 (Berlin [u. a.] 1987) 271–280
NAOGEORG 1558	*Sophoclis Tragoediae Septem, Latino carmine redditae, & Annotationibus illustratae per Thomam Naogeorgum Straubingensem ...* (Basileae: Oporinus, in fine: 1558; SUB Göttingen 8 Auct. gr. II, 6303)
PAZZI 1536	*Aristotelis Poetica per Alexandrum Paccium ... in latinum conversa* (Venetiis ^{1}1536); edition used: *Aristotelis Stagiritae Poetica Alexandro Paccio Patritio Florentino interprete* (Parisiis: In Officina Christiani Wecheli, 1538; SUB Göttingen 4 Auct. gr. IV, 852-b)
RATALLER 1550	*Sophoclis Aiax Flagellifer, et Antigone Eiusdem Electra Georgio Ratallero [sic] interprete* (Lugduni: apud Seb. Gryphium 1550; John Rylands Univ. Library of Manchester, Christie Coll. /21 f 4)
RATALLER 1570	*Tragoediae Sophoclis quotquot extant carmine Latino reddita Georgio Ratallero ... interprete* (Antverpiae: Ex officina Gulielmi Silvij, ^{1}1570, SUB Göttingen 8 Auct. gr. II, 6304; ^{2}1576; ^{3}1584)
RICCIUS 1566	St. Riccius, «Epistola dedicatoria in comoedias Terentii», in: *In P. Terentii comoedias sex Novus Commentarius, ex publicis praelectionibus doctissimorum virorum, qui olim in celeberrima Academia VVitenbergensi floruerunt, ... collectus, et nunc primum editus a M. Stephano Riccio*, t. 1 (^{1}1566; edition used: Mulhusii: Georgius Hantzsch 1568; ULB Halle Ci 3595, 1) A2^r–[A8^r]
ROBORTELLO 1548	*Francisci Robortelli Utinensis In librum Aristotelis de arte poetica explicationes, paraphrasis in librum Horatii, qui vulgo de arte poetica ad Pisones inscribitur* (Florenz 1548; repr. München 1968)
STIBLIN 1562	*Euripides Poeta Tragicorum princeps, in Latinum sermonem conversus, adiecto e regione textu Graeco: Cum Annotationibus et Praefationibus in omnes eius tragoedias: autore Gasparo Stiblino ...* (Basileae: Oporinus, in fine: 1562, Mense Martio; SUB Göttingen 4 Auct. gr. III, 1367)
TERRASSON 1715	J. Terrasson, *Dissertation critique sur l'Iliade d'Homère, où à l'occasion de ce Poëme on cherche les regles d'une Poëtique fondée sur la raison & sur les exemples des Anciens & des Modernes* (Paris 1715; repr. Genève 1971)
VETTORI CA. 1550 (?)	P. Vettori, *Argumenta in Euripidis et Sophoclis Tragoedias* (before 1550); first published by M. Pratesi, «Gli ‹Argumenta in Euripidis et Sophoclis Tragoedias› di Pier Vettori», *Rinascimento* 25 (1985) 139–196
VETTORI 1560	*Petri Victorii Commentarii in primum librum Aristotelis de Arte Poetarum* (Florentiae 1560; repr. München 1967)

WINSHEMIUS 1546   *Interpretatio tragoediarum Sophoclis ad utilitatem iuventutis quae studiosa est graecae linguae edita a Vito VVinshemio* (Frankfurt ¹1546; edition used: Francofurti: Petrus Brubachius, Mense Martio ²1549, ULB Halle AB 150304; ³1551)

2. Works of Modern Criticism

AVEZZÙ, G., «Eschilo e l'ars critica di Pier Vettori, Note preliminari», *Lexis. Poetica, retorica e comunicazione nella tradizione classica* 19 (2001) 93–107
BORZA, E., «Sophocles Latinus. Étude de quelques traductions latines de Sophocle au XVIe siècle», *NlatJb* 3 (2001) 29–45
BORZA, E., «Catalogue des éditions imprimées de Sophocle au XVIe siècle», in: *Offrir un livre. Les dédicaces à l'époque Humaniste*, Nugae Humanisticae sub signo Erasmi 3 (Bruxelles, Musée de la Maison d'Erasme 2002) 97–139
BORZA, E., «Sophocle et le XVIe siècle», in: G. Avezzù (a cura di), *Il dramma sofocleo: testo, lingua, interpretazione* (Stuttgart/Weimar 2003) 49–58
BORZA, E., «Catalogue des travaux inédits d'humanistes consacrés à Sophocle, jusqu'en 1600», *Humanistica Lovaniensia* 52 (2003) 195–216
DASKAROLIS, A., *Die Wiedergeburt des Sophokles aus dem Geist des Humanismus. Studien zur Sophokles-Rezeption in Deutschland vom Beginn des 16. bis zur Mitte des 17. Jahrhunderts* (Tübingen 2000)
DE SMET, I. A. R., «Giants on the Shoulders of Dwarfs? Considerations on the Value of Renaissance and Early Modern Scholarship for Today's Classicists», in: Harrison (2001) 252–264
EASTERLING, P. E. (ed.), *The Cambridge Companion to Greek Tragedy* (Cambridge 1997)
GARLAND, R., *Surviving Greek Tragedy* (London 2004)
GARNIER, B., *Pour une poétique de la traduction. L'Hécube d'Euripide en France, de la traduction humaniste à la tragédie classique* (Paris 1999)
GREGORY, J., *A Companion to Greek Tragedy* (Blackwell 2005)
GRUYS, J. A., *The early printed editions (1518–1664) of Aeschylus. A Chapter in the History of Classical Scholarship* (Nieuwkoop 1981)
HARDWICK, L., *Reception Studies*, Greece & Rome. New Surveys in the Classics 33 (Oxford 2003)
HARRISON, S. J. (ed.), *Texts, Ideas, and the Classics. Scholarship, Theory, and Classical Literature* (Oxford 2001)
HEATH, M., «‹Jure principem locum tenet›: Euripides' *Hecuba*», *BICS* 34 (1987) 40–68: repr. in: J. Mossman (ed.), *Euripides. Oxford Readings in Classical Studies* (Oxford 2003) 218–260
[HIERONYMUS, Fr. (Hrsg.)], ἐν Βασιλείᾳ πόλει τῆς Γερμανίας: *Griechischer Geist aus Basler Pressen*, Publikationen der Universitätsbibliothek Basel 15 (Basel 1992)
KALLERGIS, I., «Die kritische Arbeit des Humanisten Franciscus Portus am Text des Aischylos», *Sphairos*. FS H. Schwabel 2, *WS* 108 (1994–1995) 639–646
KANNNICHT, R., Euripides, *Helena*, hrsg. und erkl. von R. Kannicht, Bd. 1-2 (Heidelberg 1969)
LACHMANN, V. R./ F. E. Cranz, «Aeschylus», in: P. O. Kristeller/F. E. Cranz (edd.), *Catalogus translationum et commentariorum*. vol. II (Washington 1971) 6–25
LOEHR, J., «Melanchthons Übersetzungen griechischer Dichtung», in: W. Ludwig (Hrsg.), *Die Musen im Reformationszeitalter* (Leipzig 2001) 209–245
LURJE, M., *Die Suche nach der Schuld. Sophokles' Oedipus Rex, Aristoteles' Poetik und das Tragödienverständnis der Neuzeit* (Stuttgart/Leipzig 2004)
MASTROIANNI, M., *Le Antigoni sofoclee del Cinquecento francese* (Firenze 2004)

MICHELINI, A. N., *Euripides and the Tragic Tradition* (Madison, Wis. 1987)
MILLS, S., *Euripides: Hippolytus* (London 2002)
MUND-DOPCHIE, M., *La survie d'Eschyle à la Renaissance. Éditions, traductions, commentaires et imitations* (Louvain 1984)
MUND-DOPCHIE, M., «La survie d'Eschyle à la Renaissance: vingt ans après», *Lexis* 19 (2001) 67–77
NIEFANGER, D., «Tragödie/Tragödientheorie», DNP 15/3 (2003) 533–543
PERTUSI, A., «La scoperta di Euripide nel primo Umanesimo», *Italia Medioevale e Umanistica* 3 (1960) 101–152
PERTUSI, A., «Il ritorno alle fonti del teatro greco classico: Euripide nell'Umanesimo e nel Rinascimento», *Byzantion* 33 (1963) 391–426
PETRINA, G., «Euripide nel Cinquecento: l'edizione di Willem Canter (1571)», in: G. Avezzù (a cura di), ΔΙΔΑΣΚΑΛΙΑΙ. *Tradizione e interpretazione del dramma attico* (Padova 1999) 211–242
PÖGGELER, O., *Schicksal und Geschichte. Antigone im Spiegel der Deutungen und Gestaltungen seit Hegel und Hölderlin* (München 2004)
PORRO, A., «Volgarizzamenti e volgarizzatori di drammi euripidei a Firenze nel Cinquecento», *Aevum* 55 (1981) 481–508
PORRO, A., «La versione latina dell'*Ecuba* euripidea attribuita a Pietro da Montagnana», in: M. Cortesi/E. V. Maltese (a cura di), *Dotti bizantini e libri greci nell'Italia del secolo XV* (Napoli 1992) 343–362
PRATESI, M., «Gli ‹Argumenta in Euripidis et Sophoclis Tragoedias› di Pier Vettori», *Rinascimento* 25 (1985) 139–196
REEVE, M., «Introduction», in: Harrison (2001) 245–251
RHEIN, St., «Melanchthon and Greek Literature», in: T. J. Wengert/ M. P. Graham (eds.), *Philip Melanchthon (1497–1560) and the Commentary* (Sheffield 1997) 149–170
RHEIN, St., «Philipp Melanchthon als Gräzist», in: G. Wartenberg/M. Hein (Hrsgg.), *Werk und Rezeption Philipp Melanchthons in Universität und Schule bis ins 18. Jahrhundert* (Leipzig 1999) 53–69
RITOÓK-SZALAY, Á., «Enarrat Electram Sophoclis», in: J. Loehr (Hrsg.), *Dona Melanchthoniana. FS H. Scheible* (Stuttgart/Bad Cannstatt 2001) 325–337
SCHMIDT, D. J., *On Germans & other Greeks. Tragedy and Ethical Life* (Bloomington 2001)
SICHERL, M., *Griechische Erstausgaben des Aldus Manutius. Druckvorlagen, Stellenwert, kultureller Hintergrund* (Paderborn 1997)
STEINER, G., *The Death of Tragedy* (London 1961)
STEINER, G., *Antigones* (Oxford 1984)
STONE, D., *French Humanist Tragedy: a Reassessment* (Manchester 1974)
THOMAS, D. A., *Aesthetics of Opera in the Ancien Régime, 1647–1785* (Cambridge 2002)
WETZEL, R., «Melanchthons Verdienste um Terenz unter besonderer Berücksichtigung ‹seiner› Ausgaben des Dichters», in: St. Rein [et al.] (Hrsgg.), *Philipp Melanchthon in Südwestdeutschland. Bildungsstationen eines Reformators* (Karlsruhe 1997) 101–128
ZIMMERMANN, B., «Griechische Tragödie», DNP 14 (2000) 316–323

Ivana Petrovic

Delusions of Grandeur:
Homer, Zeus and the Telchines in Callimachus' *Reply* (*Aitia* Fr. 1) and *Iambus* 6[*]

The visual representations of Homer were often modelled upon those of Zeus. Furthermore, not only in the visual arts, but in poetry as well Homer was often in one way or another brought in connection with Zeus. This article discusses the modes of representation of Homer in the visual arts and literature and Callimachus' usage of the metaphors ‹Zeus› and the ‹Telchines› in the preface to the *Aitia* and in the sixth *Iambus*. The discussion of the *Reply* investigates a hitherto neglected characteristic of the Telchines, namely their expertise as visual artists and its implication for the interpretation of the passage and the picture of Callimachus' critics.

Based on the discussion of the *Reply* and on the analysis of the modes of representation of Homer in Greek literature and in the visual arts, I propose a new, allegorical interpretation of the sixth *Iambus*: the statue of Zeus stands for Homeric poetry and the speaker of the poem is a Telchine. The description of the statue of Zeus in the sixth *Iambus* is intended to mimic, with sarcastic implications, the logic of the critics who can only value huge size and the imitators who want to follow Homer so closely they might as well tape-measure him.

1. Visual representations of Homer

In the year 1827 Ingres completed a painting *Apotheosis of Homer* the Louvre commissioned from him as a ceiling decoration. The majestic figure of Homer with a sceptre in his left hand and a scroll in his right occupies the centre of the painting. He is seated on the highest step in front of an Ionic temple and is being crowned with a laurel wreath by a winged Victory. The wreath is on the same level as the inscription on the architrave of the temple: ΟΜΗΡΟΣ and, if one looks closely, partially hidden behind the wreath stands the word ΘΕΟΣ.

On the stairs leading to the temple numerous figures of ancient and modern artists flock around the seated Homer.[1] Beneath Homer the personifications of the *Iliad* and *Odyssey*

---

[*] It is a pleasure to acknowlege by name those colleagues who have helped me with this paper. First and foremost I owe my wormest gratitude to Marco Fantuzzi, both for his sceptical, probing questiones and lucid comments. For helpful comments on various stages of the paper, I am indebted to Barbara Borg, Angelos Chaniotis, William Furley, Richard Hunter, Helmut Krasser, Ted Lendon, Peter v. Möllendorff and Andrej Petrovic.

[1] Parts of the paper were presented at conferences *Bildtext* (Giessen, July 2004) and *Visualising Epic* (Nottingham, September 2005). I wish to thank all those who participated in the discussion. I also thank the British Museum for permission to publish the photographs of the Archelaos Relief.
On the identification of the figures, Rosenblum (1985), pp. 130-133.

are sitting on the steps leading to the temple. They are flanking the inscription beneath Homer's feet: ΑΝΔΡΩΝ ΗΡΩΩΝ ΚΟΣΜΗΤΟΡΙ.

On the step beneath yet another inscription can be read. It is the anonymous epigram from the *Palatine Anthology* (16, 301):

> εἰ θεός ἐστιν Ὅμηρος, ἐν ἀθανάτοισι σεβέσθω
> εἰ δ' αὖ μὴ θεός ἐστι, νομιζέσθω θεὸς εἶναι.
> ‹If Homer is a god, he should be worshipped among the immortals,
> But again, if he is not a god, he should be acknowledged to be one.›

On the lowest step, two further inscriptions can be read. With an almost philological accuracy, the Latin passage is cited as Quintilianus, *Inst.Or.* Lib X Cap 1. The text runs as follows:

> *modesto tamen et circumspecto iudicio de tantis viris pronuntiandum est, ne, quod plerisque accidit, damnent quae non intellegunt. Ac si necesse est in alteram errare partem, omnia eorum legentibus placere quam multa displicere maluerim.*
> ‹However, modesty and circumspection are required in pronouncing judgement on such great men, since there is always the risk of falling into the common fault of condemning what one does not understand. And, if it is necessary to err on one side or the other, I should prefer that the reader should approve of everything than that he should disapprove of much.›[2]

The Greek text on the left is simply titled *Longinus*:

> Ἐνδείκνυται δ' ἡμῖν οὗτος ἀνήρ, εἰ βουλοίμεθα μὴ κατολιγωρεῖν, ὡς καὶ ἄλλη τις παρὰ τὰ εἰρημένα ὁδὸς ἐπὶ τὰ ὑψηλὰ τείνει. ποία δὲ καὶ τίς αὕτη; ἡ τῶν ἔμπροσθεν μεγάλων συγγραφέων καὶ ποιητῶν μίμησίς τε καὶ ζήλωσις. καί γε τούτου, φίλτατε, ἀπρὶξ ἐχώμεθα τοῦ σκοποῦ.[3]
> ‹This writer[4] shows us, if only we were willing to pay him heed, that another way (beyond anything we have mentioned) leads to the sublime. And what, and what manner of way, may that be? It is the imitation and emulation of previous great poets and writers. And let this, my dear friend, be the direction in which we firmly point our gaze.›[5]

The painting could be seen as an attempt to answer the tantalising question posed in the epigram inscribed on the step beneath the *Iliad* and the *Odyssey* – Is Homer a mortal or a god? The ancients asked the same question and answered it: What makes a poet a god? What makes *anyone* a god? The divine honours bestowed upon him. For artists who look up to Homer as the ideal of perfection, he *is* a god, because they strive to emulate him; he is the one that, in the words of Longinus, ‹leads them to the sublime›.

The road that leads to the sublime is the imitation and emulation – μίμησίς τε καὶ ζήλωσις – of previous great poets and writers. Of all great artists, Homer is the greatest, a god among lesser gods and heroes. The godly status of Homer is signified not only through the textual citations in the painting, but also through the overall stylisation of his figure – he not only holds a papyrus roll, but also a sceptre, he is being crowned by Nike, he has a temple with the inscription ‹Homer (is a) god›, he is clad in a godly manner and the ultimate symbol of Zeus, the eagle, is spreading his wings on the tympanum directly above his head.

---

[2] Slightly addapted translation of Butler (1961).
[3] *De Subl.* 13. 2. 1.
[4] Longinus is discussing Plato.
[5] Modified translation of Rhys Roberts (1907).

In fact, as is suitable for an academic painting, this particular representation of Homer is in many respects similar to the chryselephantine statue of Olympian Zeus as described by the ancient sources.[6] The overwhelming seated Zeus was so big that the observer had the impression he would break through the roof of his own temple if he decided to stand up. According to Pausanias,[7] the god held a sceptre in his left hand and a Nike with a wreath in his right hand. Seated on a sceptre was his bird, the eagle.

But where does the conception of Homer as Zeus originate? Ingres was hardly the first to come up with this idea. In fact, his sophisticated painting alludes to numerous previous representations of Homer's divinity, most notably the famous relief by one Archelaos of Priene, now in the British Museum (Brit. Mus. 2191, plate 1).

Due to the resemblance of the figure of Homer on this relief to that of Zeus, immediately after its discovery in Italy in the 17th century the relief was titled *The Apotheosis of Homer*.[8] Firm dating of the relief has proved to be very difficult,[9] but recent studies suggest the late third century BC[10] and link the work with Alexandria, on the basis of the similarity of two figures to portraits of Arsinoe III and Ptolemy IV Philopator.[11] Since it was Ptolemy IV who founded a shrine in honour of Homer in Alexandria[12] placing a majestic seated statue of Homer in it, recent studies[13] connect relief to this sanctuary and suggest an Alexandrian context for its creation.

The relief was probably a votive monument dedicated by a poet as commemoration of a victory in a poetic contest.[14] It shows 27 figures in four tiers and two settings.[15] The lowest register is a typical representation of a sacrifice, but the worshippers and the god are unusual: as identified by inscriptions beneath, the seated Zeus-like figure with a scroll in his right hand and a sceptre in the left is Homer. He is receiving a sacrifice of a cow from a boy labelled as ‹Myth› and a female labelled ‹History› who are stylized as an altar boy and a priestess;[16] behind them more labelled figures (Poetry, Tragedy and Comedy) make offerings on the altar and Physis, Arete, Mneme, Pistis and Sophia observe the sacrificial ritual. On either side of Homer, the personifications of the *Iliad* and *Odyssey* kneel. Behind Homer

---

[6] For *testimonia* see Overbeck (1959) T 692–754.
[7] Paus. 5. 11. 1.
[8] G. Cuper first entitled it *Apotheosis* in his publication *Apotheosis vel consecratio Homeri* (1671). The literature on it is immense. See Pinkwart (1965a; 1965b); Richter (1965), Vol. I, pp. 53–4; Pollitt (1986), pp. 15–16; von Hesberg (1988); Ridgway (1990), pp. 257–268; Smith (1991), pp. 186–7; Cameron (1995), pp. 273–7; Zanker (1995), pp. 154–158; Clay (2004), pp. 91–92.
[9] See Richter (1965) Vol. I, p. 54 for a summary of attempts at dating the relief.
[10] See Pollit (1986), pp. 15–16; Smith (1991), pp. 186–87.
[11] On the identification of Chronos and Oekumene, La Rocca (1984), p. 538 (with further literature). The most complete survey of all suggested identifications with Hellenistic rulers is still Pinkwart (1965a), pp. 36–42.
[12] On Homereion of Alexandria, Clay (2004), p. 74 and *testimonia* in the Appendix *Homer* (T6) p. 139.
[13] Richter (1965), Vol I, p. 54; Pollit (1986), pp. 15–16; Smith (1991), pp. 186–87. Other suggestions have been made, namely the temple of Homer in Smyrna: Pinkwart (1965), p. 90. Voutiras (1989) suggests a Stoic interpretation and connects the relief with Pergamon, but see the objections in Zanker (1995), p. 340 n. 15. Ridgway (1990), pp. 264–6 considers the possibility of a Roman context, notably Bovillae and its general area (where the relief was found) and connects the relief with the *Tabulae Iliacae*, dating it as late as the first century BC.
[14] It takes a poet to recognise a poet – J. W. von Goethe (1827), p. 28 was the first to suggest a commemorative relief of a victorious poet, whereas previously one tended to see the relief simply as an allegorical representation of Homer's apotheosis. See Pinkwart (1965), pp. 16–17 for the overview of interpretations proposed thus far.
[15] For the detailed description see Pinkwart (1965b), pp. 55–57.
[16] Pinkwart (1965b), p. 57.

two figures are standing, identified by *tituli* as Inhabited World (Oikoumene) and Time (Chronos) and taken to be the cryptoportaits of Arsinoe III and Ptolemy IV.

The second scene, above, is a mountainous area, represented in three slope-like registers. The highest register is occupied by a stately figure of a reclining, half-naked Zeus, with a sceptre in his right hand and an eagle by his side. Slightly beneath Zeus is the mother of the Muses, Mnemosyne. On her left side a Muse is descending the slope and approaching the second register, where her four sisters with their respective attributes are represented. On the third slope there are four Muses and, on the far right side, a statue of the victorious poet with a tripod. The poet is holding a scroll in his right hand. His head, now badly damaged, could once have been a portrait. On his right side is a cave where Apollo *Musagetes* is playing the lyre next to the Delphic Omphalos.

The mountain setting of the upper three registers suggests Parnassos (due to the Omphalos) or Helicon (a more attractive interpretation, since it would place the relief more firmly in the Alexandrian setting[17]).

Pollitt (1986), p. 16 proposes the following interpretation of the relief:

‹Inspiration springs from Zeus (…) and Memory and is passed from heaven to earth by the Muses. Its foremost recipient was Homer, both a patron god and symbolic ancestor of the victorious poet for whom the relief was made. Homer's epics will last for all times and are universal (hence he is crowned by Chronos and Oikoumene); they celebrate both myth and history. They are the fountain head of the literary genres that came after epic (lyric poetry, tragedy and comedy, arranged, in an appropriately learned fashion, in the historical order of their invention) and they have bestowed, like all worthy poetry, essential moral virtues upon human nature.›

What makes this representation of Homer so similar to Ingres' painting is not only the general subject – the road to the divine through imitation and emulation of the great predecessors – but also the conception of Homer as Zeus. While Ingres avoided representing Homer and Zeus together, Archelaos is by this very device stressing the similarity of the two characters. Homer is a mirror-image of Zeus, since he himself is also a patron god from whom inspiration flows. The ‹double projection› of some of the figures in both scenes underlines this: History, Tragedy and Comedy appear as Muses in the upper setting[18] *and* as worshippers of Homer on the lower setting.

The allegorical representation of Archelaos is not the earliest example of a Zeus-like Homer. Even though our knowledge of Homer's cult statues from his sanctu-

---

[17] Ptolemy IV Philopator and his wife Arsinoe III promoted the cult of Muses in Thespiai and were involved in reorganisation of the *Museia*. On this see Schachter (1986), p. 160 and 164–166; SEG XXII, 376.

[18] The identification of individual Muses on the relief is a notoriously difficult problem. Pinkwart (1965a), pp. 79–80 is balanced to a fault, arguing against individualisation of the Muses and tentatively suggesting only two identifications, namely Urania (Muse with the globe in the second register) and Calliope (the far right Muse in the second register). However, her discussion of the specialisation of the Muses is, at least as far as texts are concerned, deficient (Pinkwart (1965a) Exkurs II, pp. 174–182): She neglects several important Hellenistic passages, for example several occurrences of Καλλιόπη and Κλειώ in Callimachus' *Aitia* (most notably *Fr*. 43. 56 Pfeiffer where Κλειώ provides information about Sicilian cities; *Fr*. 7. 22 Pfeiffer: Καλλιόπη provides information about cult idiosyncrasies on Rhodes and Anaphe; and Fr. 75. 77 Pfeiffer). Ascribing particular domains to individual Muses, at least as far as history, tragic and comic poetry are concerned is surely attested for the early third century BC and arguable as early as the fifth. (Pinkwart does not discuss a single line from Aristophanes and does not consider Plato *Phdr*. 259c–d to be enough evidence for the individualisation of the domains of the Muses).

aries[19] is tantalisingly limited, it is possible that the cult statue from the *Homereion* in Alexandria resembled Homer on Archelaos' relief. According to Aelian (*Var.Hist.* 13. 22) the Alexandrian temple featured a ‹magnificent seated Homer› in the centre and, in a circle around him, all the cities that claimed Homer as their own. The ‹road to the divine through the emulation of great predecessors› message was transmitted with what would to many a modern observer appear to be a rather repulsive literalness: The painter Galaton drew Homer vomiting and the other poets collecting the vomit.[20]

A similar representation of Homer surrounded by his devotees could be seen in Memphis: In the exedra of the Sarapeion, the over life-size statue of seated Homer was surrounded by (or rather, flanked by, if one accepts the semicircular arrangement of the figures proposed by Picard[21]) the statues of great philosophers and writers: Protagoras, Thales, Heraclitus, Plato, Aristotle on the right side, and Hesiod, Orpheus, Demetrios of Phaleron and Pindar on the left side. The identification of the figures as well as the date of the sculptural complex has been debated: Instead of construction in the time of Ptolemy II, as argued by Picard and Lauer,[22] recent scholarship is more inclined to date the group at the first or the second half of the second century BC[23] and to identify some of the figures as Alexander the Great, Indian Dionysos and Diogenes. However, the identification (and the positioning) of Homer is not in question.

If some of the statues are correctly identified as members of the Ptolemaic dynasty,[24] the significance of Homer's position in the Hellenistic pantheon and the importance of his cult for the self-presentation of the rulers in the Hellenistic period is additionally stressed: Homer is not only the ultimate source of inspiration for any artist, but also for the divinised rulers.[25] This points towards the tendency to perceive Homer not only as a god, but as a presiding divinity in his own pantheon.[26]

The unique standing of Homer's cult in Alexandria is further supported by the anonymous epigram addressed to Ptolemy IV Philopator probably contemporary to the founding of the cult of Homer.[27]

As the institution of the cult of Homer in Alexandria was not only a way to pay respect to the best of the poets, but also played an important role in the self-presentation of the Ptolemies as the patrons of arts and as such contributed to their own prestige,[28] it was

---

[19] On the cult and sanctuaries of Homer, Clay (2004) pp. 74–76 and *Testimonia* 136–143.
[20] One might note that in the Louvre, the image of the poet surrounded by cities that claimed his birth is repeated: Beneath the painting of Ingres there are seven female figures, representing Smyrna, Chios, Kolophon, Argos, Salamis on Cyprus, Athens and Rhodes. The painting's placement in the Hall of *Egyptian* antiquities is rather intriguing as well.
[21] Picard / Lauer (1955), p. 153.
[22] Picard / Lauer (1955), pp. 38–47, 48–171.
[23] See the discussion in Ridgway (1990), pp. 131–134 with further literature.
[24] Matz (1957) identified Ptolemy Philometor in one of the heads; Pietrzykowski (1976) identifies one thus far unidentified figure as Ptolemy I.
[25] Zanker (1995), pp. 166–7.
[26] In the Hellenistic age, the divinity ascribed to poets by poets became a commonplace. See Gabathuler (1937) for epigrams on this subject and Clay (2004) for cults of poets.
[27] SH 979.
[28] The relief of Archelaos is a significant indicator for the Ptolemaic modes of self-representation, since Ptolemy IV and his wife are the ones that are crowning Homer. One wonders if the *titulus* Oecumene hints at the attempts of the Ptolemies to conquer a significant part of the Mediterranean, and if the *titulus* Chronos

probably the aspect of prestige that prompted the individual cities to establish cults of Homer.[29]

The cities who claimed Homer as their own tended to establish his shrines and to issue coins honouring him. There is evidence for his cult in Argos, Chios, Smyrna and Ios. Smyrna, Chios, Kolophon, Kyme, Nikaia, Temnos, Ios and the colony of Smyrna, Amastris issued coins representing Homer. The earliest sources for the cult come from the fourth century BC (Argos, Chios). Ios issued coins with Homer in the fourth century BC and his cult in Smyrna was founded in the early third century BC.[30]

How did the cities represent Homer in their shrines? Of this, we posses frustratingly little information. There was a bronze statue of him in Argos;[31] Strabo mentions a *xoanon* in the temple of Homer in Smyrna[32] – the word implies a particularly old, perhaps wooden statue.[33] The iconographical characteristics of the statues are not discernible, but some impression of what they might have looked like might perhaps be gained from the coins issued in honour of Homer.[34]

Coins from Smyrna, Kolophon, Chios, Nikaia and Cyme depict a bearded, seated Homer who is wearing a mantle and holding a scroll, often with one hand raised to his chin. Especially interesting are the coins from Smyrna, since some of them represent Homer with a staff or sceptre in one hand and a papyrus roll in the other.[35] Esdaile (1912) argued that this series unquestionably reproduces the bronze statue in the *Homereion* at Smyrna. Even if this statement is too enthusiastic,[36] the seated Zeus-like Homer was, according to Zanker, the preferred representation of Homer on the coins of Smyrna.[37]

The representation of a seated, Zeus-like Homer holding a sceptre and scroll is also attested on the coin from Cyme.[38]

The striking similarity with Zeus is a feature of Homer's portrait on the coin of Ios (4th century BC).[39] Zanker claims that without the inscription ‹Homer› everyone would think that the image represents Zeus and concludes (p. 160): ‹Man sieht daran, wie früh Homer

---

stands for their efforts to preserve the literary legacy of the Greeks by instituting and supporting the Museum and the Library.

[29] On the cults of Homer see now Clay (2004), pp. 74–5 and *Testimonia*, pp. 136–143. See also the survey in Pinkwart (1965a), pp. 169–173.
[30] Pinkwart (1965b), p. 172.
[31] Clay (2004) T 10 = *Cert.Hom.Hes.* 302-4 Allen.
[32] Strabo 14. 37 = Clay (2004), T 20.
[33] Zanker (1995), p. 157.
[34] For the coins, Esdaile (1912); Richter (1965) Vol. I, pp. 55–6; Heyman (1982); Klose (1987), Clay (2004), p. 82.
[35] Richter (1965) Vol. I, fig. 127; Zanker (1995), fig. 88b.
[36] Schefold (1943), p. 219 argues against it: ‹Als man nach der Schlacht bei Magnesia 188 zuerst Homer auf die Münzen setzte, entsprach das Kultbild im Homereion nicht dem hochhellenistischen Geschmack. Man griff deshalb auf einen zeusähnlichen Typus (…) ähnlich der Homerstatue im Homereion von Alexandria. Die Gemeinsamkeit des Herrschersymbols, des Szepters, spricht sogar für direkte Abhängigkeit›. See also Zanker (1995), p. 160: ‹Nicht alle diese Bilder können auf tatsächlich existierende Statuen oder gar «Kultstatuen» zurückgehen, aber ihre Vielfalt bezeugt, wie intensiv man sich mit Homers Gestalt beschäftigte.›
[37] Zanker (1995), p. 160: ‹Am beliebtesten war auch in Smyrna das Bild eines zeusähnlich thronenden Homer, der wie auf dem Archelaos-Relief ein hohes Szepter und (statt des Blitzes!) eine Buchrolle hält. Auf einer der frühesten Prägungen war er Zeus noch mehr angeglichen, hatte wie dieser einen nackten Oberkörper und streckte seine Rechte mit der Rolle gebieterisch aus.›
[38] Esdaile (1912), Plate V, 9.
[39] Zanker (1995), fig. 87.

selbst zu einer mythischen Gestalt wird und dass die Angleichung des Homerbildes und das des Zeus auf alte Vorstellungen von der einzigartigen Bedeutung des Homer zurückgeht. Die Gestalt des Sängers verschmilzt mit der der Götter und Heroen, von deren Welt er kündet.›

Since the general characteristic of the portraits of Homer in antiquity was ‹a dignified, Zeus-like aspect with long hair and beard› (Richter (1965), Vol. I, p. 56) it may have been argued that the cult statues of the poet emphasised the Zeus-like aspect as a matter of course.

2. What do poets talk about when they talk about Zeus?

We have seen that Homer was worshipped as god and probably represented in a Zeus-like manner in his shrines. One could argue that, in the manner of other Greek divinities, he instituted and, in a way, took care of his own cult: he called the singers in the epics θεῖοι ἀοιδοί[40] and θεῖος ἀοιδός soon came to be his own other name.[41] But then, other poets did the same, as well: they either called themselves θεῖος (not surprisingly, Bacchylides,[42] the ‹Cean nightingale› is one among them) or were pronounced by others to be ‹divine› and so many θεῖοι ἀοιδοί came into beiing. Numerous praises of Homer as the greatest poet, the offspring of Muses, the messenger of the gods are to be found in Greek literature, and equally numerous are the assertions of his special status among the poets,[43] but comparisons with Zeus are more difficult to find, especially in the classical period. In the Hellenistic era however, the divine status of poets seems to have been subject to inflation – so numerous are the poets to whom divinity was ascribed to, that it becomes a commonplace. This is the period when the equation of Homer with Zeus is to be expected, and, indeed, is to be found.

The oldest example for the equation of Homer with Zeus comes from the *enfant terrible* of the Greek dithyramb, Timotheos of Miletus (ca. 450–360 BC), who is enthroning Homer as Zeus only to overthrow him and declare him Kronos in the same line.[44]

Asper (1997) discusses several instances of poetic identification of Homer with Zeus.[45] The epigram of Leonidas (*AP* 9. 25) is particularly interesting, since in it the poet Aratus is being praised as ‹second to Zeus› (l. 5–6 Διὸς ... δεύτερος), a praise that would make much more sense if one takes ‹Zeus› to mean ‹Zeus of poets›, that is Homer. In an epigram which seems much like a reply to this one, Ptolemy III asserted that Aratus is not second to Zeus, but does indeed hold the sceptre himself.[46]

The motif of holding a sceptre was obviously very *en vogue* in Hellenistic epigrams on poets and could be taken to mean ‹to be the Zeus of poetry›, as in the following epigram of Antipater of Thessalonica:[47]

---

[40] On the conception of Homer's divinity in Greek literature, Skiadas (1965), pp. 64–111.
[41] See Skiadas (1965), pp. 66–8 for numerous examples.
[42] Cf. 9. 3
[43] Skiadas (1965) *passim*.
[44] PMG 796. See the discussion in Asper (1997), p. 197, n. 279.
[45] Asper (1997), p. 141 (Callimachus *Ep.* 6 Pfeiffer) and p. 197 (Leonidas *Ep.* 101.2577 *HE* = *AP* 9.25; Ps. Longinus 9. 14; Quintilian 10. 1. 46, Plutarchus *Quom. Adul.* 10. 54).
[46] *SH* 712: Many poets, including Hegesianax and Hermippus wrote on similar subjects, (V.4) ἀλλ' ὅ γε λεπτολόγος σκῆπτρον Ἄρατος ἔχει.
[47] *AP* 7. 409.

Ὄβριμον ἀκαμάτου στίχον αἴνεσον· Ἀντιμάχοιο,
ἄξιον ἀρχαίων ὀφρύος ἡμιθέων,
Πιερίδων χαλκευτὸν ἐπ' ἄκμοσιν, εἰ τορὸν οὖας
ἔλλαχες, εἰ ζαλοῖς τὰν ἀγέλαστον ὄπα,
εἰ τὰν ἄτριπτον καὶ ἀνέμβατον ἀτραπὸν ἄλλοις
μαίεαι· εἰ δ' ὕμνων σκᾶπτρον Ὅμηρος ἔχει,
καὶ Ζεύς τοι κρέσσων' Ἐνοσίχθονος, ἀλλ' Ἐνοσίχθων
τοῦ μὲν ἔφυ μείων, ἀθανάτων δ' ὕπατος·
καὶ ναετὴρ Κολοφῶνος ὑπέζευκται μὲν Ὁμήρῳ,
ἀγεῖται δ' ἄλλων πλάθεος ὑμνοπόλων.
‹Praise the sturdy verse of tireless Antimachus,
worthy of the majesty of the demigods of old,
beaten on the anvil of the Muses, if thou art gifted
with a keen ear, if thou aspirest to gravity of words,
if thou wouldst pursue a path untrodden and unapproached by others.
If Homer holds the sceptre of song,
yet, though Zeus is greater than Poseidon,
Poseidon his inferior is the chief of the immortals,
so the Colophonian bows before Homer,
but leads the crowd of other singers.›[48]

Antipater operates with a whole parallel pantheon of the poetic gods, a strategy which surely would not have been possible, if the assimilation of Homer to Zeus was not a motif already established.

The comparison of Homer to Zeus is a reflection of his standing in Greek literature as the ultimate and best poet, the measure to which every aspiring artist must be compared. The custom to praise writers by comparing them to Homer was not only reserved for the writers of epics. Herodotus, Stesichorus, Sophocles, Euripides, Plato – even Thucydides was praised as his heir[49] and, in one way or another, all literary genres were thought to have had their origin in his epics.

The relief of Archelaus presented in the language of the visual arts what was taken to be a fact in the Hellenistic period: not only literature, all arts (and artists) are indebted to Homer. But there are emulations and emulations. Not all was idyllic in the picture of Homer as the ultimate ideal. And as much as one might appreciate the serene, dignified classicism of Ingres' *Apotheosis*, it does somehow make one a bit drowsy. Ingres would probably faint at the sight of Dali's work on the same subject from 1944/5, an image of disorientation and destruction worlds apart from the tranquil certainty of Ingres' dead artists' society.[50]

---

[48] Translation: Patton (1917). This epigram celebrates the works of Antimachus in a distinctly Callimachean language, the pun being the fact that Callimachus himself was attacking Antimachus' *Lyde* vigorously. On Hellenistic epigrams against Callimachus, Hunter (2004), pp. 446–9. See also the discussion of this epigram in Skiadas (1965), pp. 118–124.

[49] Cameron (1995), p. 275.

[50] Dali's *Apotheosis of Homer* (now in *Staatsgallerie Moderner Kunst* in Munich) represents Homer as a crumbling plaster bust supported by a walking stick, a rather cleaver pun on the image of the blind bard. This compelling work of art demonstrates a conspicuous parallel to Callimachus' *Reply*: Out of the mouth of Homer's crumbling bust a child's head emerges. Chronologically it was possible for Dali to read the *Reply*, but the παῖς ἄτε parallel may well have been a product of the similarity of concepts of avant-garde rather than a product of a close reading of Callimachus.

But then again, didn't Pindar profess his choice to take ‹the road less travelled› in the fifth century BC[51] and didn't Timotheus refuse to have anything to do with Homer's Muse and told her to hit the road in the fourth? The problem for both was not the work of Homer itself, but the kind of μίμησίς τε καὶ ζήλωσις the poet should choose when producing his own poetry, which brings us to the image of Zeus in Callimachus.

3. Thundering is not my job, but Zeus'

In his programmatic preface to the *Aitia* ‹Reply to the Telchines›[52] Callimachus uses a number of notoriously cryptic metaphors.[53] One of them evokes the image of Zeus: the speaker of the *Reply* refuses to produce ‹a loud-resounding poem› (v. 19) and states: ‹Thundering is not my job, but Zeus'!› (v. 20). He claims that the Telchines (on whose insults he is not brief) are ‹constantly mumbling against his poetry› because it is not ‹one continuous poem (ἓν ἄεισμα διηνεκές)[54] in thousands of lines on kings or heroes.›[55]

The defence of the speaker is one of the most influential passages of Greek literature: after additional jabs at Telchines and naming a few examples of poems he appreciates, he goes on to refuse to produce a ‹loud-resounding poem› and advises the Telchines to ‹judge poetry by art, not by the Persian *schoinos*›[56] (Fr. 1, 17–20 Pfeiffer):

ἔλλετε Βασκανίη]ς ὀλοὸν γένο[ς· αὖθι δὲ τέχνῃ
κρίνετε,][μὴ σχοίν]ῳ Περσίδι τὴ[ν] σοφίην·
μηδ' ἀπ' ἐμεῦ διφᾶ]τε μέγα ψοφέουσαν ἀοιδήν
τίκτεσθαι· βροντᾶ]ν οὐκ ἐμόν, [ἀλλὰ] Διός.

‹Off with you, wretched race of Malice! In future (judge) fine poetry by art, not by the Persian schoinos. Do not look to me for the birth of a loud-resounding poem: thundering is not my job, but Zeus'›.[57]

The cluster of Callimachus' poetic metaphors is extremely complex and ingeniously allusive and most probably these verses were written to tease[58] – after all, they have been teasing (and tormenting) scholars for almost eighty years. The issue at stake here is obviously big vs. small[59] and the appeal to the critics to reject length and bombast as sole

---

[51] Paean 7b Fr. 52h.10–14 Snell/Maehler. For Pindar's usage of the «road» metaphor, Asper (1997), pp. 26–38; For this fragment and *Aitia* pp. 64–72. Asper is extremely cautious about accepting Callimachus' direct imitation of Pindar, but the majority are not – see Hunter (2004), p. 70 with further literature.
[52] *Reply* is a much-discussed poem indeed. See Benedetto (1993) on he history of interpretation; Asper (1997) for the fullest discussion, and now also Hunter (2004), pp. 66–76.
[53] On Callimachus' poetological metaphors, Asper (1997).
[54] On possible Aristotelian connotations of this reproach, Hunter (1993), Appendix, pp. 190–196.
[55] *Aetia Fr.* 1, 3–5 Pfeiffer.
[56] According to Pfeiffer (1928), p. 318 the ‹Persian schoinos› is the largest measure for length, equal to παρασάγγης (app. 6 km).
[57] All translations of the *Reply* are from Hunter (2004).
[58] As stated by Hunter (1993), p. 190.
[59] For a very thorough discussion of big vs. small in Callimachus' poetological metaphors, Asper (1997), pp. 135–156 with bibliography. I cannot however follow Asper's main thesis (that Callimachus' poetological metaphors cannot be deciphered because they function as *Leerstellen* (see also Asper (2001), pp. 86–8 for a synthesis of this argument). For the lack of space here I only state my main reasons for trying to

aesthetic criteria – indeed, bombast and length seem to merge into a single criterion in this passage (since the poem is characterised as μέγα ψοφέουσα).⁶⁰

The additional issue at stake in the *Reply* is the problem of self-positioning in the literary tradition. To cut a very long *Forschungsgeschichte* short:⁶¹ the Zeus from the *Reply* is not being rejected altogether, nor is his thundering seen as a negative characteristic; the speaker is simply refusing to accept the need for thundering for his own poetry.⁶² According to the speaker, the Telchines demand of him to produce a poem much like that of Zeus, and it is the closeness to the model in length and in style the speaker is unwilling to deliver.⁶³

Cameron (1992) argues that the speaker of the *Reply* is protesting against the sort of imitation which is unsophisticated because of its closeness to the model:⁶⁴ the model is not being questioned, it is the requirement to follow it too closely that is problematic.

If we take *Zeus* from the *Reply* to metaphorically stand for *Homer* – which is in my opinion the most plausible interpretation of the passage⁶⁵ – then modes of imitation and emulation of Homeric epics are being discussed here, and the Telchines are representing the view that the Homeric model should be followed very closely. Their positive example might have been the kind of epic poetry that experienced its revival with the age of Alexander and the Diadochs: historical, historical-encomiastic and historical-geographic epic, probably of the cyclic type, closely imitating Homer both in language and scope and reaching grandiose proportions⁶⁶ but it is also possible that the Telchines would have appreciated contemporary historical-encomiastic elegy, a genre that also appears to have flourished at this time and whose authors apparently also closely followed the style of the Homeric epics.⁶⁷

Both genres appear to have been characterised by heavy borrowing from Homeric language and formulaic repetition – all characteristics that Callimachus, Theocritus and Apollonius Rhodius rejected.⁶⁸ Those poets who enthroned Homer as Zeus and attempted to write exactly as he did were, according to the *Reply*, actually committing the act of hubris and, lost in their delusions of grandeur, in an attempt to thunder like Zeus produced nothing better than the ‹braying of asses›.⁶⁹

---

decipher them: They function as a system, not only in the *Reply* but in the whole opus of Callimachus and they do not function alone, but are combined with allusions.

⁶⁰ As argued by Hunter (2004), pp. 69–70 (with bibliography and the discussion of Aristophanes' *Frogs* in this context).

⁶¹ Asper's analysis of the metaphor *Zeus* in the *Reply* (1997), pp. 196–198 provides an extensive bibliography.

⁶² Asper (1997), p. 196: ‹Der ausschließliche Nexus des Donners mit Zeus impliziert nicht nur eine Ablehnung des Donnerns für Kallimachos selbst, der nicht Zeus ist, sondern auch für alle anderen, die ebenso wenig Zeus sind. Der Gedanke ist also apologetisch und polemisch zugleich.›

⁶³ As discussed in Hunter (2004), pp. 69–72 (with further literature).

⁶⁴ Cameron (1992) and (1995), pp. 268–302 argues that the genre in question is elegy, not contemporary epic, but see n. 66.

⁶⁵ See Asper (1997) p. 196 for this interpretation (with bibliography).

⁶⁶ Cameron (1995) questions the very existence of Hellenistic traditional epic as postulated by Ziegler (1965); however, we do possess Hellenistic inscriptions honouring the poets for works of this kind. See the discussion of inscriptions in Chaniotis (1988); on traditional epic in the Hellenistic age, Fantuzzi (1988) XXXIV–XLI; Lehnus (1999); Fantuzzi (2004) pp. 21–23; 246–9.

⁶⁷ On Hellenistic encomiastic elegy see now the extensive study of Barbantani (2001). (On p. 25 Barbantani suggests itinerant elegiac poets as the target of Callimachus' attack in the *Reply*.)

⁶⁸ On this see Fantuzzi (2004), pp. 246–9 (with bibliography).

⁶⁹ Fr. 1, 29–30 Pfeiffer: ἐνὶ τοῖς γὰρ ἀείδομεν οἳ λιγὺν ἦχον / τέττιγος, θόρυβον δ' οὐκ ἐφίλησαν ὄνων.

Instead of trying to reproduce Homeric thunder (sc. stylistic grandeur), Callimachus rather chose to pay respect to the god of poets by selective use of Homeric words and avoidance of the formulae, thus creatively changing his language and adapting it to his own, thematically and stylistically different kind of poetry. This applies to Theocritus and Apollonius Rhodius as well: in the words of Fantuzzi (2004) p. 249, they ‹set up the dialectic between «formularity», allusion, and innovation which characterises their work and distinguishes them from the more unimaginative imitators of Homer›.

The image of the Telchines from the *Reply* adapts well to the idea of hubris: in Greek mythology, the Telchines are a race of demonic creatures skilled in all manner of metalwork, but (or rather: therefore) also in magic, invidious and dangerous, having the Evil Eye. On account of their rendering the soil (mostly on Greek islands) infertile or demonstrating lack of respect for the gods, they were destroyed by one of the greater gods, Zeus, Poseidon or Apollo.[70]

Pfeiffer tentatively suggested that in the *Reply* Callimachus was alluding to a legend, according to which the hubris of the Telchines was punished by Apollo in the form of a wolf – hence his epithet Λύκειος.[71] Since in the *Reply* Apollo Λύκιος defends Callimachus' poetical *credo* from the critish of the Telchines (who are obviously demonstrating hubris towards Zeus), the image of the vindictive god punishing the critics would fit the imagery of the *Reply* perfectly.[72]

The choice of the metaphor ‹Telchines› for critics is a very clever one, providing Callimachus with a range of negative connotations for his opponents, thus rendering his figure of the narrator more credible and winning the favour of the reader in advance.[73] But, at the same time, depicting his critics as absolute and hopeless amateurs and total bad guys would also be a mistake – why even engage in a critical discussion with someone who is totally worthless? True, the Telchines are characterised as ‹mumbling against› the speaker's poetry (v.1), as ‹ignorant and no friends of the Muse› (v.2);[74] they are addressed with the words ‹race who know how to melt your own liver (sc. with envy)› (7–8); and ‹wretched race of Malice› (17) but still, the speaker *is* engaging in a critical discussion with them, and even trying to instruct them how they should judge fine poetry in the future.

---

[70] On Telchines in Greek mythology, Herter (1934); Forbes (1950), pp 78–91; Kambylis (1965), pp. 76–7; Brillante (1993); Rakoczy (1996), pp. 166–7; 170–1.

[71] Pfeiffer (1928), p. 320 citing Servius on Verg. *Aen.* 4. 377 *sive quod in lupi habitu Telchinas occiderit* and Eust. 2. 789. 16 ἢ τοξευθέντες ὑπ' Ἀπόλλωνος ὤλοντο.

[72] And would provide a picture very coherent with the closure of the *Hymn to Apollo* (where Apollo is again defending the Callimachean poetics against Momos and Phthonos – cf. Call. *H. Ap.* 105-13 and the interpretation of Williams (1978), pp. 85–97). Epigram 21 Pfeiffer provides an additional piece for the metaphorical mosaic: There Calimachus is characterised as the one whose song was *stronger than* βασκανία (v. 4: ὁ δ' ἤεισεν κρέσσονα βασκανίης) e.g., the one whose poetry survived the test of time and invidious critics. Giangrande (1968), p. 716 argues that βασκανία here means only ‹destruction›, not ‹enviousness› but I do not see why both meanings should not be implied.

[73] For Callimachus' poetological metaphors as a strategy for *Sympathielenkung* see Asper (1997) *passim*; see also Schmitz (1999) on Callimachus' strategy of ‹luring the readers into adopting the role of the implied reader› (p. 162) in the *Reply*. I agree with both Asper and Schmitz that the *Reply* aims at defining the implied reader, but think that, just as it refers to (at that time) extant works of his predecessors, the speaker also suggests the existence of readers who would prefer different approaches to the Homeric model. The historical identity of the Telchines is not the subject of this paper. On that, Cameron (1995), pp. 185–232 (with bibliography).

[74] Magnelli (1999) offers an extensive discussion of the syntax of this difficult verse.

The accumulation of expressions like ‹envy› and ‹malice› brings to mind an aspect of the Telchines thus far largely neglected in the discussions of the *Reply*:[75] one can envy only the things that are envi*able*. Why were the Telchines so often depicted as destructive, malicious creatures? Because they were artisans themselves and their envy was directed at those who could claim the same or a higher level of craftsmanship.[76]

In ancient texts, there are two characteristics of the Telchines regularly mentioned: their envy and their craftsmanship. Their excellence in arts and crafts, particularly in metal-work is mentioned in numerous texts and some went as far as specifying them as ‹inventors of (useful) skills›,[77] or, more specifically, of the forging of metals.[78]

Especially interesting is their relationship with the gods: on the one hand, there are several traditions of them being destroyed by the gods on account of their hubris, but, on the other hand, they were credited with invention of the art of making cult statues (ἀγαλματοποιΐα).[79] Many cult statues of the gods were, according to legend, made by the Telchines – even a statue of Apollo on Rhodes.[80] Furthermore, the Telchines were, like the Cyclopes, credited with forging the arms of the gods, for instance the sickle of Cronos.[81] Their negative qualities, such as association with magic, envy and the possession of an Evil Eye, are connected with their expertise in arts and excellence as metal-workers. Their envy is actually presented as an occupational disease since they are jealous of artistic skills. They are described as φθονεροὶ ἐν τῇ διδασκαλίᾳ τῶν τεχνῶν by Diodorus (5. 55. 3) and as τεχνῖται δὲ ὄντες καὶ τὰ τῶν προτέρων ἔργα μωμησάμενοι by Nicolaus of Damascus.[82]

In my opinion, Callimachus did not want to blend out the artistic connotations of the Telchines in the *Reply*; on the contrary – he appeals to their several characteristics simultaneously: to their image as malicious, vindictive critics, to their destruction on account of hubris, and to their association with arts. This is accomplished through typical Calli-

---

[75] With one exception: in their 2002 paper, Acosta-Hughes and Stephens do discuss the artistic connotations of the Telchines, but they interpret them as ‹primitive artists› lacking artistic inspiration (p. 241). This view is based on their reading of Diod.Sic. 5. 55. 2 as a source for Telchines as ‹first statue makers, whose crude efforts were replaced over time› (p. 241). Diodorus does ascribe the invention of statue-making to the Telchines, and numbers several examples for cult statues they produced, but nowhere does he say that these were replaced. The crudeness of the statues is not mentioned in the text either: Diodorus calls them ἀφιδρύματα ἀρχαῖα. ἀφίδρυμα (as opposed to ξόανον) does not connote the crudeness of the work (for the term ἀφίδρυμα see Donohue (1988), pp. 81–82). As for the fact that their very invention of the skill of ἀγαλματοποιΐα would connote the crudeness of their work, one only need recall the image of Daedalus to see that the notion of an archaic artist does not imply aesthetic limitations, crudeness or lack of skill (to the contrary). Finally, their interpretation of the remark ‹not friends of the Muse› (v. 2) as ‹they lack artistic inspiration› is in my opinion incorrect, since the Muses were never considered to be patrons of the visual arts and artists.
[76] On the craftsmanship of the Telchines, Herter (1934), Sp. 202–207; Forbes (1950), pp 78–91. See also the *Testimonia* on the Telchines as artisans in Overbeck (1959), T. 40–55.
[77] Cf. Diod. 5. 55. 2: τεχνῶν τινων εὑρεταὶ καὶ ἄλλων τῶν χρησίμων εἰς τὸν βίον τῶν ἀνθρώπων εἰσηγηταί.
[78] See on this the texts quoted by Herter (1934), Sp. 200–202 and Overbeck (1959), T 42, 44; 48.
[79] Overbeck (1959), T 44; 45.
[80] Ovebeck (1959), T. 44; 45; 46.
[81] Overbeck (1959), T. 40; 42.
[82] Stob. *Anth*. 3. 38. 52: Τελχῖνες ἄνθρωποι ὀνομαζόμενοι τὸ ἀνέκαθεν Κρῆτες, οἰκήσαντες δὲ καὶ ἐν Κύπρῳ μεταναστάντες δ᾽ εἰς Ῥόδον καὶ πρῶτοι τὴν νῆσον κατασχόντες, βάσκανοί τε σφόδρα ἦσαν καὶ φθονεροί. τεχνῖται δὲ ὄντες καὶ τὰ τῶν προτέρων ἔργα μωμησάμενοι Ἀθηνᾶς Τελχινίας ἄγαλμα πρῶτοι ἱδρύσαντο, ὥσπερ εἴ τις λέγοι Ἀθηνᾶς βασκάνου.

machean word-play. By addressing the Telchines as φῦλον ... τήκ[ειν] ἧπαρ ἐπιστάμενον (v. 7–8), Callimachus is alluding to their reputation as experts, and to one etymology of their name: the word Τέλχις was usually etymologised as deriving either from θέλγειν ‹bewitch› or from τήκειν ‹to melt (metals)› / ‹to cause someone to pine away›.[83] By characterising the Telchines as a φῦλον ἐπιστάμενον, Callimachus is first alluding to their reputation as experts and artisans, but then he insults them with a clever etymological pun: Yes, you are fine experts in melting indeed ... but in melting your own liver! The usage of the word ἧπαρ with τήκειν is here attested for the first time,[84] an unusual combination that can be easily understood as the occasional but exceptional adaptation. This further attracts the reader's attention to the sophisticated joke Callimachus is making on Telchines' account.

By stating that the Telchines are ‹no friends of the Muse› (v. 2: νήιδε]ς οἳ Μούσης οὐκ ἐγένοντο φίλοι) Callimachus is overriding the metaphor he created in the first line: after reading the first line of the *Reply*, the reader will assume the Telchines to be a metaphor for contemporary critics, but in the second line Callimachus is describing the Telchines *qua* mythological creatures, ancient artisans specializing in the formgiving of metals and producing the weapons and cult statues of gods, since to say that they are ‹no friends of the Muse› is a learned remark about the fact that the Muses were never assumed to be patrons of *visual* arts. Telchines as artisans never *needed* to be friends with the Muses, whereas the critics should attempt to be just that.

νήιδες is another matter altogether: this word, in essence a negation of ἰδεῖν, is an etymological pun very similar to that on τήκειν from line 8: through ἰδεῖν a notion of the Telchines as *experts* is being brought into the reader's mind, and immediately negated (νη-) in the form of the insult.[85] The speaker of the *Reply* is getting carried away with insulting the Telchines and is using just the same unfair tactics everyone does when angry: He is cruelly choosing the insults that would hurt the most and is renouncing the Telchines the very characteristics they cherish the most – their expertise, their knowledge, their artistry. At the same time, he is aiming at their very heart (or liver) by pronouncing the painful truth – they were not born to be friends with the Muses. To add salt to the wound, he is

---

[83] On this etymologising, see the commentaries of Pfeiffer, Hopkinson (1988), Massimilla (1996) *ad loc*. The commentators stress the aspect of sorcery in the interpretation of the passage. Kambylis (1965) entertains the thought of *Künstlerneid* of the Telchines briefly (p. 76) but then concentrates fully on the aspect of the Evil Eye and sorcery.
In my opinion, Callimachus is making the most of the ambiguity of τήκειν and hinting at both its meanings – a strategy not unusual for him (see n. 85).

[84] See Pfeiffer (1928), p. 311, n. 5. On ἧπαρ see also Call. *Aet. Fr*. 2. 5 Pfeiffer and Pfeiffer's commentary ad loc.

[85] Magnelli (1999) analyses the meanings and the implications of the word νήιδες and offers a compelling interpretation: νήιδες was also a term used to signify a race of Greek mythological creatures, a kind of large pre-historic animals with extremely loud and powerful voices. By using this particular word to characterize the critics, Callimachus might be enriching his cluster of metaphors with an additional one pertaining to the sound.
Kaesser (2004) argues that ἀοιδή and ἀοιδός in the *Reply* are also etymological puns and that Callimachus implied different etymologies ranging from οἰδέω ‹to swell› with a *privativum* to οἶδα with α *privativum and α intensivum*. The switching between two opposed meanings of the word derived from οἶδα underlines the poet's ‹constant switching between presence and absence of knowledge in the Aitia› (Kaesser (2004) p. 41). This interpretation seems probable, especially in the light of Callimachus' play with the double etymology of Telchines.

underlining his own long-lasting friendship with the goddesses (v. 37-8) *and* with Apollo Λύκιος (v. 21-33) – their archenemy. Finally, to add insult to injury, the speaker mentions the race of Pygmies (and the ‹crane, delighting in their blood›, v. 13-14) and is thus reaching the peek of political incorrectness – the Telchines were very probably thought of as dwarfs[86] and were thus vertically challenged!

Taking the speaker's characterisation of his critics *cum grano salis* and keeping in mind their general characteristics as depicted in the *Reply* (and other poems of Callimachus) – their hubris and punishment,[87] their expertise in metallurgy,[88] and finally, their malice, enviousness and sorcery[89] – the question to be posed now is: what does one gain when the aspect of the Telchines' artistry is added to the mosaic that is the *Reply*? Do we understand their objections to the *Aitia* better and do we gain a better insight into the poetics of the author? I think we do. If Callimachus is bringing the visual arts into play in the *Reply*'s metaphors, and if we consider the fact that the Telchines as visual artists were credited especially with the production of the weapons of the gods and their ἀγάλματα, then their accusations gain a new perspective – obviously, they busy themselves with the production of *big* things that are in some way *useful* for practical purposes.

On the other hand, when one thinks of the Telchines as artists who make cult statues, it is obvious that they were bound to delight in the close imitation of dignified, elevated subjects. That is why they accuse Callimachus of being ‹childish› (v. 6: παῖς ἅτε) implying not only that the poetry of Callimachus is not grand enough, but also that his subjects are not elevated, and that he is playing for his own amusement. When one sees this accusation in the context of the Telchines being artists themselves, and furthermore, artists who possess skill, but who are also very envious of the skill of others, then their qualification of Callimachus' poetry can be seen in a new light: they notice the technical excellence of Callimachus and they can value *techne*. Since the amount of *techne* in the *Aitia* is very high, the Telchines are invidious and the only fault they can find is the subject-matter of the work. And that is why the speaker in engaging in a technical discussion with them in the first place – because the very fact that the Telchines are mumbling against his book proves that it is technically enviably good. Only the subject matter, not the poet's skill is in question. Precisely this point is the very core of the speaker's defence, since he is implying that the grandeur of the subject is less important than the artistry of the work. If the Telchines would judge solely the skill of the *Aitia*, and not the subject-matter by measuring it with the Persian *schoinos*, he would win the argument. When the speaker admonishes his critics to do just that (v. 17 f. αὖθι δὲ τέχνῃ / κρίνετε,][μὴ σχοίν]ῳ Περσίδι τὴ[ν] σοφίην), he is defending his work against someone who *can* make a good judgement of techne, not from ignoramuses oblivious to any artistic criteria.

---

[86] Herter (1934), Sp. 211.
[87] The hubris of the Telchines is also briefly mentioned in the aition *Acontius and Cydippe* (*Aet. Fr.* 75. 64-69 Pfeiffer) where Callimachus is relating the episode from Xenomedes' (lost) *History of Ceos* about the destruction of the Telchines who inhabited the island. Since the Ceian Telchines did not pay respect to the gods, they destroyed them, save for the humble Macelo.
[88] This aspect of Telchines is also mentioned in the *Hymn to Delos* v. 30-32 where Callimachus relates the legend about Poseidon who hit the mountains with a ‹trident made for him by the Telchines› (v. 31: ἄορι τριγλώχινι τό οἱ Τελχῖνες ἔτευξαν) and thus created the islands.
[89] This aspect is also mentioned in *Acontius and Cydippe*: *Aet. Fr.* 75, 64-5 Pfeiffer: ἐν δ᾿ ὕβριν θάνατόν τε κεραύνιον, ἐν δὲ γόητας / Τελχῖνας.

But, in the end, the Telchines, being what they are, cannot accept the poetry of Callimachus because they are not interested in the poetic of λεπτότης – and how could they possibly be, being specialists for ἀγάλματα and the forging of the weapons that crush mountains? They must appreciate stylistic qualities like bombast, to be able to produce an image of a god! By stating: ‹thundering is not mine, but Zeus'›, the speaker of the *Reply* is refusing to engage in a close mimesis of a god in all his grandeur and is thus signifying where exactly the difference between him and the Telchines lies. But he is also using a metaphor that can be understood in both the visual and the literary discourse. On the visual level it could mean: ‹I do not intend to make ἀγάλματα and thus am not interested in bombast›. In the discourse of literary criticism, it could mean: ‹I do not intend to pursue a close imitation of Homer›. In both cases, the grandeur is inapplicable and can thus not be applied as an aesthetic criterion to the *Aitia*.

The image of the Telchines and the image of Homer as Zeus thus come together in the *Reply* and create a cluster of metaphors poet is using to express his opinion on what poetry should be like. By perceiving the Telchines not only as malicious sorcerers, but also as visual artists, we are able to understand the *tenor* of this metaphor: the critics are professionals, they understand and can judge the *techne*, but they are at the same time artists interested in an entirely different kind of production, demanding poetry on a grand scale, that is a close imitation of Homer's epics in style and length. The aspect of ἀγαλματοποιΐα serves to explain their preferences further: whereas their objects of mimesis are big and elevated, Callimachus is nourishing the slender Muse and playing like a child (that is with small things).

Finally, by employing the metaphors from the domain of the visual arts, Callimachus is providing his readers with an apt parallel for contemporary literary disputes. The opposition between the poets such as Theocritus, Apollonius and contemporary elegists and epic poets whose works were more closely modelled upon Homer, and/or were long catalogic poetry could be compared to the situation in the visual arts, especially sculpture, where two opposite tendencies were also present at the same time: on the one hand, the immense influence of Lysippus' school with its majestic sculptures of gods and heroes, and, on the other hand, the small-scale, intricate representations of subjects such as children playing with pets or scenes from ordinary life.[90]

Perhaps one can go even further with the images of Homer as Zeus and the Telchines as visual artists. In my opinion, both motifs come together again in another poem of Callimachus. This is the much-discussed 6th *Iambus*[91] offering a curious ἔκφρασις of Pheidias' statue of Zeus – an extensive, detailed and precise summary of its dimensions. The setting of the poem is a προπεμπτικόν. According to the *Diegesis*, someone who is about to visit the Olympian sanctuary of Zeus is being instructed by his acquaintance. ‹He narrates the length, height, and breadth of the base, the throne, the footstool, and of the god himself, and how much was the expense, and that the creator was the Athenian Pheidias the son of Charmides.›[92]

---

[90] In his book on Hellenistic epic, Ziegler (1966²), pp. 44–50 discusses this phenomenon in the visual arts and its possible implications for contemporary literature. See also on Hellenistic art and literature Webster (1964); Onians (1979); Fowler (1989); Zanker (2004).
[91] The *Iambi* have recently been the subject of two monographs: Kerkhecker (1999) and Acosta-Hughes (2002).
[92] *Diegesis* 6. 25–31: Γνωρίμῳ αὐτοῦ ἀποπλέοντι κατὰ θέαν τοῦ Ὀλυμπίου Διὸς εἰς Ἦλιν διηγεῖται μῆκος ὕψος πλάτος βάσεως θρόνου ὑποποδίου αὐτοῦ τοῦ θεοῦ καὶ ὅση ἡ δαπάνη, δημιουργὸν δὲ Φειδίαν Χαρμίδου Ἀθηναῖον. Text: Pfeiffer; translation: Acosta Hughes (2002).

The fragmentary remains of this *Iambus* do not allow an extensive analysis, but, nevertheless, some impression of the poem can be gained. It is written in the Doric dialect in alternating iambic trimeters and ithyphallics. To say that it ‹perplexed modern critics› (Acosta-Hughes (2002) p. 289) is to say too little: the modern interpretations range from a parody of προπεμπτικόν and a failed or an ironic ἔκφρασις to a declamation of a tourist-guide in Elis and a ‹monstrous display of erudition›.[93]

One of the main issues for the interpretation of this poem is the identity of the speaker. We have no clues as to who he is, save the way he is treating his subject-matter. The subject is a different matter altogether – this particular statue of Zeus was one of the most celebrated works of art in antiquity, famous for its artistic qualities, the impression it left on its observer and for its technical excellence. It was one of the Seven Wonders of the World[94] and was famous as a representation of a divinity approved from the highest place – Zeus himself.[95]

The Olympian statue of Zeus was brought into close connection with the works of Homer. According to widespread tradition,[96] Pheidias' representation of Zeus was inspired by the following verses from the *Iliad* (1. 528-30):

Ἦ καὶ κυανέῃσιν ἐπ' ὀφρύσι νεῦσε Κρονίων·
ἀμβρόσιαι δ' ἄρα χαῖται ἐπερρώσαντο ἄνακτος
κρατὸς ἀπ' ἀθανάτοιο· μέγαν δ' ἐλέλιξεν Ὄλυμπον.[97]

‹As he spoke the son of Kronos bowed his dark brows, and the ambrosial locks swayed on his immortal head, till vast Olympus reeled›.[98]

Based on both Callimachus' usage of the metaphor *Homer: Zeus* and the metaphor *mythical visual artists Telchines: literary critics*, I propose a new interpretation of the sixth *Iambus*. What if the Zeus of *Iambus* VI is yet another metaphor for Homer? We have seen that in the *Reply*, Homer is being referred to as Zeus and that the issue at stake is mimesis: Zeus-Homer is being rejected as a direct model by the speaker and obviously postulated as the only desirable model by the Telchines. In the case of the statue of Olympian Zeus, so closely related to Homer in its very process of production, the identification with Homeric poetry could be even more natural. But then, why would the speaker of the sixth *Iambus* be so interested in its measurements? And why is he speaking in a Doric dialect? Who in the world would be interested in measuring Homeric verses? Well, thinking of the *Reply*, especially the verses αὖθι δὲ τέχνῃ κρίνετε,][μὴ σχοίν]ῳ Περσίδι τῇ[ν] σοφίην one could say that the Telchines might be inclined to do just that. The iambic scorn of the sixth *Iambus* would thus be directed against the Telchines: their interest in all things grand and thundering is being ironically exaggerated to the point of absurdity. A poem describing one of the most celebrated statues of the classical world without (apparently) a word of proper description of its aesthetic peculiarities is intended to mimic, with sarcastic implications, the logic of the critics who can only concentrate on huge size and the imitators who want to follow Zeus/Homer so closely, they might as well tape-measure him.

---

[93] Thus Zanker (1987), pp. 64–5. Both Kerkhecker (1999), pp. 166–181 and Acosta-Hughes (2002), pp. 288–294 offer an extensive survey of interpretations proposed thus far.
[94] On the Seven Wonders, Ekschmitt (1996).
[95] Cf. Paus 5. 11. 9.
[96] See T 692–754 in Overbeck (1959).
[97] Text: Monro / Allen.
[98] Translation: Butler (1898).

This interpretation would explain why this ‹description› is so infused with the language of the rivalry and greed[99] – this fits perfectly with the image of Telchines in Callimachus and hints at their interest in grandeur and their envy and malice. On the other hand, if one was about to produce an exact imitation of the statue, one would obviously want to know not only its measurements, but also the cost.

One could, perhaps, take the last point further. It is reported anecdotally that writers of Hellenistic historical epic were so greedy, that some of them requested a pay *per verse*. The longer the poem, the better their wage.[100] This could explain the greedy thirst for knowledge of *just how costly* Zeus / Homer was.

On taking a closer look at the fragments of the 6th *Iambus*, some expressions and motifs gain an additional nuance of meaning when one imagines one of Telchines as its speaker.

The very opening brings to mind the connection of Telchines with the statues of the gods and their envy of *techne* (*Fr*. 196. 1 Pfeiffer):

Ἀ]λεῖος ὁ Ζεύς, ἁ τέχνα δὲ Φειδία.
‹The Zeus is of Elis, the skill of Pheidias.›[101]

One would now expect to hear more about what is so special about the *techne* of Pheidias and what makes the statue so famous, but the rest of the poem seems to enact the motto ‹size matters› (Fr. 196. 37–38 Pfeiffer):

αὐτὸς δ᾽ ὁ δαίμων πέντ[ε] τ[ᾶ]ς ἐφεδρ[ί]δος
παχέεσσι μάσσων·
‹and the god himself is taller than the throne by five cubits.›

Kerkhecker (1999) pp. 157–8 discusses the strange wording in this fragment: Callimachus is not using the common word for throne (θρόνος), but a hapax ἐφεδρίς. Unfortunately, one can not even say wether the expression is a technical or a poetic one but it is surely connected to ἐφέδρα and ἔφεδρος ‹seat› and as such (especially considering the connotations of ἔφεδρος) strikes a competitive note.[102]

The primary meaning of the verses would be that the image of the seated god is taller than his seat by precisely five cubits. If however, we imagine one Telchine describing the statue to another, the implication of this verse would be (self)ironic: however hard they might try to immitate his grandeur, the god (Homer) is still grander than his successors.

The next passage is also infused with the motifs and language of the rivalry – the word μειονεκτεῖν ‹to be at disadvantage› evokes a rather jousting atmosphere. Even the Seasons and Graces are taking part in a size contest (Fr. 196. 42–4 Pfeiffer):

παρθένοι γὰρ Ὧραι
τᾶν ὀργυιαιᾶν ὅσσον οὐδὲ πάσ[σα]λο[ν
φαντὶ μειονεκτεῖν.

---

[99] For the language of the *Iambus* see Kerchecker (1999), pp. 151–163 and Acosta-Hughes (2002), p. 290.
[100] Cf. Suid. s.v. Χοιρίλος: ἐφ᾽ οὗ ποιήματος κατὰ στίχον στατῆρα χρυσοῦν ἔλαβε (about Alexander's poet Choerilus of Iasus).
[101] All translations of Callimachus' *Iambi* are Acosta-Hughes' (2002).
[102] Cf. LSJ s.v. ἔφεδρος 4: ‹the third competitor in contests, who sits by to fight the conqueror and (5) generally, one who waits to take another's place, a successor.›

‹For the virgin Seasons[103] say they do not fall short of the women who are one fathom high by so much as a peg.›

Since the measurements obviously do not satisfy the addressee's thirst for knowledge, he inquires about the costs (Fr. 196. 45–46 Pfeiffer):

τ[ὸ] δ' ὧν ἀναισίμωμα - λίχνος ἐσσὶ [γὰρ
καὶ] τό μευ πυθέσθαι

‹And as to the expense of these – for you are greedy to learn this too of me.›

Kerkhecker (1999), p. 161 notes that the word ἀναισίμωμα ‹the cost› is unusual in two ways: First, it is a rare expression and secondly, it is a markedly Ionic word (from the verb ἀναισιμόω[104]) in a literary Doric context.

Could it be that this unusual word usage is intended to attract the reader's attention? Kerkhecker (p. 162) further notes its prominent placement: ‹After ἀναισίμωμα, the sentence breaks off: the word is left to ring out, the shock to settle in the reader's mind. Protestations of urgency heighten the sense of incongruity. Direct address signals the importance of this most fascinating item.›

I suppose that, faced with an unusual word, one could try to etymologise, and, bearing in mind just how fond Callimachus is of etymological word-play, this just might prove to be a fruitful approach. So, what do we get when we deconstruct this word? We could try with an α *privativum* / αἶσα / μῶμος. Now, μῶμος is a familiar enough occurrence in Callimachus[105] and ἀναίσιμος ‹unseemly› is attested elsewhere. Could we decipher this expression as ‹unseemly criticism›? Another (self)ironical utterance of the speaker of the *Iambus*, perhaps another joke at the cost of the Telchines and their unseemly modes of criticising great works of art.

Maybe the text of the whole *Iambus* was pervaded with double-edged expressions that could hint to the careful reader at the true nature of the speaker and his aesthetic criteria. The subject of aesthetics and the modes of criticism connect this poem to the *Reply*, where Callimachus not only used ‹Zeus› as a metaphor for ‹Homer›, but also introduced the discourse of literary criticism through the metaphorical entrance of the Telchines. Finally, the demand not to judge fine poetry by length brings the *Reply* and the sixth *Iambus* together and, in my opinion, provides a hint for the interpretation of the *Iambus*. Here we have the critics who are demonstrating *in vivo* what unseemly criticism looks like – a strategy very appropriate to the iambic genre.

Seeing that the sixth *Iambus* fits well into the general tone of the programmatic passages of Callimachean poetry, it remains to be seen how this interpretation suits the corpus of the *Iambi*. Acosta-Hughes (2002) persuasively argued that the programmatic first *Iambus* with its *persona loquens* Hipponax introduces the discourse of literary criticism as one of the main subjects of the book. Furthermore (and very significant for the proposed interpre-

---

[103] Behind the throne of Zeus the Seasons and Charites were represented.
[104] Cf. Schmitt (1970), p.103 n. 26 on ἀναισίμωμα: ‹Das wie das zugrunde liegende ἀναισιμόω nur bei Herodot belegte Wort ist ein speziell ionischer *terminus technicus* für «Kosten», dessen Verwendung in einem dorisierenden Text auffällt›. See also Kerkhecker (1999), p. 161 n. 78.
[105] The programmatic closure of the *Hymn to Apollo* features Apollo defending the Callimachean poetic from Phthonos and Momos. In the fragmentary epigram (Fr. 393 Pfeiffer) Momos is poking fun at the philosopher Diodorus of Iasus.

tation of the sixth *Iambus*) the figure of Hipponax can be seen as the positive foil of the Telchines, since he, too, is a literary critic, but also has connotations with the *visual* arts.

As argued by Acosta-Hughes (2002), pp. 32–47, Callimachus is using the figure of Hipponax as a critic because Hipponax was famous for his attacks of the sculptors Bupalus and Athenis and a painter named Mimnes – all artists. Hipponax attacks them because of the aesthetic faults of their works and thus presents himself as a *critic of aesthetics*. What Callimachus is doing by introducing the figure of Hipponax as a *literary critic* is a shift in discourse – while the poet Hipponax criticized visual artists, the Callimachean Hipponax *redivivus* is criticizing Alexandrian poets. Callimachus ‹employs the choliambic line (...) as a medium for the criticism of a poetic composition›.[106]

But the shift in discourse is not complete, precisely as it is not complete in the case of the Telchines in the *Reply*, where Callimachus does not blend out the Telchines' connection with the visual arts. In his book of *Iambi*, literary criticism is an explicit subject in several poems,[107] but in others, works of plastic art are being discussed[108] and in at least two of these,[109] the sculptures are metaphors for literary genres.

In the sixth *Iambus*, the description of a sculpture could be interpreted as an allegory for literary criticism. By depicting the Telchines' way of viewing of the statue of Zeus Callimachus is satirically portraying their way of reading and imitating Homer. Here, Callimachus is further exploring the possibilities of the Telchines as a metaphor for critics. Their connection with the visual arts, especially with the statues of gods, enables Callimachus to satirize their aesthetic criteria by letting them speak of the statue of Zeus as they would be speaking of poetry of Homer.

It remains to be seen *how exactly* the Telchines see the poetry of Homer. The ancient and modern readers of the sixth *Iambus* did not fail to notice the excessive accuracy as the main characteristic of the discussion of the statue. Hunter (2003) persuasively argues that accuracy (ἀκρίβεια) was perceived as a positive stylistic characteristic in the circles of the learned poets of Alexandria. In the classical period, however, this particular quality was perceived as a typical characteristic of prose, most notably of rhetorical and historical writings. In the domain of rhetoric was especially important for the judicial speeches delivered in courtroom, as opposed to the speeches written for delivery before the assembly;[110] in the domain of history, ἀκρίβεια was postulated by Thucydides to be the most important quality in relating and interpreting of events.[111]

The dichotomy between the poets who create their poems thanks to divine inspiration and those who rely on labour and strive to achieve a true and accurate account of events, famously postulated in the ‹method chapters› of Thucydides' *History*, reaches its peek in the domain of accuracy: a bard claiming divine inspiration relates his poetry orally and is thus able to transfer his enthusiasm to his audience, that is to say to *elevate* it – and this is the point where orality and inspiration come together forming the very notion of gran-

---

[106] Acosta-Hughes (2002), p. 35.
[107] Iambi 1, 2, 13.
[108] Iambi 6, 7 and 9.
[109] In a forthcoming article, I argue that the statue of Hermes in *Iambus* 7 is a metaphor for the iambic genre.
[110] In *Rhetoric* 3. 12 Aristotle explicitly links precision with judicial speeches. On this passage, see Hunter (2003), pp. 218–19.
[111] Th. 1. 20–23, esp. 1. 22. 1–3. For an overview of the concept of ἀκρίβεια in the fifth and fourth century BC, see Kurz (1970).

deur – yet, he is not as obliged to the principle of accuracy as a historian writing to be read, since the main objective of a historian (as seen by Thucydides) is not to produce an effect on his audience (or ‹mere entertainment›[112]) but rather to relate the information as accurately as possible[113] and to educate the reader.

It seems that early on, the ideal of akribeia became closely connected with literature *for reading* as opposed to orally transmitted poetry, which is dependant on delivery and aims at grandeur.[114] Hunter argues that in the domain of prose, a higher level of akribeia was demanded in the cases when delivery did not play an important role, that is in the speeches delivered before one judge or those commissioned from the professional speech-writer.[115] The grandeur on the other hand, was perceived as lacking in (or, more precisely: not *needing*) akribeia. However, things became different with the arrival of Hellenistic book poetry. Since it did not depend on delivery, poetry written for reading could require more precision. Equally important for admission of akribeia into the domain of poetry was the learned aspect of the Hellenistic poetry. The self-stylization of poets like Callimachus, Theocritus and Aratus as diligent philologists and their introduction of the idea of labour as an artistic prerequisite for creating poetry and the narrative strategy of insisting on closing, rather than opening their works to the general public resulted in the final admission of akribeia into poetry. Hellenistic poets are only too happy to state that they have learned something (preferably by reading a book) and the amassing of information not only was not perceived as unworthy of poetry, it was the very subject (and a narrative frame of the first half) of most Hellenistic of all poetry books – the *Aitia*.

So how is a high level of akribeia to be explained in a poem by Callimachus, where the speaker is not really his *persona*, but the hated Telchines speak through his voice?

If one recalls the image of the Telchines from the *Reply*, especially their possession of *techne*, one will understand why the technical virtuosity with which they are stating the measures of the Olympian Zeus is actually in keeping with their general image in Callimachean poetry. What is ridiculed in the sixth *Iambus* is the fact that they so stubbornly insist on imitating Homer and yet manage to ignore the crucial characteristic of his style: the grandeur that not only does not need accuracy, but is radically opposed to the very idea of precision and meticulous learning. Grandeur cannot be learned, nor can it be imitated.

The Telchines are desperately trying to re-create the poetry that belongs in a different era and whose production and performance is radically different from the Hellenistic circumstances. The idea of transferring enthusiasm to an audience by meticulously stating data is hilarious. Callimachus really knew how to drive a point home.

Thus the game of guessing the speaker of *Iambus* Callimachus which is playing throughout the book[116] reaches its peek in the sixth *Iambus*, where the reader should demonstrate

---

[112] This is admittedly a rather daring translation of ἀγώνισμα ἐς τὸ παραχρῆμα ἀκούειν (Thuc. 1. 22. 4). I wonder though if this sentence could be seen as the first instance of highbrow smirking at popular culture.
[113] Thuc. 1. 22. 3 professes his goal of relating the events with ‹as much accuracy as possible›: ὅσον δυνατόν ἀκριβείᾳ.
[114] Hunter (2003).
[115] Hunter (2003), pp. 218–19.
[116] Cf. Fantuzzi (2004), p. 11 on the voice of the *Iambi*: ‹In these poems, moreover, Callimachus plays some very iambic variations on the game of masking the persona loquens, thus concealing, as Aristotle thought iambic authors did, his own identity when impersonating a series of more or less embarrassing roles›.

not only his thorough knowledge of other works of Callimachus, but should also remember that the Telchines were always connected with Rhodes and Crete[117] – areas where Doric was spoken, so explaining the Doric dialect of this poem.

The guessing game is not made easy (but then again, what is *ever* easy in Callimachus?): the motifs of προπεμπτικόν and ἔκφρασις play an important role in this poem and Doric was also spoken in Olympia, but Callimachus is not playing unfairly, either. It is clear (even from the extant fragments, without the help of *Diegesis*) that the addressee is about to leave for Olympia and is not yet there, which would rule out the dialect of Elis for the sixth *Iambus*. The motifs of προπεμπτικόν and ἔκφρασις, on the other hand, are not obstacles to an allegorical interpretation. In his other *Iambi*, Callimachus very successfully introduces different genres into the iambus: one finds fables, epigrams, aitia, even an epinician scattered throughout the book.[118]

Since the opening and the closing *Iambi* of the collection evoke the atmosphere of contemporary Alexandria, address the *literati*, and engage in a discussion of literature, the appearance of Telchines in the sixth *Iambus* should not come as a great surprise. I might be suffering from a delusion myself but I suggest that one actually expects them to make an appearance and furthermore that it would be very Callimachean to let them enter unannounced. Not revealing their identity explictly also fits in with the general tone of the *Iambi*, since Callimachus is avoiding personal invective and is rather presenting types of personality of behaviour.[119]

4. σὺ δ' οὐ θάνες, ἐσσὶ γὰρ αἰεί

I do not intend to propose that Callimachus' *Hymn to Zeus* is also an allegory of Homer (although this verse (9) does indeed tease) but to pose a different question: If Archelaos' *Apotheosis of Homer* were really ordered to celebrate the literary achievements of Callimachus, as Cameron tentatively sugested[120] how would he be presented? If we carefully examine the representation of the poet on the relief (plate 2), we will notice that the only other similar figure is Apollo *Musagetes*. Both have the same posture and both are holding a scroll in their left hand.[121] Between them, there is a Muse (Calliope) holding a scroll in her right hand. Pinkwart interprets her gesture as presenting the scroll to Apollo.[122] But, what if she is receiving the scroll *from* Apollo in order to give it to the poet? Could it be that the second register of the relief is depicting the poet who receives his poetical manifesto from Apollo directly – as Callimachus claimed to have done in the *Reply*?

---

[117] For the sources see Herter (1934). The association of Telchines with Rhodes would provide an additional parallel with the world of the visual arts: The pupil of Lysippus, Chares of Lindus produced the biggest statue of antiquity for his home island, Rhodes, and had his school there.
[118] See Fantuzzi (2004), pp. 10–17 with further literature.
[119] Acosta-Hughes (2002), pp. 32–47
[120] Cameron (1995) pp. 276–7 suggests the identification of a poet with Callimachus or Erathostenes.
[121] Cf. Pinkwart (1965b) p. 63: ‹Die Statue wird nicht nur durch diesen Standplatz isoliert, sondern auch durch das Schreitmotiv nach rechts von den übrigen Figuren getrennt. Schwacher Bezug zur Apollongruppe sind ihre Kopfwendung und ihre Haltung, die die des Apollon fast getreu wiederholt.›
[122] Pinkwart (1965b), p. 61.

We may never know when this relief was made, who ordered it and where (and if) it was dedicated. Maybe this is a significant part of its allure. Nevertheless, this allegorical representation of Homer's apotheosis is in many ways illustrative of the Alexandrian, especially Callimachean concepts of imitation: There was no poet greater than Homer and his poetry was acknowledged as immortal. But, whereas the personifications of History, Poetry, Myth, Tragedy, Comedy, Human nature, Arete, Mneme, Pistis and Wisdom are paying him respect and offering sacrifices on his altar, the fellow poet is curiously absent from this group. He is on a different level, and, although close to Apollo and Calliope, he stands alone. We do not know if he was looking at Homer, or turning his head towards Apollo. Maybe, just maybe he was looking in a different direction altogether, searching for his own way.

Bibliography

HE = A.S.F. Gow / D.L. Page (edd.): The Greek Anthology. Hellenistic Epigrams, 2 Vols. Cambridge 1965
PMG = D. L. Page (ed.), Poetae Melici Graeci, Oxford 1962
SH = H. Lloyd-Jones / P. Parsons (edd.): Supplementum Hellenisticum, Berlin, New York 1983
Pfeiffer = R. Pfeiffer (ed.): Callimachus, 2 Vols. Oxford 1949-53

ACOSTA-HUGHES, B. / S. Stephens: Rereading Callimachus' Aetia Fragment 1, Class.Phil. 97, (2002), p. 238-55
ACOSTA-HUGHES, B.: Polyeideia: The Iambi of Callimachus and the Archaic Iambic Tradition (Hellenistic Culture and Society 35), Berkeley, Los Angeles, London 2002
ASPER, M.: Onomata allotria. Zur Genese, Struktur und Funktion poetologischer Metaphern bei Kallimachos (Hermes Einzelschriften 75), Stuttgart 1997
ASPER, M.: Gruppen und Dichter. Zu Programmatik und Adressatenbezug bei Kallimachos, A&A 47 (2001), pp. 84-116
BARBANTANI, S.: Φάτις νικηφόρος. Frammenti di elegia encomiastica nell' età delle Guerre Galatiche: Supplementum Hellenisticum 958 e 969, Milano 2001.
BENEDETTO, G.: Il sogno e l'invettiva. Momenti di storia dell'esegesi callimachea, Florence 1993
BRILLANTE, C.: L'Invidia dei Telchini e l'origine delle arti, Aufidus 19, 1993, pp. 7-42
BUTLER, H. E.: The Institutio Oratoria of Quintilian, With an English Translation, Vol IV, London, Cambridge 1961, 4th ed.
BUTLER, S.: Homer, The Iliad, English Translation, Mineola 1999 (1st ed.: 1898).
CAMERON, A.: Genre and Style in Callimachus, TAPhA 122 (1992), pp. 305-312
CAMERON, A.: Callimachus and His Critics, Princeton 1995
CHANIOTIS, A.: Historie und Historiker in den griechischen Inschriften: epigraphische Beiträge zur griechischen Historiographie, Stuttgart 1988
CLAY, D.: Archilochos Heros, The Cult of Poets in the Greek Polis (Hellenic Studies 6), Washington 2004
DONOHUE, A. A.: Xoana and the Origins of Greek Sculpture, Atlanta 1988
EKSCHMITT, W.: Die Sieben Weltwunder. Ihre Erbauung, Zerstörung und Wiederentdeckung, Mainz am Rhein 1996
ESDAILE, K. A.: Homeric Coin Types, JHS 32 (1912), pp. 298-325
FANTUZZI, M.: L'epos ellenistico tradizionale prima e dopo Ziegler and Epici ellenistici, in: K. Ziegler, L'epos ellenistico. Un capitolo dimenticato della poesia greca (Ital. trans. of Ziegler (1966), Bari 1988 pp. XXV-LXXXIX

Fantuzzi 2004 = R. Hunter / M. Fantuzzi: Tradition and Innovation in Hellenistic Poetry, Cambridge 2004
Forbes, R. J.: Metallurgy in Antiquity, Leiden 1950
Fowler B. H.: The Hellenistic Aesthetic, Madison, Wisconsin 1989
Gabathuler, M.: Hellenistische Epigramme auf Dichter, Basel 1937
Giangrande, G.: Das Dichten des Kallimachos im mittleren und hohen Alter, Hermes 96 (1968), pp. 710–725
von Goethe, J. W.: Entwurf zu Homers Apotheose. Werke, Sophien- (Weimarer) Ausgabe, Abt. I Bd. 49² = E. Grumach, Goethe und die Antike, Berlin 1949, Vol II, pp. 572 ff.
Herter, H.: s.v. *Telchinen*, RE V A1, 1934, Sp. 197–225
von Hesberg, H.: Bildsyntax und Erzählweise in der hellenistischen Flächenkunst, JDAI 103 (1988), pp. 309–365
Heyman, C.: Homer on Coins from Smyrna, in: S. Scheers (ed.): Studia Paulo Naster oblata, Vol. I, Leuven 1982, pp. 162–173
Hopkinson, N.: A Hellenistic Anthology, Cambridge 1988
Hunter, R. L.: The Argonautica of Apollonius. Literary Studies, Cambridge 1993
Hunter, R. L.: Reflecting on Writing and Culture: Theocritus and the Style of Cultural Change, in: H. Yunis (ed.), Written Texts and the Rise of Literate Culture in Ancient Greece, Cambridge 2003, pp. 213–234
Hunter 2004 = R.L. Hunter / M. Fantuzzi: Tradition and Innovation in Hellenistic Poetry, Cambridge 2004
Kaesser, Ch.: Callimachus, Fr. 1 Pf. on the Meaning of Song, ZPE 150 (2004), pp. 39–42
Kambylis, A.: Die Dichterweihe und ihre Symbolik. Untersuchungen zu Hesodos, Kallimachos, Properz und Ennius, Heidelberg 1965
Kerkhecker, A.: Callimachus' Book of Iambi, Oxford 1999
Klose, D. O. A.: Die Münzprägung von Smyrna in der römischen Kaiserzeit, Berlin 1987
Kurz, D.: Akribeia. Das Ideal der Exaktheit bei den Griechen bis Aristoteles, Göppingen 1970
La Rocca, E.: Philiskos a Roma. Una testa di Musa dal tempio di Apollo Sosiano, in: Alessandria e il mondo ellenistico-romano. Studi in onore di A. Adriani, Vol. III, Roma 1984, pp. 629–643
Lehnus, L.: In margine a un recente libro su Callimaco, in: Ricordando R. Cantarella: Miscellanea di studi, Milan 1999, pp. 201–225
Magnelli, E.: Quelle bestie die Telchini (sul v. 2 del prologo degli Aitia), ZPE 127 (1999), pp. 52–58
Massimilla, G.: Callimaco, Aitia. Libri primo e secondo. Introduzione, testocritico, traduzione e commentu, Pisa 1996
Matz, F.: review of Picard / Lauer 1955, Gnomon 29 (1957), pp. 84–93
Monro, D. B. / T. W. Allen (Eds.): *Homeri Opera*, 5 Vols., Oxford ³1956
Onians, J.: Art and Thought in the Hellenistic Age: The Greek World View 350–50 BC, London 1979
Overbeck, J.: Die antiken Schriftquellen zur Geschichte der bildenden Künste bei den Griechen, Hildesheim ²1959
Patton, W. R.: The Greek Anthology with an English Translation, 5 Vols., Cambridge MA 1917.
Pietrzykowski, M.: Sculptures Grecques du Sarapeum de Memphis: Etude d'iconographie, Warshaw 1976
Pfeiffer, R.: Ein neues Altersgedicht des Kallimachos, Hermes 63 (1928), pp. 302–341
Picard, C. / P. Lauer: Les statues ptolemaïques du Serapeion de Memphis, Paris 1955
Pinkwart 1965a = D. Pinkwart, Das Relief des Archelaos von Priene und die «Musen des Philiskos», Kallmünz 1965

Pinkwart 1965b = D. Pinkwart: Das Relief des Archelaos von Priene, Antike Plastik 4, Berlin 1965, S. 55–66
Pollitt, J. J.: Art in the Hellenistic Age, Cambridge 1986
Rakoczy, T.: Böser Blick, Macht des Auges und Neid der Götter. Eine Untersuchung zur Kraft des Blickes in der griechischen Literatur, Tübingen 1996
Rhys-Roberts, W.: Longinus on the Sublime, Edited with Introduction, Translation, Facsimiles and Appendices, Cambridge ²1907
Richter, G. M. A.: The Portraits of the Greeks, 3 Vols., London 1965
Ridgway, B. S.: Hellenistic Sculpture, Vol. I: The Styles of ca. 331–200 BC, Bristol 1990
Rosenblum, R.: Jean-Auguste-Dominique Ingres, New York 1985
Schachter, A.: Cults of Boiotia, Vol. II: Herakles to Poseidon, London 1986
Schefold, K.: Bildnisse der antiken Dichter, Redner und Denker, Basel 1943
Schmitt, R.: Die Nominalbildung in den Dichtungen des Kallimachos von Kyrene. Ein Beitrag zur Stellung seines Wortschatzes innerhalb des Griechischen, Wiesbaden 1970
Schmitz, Th. A.: «I hate all common things»: The Reader's Role in Callimachus' *Aetia* Prologue, HSCPh 99 (1999), pp. 151–178
Skiadas, A. D.: Homer im Griechischen Epigramm, Athen 1965
Smith, R. R. R.: Hellenistic Sculpture, London 1991
Voutiras, E.: Gedanken zum Relief des Archelaos von Priene, Egnatia 1 (1989), pp. 129–170
Zanker, G.: Realism in Alexandrian poetry: A Literature and Its Audience, London, Sydney 1987
Zanker, G.: Modes of Viewing in Hellenistic Poetry and Art, Madison, Wisconsin 2004
Zanker, P.: Die Maske des Sokrates, Das Bild des Intellektuellen in der antiken Kunst, München 1995
Ziegler, K.: Das Hellenistische Epos, Leipzig ²1966
Webster, T. B. L.: Hellenistic Poetry and Art, London 1964
Williams, F.: Callimachus, Hymn to Apollo. A Commentary, Oxford 1978

Source of Illustrations

Pinkwart, D.: Das Relief des Archelaos von Priene, Antike Plastik 4, Berlin 1965, Plate 28.

Plate 1: *The Apotheosis of Homer*, a bas-relief by Archelaos of Priene (Brit. Mus. 2191)

Plate 2: *The Apotheosis of Homer* (detail)

Alex Hardie

The Aloades on Helicon: Music, Territory and Cosmic Order*

Pausanias preserves a unique account of the worship of the Muses on Mount Helicon. The sons of Aloeus (the Aloades), he says, co-founded Ascra and were first to designate the mountain as sacred to the Muses; they instituted sacrifices and honoured three Muses named Melete, Mneme and Aoide; then a Macedonian, Pieros, came to Thespiae, changed the names, and established the canonical cult of nine.[1]

As with any mythical ‹cult› history, particularly one that deals with ‹previous ownership›, Pausanias' account raises questions about the objects of cult, the claimed founders, and the relative dating of its various phases.[2] Did this Muse-trio exist as a cult, and if so when? How much ‹historicity› is there in the Aloades' association with Helicon? And do these elements reflect long past events, or circumstances obtaining when the myth was first enunciated, or some combination of the two?[3] The Aloades themselves are better known as the brothers who grew prodigiously large and at the age of nine aspired to pile Pelion on Ossa and Olympus, assault the gods in their heaven, subvert the Olympian order, and rape virgin goddesses.[4] It is not easy to see how these extraordinary creatures might have associated with Muses, and the approach to be adopted in this study will assume the possibility, even likelihood, of an extended process of territorial association between the Aloades, Ascra and Helicon which provided a context for the myth of first worship and led towards it.

As will be seen, the Aloades (Otus and Ephialtes) were honoured as heroes. They were also identified in positive ways with Aeolian ethnic and territorial interests and were not simply the hubristic monsters so prominent in the mainstream tradition. Moreover, the competitive intrusion of a northern eponymous hero is consistent with other evidence, to be considered later, for ethnic tensions around the Heliconian cult. The myth thus offers an opportunity to explore wider issues of culture, ethnicity and territoriality from a musical perspective. It also has to do with three non-canonical Muse names which deserve fuller analysis than they have received, as a basis for judgments about technical affinities, edu-

---

* I am grateful to Dr Penelope Murray for comment on this paper.
[1] Paus. 9.29.1-4 ... θῦσαι δὲ ἐν Ἑλικῶνι Μούσαις πρώτους καὶ ἐπονομάσαι τὸ ὄρος ἱερὸν εἶναι Μουσῶν Ἐφιάλτην καὶ Ὦτον λέγουσιν, οἰκίσαι δὲ αὐτοὺς καὶ Ἄσκρην· καὶ δὴ καὶ Ἡγησίνους ἐπὶ τῷδε ἐν τῇ Ἀτθίδι ἐποίησεν [text of verse at Appendix I] ... οἱ δὲ τοῦ Ἀλωέως παῖδες ἀριθμόν τε Μούσας ἐνόμισαν εἶναι τρεῖς καὶ ὀνόματα αὐταῖς ἔθεντο Μελέτην καὶ Μνήμην καὶ Ἀοιδήν. χρόνῳ δὲ ὕστερόν φασι Πίερον Μακεδόνα, ἀφ' οὗ καὶ Μακεδόσιν ὠνόμασται τὸ ὄρος, τοῦ τον ἐλθόντα ἐς Θεσπιὰς ἐννέα τε Μούσας καταστήσασθαι καὶ τὰ ὀνόματα τὰ νῦν μεταθέσθαι σφίσι. Principal treatments: B.A. van Groningen (1948); M.T. Camilloni, (1998) 28-33.
[2] For the methodological issues involved in determining ‹historicity›, see C. Sourvinou-Inwood (1987).
[3] For mythological narrative as ‹history›, and as the ‹situation of the enunciation›, see C. Calame (1987) 176-77.
[4] Principal treatments: L. Preller and C. Robert (1894) 103; J. Toepffer (1894); K. Tümpel, *RE* V (1905) 2847, s. v. ‹Ephialtes›; K. Scherling, *RE* XVIII.1 (1942) 1879-81 s. v. ‹Otus›; E. Simon (1981). For the Aloades in the context of other monstrous, hubristic twins, V. Dasen (2005) 144-52 (I am grateful to Dr Nicholas Horsfall for this reference).

cational influence and dating. Detailed analysis of a rich and resonant musical myth will, it is hoped, help illuminate the workings of the Muses' principal Greek cult site over a period extending from the Dark Ages to the late classical era.

I: Melete, Mneme and Aoide

Melete, Mneme and Aoide differ from the canonical Muses in that they bear functional names as distinct from musical ‹speaking names›.[5] They have no genealogy or personality; and they carry no musical reference other than to song, no evaluative or aesthetic element, and no sense of the pleasures or impact of singing.[6] Rather, ‹Practice›, ‹Memory› and ‹Song› are a coherent, closely focused and carefully designed trio, each component of which will be found to interact with its two companions.

Greek interest in the origins of cults generated accounts of legendary ‹first sacrificers› at most periods.[7] But Homeric epic shows little interest in cults and festivals, and it is unlikely that the Aload cult legend as we have it was recorded in epic before the sixth century (when the ‹first sacrificer› motif appears in the Hesiodic *Catalogue* and in *Phoronis*).[8] Pausanias says the Aload ‹cult› preceded the canonical nine; and that claim has found its way into several modern accounts.[9] But this is fertile territory for retrojection, and there are in fact no grounds for assuming that Melete, Mneme and Aoide are earlier than Hesiod's Muses, still less that they represent a more primitive conception of music.[10] Indeed, as will be seen, there are lexical objections to the emergence of the trio before the late sixth century. Some scholars have suggested a later date. Frank Hieronymus, in his study of rhetorical μελέτη, stated that our Muses ‹at the earliest, Hellenistic inventions›; more cautiously, Albert Schachter wrote of the difficulty of distinguishing between ‹genuine tradition and learned theorizing› in this area.[11] There was certainly inventive interest in Muse names at all periods.[12] Among them was a group of four (Melete, Aoide, Arche and Thelxinoe), an overlap of names with our group that suggests a tradition of sorts.[13] This group was known to Aratus; and if its greater diversity of nomenclature indicates awareness and adaptation of our trio, that would yield a rough *terminus ante quem* around the late fourth century.

---

[5] For example ‹Calliope› from Muse-singing ὀπὶ καλῇ: Hom. *Il.* 1.604; *Od.* 24.60; of Circe at *Od.* 10.221; Hes. *Theog.* 68; *Hom. Hymn Apoll.* 189; Diod. Sic. 4.7.4.

[6] For the Hesiodic names, P. Murray (2004) 367 n. 5.

[7] Pausanias records two further ‹first sacrificers›: 4.3.9; 9.8.5 (Amphion/Hermes); cf. also e.g. Schol. *Il.* 2.670 with Schol. Pind. *Ol.* 7.35 (Rhodians/ Athena). A separate claim in respect of the Muses was made for the Idaean Dactyls: Schol. Hom. *Il.* 22.391.

[8] Hes. fr. 71(c) MW (Eteocles and the Charites); *Phoronis* fr. 4.2-3 B (Io and Hera); for a conspicuous interest in ‹firsts› in the *Phoronis*, *RE* XX.647-50 (Stoessl).

[9] Accepted without discussion by M. Detienne (1999) 41; similarly, E. Pascal (1985) 114-15; Van Groningen (1984) 291; G. Nagy (1989) 32 speaks of ‹the transformation of the local Heliconian Muses [i.e. our trio] into the pan-Hellenic Olympian Muses›. Camilloni (1998) offers no view on dating.

[10] Thus, O. Vox (1980) 322-23.

[11] F. Hieronymus (1970) III n. 12; A. Schachter (1986) 156 n. 1.

[12] *RE* XVI.687-91; below, n. 27.

[13] Tzetzes on Hes. *WD* 1, lines 47-49 Ἄρατος δὲ ἐν τῇ πέμπτῃ τῶν Ἀστρικῶν, τέσσαρας λέγει, Διὸς τοῦ αἰθέρος, καὶ Πλουσίας νύμφης, Ἀρχὴν, Μελέτην, Θελξινόην, καὶ Ἀοιδήν. Cf. Cic. *de Nat. Deor.* 3.54 *iam Musae primae quattuor Iove altero natae et ...*, *Thelxinoe, Aoede, Arche, Melete* (not noted by Hieronymus). There is no evident connection with Helicon.

The first datable personification of *aoide* is at Pindar *Nem.* 5.2 (483 BC), where ‹song› (i.e. the ode) is apostrophised as a traveller by ship (at *Nem.* 4.3 (473 BC), ‹songs› are ‹daughters of the Muses›). *aoide* carried a wide range of reference, including the art of song (or the capacity for singing, as bestowed by the Muses), singing as a generic activity, the performative action of singing, and ‹song› as the performed product of that action.[14] It embraces choric song as well as the performance of the individual *aoidos*.[15] *Molpe* generally denotes choric (song and dance) performance, whereas *aoide* and *aeidein* focus on sung (or recited) words and thus on song content.[16] Aoide may be taken to embrace performance and also song-content as the product of performance.[17]

Melete and *mneme* do not appear in Homer. *Melete* features in the *Works and Days*, and Hesiod's aphorism ‹*melete* assists work› (*WD* 412 μελέτη δέ τοι ἔργον ὀφέλλει) achieved motto-status among trainers and teachers.[18] But while agricultural work embraces specialist technical skills that must be learned, the extended application of μελέτη, in the sense ‹practice› or ‹training›, to the mastery of *techne*, musical or otherwise, is post-Hesiodic. In the Homeric Hymn to Hermes, μελετάω denotes ‹application› to a teachable skill, Apollo's childhood practice of *manteia*.[19] In the same passage, Apollo underlines his mastery of learned skills, as distinct from inborn, or god-given, gifts, echoing comment within the hymn on music as a *techne* to be mastered by learned skills as well as natural ability.[20] *melete* and *aoide* appear together in the early fifth century. In *Olympians* 14 (488 BC), Pindar prays to Thalia and the Graces for a favourable reception for his choric *komos*: ‹for I have come singing of Asopichos in the Lydian mode and in [songs which have been] the objects of careful preparation [μελέταις]›.[21] Some eighty years later, Aristophanes parodied a Euripidean treatment of the regular, repeated workings of the loom as ‹singing› (*Frogs* 1316): κερκίδος ἀοιδοῦ μελέτας (‹practisings of singer shuttle›; Dover), and this exploits the nuance of repetitive exercise and rehearsal.[22] Epicharmus (fr. B33 DK) spoke of

---

[14] For a full treatment, see *LfgrE* s. v. ἀοιδή.

[15] Van Groningen (1948) 290, and others assume singing by individuals, e.g. rhapsodes. Choric *aoide*: Hom. Hym. Herm. 451 (the Muses) ... τῇσι χοροί τε μέλουσι καὶ ἀγλαὸς οἶμος ἀοιδῆς; cf. *Od.* 12.44 (Sirens); Hes. *Theog.* 44; *WD* 1; *Scutum* 205 (all Muses). For individual and choric singing in Homer, M. Wegner (1968) 29–40.

[16] W.G. Thalmann (1984) 117–18; cf. *LfgrE* s. v. ἀοιδή 2. Van Groningen (1948) 290 notes the absence of Molpe.

[17] Thus (with the qualification already noted) van Groningen (1948) 290 ‹Il ne peut s'agir, en principe, que de performances rhapsodiques›; Detienne (1999) 41 (‹epic recitation, the completed poem›); and, briefly, Nagy (1989) 32 n. 62.

[18] Pind. *Isth.* 6.65–66; Himerius *Or.* 74.1 Col.

[19] Hom. *Hym. Herm.* 556–57 (Apollo on the Thriai as teachers of prophecy) ... μαντείης ἀπάνευθε διδάσκαλοι ἦν ἐπὶ βουσὶ/παῖς ἔτ' ἐὼν μελέτησα· πατὴρ δ' ἐμὸς οὐκ ἀλέγιζεν. For the date, R. Janko (1982) 133–50. For παιδομαθίη, Phocylides fr. 15 χρὴ παῖδ' ἔτ' ἐόντα καλὰ διδάσκειν ἔργα. P. Shorey (1909), at 189.

[20] H. Görgemanns (1976) 124–26; Thalmann (1984) 127–28, with n. 50.

[21] *Ol.* 14.17–18: Λυδῷ γὰρ Ἀσώπιχον ἐν τρόπῳ/ἐν μελέταις τ' ἀείδων ἔμολον. I draw on Verdenius' suggestion that at *Isth.* 5.28, *melete* means ‹the task of preparing a song›. The Loeb (Race) suggests ‹as I practise my art› (but the singing is the song actually being performed). The nuance of past practice may be present, and Fenn's ‹chanting a carefully practised ode in Lydian mode on Asopikos› is not to be ruled out. Wilamowitz (1922) 151 n. 1 adduces Muse-Melete: ‹Aber neben dem Gesange wird es komplementär die Tätigkeit des Dichters, ἐν Μούσαις κόννte dafür stehen; μελέτη ist ja selbst eine Muse.› But the poem probably pre-dates the Muse by many decades.

[22] *LSJ* s. v. II b,c. μελέται is also a derisive word-play (from ‹Aeschylus›) on Euripides' μέλη.

the superiority of *melete* (‹application›) to natural endowment (*physis*); and Pindar speaks of the ‹nurturing› power of *melete* (*Ol.* 9.107) in an ode that illustrates the wider ‹dialectic of *physis* and *techne*›.[23] The Sophists took an interest in the word, and Protagoras wrote of the interdependence of *melete* and *techne*. Later, Plato satirises that interest when he applies μελετάω to Phaedrus practising and memorising Lysias' written speech (see below on *mneme*).[24] By around 400 BC, *melete* was established in educational and rhetorical contexts as a term for ‹practice›.[25] Despite the word's history, however, our Melete appears to be its first personification. At one time, it was thought that an *aulos*-carrying woman depicted on a mid-fifth century Attic vase as ‹Melelosa›, in the company of Terpsichore and Musaeus, was in fact ‹Meletosa›.[26] Tempting though it is to re-argue the point, the case for ‹Meletosa› is too speculative to be of use as a dating indicator for Melete; nor does the figure as depicted seem to carry any iconographical connotation of ‹practice›.[27]

Mneme appears as an alternative name for Mnemosyne;[28] but it carries less ‹personality› and greater emphasis on the functioning of memory. The early Pythagoreans placed a high valuation on *mneme*, which entered their numerological system as the ‹decas›, with quasi-divine force.[29] The *Prometheus Vinctus* (461) refers to writing as μνήμην ἁπάντων, μουσομήτορ' ἐργάνην (‹memory of all things, Muse-mothering worker›), where ‹Muse-mothering› is cued by μνήμην and gives it mythical colouring. Thus the divinisation of Mneme will not have been a novelty. Less usual is the alignment of Mneme with the ‹Muses› (as distinct from the mother-daughter genealogical relationship):[30] how are we to understand her function within a configuration that implies partnership on equal terms?

The Homeric Muses ‹bring to mind›, and offer the *aoidos* access to the ‹memory› of the totality of events that lies at their disposal.[31] At the same time, ‹memory› is a function of the oral poet's capacity to articulate a narrative in performance, from his personal resources and repertoire.[32] If our Mneme has retained this frame of reference, then within the Heliconian partnership of equals, she will assist Aoide with song-content and also with production in performance. But in the early fifth century, *mneme* acquired a new dimension in association with the culture of writing. It is applied to the repository of knowledge represented by a growing store of written material, and in parallel the act of writing is found as a

---

[23] T.K. Hubbard (1985) 116–17. Cf. Bacch. 3.191 (*melete* of the trainer).

[24] *Phaedr.* 228b; cf. *Symp.* 172a; 173b; 208a. Hieronymus (1970) 48. Shorey (1909) 189, citing Protagoras fr. 10 DK ἔλεγε μηδὲν εἶναι μήτε τέχνην ἄνευ μελέτης μήτε μελέτην ἄνευ τέχνης. A central text, produced around the end of the fifth century and reacting against written texts, is Alcidamas ‹Concerning the composers of written speeches›, or ‹Concerning the sophists›, a tract advocating the facility of improvisation (text at L. Radermacher [1951] B.XXII fr. 15). For μελέτη and writing see ibid. sections 2; 11; 15; 26; 34. For *mneme* and writing see sections 18–19. *Melete* is also applied to military exercises (Thuc. 1.18; 2.39).

[25] Hieronymus (1970) 43–44; 55–59; 78–81.

[26] *LIMC* s. v. *Mousa, Mousai* 79 (= *Mousaios* 3); *RE* XV.500; 593–94.

[27] ‹Melelosa› is more likely one of several one-off ‹Muse› names found on fifth century vases: *LIMC* VI.1.679.

[28] *PMG* 941; Plat. *Euthyd.* 275d.; Diog. Laert. 6.1.14. For Mneme as original Muse mother changing her name to Mnemosyne, Philo *de Plant. Noe* 129.

[29] W. Burkert (1972) 170; Mneme/‹decad› (distinct from Mnemosyne/‹monad›): below, n. 41.

[30] The Muses themselves regularly ‹remember›: see below, and cf. e.g. Pind. *Nem.* 1.12; also the ‹Mneiai›: *RE* XVI.691-92. Plutarch (*Mor.* 743) records an etymology of Polyhymnia as μνήμη πολλῶν.

[31] *RE* XV.2257-58 (on Mneme); 2265-69 (Mnemosyne); J.A. Notopoulos (1938); E. Barmeyer (1968) 120–24; J.-P. Vernant (1983) 75–105 (‹Mythical Aspects of Memory›); Detienne (1999) 39–43.

[32] E. Minchin (2002) esp. 163–64.

symbol for the mental activity of recollection.[33] *Prometheus Vinctus* 461 (see above) projects the *techne* of writing both as ‹memory› and as a productive practitioner: ‹Muse-mothering› signifies the ‹maternal› production of new literary work, and ἐργάνην suggests a worker in a craft industry (it is a cult title of Athena).[34] The expression connects memory, craftsmanship and literary production within the emerging culture of the written word.

The *techne* of memorisation appeared in the early fifth century and was elaborated later as a rhetorical discipline.[35] It had to do with developing the memory, through practice (*melete*), to cope with the professional demands on poets and speakers, including improvised response to occasion.[36] ‹Improvisation›, although re-invented as a product of sophistic *techne*, was a link between the disciplines, skills and memory of the *aoidos* who might be required to sing to demand (or to respond to occasion), and those of the prose speaker. A wider debate about memory, writing and mnemomics explored the individual's natural capacity for recall versus artificial mnemonic stimuli to memory; as also the individual's inner capacity for memory versus the external stimuli to memory provided by written texts. In the *Phaedrus*, Plato offers a mythical exchange between an Egyptian inventor of *technai* (Theuth) and his king (Thamus). Theuth claims that writing will improve memory (*mneme*). Thamus retorts that writing will bring with it ‹lack of practice in memorisation› (*mnemes ameletesia*). The exchange highlights the centrality of *mneme* to the fifth/fourth century controversy about the impact of texts upon a predominantly oral culture. By the fourth century, the partnership of *melete* and *mneme* is a technical commonplace, and Aristotle, for example, assumes the preservation of *mneme* by *meletai* (‹exercises›).[37] The two terms are not associated in this way in fifth century texts;[38] but J.-P. Vernant has suggested that the Pythagorean discipline of memory-exercise (*mnemes gymnasia, melete*, or *epimeleia*) may be earlier.[39] He connects these ideas with Pythagorean eschatology.[40] And indeed given Pythagorean interest in Mneme and Mnemosyne as well as Muses, indirect Pythagorean influence on our trio is not to be ruled out.[41]

---

[33] R. Pfeiffer (1968) 25–26.
[34] For the mother/daughter image, cf. Pind. *Nem.* 3.3–4 αἱ δὲ σοφαί Μοισᾶν θύγατρες ἀοιδαί ...
[35] Simonides: Call. *Aet.* fr. 64.10, with Pfeiffer; Cic. *de Or.* 2.351–54. Hippias: *FVS* 86A.2; 5a; 11; 12.
[36] Some sensible comments in J.P. Small (1997) 82–84.
[37] Aristot. *Mem.* 451a αἱ δὲ μελέται τὴν μνήμην σῴζουσι τῷ ἐπαναμιμνῄσκειν· Cf. also Diod. Sic. 3.4.4. Hieronymus (1970) 47; 50–51; 55.
[38] Thuc. 5.69.2 juxtaposes the *mneme* of Spartan disciplines acquired through prior *melete*.
[39] Vernant (1983) 106–23, esp. 107–9; Diod. Sic. 10.5.1; *VP* 164.
[40] That is, with the soul's capacity to recall its past existence, and thus avoid Lethe. Burkert (1972) 213 finds this an ‹attractive conjecture›. Cf. the Platonic (Diotima) doctrine of immortality through renewal of knowledge (*Symp.* 208ab): *melete* replaces the *mneme* of departing knowledge, preserves the appearance of continuity and enables the mortal to share in immortality (208a ... μελέτη δὲ πάλιν καινὴν ἐμποιοῦσα ἀντὶ τῆς ἀπιούσης μνήμην σῴζει τὴν ἐπιστήμην, ὥστε τὴν αὐτὴν δοκεῖν εἶναι). For post-mortem *mneme*, Diog. Laert. 8.4–5; for Pythagorean memory (*mneme*) of things said and learned, and memory training, Iambl. *VP* 164. For *mneme* as the ‹greatest and finest discovery›, and for ‹hearing›, ‹practising› and ‹learning›, see the anonymous *Dialexeis* 9 (Diels-Kranz *FVS* II.416.13–22).
[41] G. Pugliese Carratelli (1999) establishes the fifth century provenance of these ideas, and evokes the quasi-religious context. Philolaus A 13 DK (on the decad) διόπερ καὶ Μνήμη λέγοιτ' ἂν ἐκ τῶν αὐτῶν, ἀφ' ὧν καὶ μονὰς Μνημοσύνη ὠνομάσθη. The four-Muse group (above) includes ‹Arche› but not ‹Mneme›: cf. Philolaus B 8 DK ἡ μὲν μονάς ὡς ἂν ἀρχή οὖσα πάντων κατὰ τὸν Φιλόλαον; idem B13 DK ἐγκέφαλος δὲ <ἔχει> τὰν ἀνθρώπω ἀρχάν («the brain <contains> the origin of man»), with Pugliese Caratelli (1999) 190.

This is a coherent threesome, conceived within a specialist environment that recognised the need for structured disciplines in the acquisition of technical proficiency. Aoide has to do with performed song and its content, and is perfected by Melete; Mneme informs Aoide and facilitates performance; Melete of heard or written Aoide enhances the bard's Mneme; performed Aoide adds to the resources of Mneme; and so on. Technical influence is evident, and embedded within our trio is the polarity of *techne* and *physis*. This bears on dating, and we need to look briefy at the balance within that polarity, as it evolved in the late archaic and classical eras. In the Homeric Hymn to Hermes (467–89), lyre-playing requires innate gifts and also practice (*ergasia*, 486), with the weighting towards the former. As Thalmann comments, ‹... there seems ... to be a suggestion that laborious practice will take the player only so far, that he needs an innate talent to handle the instrument›.[42] Pindar too can strike a sophisticated balance between craft, training, and learned disciplines on the one hand and natural talent, inborn genius and inherited gifts on the other;[43] but again the weighting is generally towards the latter. There is, nonetheless, a clear contrast with Homeric *aoidoi*: the latter do not speak of practice, or (in modern parlance) of ‹perspiration› versus ‹inspiration›.[44] They are given the divine gift of *aoide* by the Muses; they are ‹taught›, if at all, by the Muses; and it is the Muses who give them access to the accumulated resources of *mnemosyne*. Demodocus and Phemius do not speak of apprenticeship, or of learning from the songs of other *aoidoi*, or of rehearsing their own repertoire. Nor do they acknowledge the authority of earlier *aoidoi*. Our Muses, with Melete as co-equal with her companions, are further distanced from this model. They they lie a very long way from the Homeric and Hesiodic Muses, breathing divine song into the breasts of receptive bards. Indeed it is tempting to compare them with the rhetoricians' abandonment of the inspirational Muses in the name of *techne* (skills lying within human competence), and their espousal of a *paideia* that was based not on *mousike* but on *logoi*.[45] Our trio, I would suggest, belongs to the same era as that phenomenon: to the end of the fifth century, perhaps, or the first decades of the fourth. A similarly anachronistic tradition, perhaps again the product of the same era, is recorded by Pausanias (2.31.3) in his description of the *Mouseion* at Troizene: he credits Pittheus, legendary first king of Troizene, with teaching the art of *logoi* (διδάξαι λόγων τέχνην φασί) there, and writing a (surviving) handbook on the matter.[46]

A tentative dating of Aoide, Melete and Mneme to the later classical era involves a further consequence for the cult status of the trio. The Aload names cannot predate Hesiod; and it appears from Pausanias that no claim was made for the existence of this ‹cult› after Pieros changed their names. It follows that the ‹cult›, as claimed for Helicon, is most likely a fiction. We are dealing not with a real cult, but with Heliconian ideology that retrojected three Muse names back to the mythical origins of worship on the mountain, and tied them together with the presence there of the terrible twins.

---

[42] Thalmann (1984) 224 n. 50. For *ergasian* (486) as ‹practice›, and its application to *technai*, including music, see the excellent note of Allen, Halliday and Sikes *ad loc.*
[43] Hubbard (1985) 107–24.
[44] On Homeric ‹concealment› of the realities of learning and transmission, R. Scodel (1998) 171–74, with earlier bibliography.
[45] This follows an illuminating recent treatment in Murray (2004) 380–89.
[46] See C. Brillante (1994) 23–24.

II: The Aloades and Aeolian Ethnic Identity

The Aloades are Aeolian by descent, and thus constituent parts of the Aeolian ethnic identity. A recent analysis suggests that ‹a sense of Aiolian identity – together with the migration tradition that legitimated that identity- ... first arose in Asia Minor› (that is to say in the eastern Aeolis, rather than in the Aeolian speaking areas on the mainland).[47] This view does not fully reflect the evidence for the pre-Homeric history of Aeolian poetry and the Aeolian dialect. Within this obscure area, two things seem reasonably clear: first, the dialect was carried from Thessaly to Boeotia, with linguistic admixtures from elsewhere, as part of the southward movement of peoples in the late second millenium, and the arrival of the Boeotoi in central Greece;[48] and second, Aeolian-speaking poets in Thessaly and Boeotia actively developed regional epic cycles in the late Mycenaean period and later.[49] This poetry can be assumed to have recorded and transmitted the myths, traditions and sagas of the Aeolian-speaking peoples in the central-north Greece, and it will have helped forge regional loyalties, foster local pride and connect places and peoples with their heroic and divine ancestry. The sixth century ‹Hesiodic› *Catalogue*, and the regional character of the genealogical myth-groups it brings together (the products of the eighth and seventh centuries) preserves some of this inheritance.[50]

In the genealogical myths recorded in the *Catalogue*, the Aloades were descendents of Aeolos through the union of his daughter Kanake with Poseidon.[51] And Poseidon, the quintessential Thessalian god, was himself the tribal ancestor of the Aeolians.[52] The Aloades, if not literally autochthonous in the sense of earth-born (like Erechtheus of Athens), were closely associated with territory: so much is evident from Homer's description of them as nurslings of ‹cereal giving earth›.[53] This in turn reflects their Poseidonian inheritance (Erechtheus himself was assimilated to Poseidon in respect of autochthony, and also as a function of the Athenian national myth,).[54] Additionally, through their mortal father Ἀλωεύς they connect with the technology of grain production (ἀλοάω ‹thresh›; ἀλωή, ‹threshing floor›, later ‹piece of cultivated land›; ἀλωεύς, ‹cultivator›), that is to say with the extension of agricultural civilisation to the territory with which they are identified.[55]

---

[47] J. Hall (2002) 71–73.
[48] R.J. Buck (1968); idem (1969) 292.
[49] Mycenaean epic: G.C. Horrocks (1980); A. Hoekstra (1981); M.L. West (1988) 156–59. Aeolian epic and regional cycles in Thessaly and Boeotia: E. Bethe (1927) III.79–83; West, art. cit. (*supra*) 159–62.
[50] M.L. West (1985) 137–71 (esp. 164–71). For the centrality of ‹fictive kinship and descent›, including genealogical myth, in creating ethnicity, see Hall (2002) 10; 15; 25–29.
[51] Hes. Fr. 19–21 M-W; West (1985) 61–62.
[52] L.R. Farnell (1907) 14–15; 23–27; cf. W. Burkert (1985) 136; *LIMC* VII.1.446 (E. Simon).
[53] *Od.* 11.309 οὓς δὴ μηκίστους θρέψε ζείδωρος ἄρουρα; compare especially *Il.* 2.547–48 on autochthonous Erechtheus (a likely sixth century interpolation, later than the Odyssean Aloades) ... Ἐρεχθῆος μεγαλήτορος, ὅν ποτ' Ἀθήνη/θρέψε Διὸς θυγάτηρ, τέκε δὲ ζείδωρος ἄρουρα. The proximity was explicitly recognised in Eratosthenes' assimilation of them to γηγενεῖς (Schol. Apoll. Rhod. 1.482).
[54] For the myth of Athenian autochthony and its patriotic exploitation, R. Parker (1987) 193–95. For Poseidon, cf. Plato's portrayal of Atlantis in the *Critias* (113–14): Poseidon marries Cleito, daughter of an earth-born mountain dweller; one of their children is Autochthon. The Athenians too are autochthonous in the *Critias* (109d). For the cult of Poseidon Erechtheus, see Eur. *Erechth.* fr. 370.93–94 K, with Cropp's note ad loc.
[55] Less persuasive are the suggested ‹grain› connections of their own names, through ὠθέω and ἐφιάλλομαι, *pace* Preller and Robert (1894) and Toepffer (1894) 1590. For traces of the cereal tradition, cf. an allegorical

The Aloades had a presence in Thessaly and Boeotia, and with Aloeus are associated with city-foundation and place names.[56] They founded Aloion in the vale of Tempe, otherwise unknown;[57] also a town called Alos that features only in the Homeric Catalogue, suggesting a Mycenaean establishment that did not survive into historical times.[58] They were, then, civilising organisers of space.[59] At the same time, they pursued Thessalian ethnic and territorial interests against ‹Thracians›. The foundation of Aloion at the natural boundary between Thessaly and the Mount Olympus massif to the north is associated with defeat of ‹Thracians›.[60] A pattern of ethnic confrontation between Greek-speaking Thessalians and tribes lying to the north is indicated in a later account of their imprisonment of Ares: as ‹kings of Hellas›, they conquered much barbarian land, subdued opposition, enforced a general state of peace and thus ‹seemed to have confined Ares›.[61] On one version, the binding of Ares took place in Thrace, in which context it may be right (with *RE* I.1592) to recall Ares' Thracian identity, making him a natural enemy of the Thessalian Aloades. Thracian rivalry is combined in Diodorus (5.50-51) with what appears to be an early association with Naxos: Aloeus sent his sons to rescue Iphimedeia from Thracian confinement there, leading to conflict over control of the island.[62] This may reflect events in the late 10th/early 9th centuries when Thessalian influence spread through Euboea to the Cyclades and Naxos.[63] The Aloades have taken on the character of autochthonous heroes, defending Thessalian territorial interests against Thracians; and we may even have traces, in the regal titles, of an autochthonous kingship comparable to those at Athens (above) and Sparta.[64]

---

reading of Ares/Aloades (Schol. D *Il.* 5.385) identifying Ares with zodiacal Leo and heat, that leads to ‹fields appearing empty of corn ears›. For cereal cultivation within a genealogical representation of the regal organisation of territory at Sparta, see Calame (1987) 159-61 on ‹Myles› (‹the millar›), at Alesiai. For agriculture and autochthony, Apollodorus on the Athenians *FGrHist* 244 F 106 κληθῆναί φησιν αὐτοὺς αὐτόχθονας, ἐπεὶ τὴν χθόνα, τουτέστιν τὴν γῆν, ἀρχὴν οὖσαν πρῶτοι εἰργάσαντο· Camilloni ([1998] 30) offers unpersuasive etymologies of Aloeus to suggest a connection with ‹exile›.

[56] *RE* I.1592 (Toepffer); rightly noted by Camilloni (1998) 29-31; 33.
[57] Steph. Byz. s. v. Ἀλώιον, πόλις Θεσσαλίας ἐπὶ τῶν Τέμπεων, ἣν ἔκτισαν οἱ Ἀλωάδαι καθελόντες τοὺς Θρᾷκας. ὡς εἶναι αὐτὴν ἀπὸ Ἀλωέως. τὸ ἐθνικὸν Ἀλωεύς.
[58] Hes. Fr. 19 M-W (Schol. Apoll. Rhod. 1.482) Ἀλωέως εἰσὶν υἱοί. Ἡσίοδος δὲ Ἀλωέως καὶ Ἰφιμεδείας κατ' ἐπίκλησιν, ταῖς δὲ ἀληθείαις Ποσειδῶνος καὶ Ἰφιμεδείας ἔφη, καὶ Ἄλον πόλιν Αἰτωλίας ὑπὸ τοῦ πατρὸς αὐτῶν ἐκτίσθαι, ἧς Ὅμηρος μνημονεύει· ‹οἵ τ' Ἄλον εἶχον›. The Laurentine scholia record a variant: the Aloades founded the town for their father; West (1985) 61. For the disappearance of Mycenaean towns named in the Catalogue, cf. J. Latacz (2004) 238-47.
[59] Compare the civic component within the Spartan genealogies: Calame (1987) 162-64.
[60] Steph. Byz. s. v. Ἀλώιον (cited above, n. 57).
[61] Schol. D *Il.* 5.385 Ἄλλοι δὲ ... τοὺς Ἀλωείδας τούτουςφασὶ γενέσθαι βασιλεῖς τῆς Ἑλλάδος. Πολλῆς δὲ καὶ βαρβάρου γῆς ἐπικρατήσαντας, καταπαῦσαι τὸν πόλεμον, καὶ τὰς εἰς αὐτὸν παρασκευὰς, καὶ ἐν εἰρήνῃ ποιῆσαι βιοτεύειν τοὺς ἀνθρώπους. Διὰ τούτου ἔδοξαν δῆσαι τὸν Ἄρην, τουτέστι, τὸν πόλεμον. The imprisonment itself is early: *Il.* 5.385-91; for likely near eastern origins, see J. Harmatta (1968); but the above version is not earlier than C5. Ephialtes as ἄναξ, Pind. *Pyth.* 4.89. For Aloades as Thessalian ‹tyrants› Ps.-Nonn. *Or.* 4 *Hist.* 85 οὗτοι δὲ ἦσαν υἱοὶ μὲν Ἀλωέως, τύραννοι δὲ τὴν φύσιν. ἐγένοντο δὲ περὶ Θετταλίαν. οὗτοι ἀνταρσίαν ἐμελέτησαν κατὰ τῶν θεῶν.
[62] Cf. also Parthen. *Erot. Path.* 19.1 οἱ Θρᾷκες ὁρμήσαντες ἀπὸ νήσου τῆς πρότερον μὲν Στρογγύλης, ὕστερον δὲ Νάξου κληθείσης, ἐληΐζοντο μὲν τήν τε Πελοπόννησον καὶ τὰς πέριξ νήσους· προσχόντες δὲ Θεσσαλίᾳ πολλάς τε ἄλλας γυναῖκας κατέσυραν, ἐν δὲ καὶ τὴν Ἀλωέως γυναῖκα Ἰφιμέδην καὶ θυγατέρα αὐτῆς Παγκρατώ.
[63] *CAH* III².1.671 (Snodgrass); 767 (Boardman).
[64] For Sparta, see Calame (1987) 156-59.

Evidently, then, a series of spatial and civilising myths accumulated around the Thessalian Aloades, articulating processes that elsewhere might typically be expressed through an extended genealogy.[65]

Moving south, now, to Boeotia, we again find Poseidon in the role of tribal ancestor, father of Boeotos and divine parent of the founders of ethnic groups and towns.[66] He may have been established at Onchestus in Boeotia in the Bronze Age.[67] The ‹Hegesinous› text makes him father of the co-founder of Ascra, Oioklos, by the nymph Ascra.[68] The cult name Ἑλικώνιος may signify an early association with Helicon; but Achaean Helike is also a candidate, and an ancient dispute on the matter remains unresolved (the balance of modern opinion favouring the mountain).[69] Poseidon was not associated with mountain-top cult; but an interest in mountain terrain is evident from his Thessalian cult name Πετραῖος (‹of the rocks›) and from representations of him with one foot resting on a rock/mountain.[70] This has to do with mountains as sources of water, and it finds expression in equine myth: the genesis of the first horse from rock; and the production of water by a horse from the rocky side of a mountain.[71] We think especially of Pegasos, horse-son of Poseidon, who struck his hoof on Helicon and caused Hippocrene to flow.[72]

The Aloades established a presence on the north coast of Boeotia. Otus was evidently credited with the foundation of a κώμη in that area;[73] and their tombs were displayed at Anthedon.[74] Anthedon itself was reputedly a Thracian foundation (Steph. Byz. s. v.), and so there may lurk a further identification of the Aloades with territorial interests (embodied in tomb cult) against alien Thracians.[75] Moreover, the proximity of the Aloades' tombs

---

[65] Again, as at Sparta: Calame (1987), esp. 178.

[66] *RE* XXII.482 (‹P. als Gründer von Städten, Stämmen, Völkern›). Poseidon/Boeotos: A. Veneri (1990) 130, with n. 15. For genealogical associations with Minyan Orchomenos, *RE* XV.2015-18. Cult: Schachter (1986) 206-25; *LIMC* VII.1.447 (E. Simon).

[67] Schachter (1986) 212-13, noting similarities to inland sites in Thessaly, and registering the possibility that he was not imported into Boeotia until later.

[68] Paus. 9.29.1 (below, Appendix I).

[69] For the cult name, cf. esp. *Il.* 20.403-4. Etym. Magn. 547.16 Ἑλικώνιον τὸν Ποσειδῶνα εἴρηκεν ἀπὸ Ἑλικῶνος, ὡς Ἀρίσταρχος βούλεται· ἐπεὶ ἡ Βοιωτία ὅλη ἱερὰ Ποσειδῶνος· οὐ γὰρ ἀρέσκει ἀπὸ Ἑλίκης; for Poseidon and Helicon, cf. *Epigr. Hom.* 6.2; *Hom. Hym.* 22.3. For the uncertainties, Schachter (1986) 206-7, 214. Contrast Farnell (1907) 29-33; U. von Wilamowitz-Moellendorf (repr. 1959) I.208; *RE* XXII.497; Veneri (1990).

[70] *Petraios*: Schol. Apoll. Rhod. 3.1244. Etym. Magn. 473.46 Ἵππιος ὁ Ποσειδῶν: Ὅτι δοκεῖ πρῶτον ἵππον γεγεννηκέναι Σίσυφον ἐν Θεσσαλίᾳ, τῇ τριαίνῃ πέτραν παίσας· ὅθεν ἱερὸν Ποσειδῶνος Πετραίου καθίδρυται ἐν Θεσσαλίᾳ. *LIMC* VIII.1.575, s. v. Equi. Rock/mountains: *LIMC* s. v. Poseidon, nos. 34-38; ibid. VII.1.478 (E. Simon); Farnell (1907) 66-67.

[71] Farnell (1907) 30; Wilamowitz (repr. 1959) I.208; Burkert (1985) 138.

[72] *RE* XIX.56-59, s. v. Pegasos; M. Ninck (1921) 18; *LIMC* VII.1.229-30. For Poseidon/Pegasus/ Helicon, cf. Anton. Lib. 9.2 (Helicon's reaction to the Muses in the contest with the Pierides): ὁ δ' Ἑλικὼν ηὔξετο κηλούμενος ὑφ' ἡδονῆς εἰς τὸν οὐρανόν, ἄχρις αὐτὸν βουλῇ Ποσειδῶνος ἔπαυσεν ὁ Πήγασος τῇ ὁπλῇ τὴν κορυφὴν πατάξας.

[73] P.Mich. 4913.13 as read by Jacoby (*FGrHist* 376F1).

[74] Paus. 9.22.6; A. Schachter (1981) 17-18. These tombs will presumably have been rather large; and one wonders whether they were (modified) natural features. A variant tradition makes Minyas, the founder of Orchomenos, a son of Aloeus: Schol. Pind. *Isth.* 1.56. Poseidon is prominent in the genealogy of Minyas and Orchomenos: *RE* XV.2015-16 (Stier).

[75] Tombs and territory: cf. A. M. Snodgrass (1980) 38-39.

to the sanctuary of Dionysus at Anthedon, taken together with the status of their mother (Iphidemeia) and sister as ‹nurses of Dionysus›, their capture by the Thracians of Naxos and rescue by the Aloades' seaborn expedition, has led Schachter to posit an ancient cultic connection between tombs and sanctuary. Schachter also notes the parallel situation on Naxos, a major centre of Dionysiac cult where the Aloades were honoured as heroes.[76] Here, then, there emerges a cluster of territorial, defensive and cultic interests, with sea-going as an additional element. We may surmise that the Aloades came from Thessaly to Boeotia by sea, re-established their pattern of city-founding activity there too, and acquired or extended a cultic role in support of the worship of Dionysus.

At some point, the Aloades came to be associated with Ascra, as co-founders. This cannot be assumed to be a direct extension of their coastal presence, and it could be a separate phenomenon, brought from the north over mountain routes (see below). It might be part of the wider pattern of dissemination of Thessalian identities in Boeotia (see below);[77] but as was seen earlier, Poseidon may have established a very early connection with Helicon, in addition to his oracular presence at Onchestos, and for all we know, his sons' presence at Ascra may pre-date that on the northern coast. At all events, there are solid reasons for thinking that Pausanias' report of their presence in Boeotia represents a genuine and ancient tradition. Indeed Jacoby himself was moved to speculate that the Aloades' role in Boeotian legend may have been much greater than is apparent from the evidence available to us.[78]

Pausanias' statement (9.29.1) that the Aloades were first to declare Helicon sacred to the Muses is directly at odds with Strabo who surmises (9.2.25) that the Thracians were first to dedicate Helicon to the Muses. The discrepancy is underlined in Pausanias' suggestion that ‹Pieros› may have been acting under Thracian influence. Strabo (9.2.25; 10.3.17) adduces the replication of Thessalian and Pierian place names in Boeotia, and there is indeed cumulative evidence of the north-south migration of toponyms and cultic epithets: Thourion/Thourides (probably from Macedonia); Helicon, Leibethrion, and perhaps a stream Piera, from Pieria;[79] Zeus Homoloios from Thessaly;[80] and Onchestos and Thespiae from likely homonyms in Thessaly.[81] That phenomenon, together with the concentration of female pluralities (nymphs and Muses) in Boeotia, might rather be the cumulative outcome of the southwards drift of other peoples, including the Boeotoi, over an extended period of time.[82] But Strabo's contention that the ‹Pieres› and ‹Pieria› were themselves originally ‹Thracian› commands attention. The interplay of Pieria, Macedonia and Thrace in myth and tradition appears to reflect, albeit it at some distance in time, the historical incursion of ‹Thracian› peoples into Greek-speaking Pieria in the late Bronze age, and their penetration

---

[76] Schachter (1981) 17. The ‹nurses› myth has an analogue in Thracian Lycurgus' attack on the nymph-nurses of Dionysus Hom. *Il.* 6.132–37. For Dionysus' role in supporting ‹Boeotoi› against Thracian invaders, cf. also Paus. 9.16.2; Suda s. v. Λύσιοι τελεταί.
[77] Thus, tentatively, Schachter (1986) 188 n.2.
[78] In his comments on Kallippos, *FGrHist* 385F1.
[79] Thourion: inferred from Macedonian *Thourides* (Hesychius s. v.); cf. Schachter (1986) 146. ‹Piera› depends on an emendation of Pausanias 9.34.4: Schachter (1986) 187 n.2.
[80] For the Thessalian origin of Zeus Homoloios, A. Schachter (1994) 120–22.
[81] Onchestos: *RE* XVIII.1.417. Thespiae: A. Schachter (1996) 111. Thespiae later acquired an Athenian oikist, marking Athenian input into its re-establishment after 479: ibid. 116, citing Diod. 4.29.2.
[82] Schachter (1986) 187–88; for a summary of female groups and toponyms related to migration patterns, see J. Larson (2001) 138–39. For further examples, Buck (1968) 278, n. 80.

at least as far as the Peneius river and the Vale of Tempe.[83] They were eventually expelled from Pieria, to become the ‹Pieres› in the territories east of the Strymon.[84] N.G.L. Hammond dated that occupation from around 1300 to around 650 BC and suggested that ‹it was during this long time that Thracian influences in music and religion percolated into Greece from Pieria›.[85] He further suggested that Pausanias' ‹Pieros› and the hypothesised Thracian influence on his Muses ‹may be a confused memory of a time when Thracians occupied Pieria›.[86] Now, the southern migration of Boeotoi may account for the introduction of Pierian/Thracian influences to Mount Helicon, and by extension for the Heliconian legend of Pieros; but it would not immediately account for the tradition of the Aloades' prior presence in the area, and for that we need to consider the wider pattern of sub-Mycenaean migration and invasions.

There is a historiographical tradition that Thracian invaders actually penetrated central Greece around the time of the Trojan War, or a little later. Differing versions, reflecting the local interests of the narrators, give differing timings, achievements and scenes of conflict;[87] but there is little doubt that the tradition reflects historical events which unfolded at some point in the twelfth century. The Thracians encountered resistance and were repelled. The question for us is whether memories of this invasion could have given rise to the Aload tradition at Ascra/Helicon, possibly as an analogue of their defence of Greek-speaking interests at Tempe. We have already seen one ‹out of area› action involving Thessalian Aloades and Thracians, in Naxos (above), with implications for the cultic association of Aloades and Dionysus on Naxos and at Anthedon. Ascra itself commanded a strategic position on an north east/south west invasion route at the point where it descends from Helicon to the central lowlands, and the hill now known as Purgaki offered a commanding point of defence of the fertile plains of the Thespike against hillman invaders.[88] There is evidence of a substantial early Bronze Age settlement in the area. So Ascra, if anywhere, would have been a likely locality for the Aloades to put down early roots as champions of resistance to ‹Thracians›.[89] We cannot hope to know who brought them there, and when; but the Boeotoi were not the only migrants from Thessaly to central Greece; and from

---

[83] For the archeological evidence and its bearing on the myths, N.G.L. Hammond (1972) 416–18. Hammond (ibid, 417) warns that in Greek sources, ‹Thracian› may have ‹geographical and linguistic meaning rather than an ethnographic association›.
[84] Thuc. 2.99.3; Hammond (1972) 417.
[85] Hammond (1972) 417; cf. Larson (2001) 169. Given the tradition of expulsion of the ‹Thracians› (next note), hence incomplete miscegenation, that period seems rather long; but Hammond's basic thesis of Thracian occupation and southwards influence remains unchallenged in essentials.
[86] Paus. 9.29.3-4 χρόνῳ δὲ ὕστερόν φασι Πίερον Μακεδόνα, ἀφ' οὗ καὶ Μακεδόσιν ὠνόμασται τὸ ὄρος, τοῦτον ἐλθόντα ἐς Θεσπιὰς ἐννέα τε Μούσας καταστήσασθαι καὶ τὰ ὀνόματα τὰ νῦν μεταθέσθαι σφίσι. ταῦτα δὲ ἐνόμιζεν οὕτως ὁ Πίερος ἢ σοφώτερά οἱ εἶναι φανέντα ἢ κατά τι μάντευμα ἢ παρά του διδαχθεὶς τῶν Θρᾳκῶν· δεξιώτερον γὰρ τά τε ἄλλα ἐδόκει τοῦ Μακεδονικοῦ τὸ ἔθνος εἶναι πάλαι τὸ Θρᾴκιον καὶ οὐχ ὁμοίως ἐς τὰ θεῖα ὀλίγωρον. εἰσὶ δ' οἳ καὶ αὐτῷ θυγατέρας ἐννέα Πιέρῳ γενέσθαι λέγουσι καὶ τὰ ὀνόματα ἅπερ ταῖς θεαῖς τεθῆναι καὶ ταύταις, καὶ ὅσοι Μουσῶν παῖδες ἐκλήθησαν ὑπὸ Ἑλλήνων, θυγατριδοῦς εἶναι σφᾶς Πιέρου·
[87] The evidence is reviewed by Buck (1969) 289–91.
[88] P.W. Wallace (1974). Schachter (1986) 212 notes a pattern of Poseidon's sanctuaries in Thessaly (and Onchestus) ‹situated so as to control heights and/or routes›.
[89] Early settlement: J. Bintliff (1996) 196. A.T. Edwards (2004) 167–70 (without analysis of the foundation role of the Aloades). For the invasion route, see A.R. Burn (1949) 316–22; for the strategic position of Ascra, R.M. Kallet-Marx (1989) 301–4.

what has been said about Poseidon's early presence in the area, the Aloades could well have pre-dated the Boeotoi.[90]

At all events, there are grounds for taking the Aloades' foundation of Ascra as a genuine tradition reflecting Thracian incursion and autochthonous defence. Given the extreme difficulty of reconstructing anything like a reliable picture of northern incursions in the sub-Mycenaean period, this reading is necessarily speculative, and it involves only the barest account of what must have been messy and complex ethnic moves, countermoves and alliances over an extended period.[91] Nonetheless, the historiographical tradition offers a Thracian invasion (repelled) followed by migrating Boeotoi.[92] Our myth (Aloades' foundation of Ascra, followed by Pieros' arrival at Helicon) broadly follows the same order. Leaving aside, for the present, the Aloades' worship of the Muses, this parallel sequencing offers some encouragement for seeing within Pausanias' account a substratum of myth that corresponds to early events, and movements of peoples, around the territory of Ascra.

If that is right, then we might expect the first account of those events to have been composed during the archaic era, and to have been transmitted, with more or less elaboration, in verse, prose and oral tradition until it acquired the form that was summarised by Pausanias. That process is now irrecoverable. Nonetheless, comparative material from the same conceptual area may help illuminate what remains; and to understand how the ‹territorial› Aloades might have evolved from founder-defenders of Ascra to worshippers of ‹Muses›, and how ‹Pieros› succeeded them, we need to pause, digress, and consider the Greek interest in the relationship between territory and music in greater detail. This is the subject of the next section.

III: Music and Territory

We are familiar with the identification of music and flowing water, with mountains that sing, and with water or rock nymphs that prophesy, or inspire the musician.[93] The passages adduced in this section will illustrate these and other ways in which music could be thought of as a product of landscape and territory, and how this concept lent itself to figurative or actual association with territorial aggression and defence. They do not provide a comprehensive treatment (relevant archaic material, such as the myth of Thamyris the Thracian, is omitted, although one early antecedent will be noted in the following section). But they will highlight topics and narrative patterns relevant to the place of the Aloades on Helicon; and the final passage, from Ovid's *Metamorphoses*, includes another version of the myth of Pieros and the *Pierides*.

In a polemic on the rise of Asianic rhetoric, Dionysius of Halicarnassus wrote in terms of invasion and expulsion (*de Ant. Rhet.* 1): the ‹ancient, autochthonous Attic Muse› (ἡ ...

---

[90] Schachter's (1986) comments (212-13) about the date and manner of Poseidon's arrival at Onchestus are relevant to the Aloades at Ascra.
[91] There is, for example, a record of conflict between Boeotoi and Thracians, with the latter on one version encamped around Helicon: Ephorus *FGrHist* 70F119.3; Polyaen. *Strat.* 7.43; Buck (1969) 297.
[92] Buck (1969) 292-94; idem (1968) 278-79, suggesting absorption of indigenous population.
[93] For evidence for these central issues of landscape, music and inspiration, see S.H. Lonsdale (1993) 262-68 (Pan's dance as a territorical marker); A. Hardie (1996) 223-31; idem (1998) 241-42; idem (2002) 187-89; A. Kambylis (1965) 27.

Ἀττικὴ μοῦσα καὶ ἀρχαία καὶ αὐτόχθων), he says, is driven out of public affairs as the Asian Muse arrives and assumes control of Greek cities. The ‹Muse›, personifying the Attic style, is herself an ancient product of the Attic soil and is figuratively driven out of the *poleis* by an Asian usurper. Much earlier, when Bacchylides wanted to celebrate a Cean victory at Nemea with an ode composed and sung on the spot (the second epinician), he too used the language of excursion and invasion, this time with his own ‹native Muse› (Μοῦσ' αὐθιγενὴς, 11) on foreign soil. She invites celebration of a ‹battle-victory› at Nemea (4–5), and of the record of victorious Cean excursions there (8–10). In this patriotic ode, recalling Ceos' mythic ancestry at 8, the Muse (that is, the Cean poet) has herself figuratively travelled and is in Nemea spontaneously honouring athletic *nike* (expressed in terms of conquest) with *epinicia*.

Euripides' *Bacchae* (408 BC), written in Macedonia, dramatises the arrival in Greece of a maenadic *choros*, that dances to eastern music and challenges established order at the Theban *polis*.[94] The *choros* complains (519–36) that Theban Dirke is resisting their *thiasoi*, despite the stream's physical involvement in Dionysus' birth (paradoxical autochthony). The *choros* then blesses Pieria (565), obliquely acknowledges the Muses' presence there (563; cf. 410), and pictures Dionysus leading maenads across Macedonian rivers in order to ‹set you [sc. the geographical region of Pieria] to dancing with bacchic revelries› (565–75; cf.114 for the ‹entire land dancing›). Pieria, the *choros* suggests, had once been musically tamed by lyre-playing Orpheus' creation of natural, proto-Dionysiac, *thiasoi* on Olympus, from trees and animals (561–64).[95] As a function of their Dionysiac incursion, therefore, the *choros* re-enacts the introduction of music through Pieria to Greece. It does this by physically assimilating the territory of Pieria and its natural features to the sacral-choric character of a new, thiasos-based musical regime; and Orpheus' taming of the wild landscape becomes an analogue for Dionysus' taming of the ‹wild› element within the Theban establishment.[96] The topographical references have generally been understood as compliments to Euripides' Macedonian host, Archelaos, and to the latter's interest in Orpheus, Muses and Greek drama, a topic to which we shall return (below, IV).[97] At the end of the play (1330–39), a real invasion is envisaged in Dionysus' prediction of Cadmus' exile and return with Harmonia at the head of a barbarian army that will be checked at Delphi. Musical ‹incursion›, identified with territory, is thus a component of the successful intrusion of an irresistible cult; and their success contrasts with the real invasion that is doomed to fail.

The central Hellenistic treatment of music and poetry allied to territoriality and invasion is Callimachus' *Hymn to Delos*. Ares, acting for Hera, terrifies the Greek lands into refusing to let the wandering Leto give birth to Apollo. He is perched menacingly on ‹Thracian Haemus› and terrifies the mainland regions with the cacophonous clashing of spear on shield; and in a central section of Apolline prophecy, he is identified with the invading Gauls, the ‹late-born Titans› from the west who, in a modern Titanomachy, will bring ‹Cel-

---

[94] C. Segal (1997) 70–77; 118–24.
[95] The repeated σύναγεν (563–64) of Orpheus drawing together the trees on Olympus (560–61) and its wild beasts is a technical term for assembling a *thiasos*: A. Heinrichs, (1969) 235; the allusion is cued by Dionysiac θιάσους on Nysa (558). Orpheus creates his ‹*thiasoi*› μούσαις (563) i.e. ‹by music› and ‹for the Muses›; wild nature is thus tamed and ordered by music, and worships the Muses.
[96] Segal (1997) 74–75; 153–54. For Macedonian Orpheus' taming music as an analogue for civilising conquest, see below, IV.
[97] E.R. Dodds (1960) xxxix–xl; 126; 147. Segal (1997) 122.

‹tic Ares› to the Greeks (172–74) and meet defeat at Delphi. In an elemental confrontation (105–52), the river Peneius alone of mainland locations defies Ares, parallel in that sense to Delos who ultimately accepts Leto. When Apollo is born, Apolline choric music is created with him, cacophony is replaced by harmony, and chaos by order (249–59; cf. 300–1).[98] Again, the triumph of new music, identified with territory, is juxtaposed with a doomed military invasion from the north. In a metapoetic reading of the central rivalry between Ares and Apollo, Peter Bing has shown that among Callimachus' subjects is poetry itself: so that the poet has implicitly juxtaposed his own ‹Apolline› music with homerising ‹war› epic (Ares). The ‹territorial› terms of the musical confrontation derive from earlier conceptions of culture and territory: at one level, Apolline music is identified with the territorial integrity of the Greece lands against the menaces of Ares (and ‹Celtic Ares›), with the river Peneius, inspired to courage by Leto, playing a conspicuous ‹border› role at the Vale of Tempe. At another level, music is literally identified with Greek territory and landscape/seascape: Thessaly itself ‹dances in fear› to Ares' cacophony (139–40);[99] the Cyclades form a choric circle around Delos as Apollo is born (300–301). Then we have the nymphs in their traditional role, embodying landscape features: the Delian nymphs, offspring of a river, who sing as Apollo is born (256–57); the Thessalian nymph-daughters of river Peneius (109); and above all Melia, identified with the trees at the summit of Helicon, who, frightened to see the summit trees shaking, breaks off from her *choros* (79–82).[100]

Melia returns us to Helicon and the Muses. She is αὐτόχθων Μελίη, ‹autochthonous Melia›, or ‹native Melia› (80); and she is integral to the physical topography of Helicon in a way that the Muses are not, for their birth, we have been reminded (7–8), is associated with Pimpleis, in Macedonian Pieria.[101] The Muses themselves, we infer, are Pierian/Macedonian incomers to Helicon; and the poet's break-off apostrophe (82–83) to the Muses as ‹my goddesses› (seeking earnestly to clarify the precise nature of the nymphs' co-eval tree status) further reveals that their pan-Hellenic role has now extended to embrace the scholarly pursuits of the *Mouseion* at Egyptian Alexandria.[102] Here, then, an autochthonous, pre-Apolline *choros is* identified with Helicon; but Melia and her *choros* were helpless without the championship of incoming Leto-Apollo (as accepted at Delos), and without the Heliconian presence of the pan-Hellenic Muses associated with Apollo's leading role. Callimachus' treatment of music, landscape and territory, although contemporary in detail and in Ptolemaic application, draws deeply on the literary tradition;[103] and it does so in a

---

[98] For an excellent account of the Apolline music, its circular symbolism and its role in restoring cosmic order (parallel to the defeat of the Gallic forces of chaos at Delphi), see P. Bing (1988) 124–31.
[99] There is a nuance of earthquake, accentuating Poseidonian features in Ares: cf. esp. Eur. *Erechth*. fr. 370.48–49 [ ]ἄτας· ὀρχεῖται δὲ π[ό]λεος πέδον σάλωι·/].ἐμβάλλει Ποσειδῶν πόλει· See below, and Appendix I (n. 165) for ‹shaking› Helicon.
[100] The trees are described as ‹hair› χαίτην; for oaks as hair (on Ida), cf. Dionys. Perieg. *Orb. Descr* 504. Ἴδη, καλλικόμοισιν ὑπαὶ δρυσὶ τηλεθόωσα; and for the ‹hair› of personified Helicon, see the relief at *LIMC* s. v. Helikon I no. 1 (discussed below, V)
[101] For the contemporary, Macedonian implications of this name, see below, IV.
[102] *Mouseion*: Mineur ad loc. Co-eval status: ἥλικος (81), suggesting etymological ‹integration› of co-eval nymph with ‹Helicon› itself. The juxtaposition of Melia with Ismenos (77) and Thebe (88) recalls the proem to Pindar's first Hymn (fr. 29 Ma.): Pindar's identification of the terrestrial origins of Apolline music with Thebes (for which see A. Hardie [2000] 19–40) is implicitly rejected in Apollo's attack on Thebe (88–98); that honour is, of course, now to go to Delos.
[103] Bing (1988) 128–39.

poem that marks the extension of Greek cultural frontiers into Pharaonic Egypt by a Macedonian ruler (cf. 167).

The final passage to be considered is another account of the Muses at Helicon. In *Metamorphoses* 5, Ovid narrates an encounter between the Heliconian Muses and Athena. In an elaborate *partheneion* (virgin song), the Muses speak of two external threats to themselves.[104] First, an invading Thracian king, Pyreneus, met them as they were proceeding through Phocis, confined them and threatened rape, and when they escaped on wings, sought to fly after them, with fatal consequences. Pyreneus is unknown to history; but his presence in Phocis may echo real events.[105] There is no musical component to this part, but simply a barbarian invasion combined with hubristic conduct (the threat of sexual violence towards goddesses, and an attempt to fly). The Muses' second narrative introduces the daughters of Macedonian (Pellaean) Pieros. These ‹Pierides› are a chorus of mortal singers who hubristically challenge the Muses to a singing contest. Like an invasion force, they proceed south through Greek lands and *urbes*. They commit themselves to ‹battle› with the Muses (*proelia*, 307), seek to usurp their divine role, and in a telling reflection of wider ethnic/territorial disputes, aspire to control of Helicon itself (311-12). Here, then, we have a Thracian invasion (no musical content), followed by a Pierian/Macedonian musical attempt to take over indigenous Muses (*Thespiades*; 310; *Aonides*; 333). The parallel with the sequence of events postulated earlier (above, II) for the Ascraean Aloades is striking.

Ovid's twin narratives associate territorial invasion with musical ‹invasion›; and by corollary, resistance to musical challenge is associated with defence of territory. Moreover, the Pierides' own song is symbolic of their hubristic challenge to the divine order, for it praises the giants' assault on heaven and celebrates the flight of the gods (319-31); and thus their defeat parallels the defeat of the giants (cf. 346-55) and the restoration of cosmic order.[106] Then again, the ‹judges› in the contest are nymphs immanent within physical features of the mountain, its streams and rocks (314-17). The ‹living landscape› (cf. *vivo ... saxo*, 317) of Helicon pronounces victory, in a unanimous concord (*concordi sono*, 664), that recalls the concord of the Muses' own *choros* (and in contrast to the *convicia* of the defeated ‹Pierides›).[107]

To summarise: music is associated with territory through personified landscape features who/which themselves make music; this extends to the ‹autochthonous› Muse, the personification of music-making as the native product of territory. Local Muses, music and musicians may encounter, or be challenged by, external equivalents, and that process may be expressed figuratively in terms of invasion and conquest, or may parallel actual hostilities. Equally, local music-making and associated nymphs/Muses may acquire pan-Hellenic status, and the capacity to cross borders and travel. Thus, music and musicians may

---

[104] ‹Partheneion›: thus the scene (*virgineum Helicona*, 254), the Muses' virginal fears of threats (273-74) *omnis terrent/virgineas mentes*; the Muses' choice of the rape of Proserpina as their song; and a parallel reference to the virginal Sirens (552-55).

[105] For Thracian invaders in Phocis and Daulis, cf. Buck (1969) 290-91. K. Zeigler (*RE* XXIV.18-19) takes the episode to be a Hellenistic invention rather than the product of local saga; we might rather postulate an extended process of transmission.

[106] Thamyris sang a Titanomachia (ps.-Plut. *Mus.* 3); cf. Vox (1980) 324-25: ‹sembra quasi la tematizzazione poetica della loro stessa esperienza di scontro vano e duramente represso dalle Muse.›

[107] Concord: A. Barchiesi (1991). For home territory as ‹judge›, Verg. *Ecl.* 4.57-58 (*Arcadia ... iudice*), again in a poet's boasting versus gods/heroes.

define both ‹native› and ‹other›, as a sub-set of the Greek polarity of autochthony and territorial externality.[108] Confrontation and challenge may arise between the two, and this may be resolved in rejection of the intruder, or displacement of the native, or assimilation of the two.

IV: Aloades and Muses

The Aloades' ‹foundation of Ascra› was in all probability unconnected with the Muses, and as we have seen, the Muse-names credited to them cannot be early. Yet it would be unwise on those grounds to dismiss altogether their association with deities on the mountain. It is entirely likely that the canonical Muse cult was preceded by a sacred site (or sites), oracular in character and focused on the natural features of the mountain and its water-sources.[109] Oracular sites of this kind are particularly well-attested in Boeotia, and there is no reason to suppose that they acquired their sanctity only with the arrival of the Boeotoi.[110] The belief in springs as sources of wisdom is very ancient. It derives from the elemental association of water with truth and infallibility, and more specifically from the status of springs as points of emanation from the earth and the underworld.[111] Boeotian oracular sites will no doubt have supplied the needs of the community as well as of individuals, in peace and war; and local leaders will have taken care to ensure the support of indigenous sources of wisdom in times of external peril or uncertainty in the *chora*.[112] Within this early identification of landscape, its natural features and immanent divinities on the one hand, and the infallible guidance of the oracle on the other, lies one antecedent for the identification of territory and music illustrated earlier (above, III); and so, we might speculate, a primitive oracular cult around a high source such as Hippocrene may have evolved in time into a defined ‹musical› cult involving imported *Mousai*.[113] The Aloades are not oracular heroes. But as will be seen (below, V) they have a vestigial ‹mountain› character; and on one version they were fathered by the (sea) water that Iphidemeia poured into her own lap.[114] Their putative identi-

---

[108] See Calame (1987) 158–59.

[109] For a possible reference to a Heliconian river Lamos in Theban Linear B tablet Of 38, see Schachter (1996) 110, with bibliography. Archeological finds, as published, do not help much, but are consistent with a presence in the Valley of the Muses from some point between the eighth and sixth centuries: A. De Ridder (1922) 288–90 (nos. 145–49; 151); 298–300 (nos. 197–201; 302 (n. 205); 303 (nos. 211–13).

[110] Nymph (mountain/water source) oracles in Boeotia: Schachter (1986) 185–86 (Sphragitides on Cithaeron); 187–88 (Leibethrides on Leibethrion); Schachter (1994) 60–62 (Tilphossa); P. Bonnechère (1990) 58–59.

[111] The fullest treatment remains that of Ninck (1921) 1–46 (‹Die chthonische Natur des Wassers›); and 47–99 (‹Wasser und Weissagung›). W.R. Halliday (1913) 116–44 is still worth consulting.

[112] From a different context, compare the oracular support of an *epichorios daimon* (Faunus) for admission of Trojan incomers to the Latin *chora* (Dion. Hal. 1.57.4) λέγει τις ... ἐπιχώριος δαίμων δέχεσθαι τοὺς Ἕλληνας [in fact, Trojans] τῇ χώρᾳ συνοίκους· ἥκειν γὰρ αὐτοὺς μέγα ὠφέλημα Λατίνῳ καὶ κοινὸν Ἀβοριγίνων ἀγαθόν· Compare also the ‹territorial› divinities to whom Aristides was required by Delphi to sacrifice before Plataea (Plut. *Aristides* 11.3): Zeus; Hera of Cithaeron; Pan; the Sphragitic nymphs (sc. of Cithaeron: n. 110); and six Plataean heroes. The key in both cases is the support of the territory itself.

[113] For the relationship between nymphs/water sources and Muses, see RE XVI.692–93; 709; W.F. Otto (2005) 33–35; J. Larson (2001) *General Index*, s. v. ‹Muses: conflated with nymphs›.

[114] Apollod. 7.4.2; Ninck (1921) 25; 30. For a Boeotian analogue, cf. the spring at Thespiae reputed to cause conception (Plin. *Nat.* 31.10).

fication with a pre-Muse mountain cult thus offers an attractive model for the future harnessing of ‹music›, landscape and territorial defence.

Early cultic activity, on this hypothesis, will then be overlaid and supplanted by the arrival of the ‹Muses› from the north. This brings us to Hesiod's Muses. They are developed, pan-Hellenic goddesses, capable of travelling and operating in different geographical areas.[115] The *Heliconiades* are identified in the proem to the *Theogony* as daughters of Zeus and as ‹Olympian› Muses, a title they share with their father alone; and their birthplace is Pieria. This imported northern component is however combined with a retained locality: they celebrate a Heliconian cult of Zeus (4); their mother, Mnemosyne, has her cultic seat ‹on the hills of Eleuther› (Eleutherai on Cithaeron);[116] and above all, they are active (washing and dancing) around the water sources of Helicon. One tradition, perhaps early, makes Pieros, the eponymous hero of Pieria, a son of Eleuther.[117] This is not necessarily connected with the Muses (Eleuther is first and foremost a Dionysian figure); but Hesiod may perhaps have had it mind in phrasing his reference to Mnemosyne as he did.[118] Later, Pieros is given an explicitly literary genealogy, as son of Linos and ancestor of Homer.[119] The earliest attested connection between Pieros and Muses seems to be Epicharmus fr. 41K (Pieros and Pimpleis as Muse-parents), which likely draws on some lost authority. Later accounts variously credited him with poems about the Muses, and with the consecration of a temple to the Leibethrian Muses, in Boeotia.[120] This last exploit forms part of the evidence for efforts, perhaps already visible in Hesiod, to supply a mythological basis for the appearance of the Pierian Muses in Boeotia. Of especial interest is a version recorded by Cicero at *de Natura Deorum* 3.54, describing the Muses as daughters of Pieros and Antiope. The latter was a daughter of Thespios (and mother of Amphion and Zethos). This must derive from a Thespiaean account, and it is evidence for late classical or Hellenistic interest in attaching the Pierian Muses as closely as possible to that city. The most likely context for such mythologizing is the establishment of the official cult of the Heliconian Muses under the civic control of Thespiae, dateable to the start of the fourth century.[121] It is of great value for understanding Pausanias' statement that Pieros ‹came to Thespiae› and changed the names of the Aload Muses, for it helps account for the apparent absence of confrontation in that process, and it supplies a clear dating indicator for that part of our myth. By contrast, Ovid makes the hostile ‹Pierides›, the usurping daughters of Pieros of Pella, address the Muses as ‹Thespiades› (*Met.* 5.310), thereby identifying them simply and solely with that locality.[122] They speak of themselves as ‹Aonides› (333), a name derived from the pre-Boeotian Aones and adopted by Callimachus with reference to water-sources and nymphs

---

[115] Comparable in that respect to the Delphian ‹Muses› of the oracular spring Cassotis: Hardie (1996) 232–33; for another such cult of water-source Muses, cf. Pind. *Isth.* 6.74–75 (Dirke).

[116] *Theogony* 54 with West's note; Schachter (1986) 144.

[117] Schol. *Il.* 14.226; Eustathius on *Il.* 14.226 Πιερίαν δὲ οἱ μὲν ἀκρώρειάν τινα εἶπον Ὀλύμπου, οἱ δὲ χώραν ἀπὸ νύμφης ὁμωνύμου, ἢ ἀπὸ Πίερος υἱοῦ Ἐλευθῆρος, οἱ δὲ πόλιν.

[118] Pieros (or Pier): *RE* Suppl. VIII 498–99. Eleuther: *RE* V.2343–44; 2345.

[119] Suda s. v. Ὅμηρος; *Certamen* line 47 Allen.

[120] [Plut.] *de Mus.* 1132a; Serv. *Ecl.* 7.21.

[121] The evidence is clearly assembled and intepreted by Schachter (1986) 156–58.

[122] Thespiae and the Muses must have been explicitly connected in a lost Hellenistic source, whence (the highly Callimachean) Cat. 61.27–30 *perge linquere Thespiae/rupis Aonios specus/nympha quos super inrigat/frigiferans Aganippe*. H.P. Syndikus (1990) 6; Call. *Aet.* frr. 3.6, 9 M., with Comm Ox. ad loc. 16, 30 (for Thespiae, Call. *Hymn* 5.60; 71).

on Helicon (fr. 3.9 M.).¹²³ The learned epithet and its interplay with ‹Thespiades› hints, strikingly, at a primordial, autochthonous character and suggests Hellenistic interest in and understanding of this dimension.

I would envisage our myth evolving in stages, in something like the following sequence: first, the Aloades found Ascra, as defenders of territory against Thracians; next, in the same context, they associate with a local water-source cult on Helicon; that cult is subsequently overlaid by the arrival of the ‹Muses›, brought by the Boeotoi from the north; and then a two-part musical myth gradually takes shape, distantly reflecting Thracian invasions and Boeotian migration. As we now have it, however, the myth looks like a formation shaped round the encounter of native (Aloades) and foreign (Pieros/Pierides). It may be an attempt consciously to resurrect an ancient tradition, and primordial territorial heroes, in order to assert Aeolian primacy at the Muses' central Greek cult site, as also the primacy of Helicon over Pieria and Olympus as the birthplace of Greek *aoide*. But as already noted, Pausanias does not speak of confrontation between ‹old› Muses and Pierides, and it may be that what is being summarised is a myth of succession and assimilation rather than forcible usurpation.

For early Hellenistic interest in musical cult myths, and their ancient attachment to ethnic and territorial enmities, we cannot do better than compare the end of Theocritus *Idyll* 16, addressed to the Charites of Orchomenos (104-5):

ὦ ᾿Ετεόκλειοι Χάριτες θεαί, ὦ Μινύειον
᾿Ορχομενὸν φιλέοισαι ἀπεχθόμενόν ποτε Θήβαις

(‹O goddess Graces of Eteocles, you who love Minyan Orchomenos that was once hateful to Thebes›). Theocritus alludes to the Eteocles, legendary king of Orchomenos, as founder of the cult of the Charites, together with the city's Minyan genealogy and its ancient rivalry with Thebes for control of Boeotia. In doing so, he alludes to Pindar, who speaks of the musical and festive Charites as παλαιγόνων Μινυᾶν ἐπίσκοποι (*Ol.* 14.4) (‹guardians of the ancient-born Minyans›).

Our myth, in its final form, falls in time between Pindar and Theocritus. Their references to the Charites are reminders that one medium for the promulgation of this piece of cult ideology would have been a poem recited at Helicon, or Thespiae. Poems and speeches in honour of the Muses were a central event at the Mouseia festival, as reorganised in the late third century.¹²⁴ The earlier history of musical contests on Helicon is shadowy; but there are clear pointers to the foundation of an *agon* by the early years of the fourth century, again coinciding with the period when Thespiae was establishing civic control over the cult.¹²⁵ A date in the first decades of the fourth century would suit our trio well enough; and this is the context into which their aetiology, and its ‹modern› conception of *aoide*, may most readily be fitted. The same period would also comfortably accommodate the *Atthis* of ‹Hegesinous›, and its verses on the foundation of Ascra (Appendix I).

A dating to the early fourth century opens up the question of a possible political context. In the last decade of the fifth century, the Macedonian court, for politico-cultural reasons of its own, started to take an active interest in the Pierian Muses. Archelaos founded a major festival in honour of Zeus and the Muses at the coastal town of Dion, on the east flank of

---

[123] Strabo 401; Pfeiffer on Call. fr. 572.
[124] Schachter (1986) 164–66.
[125] Schachter (1986) 156 n. 4; 157; 158; 163.

Olympus.¹²⁶ The site was chosen for its associations with Zeus and for its central location in the Pierian territory associated with the Muses. The river Helicon lay ten miles to the north. Leibethra lay a similar distance to the south, and achieved prominence as the central site of Orpheus, son of Calliope.¹²⁷ The village of Pimpleia, another site associated with Orpheus, lay within its *chora*.¹²⁸ The water-nymph Pimpleia had been canvassed by Epicharmus (fr. 41K.) as a local Muse-mother; but the territorial association achieves mainstream currency in the third century, most probably through Macedonian influence. The local legends of Orpheus at Pimpleia, Leibethra and Dion project him as a secret initiator of a warrior caste, a characterisation that suggests some contemporary colouring at the behest of a militaristic regime.¹²⁹ Poets were invited to Archelaos' capital, Aegae. Euripides reciprocated hospitality with a play, the *Archelaos*, which supplied his host with an Argive ancestry, and which was perhaps staged at the dramatic festival at Dion. Then, in the *Bacchae*, he honoured Macedonian Pieria, and Orpheus' Pierian/Olympian role as the civilising creator of Greek music (above, III). These cults were later given an aggressive slant when Alexander, on the eve of departure on campaign, celebrated the festival of Zeus and the Muses. The ancient cult statue of Orpheus at Leibethra, surrounded by the Muses and figures of beasts, broke into sweat. One seer claimed the omen portended that Alexander's exploits, achieved with much exertion, would be celebrated by poets. A variant (reminiscent of the *Bacchae*) had it that he would subject barbarian nations and Greek cities, even as Orpheus' music had tamed beasts and won over Greeks and barbarians.¹³⁰

Archelaos thus set the pattern for harnessing the Muses and their cult to the cultural requirements of kings. He gave the Muses a spectacular new focus in their original homeland; he asserted his court's claim to be a centre of Greek culture (rather than of exotic barbarism); he provided himself with a Greek pedigree; and with Euripides' help, he reinvented the first poet as a musical model for civilising incursion and perhaps also as warrior-shaman. At the same time, Archelaos was setting about the reorganisation of the Macedonian army. Within a generation, the weakness that had characterised the reign of his predecessor Perdiccas had been reversed. Then at some point around 400 BC, Macedonian nationalism took an expansionist turn. Archelaos took advantage of internal *stasis* in Larissa to cross the Peneius and occupy the town. The occupation was short-lived, for Archelaos was killed in 399 BC; and his immediate successors failed dismally to build on the strong lead he had given. But it was a memorable event that prompted local calls for defensive alliance with the ascendant Spartans; and it was recorded in a well-known speech ‹In support of the Larissaeans›, by Thrasymachus of Chalchedon, who impishly echoed Euripides in speaking of ‹Greeks in slavery to barbarian Archelaos›.¹³¹

---

[126] Diod. Sic. 17.16.3–4 (Alexander) ... πρὸς τοὺς ἀγῶνας θυσίας μεγαλοπρεπεῖς τοῖς θεοῖς συνετέλεσεν ἐν Δίῳ τῆς Μακεδονίας καὶ σκηνικοὺς ἀγῶνας Διὶ καὶ Μούσαις, οὓς Ἀρχέλαος ὁ προβασιλεύσας πρῶτος κατέδειξε. τὴν δὲ πανήγυριν ἐφ' ἡμέρας ἐννέα συνετέλεσεν, ἑκάστῃ τῶν Μουσῶν ἐπώνυμον ἡμέραν ἀναδείξας. Arrian *An.* 1.11.1 (celebration attended by Alexander). L. Rossi (1996) 63–64.
[127] F. Graf (1987) 87–90.
[128] Sources in *RE* XX.1387–89.
[129] Conon fr. 45 (O. Kern (1922) *test.* 115); Cf. Graf (1987) 87–90.
[130] Kern (1922) *test.* 144.
[131] Clem. Alex. *Strom.* 6.16 Θρασυμάχος ἐν τῷ ὑπὲρ Λαρισαίων λέγει· ‹Ἀρχελάῳ δουλεύσομεν Ἕλληνες ὄντες βαρβάρῳ;› The same occasion also underlies a Roman-era exercise piece ascribed to Herodes Atticus, in which the desirability of alliance with the Spartans is canvassed: *RE* VIII.952–54.

Thespiae and their Spartan patrons may not have been responding directly to these new manifestations of politicised Muse cult when they brought the Heliconian cult under civic control, and established a musical *agon* at Thespiae. Yet these are manifestly parallel developments, Thespiae following Archelaos by, at the outside, thirty years. The effect, if not the intention, will have been to re-assert the centrality of Helicon and the Thespike in the divine patronage of Greek music and poetry. Again, the uncertainty in the Heliconian tradition as between peaceful assimilation and hostile, hubristic usurpation by ‹Pieros› is noteworthy; and Ovid's ‹Pieros›, *Pellaeis dives in arvis* (*Met.* 5.302) surely derives ultimately from a hostile Hellenistic allusion to Pella as the site of the re-located Macedonian court.[132] It may therefore be right to think in terms of an emerging rivalry between a Macedonian cult that exploited territorial identification with Thracian Pieria and the Heliconian cult. In those circumstances, the Aloades, as legendary defenders of the Aeolian lands against ‹Thracians›, would readily find a prominent place in a local projection of an indigenous (non-Thracian) foundation as the ‹true› origins of Muse-worship in Greece.

V: *Muses, Paideia and Cosmic Order*

Among the statues in the Valley of the Muses stood Iphimedeia. The statue epigram, in three couplets, has survived and it shows that she was honoured (by whom is unknown) as the mother, by ‹the lord of the sea›, of the terrible twins.[133] The latter, not named, are designated ‹the boastful twofold [embryo] of sons›.[134] There is no reference to Muses. Rather, the epigram alludes to the Aloades' two appearances in Homer (4–6): ‹now even dire Ares knows the strength of her children; and high heaven too, which, piling mountain upon mountain, they essayed to make accessible to men›. The tone is somewhat ambiguous, but is more suggestive of awed respect than of disapproval. In the concluding couplet, οὐρανὸς ... ὃν οὔρεσιν οὔρεα θέντες/ἄμ]βατον ἀνθρώποις εἴεσαν ἐκτελέσαι, the οὔρ-form of ὄρος resonates with οὐρανὸς to suggest a linguistically appropriate action; and while ἄμ]βατον echoes *Od.* 11.316, ἀνθρώποις hints at a Promethean attempt to benefit mankind. The presence of statue and epigram on Helicon mean that we must now attempt to reconcile the Aloades' attempted assault on heaven with their submission to Muses.

Given the Muses' conventional embodiment of harmony and order in a stable cosmic dispensation, the Aloades' submission to their divine authority is unlikely to be accidental;[135] and the confrontations between chaos and order within the treatments of ‹musical incursion› surveyed earlier underline the paradox presented by the Aloades' prodigious, horizontal and vertical, growth, and its threat to good order. Within the literary tradition, the possibility that Alcman refers to the Aloades as an *exemplum* of hubristic conduct at fr. 1.22–35 PMGF, juxtaposed with the heavenly Charites, suggests that the Aloades might be

---

[132] *dives* etymologises Pieros from Pieria as ‹rich land›; cf. πίειρα; Hammond (1972) 416; cf. Tzetzes on Hes. *WD* 1, lines 138–39. Anton. Lib. 9 speaks of these daughters of Pieros as ‹Emathides›, i.e. Macedonians, and of Pieros himself as an ‹autochthonous› king of Emathia (ἐβασίλευε Πίερος αὐτόχθων Ἠμαθίας).
[133] A. Plassart (1926) 406–8 (no. 21).
[134] The supplement κῦμα (for which, of twins, cf. *AP* 6.200.4) may also mean ‹wave›, and would allude to Iphimedeia's water-borne conception by the sea (above, n. 114).
[135] The *locus classicus* for the Muses' hatred of primordial threats to the Olympian order is Pindar *Pyth.* 1.13–14.

perceived as a threat not simply to the gods in general but also to the musical order immanent in the celestial domain.[136] An analogous alignment of a threat to cosmic order with a challenge to Muses is implicit in the songs of Thamyris (Titanomachy) and of the Pierides (Gigantomachy) in their respective contests with the Muses;[137] and at the metapoetic level, Theocritus' famous image of the poet-architects, ‹cocks of the Muses›, who challenge Homer to construct their poem-buildings ‹as high as Mount Oromedon› (*Idyll* 7.45–48) derives from the same body of ideas.

Otus and Ephialtes are pre-Olympian entities belonging to a generation of monstrous Poseidonian offspring that include the Cyclops and Orion. They may represent an earlier conception of the shaping of land and sea than the giants.[138] But they are nurtured by the land (*Od.* 11.309–10) and were eventually identified with the γηγενεῖς.[139] True sons of the ‹earth shaker›, they inherited Poseidon's instinct for mixing the elements: they threatened to cast mountains into the sea, and to admit the sea on to land (Apollod. 1.7.4). They threatened much but accomplished few if any of their threats, hence a tradition (Eustathius on *Od.* 11.315) that they were simply braggarts. Yet their prodigious growth was inherently threatening to the natural order of things. When Homer describes them (*Odyssey* 11.309–10) as figures ‹whom the cereal-giving earth nurtured as the tallest, and by far the most beautiful after famous Orion› there seems (in addition to autochthony) to be an implicit comparison to the exuberant natural growth and the threat of such unrestrained ‹verticality› to reach heaven.[140] The suggested analogue with vegetal or cereal ‹verticality› is supported by accounts that gave the Aloades a sister, Elate or ‹fir tree›, herself ‹high as heaven› (οὐρανομήκης).[141] The mountain assault on heaven has been compared to the Hurrian myth of Ullikummi, a rapidly-growing giant who was himself a tower of rock that threatened to reach heaven.[142] A powerful Near Eastern image, articulating a universal concept (the inaccessibility of heaven), has attached itself, in adapted form, to a pair of Hellenic host figures.[143] Although not themselves ‹mountains›, Otus and Ephialtes are associated with mountainous landscape, in what is evidently a trace element of their Poseidonian in-

---

[136] Calame ad loc.; P. Janni (1965) 69. Within the *Partheneion* there is parallelism between the hybris of flying to heaven and assaulting goddesses (15–19), with the gods' venegeance (ἔστι τις σιῶν τίσις, 36), and the concluding choric piety towards the gods, including a humble disclaimer of superiority in song to the Sirens: ‹for they are goddesses› (98).

[137] Above, n. 106. For an archaic antecedent for Titanomachy versus *cosmos* and *eunomia*, cf. Xenophanes' alignment of these bellicose subjects, as sung at the symposium, with hubristic behaviour offending the orderly, pious symposium (fr. 1.15–24). A. Ford (2002) 54–58; 58–66.

[138] So Simon (1981); but for the thesis of pre-Hellenic, Aegean origins for the earth born Giants, see F. Vian (1952) 282–83.

[139] Schol. Apoll. Rhod. 1.482. Compare Amycus, king of the Bebrycians, described in Apollonius (2.1–4) as son of Poseidon Genethlios and Melia, then (38–40) likened to an earth-born monster.

[140] *RE* I.1592; cf. *RE* XVIII.1.1879. For the related phenomenon of the autochthonous Athenians receiving corn from Demeter, see R. Parker (1996) 138–39.

[141] *RE* 5.2236; Lib. *Prog.* 2.39.1; Eustathius on *Il.* 5.560, 14.287. For the heaven-high fir tree, *Od.* 5.239; and for its symbolism as a vertical link between earth and heaven, Eur. *Bacch*. 1064 (the fir on which Pentheus is placed), with Segal (1997) 144–45.

[142] M.L. West (1997) 121–22. The similarities include the prominence of the figure nine in their measurements: Ullikummi was nine thousand leagues in both height and width. On the Hittite background to the identification of man as mountain, see also M. Clarke (1997) 74–75.

[143] The legend that the Aloades imprisoned Ares in a jar for 13 months may also be near eastern in origin: see Harmatta (1968).

heritance. A comparable identification is preserved in similes comparing the Cyclops Polyphemus to a mountain;[144] and a Cretan tradition that a body seventy feet high, revealed by an earthquake in the centre of a mountain, was that of Otus or (another Poseidon son-giant) Orion, further associates the outsize body with mountains.[145]

One approach to the central issue would be take the archaic Aloades, in this ‹mountainous› aspect, as representing raw nature. But, as has been seen, the Aloades are also civilisers: city founders, rulers and possibly agricultural figures, and so these are beings that combine the exuberance and the violence of natural existence on the one hand, and the civilising constraints of emerging culture on the other. We can compare the treatment of their Poseidonian relations, the Cyclopes, in the *Odyssey*.[146] As analysed by Geoffrey Kirk, the Cyclopes inhabit a place that ‹represents nature in its ideal and benign form, not as opposed to culture, not as savage and repellent, but as waiting to be developed by culture›. The Cyclopean cultural picture is however complex, and Kirk goes on to speak of contradictions within the character of Polyphemus, of ‹ambivalent culture and ambivalent nature›, and of the Cyclopes themselves as ‹an extraordinary mixture of the divine and the brutish›, blasphemers against Zeus and yet (in another segment of the tradition) decisive in supporting his rule against challenges from Titans and Giants. Kirk's analysis is primarily focused on a unitary Homeric narrative (albeit the product of multi-layered, bardic elaboration), rather than on the disparate records of a cumulative tradition; and there is of course no question of the Aloades as known to us being modelled on the Homeric Cyclopes. But in dealing with the Aloades, it is difficult to set aside Kirk's conclusion that in that Odyssean narrative, ‹various aspects of nature and culture are being manipulated into proximity›. Preller-Robert perspicuously included the Aloades within their treatment of the myths of emergent mankind, alongside the Titanic, civilising figure of Prometheus. The claim that the Aloades were first to dedicate Helicon to the Muses credits them with being the first mortals to recognise the divine nature of music; and in recognising the goddesses of *mousike*, they were advancing their own civilised existence and that of the territory which they represented.

The juxtaposition of raw nature and *mousike* at Helicon turns up again in a third century BC votive relief. Dedicated to the Muses, it depicts Helicon as a gigantic old man with wild, flying hair.[147] The relief is accompanied by three epigrams, of which the second is an oracular pronouncement spoken by Helicon. He refers to his own great age and similarity in that respect to mortals.[148] Despite his wildness, he is ‹not ignorant of the Muses›. His oracle is to the effect that ‹for mortals who obey Hesiod's injunctions, there will be good order (*eu-*

---

[144] *Od.* 9.190-92; cf. 481-82; Call. *H.* 3.51-52. For a survey of such mountain-motifs in relation to gigantomachy, see P. Hardie (1986) 100-101.

[145] Plin. *Nat.* 7.73 *in Creta terrae motu rupto monte inventum est corpus stans XLVI cubitorum, quod alii Orionis alii Oti esse arbitrabantur.*

[146] G.S. Kirk (1970) 162-71.

[147] *LIMC* s. v. Helicon I no. 1 with earlier bibliography; A. Hurst (1996); A. Veneri (1996) 73-86. With the hair, cf. Call. *H.* 4.81-82; also Verg. *Ecl.* 5.62-63 (Hurst [1996] 66-67). Is he identical with the ‹old man› associated with a Heliconian spring known locally as ‹i Trypa tou Gerou› about 100m below Hippokrene (reported in V.L. Aravantinos [1996])?

[148] Combined with oracular powers in a natural element, ‹old age› has a parallel in the wisdom of the ‹old man of the sea›: for Nereus, see *RE* XVII.24-28 (Herzog-Hauser); *LIMC* VI.1.824-37 (Pipili); West on Hes. *Theog.* 233; for Nereus, foreknowledge and infallibility in Nereids, J.M. Barringer (1995) 7; and for further comment on chthonic agents of prophecy, see Kambylis (1965) 26.

nomia) and a land brimming with produce›. This belongs to the larger topic of oracles (sought or given) enjoining honours on dead poets;[149] and it here identifies the mountain with the precepts of the *Works and Days*, which is itself thereby endowed with quasi-oracular status. Helicon, as the third epigram implies, is indebted to Hesiod for its fame as a ‹divine› mountain (notwithstanding the man-mountain's ‹mortal› appearance). We are thus reminded of what Kirk described as the ‹mixture of the divine and the brutish› in the Cyclops; and it cannot be coincidental that Helicon carries an unmistakeable Cyclopean aperture on his forehead.[150] The brutish relief is however ‹adorned in verse› by the dedicator (κοσμήσας ἔπεσιν) and is thus rendered appropriate for the dedicatee Muses, by a latter-day successor of Hesiod; indeed in speaking in verse, this extraordinary creature aligns himself with the Muses to whom he is sacred;[151] and his ‹poetic› speech helps resolve the paradox of a wild mountain's oracular advocacy of civic order and agricultural plenty through obedience to the ‹oracular› poetry of Hesiod. We thus have an resonant trio comprising poetry, governance and plenty: the alignment of musical *cosmos* with civic *eunomia* echoes a well known cluster of ideas around ‹good order› that was already fully developed in the archaic era;[152] and the alignment of good governance with the fruitfulness of the land draws on the idea, articulated at *Works and Days* 225-37, that the justice of the ruler is rewarded by the fertility of the natural world around him.[153]

It would be easy to dismiss this quaint monument as late, local and inconsequential. Yet here was the initiative of a man of local standing, probably a member of the guild of ‹Hesiodistai› with a well-defined interest in the Muses and Helicon's most famous poet.[154] The iconography of his relief can still help in understanding the Aloades, for the oracular man-mountain represents, in explicit terms, the identification of oracular *mousike* with landscape which has been highlighted in this paper. He also represents the capacity of the Muses and music to create good order, *cosmos*, from wildness. Helicon remains brutish and unkempt; but dedicated to the Muses, he shares their divinity and becomes an agent for promulgating *cosmos* on the territory that he represents. This capacity supplies another line of approach to the Aloades as first worshippers of the Muses on Helicon. Their acknowledgement of the divinity of the Muses transforms the negative aspect of their personality, their potential for destabilisation and chaos, and subsumes them into a cult context dedicated to good order.

There are parallels in the incorporation of Gaia into Delphian cult-ideology as first owner of the oracle:[155] as analysed by Christiane Sourvinou-Inwood, this represents the ‹integration of the primordial powers in the new order›, in a subordinate position; Gaia's chthonic/prophetic powers are harnessed to Apolline purposes; and the myth expresses

---

[149] Cf. esp. Posidonius *SH*. 705 (118AB) 12-16.

[150] For this feature, see Veneri (1996) 76 n. 9.

[151] Compare Theocr. *Idyll* 11 (Cyclops as musician), which derives from Philoxenus' *Galatea*, composed around the turn of the fifth/fourth century.

[152] Ford (2002) 35-39 (‹*Kosmos:* Sympotic Order›) traces the conceptual links between orderly sympotic behaviour, appropriate singing and *eunomia* /civic harmony.

[153] See West's note ad loc, comparing *Od*. 19.109-114 and Call. *H*. 3.122-35; cf. also Richardson's note on Hom. *Hym. Dem*.470-82.

[154] The dedicator, Euthykles, has been plausibly placed as a member of the Heliconian guild of ‹Hesiodistai›: see Schachter (1986) 160-61; Hurst (1996) 64.

[155] Sourvinou-Inwood (1987) 225-28.

‹the perception that at Delphi the chthonic, dangerous and disorderly aspects of the cosmos have been defeated by, and subordinated to, the celestial guide and lawgiver›. The conversion of threats to the Olympian order into essential elements sustaining the stability of that order is a very old idea, seen most vividly in the conversion of the Titan Atlas into a mountain-pillar of heaven.[156] There, the ‹verticality› of the mountain that reaches towards heaven becomes the prop that separates and stabilises the two elements. So, the Aloades' past threat to the *cosmos* is converted to active support of established order, through the agency of the Muses and their *mousike*. Mankind may acquire access to the heavens not physically, by piling Pelion and Ossa on Olympus, but intellectually, through the Muses of song and their sacred mountain.[157]

The civilising qualities of the Aloades are now to the fore, and these undisciplined *paides* have embraced *mousike* informed by contemporary *paideia*. They are ‹tamed› by aoidic training; they recognise the power of Aoide and they worship it.[158] This ‹educational› conception of the Aloades on Helicon finds a striking sequel in an allegorical reading of their imprisonment of Ares (Appendix II for detail). The Aloades there stand for *logoi* in *paideia*, versus the appetitive instincts: Otus for the *logos* acquired by learning (*techne*), and Ephialtes for the innate or spontaneous *logos* springing naturally to the mind (*physis*). True to their Aload nature, however, these *logoi* may serve, not to suppress the appetitive *thumos* but to excite it to bravery on those occasions when the homeland faces the external threat of invasion and conquest.

VI: Overview

The Aloades are complex characters: gigantic yet beautiful, sinners yet heroes. It is surprising that more was not made of them in the classical era. Our Muse myth, at all events, comprises four main elements: the Aloades' co-foundation of Ascra; their ‹sacral› association with Helicon; the ‹cult› of the Muse-trio; and the intrusion of Pieros. These elements are not the product of a single act of ideological construction and retrojection. Rather, they emerged piecemeal over a long period of time, starting in the Dark Ages and extending to the fourth century. Old interests, ethnic and territorial, combine with modern developments in *mousike* and *paideia*; and the myth emerges not as a simple ideological statement about the Helicon of its day, but as a layered composition, at once archaic and new. Within the Aloades, their quintessential association with landscape, territory and growth, and also their cultic activity on Helicon, we may recognise an early precursor of what later developed into a mature identification of music and territory. And within the two-part myth as we have it, we may recognise the resurrection of an ancient tradition to serve the modern purposes of transnational Muse-cult in the pre-Hellenistic era.

---

[156] For its presence in Hesiod and exploitation in the mid-fifth century, see Hardie (2000) 29.
[157] R.M. Jones (1926); Hardie (2002) 191–92. For the juxtaposition of the giants' assault on heaven with intellectual penetration of the cosmos, cf. Hor. *Odes* 1.28.5, with NH; Ov. *Fast.* 1.295–310.
[158] Compare Orpheus' taming Pieria *mousais* (*Bacchae*, 563): ‹with music›; and ‹for the Muses› (above, n. 95). Cf. also Philostr. *Her.* 730 O. (Achilles' education) possibly preserving authentic practice in educational *Mouseia*: ἤκουσα δὲ κἀκεῖνα, θύειν μὲν αὐτὸν τῇ Καλλιόπῃ μουσικὴν αἰτοῦντα καὶ τὸ ἐν ποιήσει κράτος ...

Appendix I: ‹Hegesinous›, the *Atthis* and the Aloades

There are difficulties, both general and specific, with Pausanias' citation of sources.[159] He cites Callippus of Corinth (an undatable historian of Orchomenos), and through him, a poet named ‹Hegesinous›, for the foundation of Ascra. Doubts about authenticity have been consistently advanced since Carl Robert and Wilamowitz concluded that Hegesinous and the *Atthis* were both fictions, concocted by Pausanias' source Callippus of Corinth.[160] Bernabé succinctly describes Hegesinous as *poeta a Callippo fictus*, and notes Jacoby's suggestion that the Corinthian got the name from an attested author of *Cypria*. The issue of authenticity is further tied up with Pausanias' citation of lines (again dealing with Poseidon, and again cited from Callippus) from one Chersias of Orchomenos. Callippus himself is only named by Pausanias (9.29.2; 9.38.9), as the author (undated) of a history of the people of Orchomenos.

But perhaps too little attention has been paid to the quality and sources of ‹Hegesinous'› lines, and a closer analysis suggests that they may after all be relatively early in date. Here they are (Pausanias 9.29.1):

> Ἄσκρῃ δ' αὖ παρέλεκτο Ποσειδάων ἐνοσίχθων,
> ἣ δή οἱ τέκε παῖδα περιπλομένων ἐνιαυτῶν
> Οἴοκλον, ὃς πρῶτος μετ' Ἀλωέος ἔκτισε παίδων
> Ἄσκρην, ἥ θ' Ἑλικῶνος ἔχει πόδα πιδακόεντα.

(‹and moreover Poseidon the earth shaker lay with Ascra, she who, in the wheeling fullness of years, bore him a son Oioklos, who first, with the sons of Aloeus, founded Ascra, and she who holds the foot of Helicon, full of springs.›). This is a competent piece of versifying that reveals wit, learning and close acquaintanceship with Homeric phrasing. It deploys three relative clauses, of which the first two (ἥ ... ὅς) replicate Homeric syntax found in the catalogue of women in *Odyssey* 11 (of the type ‹I saw X, who bore Y, who ...›);[161] the third relative clause varies the pattern by adding a clause parallel to the first (so that ἥ θ' ... depends not on Ἄσκρην the town (4), but her eponymous heroine, Ἄσκρη (1)). The poet has elegantly modelled ‹Poseidon fathering Oioklos› on Odysseus' catalogue account of Iphimedeia, wife of Aloeus and mother, by Poseidon, of the Aloades.[162] Furthermore, πρῶτος ... ἔκτισε recalls and varies the only other occurrence of this pleonastic combination in the whole of Greek literature, also within the Odyssean catalogue (*Od.* 11.263; the twins Amphion and Zethus founding Thebes).[163] Ἀλωέος ... παίδων, however, appears to echo Homer's only other (Iliadic) reference to the Aloades, as παῖδες Ἀλωῆος (*Il.* 5.386).

The vocabulary is not exclusively Homeric. The rare genitive Ἀλωέος varies Homeric ' Ἀλωῆος (*Il.* 5.386; cf. *Od.* 11.305). πιδακόεντα is unhomeric: its only other appearance is

---

[159] For Pausanias' methods, especially in relation to claimed citation of early epic, see N. Horsfall (2003) 469–70; I am grateful to Dr Horsfall for advice.
[160] U. von Wilamowitz-Moellendorf (1884) 338–39
[161] *Od.* 11.260–65; 281–84; 298–301; 305–10 (Iphimedeia and the Aloades).
[162] Thus ἥ δή (2, 306); τέκε παῖδα (2)/ἔτεκεν δύο παῖδε (307); Ποσειδάων (2)/Ποσειδάωνι (306); Ἀλωέος (3)/Ἀλωῆος (305).
[163] Within the catalogue, the Antiope (Amphion and Zethus) and Iphimedeia (Otus and Ephialtes) sections are closely comparable in wording, structure and content. Less clear (given other early epic parallels) is the relevance of περιπλομένων ἐνιαυτῶν (*Od.* 1.16, another *hapax*), to line 2; cf Hes. *Theog.* 184 (birth of the giants). It may be formulaic padding.

at Euripides *Andromache* 116 πιδακόεσσα. The word combines two Homeric adjectives applied to Ida: πολυπῖδαξ (πολυπίδακος Ἴδης, *Il.* 8.47, etc.) and πιδήεις (Ἴδης ... πιδηέσσης, a *hapax* at *Il.* 11.183). Euripides uses the word allusively in an implicit comparison of the weeping Andromache to Mount Ida and its streams (guaranteed by her parallel lament for Troy).[164] Our πιδακόεντα is transferred from mountain to (watered, therefore fertile) plain, but may yet carry associations with Ida: for the combination with πόδα, cf. *Iliad* 20.59-60 (earthquake), πάντες δ' ἐσσείοντο πόδες πολυπίδακος Ἴδης/καὶ κορυφαί ‹and all the foothills of well-watered Ida shook, and the peaks›). That earthquake is caused by ‹earth-shaking Poseidon› (Ποσειδάων ἐνοσίχθων, 63), who appears also in our passage (2). We may reasonably sense a reference through the Helicon of ‹Hegesinous› to Homer's Ida.[165] Whether, in that case, we have the full intertextual history before us is another matter: a lost source, in which Homeric πολυπίδακος and πιδηέσσης were first combined into πιδακόεις as an epithet for Ida, might be common to ‹Hegesinous› and Euripides' *Andromache*. Equally, our poet could have been the first to effect the combination, underlining the neologism in a jingle (πόδα/πιδα-) that plays on the jingle between Ἴδη and πιδα-/πιδη- that was integral to the Homeric formula. It is worth noting that Quintus Smyrnaeus, in echoing the earthquake on Ida at *Iliad* 20.59-60, introduces yet another jingle (1.688: shaking ground under Ares' feet) καὶ ποταμοὶ καὶ πάντες ἀπειρέσιοι πόδες Ἴδης.

Oioklos is otherwise unknown. The name appears to be unique, and one wonders whether the poet is perpetrating a play on οἶος (‹alone›). If so, for his joint foundation of Ascra, compare the epic formula ‹X not alone, but Y together with him›: *Il.* 2.822-23 (Aeneas' does not command the Trojans alone, but together with him the sons of Antenor ...) οὐκ οἶος, ἅμα τῷ γε δύω Ἀντήνορος υἶε/Ἀρχέλοχός τ' Ἀκάμας ...[166]

The contention that Callippus himself made up these verses for the purposes of his history of Orchomenos starts to look threadbare. The learned echoes and combinations of well-known epic passages would in themselves be consistent with composition as early as the sixth century.[167] Moreover, when his point relates to the presence of Poseidon and his sons (Oioklos and the Aloades) in Boeotia, why should Callippus claim that his careful fabrication comes from a poem about Attica? On the other hand, there is an obvious reason for interest in Poseidon, his sons and territorial extension in such a poem, namely their prominence in the struggle for control of Attica and Eleusis.[168] ‹Atthis› as a term of local

---

[164] For the Homerising allusion to Ida (and Andromache's home) in πιδακόεσσα, see Stevens' excellent note ad loc.
[165] The case for an intertextual connection between our Heliconian passage and the Homeric earthquake on Ida is strengthened by a twin-reminiscence of the latter in Callimachus' *Hymn to Delos*: 81-82 (sc. the nymph Melia afraid for the life of her coeval oak tree on the summit of Helicon) ὡς ἴδε χαίτην/σειομένην Ἑλικῶνος (‹when she saw the shaking hair [i.e. trees at the summit] of Helicon›). ibid. 142 σείονται μυχὰ πάντα (of Aetna, combined with reference to Pind. *Pyth*. 1.21-23 [streams from the μυχοί] τᾶς ἐρεύγονται μὲν ἀπλάτου πυρὸς ἁγνόταται/ἐκ μυχῶν παγαί). For oaks as hair on Ida, cf. Dionys. Perieg. *Orb. Descr* 504. Ἴδη, καλλικόμοισιν ὑπαὶ δρυσὶ τηλεθόωσα; and for etymological allusion to Mount Ida in ἴδε cf. Etym. Gud. P. 270.22 s. v. Cf. also Verg. *Aen*. 2.696-97, where hair, trees and ‹etymological› sight are associated with Ida.
[166] Cf. *Il.* 2.75; 24.573; *Od.* 2.11; 15.100; Quint. Smyrn. 9.63
[167] Compare West (1988) 128-30 for imitation of Hesiod in the *Catalogue*. Cf. esp. fr. 26.18-20, where in describing Porthaon's daughters dancing in the mountains with nymphs and Muses, the poet draws on and adapts three separate passages from the *Theogony* dealing with the Muses.
[168] Cf. Hellanicus *FGrHist* 1a, 4, F 42b (the *Atthis*: *RE* VIII.141.60-61). For its wide ranging topographical interests, cf. F 3b,323a F 7 (reference to Megara).

historiography belongs, at the earliest, to the last years of the fifth century or the first years of the fourth (Hellanicus of Lesbos), and it is not attested as a name for Attica itself before Euripides. If our passage were to come from an archaic poem, then the *Atthis* title will presumably have been given to it at a later date; but if the title is the poet's own, it can scarcely be dated before the end of the fifth century. The latter on balance seems the more likely, and the lines we have may be roughly contemporary with the invention of the Aloades' cult of the Muses.

Appendix II: the Aloades and Education

An allegorical interpretation of Homer on the Aloades' confinement of Ares provides a cross bearing for the ‹educational› conception offered here.[169] Ares is allegorically identified with *thumos* and the Aloades with *logoi* in education (τοὺς ἐν παιδείᾳ λογους) that restrain the *thumos*, anger and the appetitive desires. Otus (etymologised from ‹ears›) is identified through hearing with the *logos* that is the product of learning and teaching, and Ephialtes (etymologised from ‹springing upon›) with the *logos* that is innate and springs spontaneously and naturally to human thought processes. This is the product of late Hellenistic or early Imperial allegorising, along the lines of Heraclitus' *Homeric Problems: Homer's Allegories Concerning the Gods*.[170] The anonymous allegorist cited by the scholiast has not himself conceived the connection of Aloades with *paideia*, but has pressed into service an existing association in order to explain away their reported besting of Ares. There are obvious parallels between the allegory and the theories underpinning the Aloades' Muses, including the polarity of *physis* and teaching/learning within the context of *paideia*. So when our commentator goes on to say that *logoi* do not always restrain the *thumos*, it is tempting to suspect a reflection of the Aloades' defence of the homeland against invaders:[171] when there is a need to defend *patris*, family, belongings and *politeia* against enemies, he says, ‹*logos* will not constrain the *thumos* from deploying its inherent (*oikeia*) power; it will exhort and urge it to use [sc. that inherent power] against those who are not native (*oikeion*, again), but rather our bitterest enemies ...›[172]

---

[169] The allegory is developed at length in Schol. D on *Il.* 5.385. Cf. esp. Τὸν μὲν οὖν διὰ τῆς μαθήσεως διδασκόμενον λόγον, Ὦτον προσηγόρευσεν, ὅτι διὰ τῶν ὤτων αὐτὸν καὶ τῆς ἀκοῆς ἐκμανθάνομεν παιδευόμενοι. Τὸν δὲ ἐνδιάθετον, καὶ ἐκ φύσεως παρεπόμενον τοῖς ἀνθρώποις, Ἐφιάλτην ὠνόμασεν, οἷον τὸν αὐτομάτως ἐφαλλόμενον, ἤτ' οὖν ἐπερχόμενον ταῖς διανοίαις ἡμῶν.

[170] For an overview, D. Dawson (1992) 38–52. For dating, and separation from the Stoic tradition, A.A. Long, (1992) 45–48. It is not the work of Heraclitus himself: cf. *Hom. Prob.* 32.1–2 (with some overlap in the interpretation of *stasis* within the Aload household, leading to Ares' release).

[171] Schol. D *Il.* 5.385: ἐπειδὴ πολλάκις ὁ λόγος ἐξουσίαν δίδωσι τῷ θυμῷ, χρῆσθαι τῇ οἰκείᾳ ῥώμῃ, ὅτ' ἂν ὑπὲρ πατρίδος δέοι, καὶ ὑπὲρ παίδων, καὶ γονέων, καὶ κτημάτων, καὶ πολιτείας, πρὸς πολεμίους ἀγωνίζεσθαι. τότε γὰρ ὁ λόγος οὐκ ἔτι κατέχει τὸν θυμὸν, οὐδὲ εἴργει χρῆσθαι τῇ οἰκείᾳ δυνάμει. ἀλλὰ τοὐναντίον αὐτὸν παρακελεύεται καὶ προτρέπεται χρῆσθαι κατὰ τῶν μὴ οἰκείων, μᾶλλον δὲ τῶν ἐχθίστων, ἵνα μὴ ὑπὸ τῶν πολεμίων ληφθέντες κακῶς πάθωμεν.

[172] A debated point: contrast Plut. *Mor.* 458b ἀφαιροῦσι γοῦν αὐλοῖς τὸν θυμὸν οἱ Λακεδαιμόνιοι τῶν μαχομένων, καὶ Μούσαις πρὸ πολέμου θύουσιν ὅπως ὁ λόγος ἐμμένῃ· καὶ τρεψάμενοι τοὺς πολεμίους οὐ διώκουσιν, ἀλλ' ἀνακαλοῦνται τὸν θυμόν ...

Literaturverzeichnis

ARAVANTINOS, V. L., ‹Topographical and Archaeological Investigations on the Summit of Helicon›, in Hurst and Schachter (edd.) (1996) 191.
BARCHIESI, A., ‹Discordant Muses›, *PCPS* 37 (1991) 1-21.
BARMEYER, E., *Die Musen: ein Beitrag zur Inspirationstheorie* (Munich, 1968).
BARRINGER, J. M., *Divine escorts: Nereids in archaic and classical Greek art* (Anna Arbor, 1995).
BETHE, E., *Die Sage vom Troischen Kriege: Homer-Dichtung und Sage* (Leipzig and Berlin, 1927).
BING, P., *The well-read Muse: present and past in Callimachus and the Hellenistic poets* (Göttingen, 1988)
BINTLIFF, J., ‹The Archeological Survey of the Valley of the Muses and its Significance for Boeotian History›, in Hurst and Schachter (edd.) (1996) 193-224.
BONNECHÈRE, P., ‹Les Oracles de Béotie›, *Kernos* 3 (1990).
BREMMER, J., *Interpretations of Greek mythology* (London, 1987).
BRILLANTE, C., ‹Poeti e re nel proemio della *Teogonia* esiodea›, *Prometheus* 20 (1994) 14-26.
BUCK, R. J., ‹The Aeolic Dialect in Boeotia› *Cl. Phil.* 63 (1968) 268-80.
IDEM, ‹The Mycenean Time of Troubles›, *Historia* 18 (1969) 276-98.
BURKERT, W., *Lore and science in ancient Pythagoreanism* (Eng. trans., E.L. Minar Jr.) (Cambridge, Mass., 1972).
IDEM, *Greek religion* (Eng. trans. J. Raffan) (Oxford Blackwell, 1985).
BURN, A. R., ‹Helicon in History: a Study in Greek Mountain Topography›, *BSA* 44 (1949) 313-23.
CALAME, C., ‹Spartan Genealogies: The Mythological Representation of a Spatial Organisation›, in Bremmer (ed.) (London, 1987) 153-86.
CAMILLONI, M. T., *Le Muse* (Rome, 1998).
CLARKE, M., ‹Gods and Mountains in Greek Myth and Poetry›, in A.B. Lloyd (ed.) *What is a god: studies in the nature of Greek divinity* (London, 1997) 65-80.
DASEN, V., *Jumeaux, jumelles dans l'antiquité grecque et romaine* (Zurich, 2005).
DAWSON, D., *Allegorical readers and cultural revision in ancient Alexandria* (Berkeley etc., 1992).
DETIENNE, M., *The masters of truth in archaic Greece* (Eng. trans. J. Lloyd) (New York, 1999).
DODDS, E.R., *Euripides*, Bacchae^2 (Oxford, 1960).
EDWARDS, A.T., *Hesiod's Ascra* (Berkeley, 2004).
FARNELL, L.R., *The cults of the Greek states* Vol. IV (Oxford, 1907).
FORD, A., *The origins of literary criticism: literary culture and poetic theory in classical Greece* (Princeton and Oxford, 2002).
GÖRGEMANNS, H., ‹Rhetorik und Poetik im homerischen Hermeshymnus›, in *Studien zum antiken Epos* (Meisenheim am Glan, 1976) 113-28.
GRAF, F., ‹Orpheus: a Poet among Men›, in Bremmer (ed.) (London, 1987) 80-106.
VAN GRONINGEN, B. A., ‹Les Trois Muses de l'Hélicon›, *AC* 17 (1948) 287-96.
HALL, J., *Hellenicity: between ethnicity and culture* (Chicago and London, 2002).
HALLIDAY, W.R., *Greek Divination: a study of its methods and principles* (London, 1913).
HAMMOND, N. G. L., *A history of Macedonia* I (Oxford, 1972).
HARDIE, A., ‹Pindar, Castalia and the Muses of Delphi›, *PLLS* 9 (1996) 219-57.
IDEM, ‹Juvenal, the *Phaedrus* and the Truth about Rome›, *CQ* 48 (1998) 234-251.
IDEM, ‹Pindar's «Theban» Cosmogony (the First Hymn)›, *BICS* 44 (2000) 19-40.
IDEM, ‹The *Georgics*, the Mysteries and the Muses at Rome›, *PCPS* 48 (2002) 175-208.
HARDIE, P., *Virgil's* Aeneid*: cosmos and imperium* (Oxford, 1986).
HARMATTA, J., ‹Zu den kleinasiatischen Beziehungen der griechischen Mythologie›, *A.Ant.Hung.* 16 (1968) 57-76.
HEINRICHS, A., ‹Die Maenaden von Milet›, *ZPE* 4 (1969) 223-41.
HIERONYMUS, F. *ΜΕΛΕΤΗ: Uebung, Lernen und angrenzende Begriffe* (Basel, 1970).

Hoekstra, A., ‹Epic Verse and the Hexameter›, in *Epic verse before Homer: three studies* (Amsterdam, 1981) 33-53.
Horrocks, G. C., ‹The Antiquity of the Greek Epic Tradition: Some New Evidence›, *PCPS* 26 (1980), 1-11.
Horsfall, N., *Virgil, Aeneid 11: a commentary* (Leiden and Boston, 2003).
Hubbard, T. K., *The Pindaric mind* (Leiden, 1985).
Hurst, A., ‹La Stèle de l'Hélicon›, in Hurst and Schachter (edd.) (1996) 57-71.
Hurst, A. and Schachter, A. (edd.), *La montagne des Muses* (Geneva, 1996).
Janko, R., *Homer, Hesiod and the Hymns: diachronic development in epic dictions* (Cambridge, 1982).
Janni, P., *La cultura di Sparta arcaica: richerche I* (Rome, 1965).
Jones, R. M., ‹Posidonius and the Flight of the Mind through the Universe›, *CP* 21 (1926) 97-113.
Kallet-Marx, R. M., ‹The Evangelistra Watchtower and the Defence of the Zaqara Pass›, in H. Beister and J. Buckler (edd.), *Boiotika: Vorträge vom 5 internationalen Boötien-Kolloquium zu Ehren von Professor Dr. Siegfried Lauffer* (Munich, 1989), 301-11.
Kambylis, A., *Die Dichterweihe und ihre Symbolik* (Heidelberg, 1965).
Kern, O., *Orphicorum fragmenta* (Berlin, 1922).
Kirk, G. S., *Myth: its meaning and functions in ancient and other cultures* (Cambridge, Berkeley and Los Angeles, 1970).
Larson, J., *Greek nymphs: myth, cult, lore* (Oxford, 2001).
Latacz, J., *Troy and Homer* (Eng. trans., K. Windle and R. Ireland) (Oxford, 2004).
Long, A. A., ‹Stoic Readings of Homer›, in R. Lamberton and J.J. Keaney (edd.), *Homer's ancient readers: the hermeneutics of Greek epic's earliest exegetes* (Princeton, 1992) 41-66.
Londsdale, S.H., *Dance and ritual play in Greek religion* (Baltimore and London, 1993).
Minchin, E., *Homer and the resources of memory* (Oxford, 2002).
Murray, P., ‹The Muses and their Arts›, in P. Murray and P. Wilson (edd.) *Music and the Muses: the culture of mousike in the classical Athenian city* (Oxford, 2004) 365-89.
Nagy, G., ‹Early Greek Views of Poets and Poetry›, in G.A. Kennedy (ed.) *The Cambridge history of literary criticism: Vol I: Classical criticism* (Cambridge, 1989), 1-77.
Ninck, M., *Die Bedeutung des Wassers im Kult und Leben der Alten: eine symbolgeschichtliche Untersuchung* (Leipzig, 1921).
Notopoulos, J. A., ‹Mnemosyne in Oral Literature›, *TAPA* 69 (1938) 465-93.
Otto, W. F., *Le Muse e l' origine divina della parola e del canto* (It. trans., S. Mati) (Rome, 2005).
Parker, R., ‹Myths of Early Athens›, in Bremmer (ed.) (1987) 187-214.
idem, *Athenian religion: a history* (Oxford, 1996).
Pascal, E., ‹Muses Olympiennes et Muses Héliconiennes dans la *Théogonie* d'Hésiode›, in J. M. Fossey and H. Giroux (edd.), *Proceedings of the third international conference on Boiotian antiquities* (Amsterdam, 1985) 111-17.
Pfeiffer, R., *History of classical scholarship* (Oxford, 1968).
Plassart, A., ‹Inscriptions de Thespies›, *BCH* 50 (1926) 383-462.
Preller, L. and C. Robert, *Griechische Mythologie* I⁴ (1894).
Pugliese Carratelli, G., ‹ΜΟΝΑΣ ΜΝΗΜΟΣΥΝΗ, ΔΕΚΑΣ ΠΙΣΤΙΣ ΜΝΗΜΗ›, *PdP* 54 (1999) 186-91.
Radermacher, L., *Artium scriptores (Reste der voraristotelischen Rhetorik)* (Vienna, 1951).
De Ridder, A., ‹Fouilles de Thespies et de l'hiéron des Muses de l'Hélicon: Monuments figures›, *BCH* 46 (1922) 217-306.
Rossi, L., ‹Il testamento di Posidippo e le laminette auree di Pella›, *ZPE* 112 (1996) 59-65.
Schachter, A., *Cults of Boeotia 1: Acheloos to Hera* (London, 1981).
idem, *Cults of Boiotia 2: Herakles to Poseidon* (London, 1986).
idem, *Cults of Boiotia* 3 (London, 1994).

IDEM, ‹Reconstructing Thespiae›, in Hurst and Schachter (edd.) (1996) 99–126.
SCHERLING, K., *RE* XVIII.1 (1942) 1879–81 s. v. ‹Otus›.
SCODEL, R., ‹Bardic Performance and Oral Tradition in Homer›, *AJP* 119 (1998) 171–94.
SEGAL, C., *Dionysiac poetics and Euripides' Bacchae*² (Princeton, 1997).
SHOREY, P., ‹Φύσις, Μελέτη, Ἐπιστήμη›, *TAPA* 40 (1909) 185–20.
SIMON, E., *LIMC* I (1981) 1.570–72 s. v. ‹Aloades›.
SMALL, J. P., *Wax tablets of the mind: cognitive studies of memory and literacy in classical antiquity* (London, 1997) 82–84.
SNODGRASS, A. M., *Archaic Greece: the age of experiment* (London, 1980).
SOURVINOU-INWOOD, C., ‹Myth as History: The Previous Owners of the Delphic Oracle›, in Bremmer (ed.) (1987) 215–41.
SYNDIKUS, H. P., *Catull: eine Interpretation* II (Darmstadt, 1990).
THALMANN, W. G., *Conventions of form and thought in early Greek epic poetry* (Baltimore, 1984).
TOEPFFER, J., *RE* I (1894) 1590–92 s. v. ‹Aloades›.
TÜMPEL, K., *RE* V (1905) 2847 s. v. ‹Ephialtes›.
VENERI, A., ‹Posidone e l'Elicona: alcune osservazioni sull' antichità e la continuità di una tradizione mitica beotica›, in A. Schachter (ed.), *Essays in the topography, history and culture of Boiotia*, Teiresias Suppl. 3 (Montreal, 1990) 129–34.
VENERI, A., ‹L'Helicona nella cultura tespiese intorno al IIIsec. a.C.: la stele di Euthy[kl]es›, in Hurst and Schachter (edd.) (1996) 73–86.
VERNANT, J.-P., *Myth and thought among the Greeks* (London, 1983).
VIAN, F., *La Guerre des Géants: le mythe avant l'époque Hellénistique* (Paris, 1952).
VOX, O., ‹Esiodo fra Beozia e Pieria›, *Belfagor* 35 (1980) 321–25.
WALLACE, P. W., ‹Hesiod and the Valley of the Muses›, *GRBS* 15 (1974) 5–24.
WEGNER, M., *Musik und Tanz* (Archeologia Homerica III; Göttingen, 1968).
WEST, M. L., *The Hesiodic catalogue of women: its nature, structure and origins* (Oxford, 1985).
IDEM, ‹The Rise of the Greek Epic›, *JHS* 108 (1988) 151–72.
IDEM, *The east face of Helicon: west Asiatic elements in Greek poetry and myth* (Oxford, 1997).
VON WILAMOWITZ-MOELLENDORF, U., *Homerische Untersuchungen* (Berlin, 1884).
IDEM, *Pindaros* (Berlin, 1922).
IDEM, *Der Glaube der Hellenen*⁴ (repr. Darmstadt, 1959).

PETER HABERMEHL

Quod crimen praeter amasse?
Dido und das Hohelied der Liebe (Ovid *her.* VII)*

> «*L'altra è colei che s'ancise amorosa,
> e ruppe fede al cener di Sicheo.*»
> Dante, *Divina Commedia, Inferno* 5,61 f.

Von den allerersten Lesungen an, im intimen Zirkel am Hof des Augustus, war dem Werk ein fulminanter Erfolg beschieden. Jedem Hörer ging auf, daß hier etwas genuin Neues, genuin Römisches im Entstehen war, das nicht nur in der eigenen Literatur nicht seinesgleichen hatte, sondern sich selbstbewußt mit den gewaltigsten Schöpfungen der griechischen Hemisphäre maß, *Odyssee* und *Ilias* – und in seinen besten Partien auch messen konnte: Vergils *Aeneis*, das große Lied von der Geburt Roms aus der Tragödie Trojas, das Epos von der Sendung des Aeneas, seinem fährnisreichen Weg von der kleinasiatischen Heimat ans italische Gestade, und seinem göttlichen Auftrag, ein Reich zu gründen, das die heimgesuchte Erde befrieden werde und dem kein Ende gesetzt sei.

Doch eines jener zwölf Bücher gewann bald ein eigenes Leben: das vierte, das die tragische Geschichte vom Liebesleid und Liebestod der karthagischen Königin Dido erzählt.[1] Im ersten Buch bahnt das Drama sich an. Letztlich verschlägt reiner Zufall die troische Flotte nach Iunos Sturm an Afrikas Küste.[2] Dort aber führt göttlicher Wille Dido und Aeneas zusammen, die im so verwandten Schicksal des anderen einander erkennen.[3] Listenreich trägt Venus Sorge, die der Liebe entwöhnte königliche Witwe für den hohen Gast zu erwärmen – und Dido, ihrem «kommenden Verderben geweiht» (1,712 *pesti deuota futurae*), verliert ihr Herz an den Heros.[4]

Didos Passion erzählt das entscheidende vierte Buch: das vertrauliche Gespräch mit ihrer Schwester Anna, in dem sie von Hochzeit träumt – um sich zugleich mit einem furchtbaren

---

* Für kritische Hinweise zu diesem Text bin ich Bernd MANUWALD und insbesondere Ernst August SCHMIDT verpflichtet.
[1] Zu Didos literarischem Vorleben, das sich bis in hellenistische Zeit zurückverfolgen läßt, vgl. F. GRAF s.v. Dido, in: Der Neue Pauly Bd. 3, Stuttgart 1997, 543.
[2] Vgl. *Aen.* 1,157f. *defessi Aeneadae, quae proxima litora cursu / contendunt petere, et Libyae uertuntur ad oras.*
[3] Die leidvolle Geschichte der Königin hört Aeneas aus Venus' Mund (*Aen.* 1,338-368). Mit seinem (und Trojas) Schicksal ist Dido bereits vertraut, wie ihre Begrüßung zeigt (*Aen.* 1,565f. 615-626), mehr noch der Fries des karthagischen Iuno-Heiligtums, jene steinerne Elegie auf den Fall Trojas (*Aen.* 1,456-493). – Die epische Folie dieser Begegnung bietet die *Odyssee*: «Odysseus kommt zu Kalypso, zu Kirke und zu Nausikaa» (KLINGNER 396).
[4] Entscheidend trägt dazu Aeneas' Geschichte bei (in Buch zwei und drei), mit der er sich «in Didos Herz hineinerzählt» (HEINZE 125). Alsbald klafft in ihrem Innern Amors Wunde (*Aen.* 4,1-2 *At regina graui iamdudum saucia cura / uulnus alit uenis et caeco carpitur igni*). Schon eines von Aeneas' Gastgeschenken – das Prachtgewand der Ehebrecherin Helena (*Aen.* 1,649-652) – läßt von der ersten Stunde an Schatten über die Begegnung fallen.

Eid an ihren toten Gatten Sychaeus zu binden;[5] Amors Wunde, die sich immer tiefer in ihre Brust frißt; der Jagdausflug, bei dem Iunos Wolkenbruch Dido und Aeneas Zuflucht in jener ominösen Höhle finden läßt[6] – die Stunde der Erfüllung, die in klassischer Peripetie jäh umschlägt, als *Fama* Halbwahrheiten über die Buhlschaft der beiden ausstreut und der von Iuppiter an seine Sendung erinnerte Aeneas in aller Stille zum Aufbruch rüstet. Weder Didos Rasen noch Didos Flehen vermögen ihn zurückzuhalten, und mit seinem Schwert nimmt Dido Abschied von ihrer Liebe und ihrem Leben. Sterbend liegt sie in Annas Schoß, das brechende Auge gen Himmel gewandt, bis Iuno sich ihrer erbarmt und sie vom Todeskampf erlöst.[7]

Diese so bemerkenswerte Geschichte läßt uns miterleben, wie eine Frau von edler Herkunft und edlem Herzen, voller Majestät und Würde, vom Schicksal geläutert, einer zerstörerischen Leidenschaft zum Opfer fällt, einer dämonischen Macht, gegen die sie sich wehrt – um ihr nur um so ärger zu erliegen, und die sie von der Höhe ihres späten Glücks in Verderben und Tod stürzen läßt. Fast exemplarisch durchleidet sie alle Stationen der *nósos erotiké* (der ‹Liebeskrankheit›), ihren Affekten ausgeliefert, die sie erbarmungslos auslebt – Aeneas, vor allem aber sich selbst gegenüber.[8] In ihrer Liebe verraten und verlassen, ihrer Ehre und ihres Ansehens beraubt, zerrieben zwischen Sehnsucht, Begehren, Erniedrigung, Haß, bleibt die letzte Ausflucht der Tod.[9] Den Entschluß zum Selbstmord faßt und verfolgt sie in aller Stille, mit fast ‹männlicher› Entschiedenheit[10] – nirgendwo mehr in tragisches Licht getaucht als in ihrem Ende.

Eine veritable Tragödie entfaltet sich – die im Grunde sogar übertrifft, was einer Ariadne oder Medea widerfährt. Und damit ist mehr gemeint als die weise Beobachtung, daß hier zwei reife, ehe-erfahrene Charaktere Schiffbruch leiden.[11] Denn Dido hat eine Geschichte, ein Schicksal: den Tod ihres Gatten Sychaeus, ermordet von Didos eigenem Bruder; die Flucht aus dem heimatlichen Tyros; die Gründung des neuen Reichs. Und dieses Schicksal bewältigt sie bravourös – um zu erfahren, wie ihr Lebenswerk an den Klippen des Eros zerschellt.

---

[5] *Aen.* 4,24–29. Dido verkörpert hier das höchste römische Frauenideal, die ein einziges Mal vermählte *uniuira* (vgl. HEINZE 126). An dieses Ideal bindet sie ihr Schwur; indem sie ihn bricht, lädt sie Schuld auf sich – und läßt so ihren Tod «poetisch gerechtfertigt» erscheinen (HEINZE 125); durch den Schwur «spricht sie sich schon im voraus selbst ihr Urteil» (HEINZE 128).

[6] Um die Gründung Roms zu vereiteln, sucht Iuno Aeneas mit Dido zu vermählen – und Venus gibt zum Schein ihren Segen (*Aen.* 4,90–128).

[7] Kaum eine Sterbeszene der antiken Literatur (etwa Platons *Phaidon*, die Todesstunden, die Tacitus' *Annales* überliefern, oder auch die Passionsgeschichte der Evangelien) geht dem Leser ähnlich zu Herzen.

[8] «Die Symptome dieser Leidenschaft, die [*Aen.* 4,] 68 ff. geschildert werden, sind die aus der erotischen Literatur hellenistischer Zeit bekannten (...)» (HEINZE 130).

[9] Mehrere Vorbilder standen Dido Modell: die entehrte Heroine der Tragödie (etwa Euripides' Medea), die leidenschaftlich Liebende der hellenistischen Dichtung (etwa die Medea des Apollonios von Rhodos, oder Catulls Ariadne), vielleicht auch die verlassene Liebende des Romans (vgl. u.a. HEINZE 118f. 133; CAMPS 34; QUINN 135). Zudem treibt nicht allein unglückliche Liebe Dido in den Tod; die Scham über ihre Verfehlung, die erlittene Kränkung, der Verlust ihrer königlichen Würde und ihres untadeligen Rufes, die düsteren Vorzeichen treten hinzu (HEINZE 139f.).

[10] «Das Klagen und Jammern, das sentimentale Schwelgen im eigenen Unglück (...), all diese Inventarstücke der tragischen Monodien und hellenistischen Rührszenen sind aufs äußerste sparsam verwendet.» (HEINZE 139).

[11] Aeneas und Dido sind «nicht zu vergleichen mit jenen des Eros unkundigen Jünglingen und Mädchen, die der unbekannten Leidenschaft wehrlos anheimfallen» (HEINZE 123).

An diesem Untergang spricht Vergil Dido zumindest mitschuldig (wie später sie sich selbst): sie hat ihren Treueid gegen Sychaeus gebrochen[12] (diskreter, doch nicht minder harsch fällt das Urteil über Aeneas aus).[13] Doch das ist nur die halbe Wahrheit. Letztlich wird Dido, ihres künftigen Unglücks unkundig (1,299 *fati nescia*), zum Spielball der Götter, die sie leichthändig opfern.[14] Denn sie gerät in ein Kräftefeld, das alles Individuelle übersteigt. In diesem kosmischen Konflikt wird sie zur symbolischen, ja fast historischen Figur. Sie gründet die Stadt, die Hannibal hervorbringen wird; ihr Fluch stiftet ewige Feindschaft zwischen Karthago und Rom.[15] In diesem Sinne wird ihr Tod auch zum Bild des späteren Untergangs der romfeindlichen Mächte – die persönliche Tragödie ist fest verankert in der Heilsgeschichte des Epos.[16] Oder, wenn wir Didos Fall freundlicher lesen wollen: sie wird (wie vor ihr Kreusa, oder nach ihr Amata oder Turnus) eines der ungezählten Opfer, die in der *Aeneis* den blutigen Weg zum *Imperium Romanum* säumen. Sie symbolisiert «den Preis, den die andere Seite in der Geschichte zahlt.»[17] Daß sie sich auf weltpolitischer Bühne zuträgt, gibt dieser Tragödie ihr einzigartiges Gepräge.

Was aber vor allem anderen im Gedächtnis bleibt, ist der *Mensch* Dido, und wir können nachfühlen, warum der junge Augustin über das Los der punischen Königin bittere Tränen weinte.[18] Doch bis in die Spätantike müssen wir nicht schweifen, um ihre Wirkung zu erfahren.[19] Wie Juvenal verrät, fesselte gebildete Römerinnen beim Gedanken an die *Aeneis* vor allem *ein* Thema – Didos Selbstmord.[20] Und schon ein jüngerer Zeitgenosse Vergils

---

[12] «Jener Tag» – so einer der raren auktoriellen Kommentare Vergils – «war zuerst Ursache des Todes, zuerst Ursache aller Qual». Denn Dido übersieht geflissentlich die Umstände des verstohlenen Tête-à-tête; ihre «verstohlene Liebschaft … nennt sie Ehebund; mit diesem Namen verbrämt sie ihre Schuld» (4,169-172 *ille dies primus leti primusque malorum / causa fuit; neque enim specie famaue mouetur / nec iam furtiuum Dido meditatur amorem: / coniugium uocat, hoc praetexit nomine culpam*).

[13] Wenn wir Aeneas nach der Jagd wiedersehen (bezeichnenderweise durch die Augen Merkurs) – im orientalischen Prunkgewand, als Erbauer Karthagos (*Aen.* 4,260-264) –, hat er sich fast zum Punier verwandelt (und ähnelt damit fatal dem Zerrbild, das Iarbas 4,215-217 von ihm zeichnet). – Nachsichtiger urteilt HEINZE 123: «Wenn ein Held wie Aeneas über einem Weibe seine göttliche Bestimmung auch nur für kurze Zeit vergessen kann, wie übermächtig muß die Leidenschaft sein!»

[14] Ironischerweise sind es die Intrigen zweier Göttinnen, Venus und Iuno. Den (ungewollt) galligen Kommentar der Ereignisse liefert Aeneas' Segenswunsch (*Aen.* 1,603-605), der sich ins Gegenteil verkehrt. Letztlich sind es auch jenseitige Mächte, die in Dido den Todeswunsch wecken (4,450-473). – Die Frage, wie ernst Vergil diesen Götterapparat nimmt, ist hier nicht zu beantworten.

[15] Sie verkörpert gleichsam die romfeindliche punische Seele: sie verhöhnt Aeneas' *pietas* (*Aen.* 4,596-599) – und bricht so den Stab über die eigene; sie labt sich an grausamen Rachephantasien, die das römische Schreckbild punischer *crudelitas* evozieren (4,600-606); und nicht von ungefähr erinnert ihr Fluch (4,607-629) an den berühmt-berüchtigten Eid des jungen Hannibal (vgl. Polybios 3,11; Liv. 21,1,4 u. a.; dies scheint auch A.S. PEASE *ad Aen.* 4,625 bemerkt zu haben – und Silius Italicus, *Punica* 1,81-122). Erst diese späte Dämonisierung erklärt, warum Iuppiter Dido und ihr Volk zur freundlichen Aufnahme der Troer bewegen muß (*Aen.* 1,297-304).

[16] Vgl. ANDERSON 61.

[17] CAMPS 31. Zeitgenössische Leser fanden hier aber auch Antonius' Mesalliance mit Kleopatra wieder: den einer orientalischen Königin hörigen römischen Granden, der das Wohl des Reichs seiner Wollust opfert (vgl. Anm. 13; CAMPS 29f.). – Zur Figur Didos vgl. jetzt bes. E.A. SCHMIDT und E. KRUMMEN.

[18] *Conf.* 1,13,20 *tenere cogebar Aeneae nescio cuius errores oblitus errorum meorum et plorare Didonem mortuam, quia se occidit ab amore, cum interea me ipsum in his a te morientem* eqs. Was in der Vergilliteratur offenbar noch nicht gesehen wurde: Augustin spricht hier explizit von den *errores* des Aeneas, mit denen er – wie die Übertragung auf die eigenen «Verfehlungen» zeigt – mehr meint als die «Irrfahrten» der gängigen Übersetzungen. Für Augustin ist Aeneas sittlich schuldig – auch und gerade am Tode Didos.

[19] Noch Didos sagenhafte Schätze verdrehen Kaiser Nero den Kopf (Tac. *ann.* 16,1-3; Suet. *Nero* 31,4).

[20] Juv. 6,434f. *illa tamen grauior, quae cum discumbere coepit / laudat Vergilium, periturae ignoscit Elissae*.

stellt einmal fest, kein Buch der *Aeneis* schlage die Menschen so in seinen Bann wie eben das vierte, das Dido-Buch. Das Urteil stammt von Ovid.[21]

Nicht zuletzt in eigener Sache spricht er hier; denn vor allem ihm selbst hat der Stoff es angetan. Ihn, den wie keinen anderen römischen Autor das Ewig-Weibliche hinanzog, konnte die faszinierendste Frauengestalt kaum kaltlassen, die römische Kunst erschuf.[22] Und diese Faszination hat er weidlich bewiesen: auf Dido kommt er in seinem Werk siebenmal zu sprechen.[23] Genau genommen sechsmal. Denn einmal kommt sie selbst zu Wort, in seinen *Heroides*, den Briefen mythischer Frauen an Männer, die sie lieben – und anders nicht (mehr) erreichen können. Unter den fünfzehn Einzelbriefen lesen wir dort an siebter Stelle (also fast in der Werkmitte)[24] einen Brief Didos an Aeneas. Um ihn soll es im Folgenden gehen.[25]

> «So singt, wenn das Schicksal ruft, ins feuchte Schilf gesunken
> an den Furten des Mäanders, der weiße Schwan.
> Doch nicht, weil ich hoffe, mein Flehen könne dich bewegen,
> spreche ich dich an – ein Gott ist meinem Unterfangen abhold –,
> sondern weil ich meine Gefälligkeiten, meinen Ruf, einen keuschen Leib und ein
> reines Herz böse vergeudet habe, ist es ein Leichtes, Worte zu vergeuden.»[26]

Mit einem einprägsamen Bild beginnt der Brief: dem singenden Schwan, dessen Lied bekanntlich nur einmal erklingt – in seiner Todesstunde.[27] Der Schreiber dieser Verse stimmt seinen Leser (das «du» in Zeile drei) ein auf seinen Schwanensang. Auch er sieht sich also dem Tod geweiht (das markante, als Eröffnung eines Textes fast unerhörte *sic* erzwingt vom ersten Wort an die Übertragung).[28] Doch wie der sterbende Schwan für kein Publi-

---

[21] *Trist.* 2,533–536. «Admittedly Ovid is establishing a case for the popularity of poetry about free love» (Quinn 135 Anm. 1).
[22] Und nicht nur dies. Vergils Dido ist sogar «die einzige von einem römischen Dichter geschaffene Figur (...), die in die Weltliteratur übergehen sollte» (Heinze 133).
[23] *Am.* 2,18,25 f. 31; *ars* 3,39 f.; *rem.* 57 f.; *fast.* 3,545 ff.; *met.* 14,78–81; *trist.* 2,533–536 – und natürlich *her.* 7.
[24] Von einer ‹Werkmitte› läßt sich freilich nur unter Vorbehalt sprechen. Die ursprüngliche Reihenfolge der fünfzehn (?) Einzelbriefe läßt sich nur teilweise ermitteln.
[25] Bei der folgenden Durchsicht des Briefes gilt ein besonderes Augenmerk den meist unausgesprochenen (und nicht immer bemerkten) Bindegliedern zwischen den einzelnen Abschnitten.
[26] 1–6 *Sic ubi fata uocant, udis abiectus in herbis / ad uada Maeandri concinit albus olor. / nec quia te nostra sperem prece posse moueri, / alloquor (aduerso mouimus ista deo); / sed merita et famam corpusque animumque pudicum / cum male perdiderim, perdere uerba leue est.* – Als Text liegt die Ausgabe von P.E. Knox zugrunde (Ovid, Heroides. Select Epistles, Cambridge 1995). Konsultiert habe ich darüber hinaus die vorzügliche Loeb-Ausgabe der *Heroides* von G.P. Goold (Cambridge, Mass. 1977).
[27] Adamietz 123 liest das Schwanengleichnis (ähnlich emphatisch erscheint es am Anfang des letzten *Tristien*-Buches, 5,1,11–14) als elegische Antwort auf Vergils Mänaden-Vergleich an eben der Stelle des Epos, an der dramatisch der Brief angesiedelt ist (*Aen.* 4,300–303; vgl. unten S. 87). – Das in jüngeren Handschriften überlieferte Eingangsdistichon zerstört mit seiner plumpen Eindeutigkeit (vgl. auch Jacobson 83) den zarten Ton der Eröffnung. Ungeachtet aller argumentativen Anstrengungen von E.-A. Kirfel (Untersuchungen zur Briefform der Heroides Ovids, Bern 1969, 61–64) bestehen an seiner Echtheit ernsteste Zweifel.
[28] Jacobson 83 liest bereits das erste Distichon als Anspielung auf den geplanten Selbstmord (ähnlich Adamietz 131). Doch scheint auch *her.* 7 eher eine Dynamik zu entfalten wie die *Aeneis*. Dort ahnt und fürchtet die mit Aeneas' Verrat konfrontierte Dido zunächst ihren Tod (4,307 f. *nec te noster amor nec te data dextera quondam / nec moritura tenet crudeli funere Dido?*; vgl. Austin ad Aen. 4,308). Erst später ersehnt sie ihn (4,450 f.); zuletzt, im tiefsten Schmerz, ist sie bereit, ihn selbst herbeizuführen (4,474–476. 547. 630 f.). Als erste Anspielung auf einen möglichen Selbstmord läßt sich wohl *her.* 7,63 f. lesen (vgl. Knox *ad* 64). – Als ferne Parallele für das eröffnende *sic* vgl. das emphatische *ergo* am Beginn von *am.* 2,7.

kum singt – er singt für sich, um Abschied zu nehmen von Welt und Leben –, wenden auch diese Verse sich im Grunde an niemanden; das erste Distichon klingt wie ‹beiseite gesprochen›. Kleine Signale ergänzen das Bild. Ist das «Schicksal» auch für Schwäne zuständig? Kündigt der unerwartete «Mäander» ein Lied an, das sich weg- und ziellos verströmt?[29] Und das betont «weiße» Gefieder des Tiers – beim Singschwan (*Cygnus cygnus* Linné) geradezu sprichwörtlich –, evoziert es ein Bild der Trauer, des Todes, der Unschuld?

Das Geheimnis der dramatischen Exposition gewinnt noch dadurch, daß erst das dritte Distichon an eine Schreiber*in* denken läßt, und erst das vierte ihren Namen verrät (die antiken Ausgaben kannten wohl keine Überschriften); jetzt erst sind wir im Bilde.[30]

Das zweite und dritte Distichon (3–6) bringen keine Übertragung der Metapher (dies überläßt Dido dem Leser); sie knüpfen an das Bild an und spinnen es fort. Dido weiß, daß ihr Schwanensang ins Leere geht: ihr Flehen wird Aeneas nicht bewegen. Zugleich spüren wir eine erste feine Diskrepanz: anders als der Schwan, wendet Dido sich doch an ein ‹Du› – eben Aeneas; und ihr schillerndes *mouimus* läßt ein erstes Mal ahnen, daß sie – ihrer verschleiernden Rhetorik und einer ominösen «Gottheit» zum Trotz[31] – doch etwas ‹bewegen› will.[32] Zugleich entschuldigt sie ihr Unterfangen in fast sarkastischem Ton (aber durchaus stilvoll: quasi zeugmatisch verknüpft, trifft Klimax auf Anti-Klimax; Alliterationen und Polyptota setzen Akzente): sie habe alles verloren – auf ein paar Worte komme es also nicht mehr an.

Nach diesem eher defensiven *exordium* geht Dido unversehens zum Angriff über, mit einer ganzen Breitseite ungläubiger Fragen: willst du Karthago, unsere Ehe, deine Versprechen, willst du *mich* wirklich verlassen – um eines Phantoms willen, das Italien heißt? (7–12) Zugleich unterstellt sie Aeneas, es gehe ihm gar nicht um Italien – sie attestiert ihm ein Getriebensein, eine psychische Unrast, die (modern transkribiert) aus latenten Bindungsängsten rühre (13 f.):

> «Was getan ist, fliehst du; du suchst, was zu tun ist. Kaum ist ein Land entdeckt (*oder vielleicht besser* : Wo doch ein Land entdeckt ist),
> treibt es dich, im ganzen Erdkreis ein andres zu suchen.»[33]

Aber auch seinen italischen Traum sucht sie ihm auszureden und führt ihm anschaulich vor Augen, was die Ankunft im Gelobten Land tatsächlich bedeute (15–22). Glaube er im Ernst, man werde ihm, dem ‹Unbekannten› (16 *non notis* – welche Ohrfeige, verglichen mit Didos rühmender Begrüßung im Epos!),[34] das Land einfach überlassen? Mit messerscharfer Logik greifen ihre Argumente ineinander: Du weißt nicht einmal, wo dein Wolkenkuckucksheim liegt! Angenommen, du *findest* dorthin: wer gibt dir Land? Angenommen,

---

[29] Vgl. zu diesem Fluß PALMER und KNOX *ad loc.*
[30] Vgl. ANDERSON 49 f.
[31] Für gewöhnlich wird diese Gottheit als Amor gedeutet (erwägenswert wäre auch Venus). ANDERSONS faszinierende These (50 f.), mit ihr sei Aeneas gemeint, den Dido damit als Gott apostrophiere, findet im übrigen Text jedoch allenfalls im zweifachen *precor* (63, 163) eine Stütze.
[32] Vgl. ANDERSON 49 f.
[33] 13 f. *facta fugis, facienda petis; quaerenda per orbem / altera, quaesita est altera terra tibi.*
[34] *Aen.* 1,565 f. *quis genus Aeneadum, quis Troiae nesciat urbem, / uirtutesque uirosque aut tanti incendia belli?*; 1,617 f. *tune ille Aeneas quem Dardanio Anchisae / alma Venus Phrygii genuit Simoentis ad undam?* eqs.

du *bekämest* Land – wie willst du eine Stadt gründen wie Karthago? Angenommen, selbst dieses gelänge (nun spielt sie ihren Trumpf aus): «Woher nimmst du eine Frau, die dich so lieben wird» wie ich? Wo findest du eine zweite Dido?[35]

Auch wenn Dido unvermittelt von der Anrede zum Monolog wechselt[36] – ein inneres Band verknüpft die vorangegangenen Verse mit den folgenden: ihre Liebe. Als suche sie sich ihre Lage anschaulich vor Augen zu führen, beschreibt Dido ihre verzehrende Leidenschaft, in einem Bild, in dem Eros und Tod höchst ambivalent verschmelzen (23f.):

> «Ich brenne, wie die in Schwefel getauchte Fackel,
> wie heilige Myrrhe, die man ins rauchende Altarfeuer streut.»[37]

Denn die Fackel (*taeda*) gehört zu Hochzeit wie Bestattung; und hinter dem Bild des auf dem Altar verglühenden Weihrauchs erscheint dunkel der Leichnam der Königin, der auf dem Scheiterhaufen zu Asche zerfallen wird.[38] Diese verzehrende Glut speist die stete Erinnerung an Aeneas, die sie nicht loswird – sein Bild verfolgt sie unausweichlich (25f.).[39] Dabei ist er «treulos», «undankbar» und straft all ihre Wohltaten mit Verachtung; eine kluge Frau gäbe einem wie ihm den Laufpaß. Sie aber hegt keinerlei Haß (anders als die leidenschaftliche Dido der *Aeneis*), sondern liebt ihn – hier klingt die erotische Elegie durch – «nur um so verzweifelter» (27–30; bes. 30 *questaque peius amo*).

Diese Verzweiflung sucht Beistand von außen. Mit einem innigen Appell wendet Dido, die «Schwiegertochter» (31 *nurui*), sich an ihre ‹Schwiegermutter› Venus (mit anderen Worten: sie möge ihren Sohn für jene Freuden erwärmen, über die sie als Göttin gebiete [vgl. 36]; *en passant* postuliert sie damit Familienbande, die als solche allenfalls faktisch geschlossen wurden, kaum jedoch vor Gott und den Menschen), vornehmlich aber an ihren Schwager Amor.[40] Er soll seinen Bruder lehren, im richtigen «Feldlager Kriegsdienst zu leisten»: im Lager Cupidos.[41] Auf witzige Weise zitiert Dido hier eines der berühmtesten Gedichte Ovids, *Amores* 1,9 – das sie also offenkundig gelesen und sich zu Herzen genommen hat: *Militat omnis amans, et habet sua castra Cupido*. Doch auch mit weniger wisse sie sich zu bescheiden: genug, wenn *sie* liebe – und er sich lieben lasse (33f.). Fast scheint es, als habe sie wieder die *Amores* im Sinn, in denen wir einem ähnlichen Räsonnement begegnen.[42] Kurzum: Dido träumt von Liebesentwürfen, wie Ovid persönlich sie in seinem Erstlingswerk durchspielt – um sich zuletzt bitter einzugestehen, daß sie ‹Luftschlösser› baut

---

[35] 22 *unde tibi, quae te sic amet, uxor erit?* (nach JACOBSON 89; vgl. ebd. 87f.). – Dieser Passus trägt die Hauptlast von VESSEYS wenig überzeugender These, *her*. 7 sei ein Spiel mit dem Mythos, das dessen dunkle Seiten ausblende: Dido habe nichts dagegen, daß Aeneas ein Reich suche – sie störe sich nur an dem Umstand, daß er keine Ahnung habe, wo es liege!
[36] Didos Worte gewinnen so an Intimität (DÖPP 28).
[37] 23f. *uror ut inducto ceratae sulpure taedae, / ut pia fumosis addita tura focis*.
[38] Dido «continues to play on the theme of her impending death» (KNOX *ad* 23).
[39] Dieses offene Bekenntnis ihrer Liebe (das in der *Aeneis* keine Parallele hat) läßt Aeneas' emotionales Versagen um so schärfer Kontur gewinnen (ADAMIETZ 124f.).
[40] Das Gebet an seine göttlichen Verwandten soll Aeneas in besonderer Weise verpflichten (ADAMIETZ 124).
[41] 31f. *parce, Venus, nurui, durumque amplectere fratrem, / frater Amor; castris militet ille tuis!* – Ein amüsantes Detail blieb bislang unbeobachtet. Wenn Dido Amor hier auffordert, Aeneas zu umarmen, will sie dem Geliebten mit gleicher Münze heimzahlen, was ihr (wie sie jetzt offenbar weiß) im Epos widerfuhr: dort umarmt ja Amor *sie* – mit den bekannten Folgen (*Aen*. 1,717–722).
[42] *Am*. 1,3,2f. *aut amet aut faciat, cur ego semper amem. / a, nimium uolui: tantum patiatur amari* (vgl. *her*. 15,96 *non ut ames oro, me sed amare sinas*).

(35 *ista mihi falso iactatur imago*): mit dem Naturell seiner Mutter hat Aeneas nichts gemein (35 f.).[43]

Mit dieser ernüchternden Einsicht kehrt sie aus der Meditation zurück zur Zwiesprache mit Aeneas. Doch in welchem Ton! (37-40):

> «Fels und Gebirg' und die auf hohem Joch entsprossene
> Eiche, wildes Raubgetier brachte dich hervor –
> oder die See, wie du sie, vom Wind gepeitscht, eben jetzt erblickst –
> und der Sturmflut zum Trotz rüstest du dich dennoch zur Fahrt.»[44]

Dieser Vorwurf ist seit Homer topisch; im Mund der vergilischen Dido kehrt er wieder: Aeneas – eine Ausgeburt wilder Naturgewalten.[45] Auch bei Ovid läßt sie sich den Gemeinplatz nicht entgehen. Doch sie ergänzt die Bilder um die (bereits in der *Ilias* erwähnte) See[46] – und leitet so geschickt über zu einem Thema, das ihr weit mehr am Herzen liegt als die Invektive: die von den Winterstürmen aufgewühlten Fluten. Auf sie lenkt sie Aeneas' Blick und führt ihm den Irrsinn vor Augen, solchen Unwettern die gerade im Winter notorisch gefährliche Fahrt nach Übersee abzutrotzen (41-44).[47] Sie würzt ihr Argument mit beißendem Spott (45-48: bin ich das wert, daß du in deinen sicheren Tod fährst, nur um mir zu entkommen?), um dann die Tücken der Schiffahrt zur Unzeit weiter auszumalen (53-56). Denn die ominöse See ist nicht allein aus meteorologischen Gründen gefährlich. Zumal der Eidbrüchige muß sie fürchten (soweit getreu antiker Vorstellung), besonders aber der, der einen Liebeseid verletzt habe (57-60):

> «Und schlecht bekommt es dem Eidbrüchigen, die See auf die Probe zu stellen.
> Jenes Reich fordert Buße für die Untreue –
> zumal, wenn Amor verraten wird. Heißt es doch,
> die Mutter der Amoren sei nackt Kytheras Gewässern entstiegen.»[48]

Da Venus dem Meer entstamme, sei es der Göttin ureigenstes Element, in dem sie jede Verletzung der Liebe unnachsichtig ahnde – so das arkane Theologem, das Dido hier launig zusammenfabuliert und das auf die Zuständigkeiten einer Aphrodite so wenig Rücksicht nimmt wie auf den Machtbereich eines Poseidon. Aeneas aber sitzt gleichsam in der Falle: fährt er, so fordert er sein Schicksal heraus; bleibt er aber, so hat er nichts zu befürchten. Vergnüglich lesen sich Didos Auslassungen auch deshalb, weil sie Aeneas nebenbei eine Nachhilfestunde zu seiner Familiengeschichte erteilten,[49] und zudem offenbar jene helleni-

---

[43] Der harte Schnitt von der Liebe zum Vorwurf sucht lt. ADAMIETZ 125 die «kalkulierte Schockwirkung».
[44] 37-40 *te lapis et montes innataque rupibus altis / robora, te saeuae progenuere ferae, / aut mare, quale uides agitari nunc quoque uentis, / qua tamen aduersis fluctibus ire paras.* – Vgl. DÖPP 28-31; JACOBSON 80-82.
[45] *Aen.* 4,365-367 (das Urbild *Ilias* 16,33-35).
[46] Auch von der Eiche weiß die epische Dido nichts. Ovid verkehrt das markige Gleichnis vom standhaften Aeneas, der vom Sturm weiblicher Leidenschaft geschüttelten Steineiche (*Aen.* 4,441-446), ins Negative.
[47] In der *Aeneis* wird dieses wichtige Argument nur angedeutet (4,309-313. 430); in *her.* 7 kehrt es zweimal wieder (73 f., 169-173).
[48] 57-60 *nec uiolasse fidem temptantibus aequora prodest; / perfidiae poenas exigit ille locus, / praecipue cum laesus Amor, quia mater Amorum / nuda Cytheriacis edita fertur aquis.* – Der nicht selbstverständliche Plural *Amorum* legt Dido womöglich philosophische Bildung in den Mund: eine Anspielung auf Eros und Anteros im platonischen *Phaidros*, oder auf Eros *sophron* und Eros *aischros* bzw. Eros *ouranios* und Eros *pandemos* im platonischen *Symposion*. Ähnlich spricht Seneca zweimal vom *geminus Cupido* (*Phae.* 275; *Oed.* 500).
[49] KNOX *ad* 59. Strenger JACOBSON 81 («ludicrous in light of the kinship mentioned»).

stischen Vignetten vor Augen hat, auf denen Venus einen unbotmäßigen Amor züchtigt – als hätte ihr sterblicher Sohn nun Gleiches zu gewärtigen.

Doch auch versöhnlichere Töne weiß Dido anzuschlagen. So gefährlich die maritimen Elemente sein mögen – selbst diese harte Naturgewalt kennt eine sanfte Seite: bald werden die Winterstürme sich legen (49f.). Sollte Gleiches nicht auch für einen ‹Sohn der See› (vgl. 39) gelten, so eine Hoffnung schöpfende Dido (51f.):

> «Wärest doch auch du so wandelbar (*mutabilis*) wie die Winde!
> Und du wirst es sein – es sei denn, du übertriffst die Eichen an Härte.»[50]

Einer der berühmtesten Verse Vergils klingt hier an: «allezeit launisch und wankelmütig ist das Weib» (*Aen.* 4,569f. *uarium et mutabile semper / femina* – warnend im Munde Merkurs), nun aber gleichsam in sein Gegenteil verkehrt. Es geht nicht länger um eine Diffamierung der weiblichen Natur – Dido hält der unbeweglichen männlichen Psyche einen kategorischen Imperativ vor Augen, ein Plädoyer für die Kraft der Metamorphose und Umkehr.

Halte er jedoch an seinem Starrsinn fest, müsse er gewärtigen, auf dem Meer zugrunde zu gehen – eine Vorstellung, die Dido ernstlich Sorge bereitet (61–64), zumal ihre Warnungen, einmal ausgesprochen, nach alter magischer Vorstellung Wirklichkeit werden könnten (vgl. 65 *nullum sit in omine pondus!*). Das ist das exakte Gegenstück zur Dido Vergils, die hofft, den Treulosen ereile auf See sein gerechtes Los (*Aen.* 4,382–384). Doch ohne einen Anflug boshafter Selbstgerechtigkeit kommt auch Ovids Königin nicht aus (63f.). Aeneas solle bitte schön am Leben bleiben, um voller Gewissensqualen die Verantwortung zu schultern – für ihren Tod.[51] Finde er freilich auf hoher See sein Ende, werde ihm zuletzt ihr anklagendes Bild vor Augen stehen (65–72).[52]

Doch soweit soll es nicht kommen. Dido schlägt einen anderen Ton an und appelliert an Aeneas' väterliche Verantwortung: wenn er schon das eigene Leben in den Wind schreibe, möge er zumindest Ascanius schonen (75–78). Indem sie ihm das Wohl seines Sohns ans Herz legt, in der Hoffnung auf einen Aufschub seiner Abreise (vgl. 41ff.) oder gar auf einen Sinneswandel (vgl. 51f., 73), kehrt Dido ein Argument gegen Aeneas, das bei Vergil Aeneas selbst vorträgt, sekundiert von Iuppiter und Merkur: daß er seinem Erben Ascanius das italische Reich schulde (*Aen.* 4,232–234. 272–276. 354f.). Sie deutet es freilich um: aus dem Reich wird das Leben und Wohlergehen des Kindes, das Dido der väterlichen Sorge ans Herz legt.[53]

---

[50] 51f. *tu quoque cum uentis utinam mutabilis esses! / et, nisi duritia robora uincis, eris*. Zur Eiche vgl. *Aen.* 4,441–446 und Anm. 46.

[51] In 64 *tu potius leti causa ferere mei* klingt *Aen.* 6,458 nach (*funeris heu tibi causa fui?*): «Was Aeneas dort erschüttert ausruft, wird hier von Dido gewissermaßen als Argument vorweggenommen» (Döpp 32f.).

[52] Wo Dido im Epos droht, sie werde Aeneas im Leben wie im Tod verfolgen (*Aen.* 4,384–387), warnt sie ihn im Brief vor den Qualen eines schuldigen Gewissens. Es geht nicht länger um (jenseitige) Rache, sondern um (diesseitige) Reue (vgl. Döpp 33f.; Knox 21). – Irritierend doppelbödig klingt die Wendung 69f. *coniugis ante oculos deceptae stabit imago / tristis et effusis sanguinolenta comis*. Dido spricht von sich selbst; doch gerade das Wort *coniunx* läßt im prophetischen Selbstbildnis ihres Todes (vgl. *Aen.* 4,663–665 *illam media inter talia ferro / conlapsam (...), ensemque cruore / spumantem sparsasque manus*) auch die Erinnerung an die tote Kreusa mitschwingen (*Aen.* 2,772f.), Aeneas' erster *coniunx*, die er – wie Dido gleich festhalten wird – ebenfalls auf dem Gewissen hat (vgl. Jacobson 85f.).

[53] Die dramatische Distanz zur *Aeneis* betont bereits Jacobson 88. Dort will Dido als zweite Prokne und Philomela dem Vater Ascanius als Ragout servieren (*Aen.* 4,601f.) – Ovids Dido hingegen bittet für den

Oder – so der unausgesprochene Übergang – will er für Ascanius so ‹sorgen› wie einst für Kreusa? Ihr verhaltener Ton ändert sich radikal; ein zweites Mal (nach 37 ff.) greift sie Aeneas frontal an. Seine Erzählung von der Rettung der Penaten und des Vaters sei nichts als Lüge und heroische Selbstinszenierung (79–82). Doch einen wahren Kern der Fabel läßt sie gelten: im brennenden Troja war Aeneas sehr wohl – sonst liefe ihre schärfste Anklage ja ins Leere (83–85):

> «Sollte jemand fragen, wo die Mutter des schönen Julus ist –
> sie kam um, von ihrem spröden Gemahl schnöde im Stich gelassen.
> Du selbst hattest es mir erzählt – und ich war gerührt!»[54]

Die so berühmte wie heikle Geschichte von Aeneas, dem auf der Flucht durch die nächtlichen Gassen Trojas seine Gattin Kreusa abhanden kommt, war immer ein dunkler Fleck auf dem so hellen Bildnis des Heroen.[55] Aus dem dunklen Fleck macht Ovids Dido ein blutiges Mal: in den Wirren jener Kriegsnacht hat Aeneas seine Frau nicht einfach tragisch verloren; er überließ sie schlicht ihrem Schicksal – und geht mit dieser Geschichte noch stolz hausieren.

Aeneas' tragisch-grandiose Erzählung vom Fall Trojas in der *Aeneis* stürzt in sich zusammen wie die brennenden Mauern der Stadt: die Rettung des Anchises und der Hausgötter ist billige Erfindung; Kreusa aber hat er bewußt dem Untergang ausgeliefert. Vernichtender könnte das Urteil über das hehre Heldenbild des Epos kaum ausfallen.[56] Doch Dido weiß ihre neue Sicht der Geschichte noch zu krönen: Den Himmel – so ihr impliziter Schluß – konnten diese Fabeln nicht täuschen, dieses Verbrechen blieb ihm nicht verborgen. Kein Wunder, daß die eigenen Götter Aeneas strafen und bereits sieben Jahre durch Länder und Meere verschlagen (87 f.). Die Odyssee des römischen Stammvaters wird zur von Roms Stammesgottheiten verhängten Strafexpedition für den feigen Verrat an der Gattin.[57]

In dem melancholischen Monolog, der diesem Ausbruch folgt, konfrontiert Dido Aeneas' Untaten (im doppelten Sinne: unterlassene wie begangene) mit den eigenen Verdiensten. Sie hat Aeneas in seiner Not großherzig aufgenommen und ihm gleichsam ihr Reich angetragen. Hätte sie es doch nur dabei bewenden lassen (89–92).[58] Schaudernd vergegenwärtigt sie sich jene verhängnisvolle Stunde in der Grotte (93–96). Bei aller Nähe zur *Aeneis*

Sohn um Schonung (75; vgl. 161). – Anders DÖPP 34: «Der Sinn des ganzen Unternehmens sei in Frage gestellt, wenn Aeneas sich jetzt leichtfertig in Gefahr begebe.» Wer aber alles so unbesonnen aufs Spiel setze, müsse ein Lügner sein (so die Überleitung zum folgenden Argument).

[54] 83–85 *si quaeras, ubi sit formosi mater Iuli, / occidit a duro sola relicta uiro. / haec mihi narraras et me mouere.* – J. DIGGLE (CQ 61, 1967, 139) begreift Vers 85 anders: «You told me this story and its effect was not lost on me (i.e. aroused my suspicions).» (so auch KNOX *ad loc.*).

[55] *Aen.* 2,735–794 (dieser Verlust sollte den Weg freimachen für Aeneas' spätere Heirat mit Lavinia). – Eine frühe kritische Stimme e. g. Tib. Claudius Donatus *ad loc.* (I 247,2 ff. Georgii).

[56] Die Moral dieser Geschichte – «Women are not a priority for this fate-driven hero. The queen of Carthage has no reason to expect better treatment than Creusa had received.» – habe die Dido der *Aeneis* nicht begriffen – im Gegensatz zur Dido Ovids (so DESMOND 61).

[57] Wie JACOBSON 89 betont, ein scharfes Argument: wer sieben Jahre durch die Welt irre, der erfreue sich göttlichen Geleits (vgl. 141 f.)? – Wo die epische Dido in epikureischem Geiste ein Eingreifen der Götter abstreitet (4,376–380: die Götter sorgen sich nicht um Menschendinge), betont sie hier die strafende Gewalt der Götter (vgl. ADAMIETZ 130).

[58] *Aen.* 1,572–574 bietet Dido Aeneas' Männern einen Teil ihres Reiches an, nachdem sie den Namen des Heros gehört hat. In den *Heroides* bietet sie es ihm persönlich an (90) – «interested in stressing her kindness to Aeneas personally» (JACOBSON 87). Vgl. auch DÖPP 36 f.

fällt jedoch eine Abweichung ins Auge: im Epos weiß der auktoriale Erzähler vom Unheil jener ‹Hochzeit›, nicht aber die hochgemute Dido. Bei Ovid hingegen ist nun Dido zu dieser Einsicht gelangt (vgl. 4,169f. *ille dies primus leti primusque malorum / causa fuit* und das Echo 93 *illa dies nocuit*).[59]

Deshalb weiß sie auch, daß die bereits bei Vergil unheimlich gestimmte Hochzeitsmusik der Nymphen, die mehr ‹heulen› denn ‹jauchzen› (4,168 *ululârunt ... Nymphae*), sich endgültig ins Düstere gekehrt hat (95 f.):

«Eine Stimme hatte ich vernommen; ich glaubte, Nymphen heulten –
die Eumeniden verkündeten im Zeichen mein Schicksal!»[60]

Diese Passage ist von entscheidender Bedeutung. Von den Eumeniden (bzw. Erinnyen) ist in der *Aeneis* einmal die Rede, und zwar im Gleichnis. Zu Didos todesträchtigen Omina gehören dort Alpträume, ähnlich denen, die den «von Sinnen gekommenen Pentheus» (4,469 *demens ... Pentheus*) oder den «gehetzten Orest» (4,471 *agitatus Orestes*) verfolgen – Wahnbilder eigener Schuld und göttlicher Rache, verkörpert von Eumeniden und Diren (4,465–473). In ihnen spiegeln Didos Schuldgefühle sich ebenso wie die beginnende innere Auflösung.[61] Was im Epos also subtiles Symbol bleibt für Didos seelische Verfassung, hinter der die göttliche Heimsuchung dunkel durchschimmert, wird in den Augen der elegischen Heroine bittere Realität: es waren wirklich die Eumeniden – die von Anfang an als Unstern über dem Liebesbund standen. Vom ersten fatalen Schritt an lag ihr Schicksal in der Hand mißgünstiger Mächte, die sie dem Verderben weihten – ein Verderben, dem sie nicht entkommen konnte. Die Schlüsselszene der epischen Romanze wird radikal neu gewichtet.[62]

Doch zu der Schuld, die eine höhere Gewalt ihr verkündet, bekennt Dido sich reumütig (97f.). Sie ist schuldig geworden an ihrer «Keuschheit» (97 *pudor*), d.h. an dem mit heiligem Eid beteuerten Versprechen, einzig einem Mann zu gehören,[63] an ihrem guten «Ruf» (97a *nec ad cineres fama retenta meos*, «und mein Ruf, den ich nicht reinhielt bis zu meinem Tod»), an ihren «Ahnen» (97b *mei manes*), v.a. aber am toten Sychaeus, zu dem sie nun «voller Scham» (98 *plena pudoris*) heimkehrt.[64]

Denn gleichsam aus dem Jenseits heraus zieht dieser letzte Vers Dido hinab in die Sphäre des Todes. Im Schrein, den sie Sychaeus' Angedenken errichtete, ruft sie der Verstorbene (99–102). Auf dieses eine Vorzeichen verdichtet sich die Vielzahl düsterer Omina bei Vergil (*Aen.* 4,452–473). Wo aber das Epos gerade jenes Omen in vages Dunkel taucht (nur von

---

[59] Vgl. DÖPP 38f.; DESMOND 62.
[60] 95f. *audieram uocem: nymphas ululasse putaui; / Eumenides fati signa dedere mei.*
[61] «Die Traumängste Didos sind wie die Wahnängste des Pentheus und des Orestes, die beide zur Strafe für ihre Sünden die Rachegöttinnen leibhaftig zu sehen vermeinen. (...) Da wird es vollends klar, daß Schuld und Gewissen ins Spiel getreten sind.» (KLINGNER 453).
[62] Angesichts dessen wirkt es fast rührend, wenn sie einen Moment lang das Rad zurückdrehen und die ganze Affäre ungeschehen machen möchte. – In der Zuspitzung dieses Motivs tritt die Erinnye als veritable Brautjungfer auf (e.g. Ov. *her.* 2,117 *pronuba Tisiphone thalamis ululauit in illis*; 6,43–46; Ps.-Sen. *Oct.* 23f. *illa, illa meis tristis Erinys / thalamos Stygios praetulit ignes*; 257–269).
[63] *Aen.* 4,24–29, bes. 27 *ante, pudor, quam te uiolo aut tua iura resoluo*.
[64] Während Dido im Epos sich insgeheim und ernstlich über ihre Schuld Rechenschaft ablegt, schmiedet sie die Schuld hier zum fast sophistischen Argument gegen Aeneas: Von ihm getäuscht (und für ihn) habe sie alles auf sich genommen. Nicht sie habe ihre *fides* gegen Sychaeus verraten – Aeneas habe seine *fides* ihr gegenüber gebrochen (ADAMIETZ 128).

rätselhaften Stimmen und Worten ist die Rede), wird Ovid zweifach konkret: in Zahl (101 *quater*, «viermal») und Wortlaut (102 *Elissa, ueni!*, «Elissa, komm!»).[65] Und Dido sichert Sychaeus nicht nur zu, ihm zu folgen (103f.) – sie sucht bei ihm (der ihr ohnehin – auf den Spuren von *Aen.* 6,473f. – den Fehltritt großmütig zu vergeben scheint) Verständnis zu wecken für den Eidbruch (105–110). Ihre Schuld war läßlich, fiel sie doch einem «edlen Verführer» (105 *idoneus auctor*) in die Hände,[66] dessen göttliche Abkunft und bewährte *pietas* ihr Vertrauen einflößten. Sie war sich gewiß, seinen Adel und seine «Verläßlichkeit» (oder «Treue», 110 *fidem*) werde er auch ihr gegenüber beweisen und ihr «Gatte bleiben, wie es sich geziemt» (108 *spem mihi mansuri rite dedere uiri* – eine nebenbei bemerkt nicht unpikante Feststellung gegenüber ihrem wirklichen Gatten, der dies zudem auch gerne geblieben wäre). Im Grunde trifft sie keinerlei Schuld – weder Sychaeus noch den Göttern gegenüber; sie war – und bleibt stets – das Opfer böser Verhängnisse.

Wie um ihre Unschuld biographisch zu begründen, reflektiert Dido das Unglück, das den Grundton zu ihrem Leben gab – und bis zuletzt geben wird (wieder klingt das Leitmotiv eines gewaltsamen Endes an; 111–128).[67] Wir hören von Sychaeus' Ermordung, von der gefahrvollen Flucht aus Tyros, von der Gründung Karthagos inmitten kriegslüsterner Völker und ehelüsterner Freier. Stets trägt sie die Farben satter auf als Vergil: Sychaeus etwa wird zum Schlachtopfer am Altar; oder als wolle sie mit Leporellos Registerarie konkurrieren, fabuliert sie von «tausend Freiern» (123 *mille procis placui*), die sie Aeneas zuliebe verschmäht habe (chronologisch ein Ding der Unmöglichkeit; wie wir aus *Aen.* 4,35–38 wissen, ging dieses Werben der Ankunft der Troer voraus)[68] – und die sich nun bitter über Didos Gattenwahl beklagten.[69]

Doch ihr dramatischer Ton hat gute Gründe: von der See wie vom Land her sieht sie sich von Feinden umringt – denen Aeneas' Aufbruch sie nun unweigerlich in die Hände spielt. Schon im Epos befürchtet sie, nach der Abfahrt der Troer könne ihr Bruder Karthago einnehmen, oder Häuptling Iarbas werde sie als Gefangene fortführen (*Aen.* 4,325f.). Im Brief führt sie Aeneas noch anschaulicher vor Augen, was er ihr antut: wo das kurze Glück mit ihm sie die unselige Vergangenheit und die unsichere Gegenwart vergessen ließ, wirft seine Flucht sie um so ärger ins vertraute Unheil zurück. Warum kröne er nicht sein Unrecht und liefere sie – so die höhnische Schlußfolgerung – Iarbas aus, oder gleich ihrem blutrünstigen Bruder?

Zumal der Mann, der Dido ohne Zögern dem sicheren Verderben überantwortet, beiden sehr wohl das Wasser reichen kann. Die «ruchlose Hand» ihres Bruders (127 *manus impia*)

---

[65] Diese taghelle Eindeutigkeit raubt dem Omen freilich fast alle Kraft. Soll Vergils dunkles Geheimnis entzaubert werden?

[66] KNOX *ad loc.* verweist auf die Doppelbödigkeit der Junktur: hinter der ‹angesehenen Autoritätsperson› (vgl. *fast.* 2,543 *Aeneas, pietatis idoneus auctor*) komme der ‹vertrauenswürdige Autor› zum Vorschein – Vergil.

[67] Vgl. JACOBSON 80; ADAMIETZ 128f.: In der *Aeneis* blickt Dido stolz auf das von ihr Erreichte zurück. Bei Ovid erscheint ihr ganzes Dasein eine einzige Kette von Leiden: ein Kreuzweg.

[68] Zumindest atmosphärisch trifft Ovid damit den Nerv der epischen Erzählung. Dort fürchtet Dido den Haß der Berberfürsten, den sie um Aeneas' willen auf sich gezogen habe (*Aen.* 4,320f.); und in Iarbas' Worten klingt unüberhörbar die Eifersucht des verschmähten Liebhabers durch (4,213f.).

[69] Das Modell liefert hier vielleicht der hellenistische Liebesroman, bes. Charitons *Kallirhoe*. Auch um Kallirhoe balgt sich ein ganzes Rudel offizieller Freier. Erst als der Außenseiter Chaireas das Mädchen gewinnt, schmiedet der gemeinsame Haß auf Kallirhoe und ihren Gemahl das Rudel zum mörderischen Komplott zusammen.

kehrt für Dido zurück in der «ruchlosen Rechten» des Aeneas (130 *impia dextra*). Mit anderen Worten: nur wenig unterscheidet den einstigen Gattenmörder vom baldigen Mörder der ‹Gattin› (129–132):⁷⁰

> «Lege die Götter nieder, und das Kultgerät, das deine Berührung entweiht!
> Schlecht huldigt eine ruchlose Rechte den Himmlischen.
> Warst du den Göttern, die den Flammen entkamen, als Verehrer erkoren,
> reut es die Götter, daß sie den Flammen entkamen.»

Mit Aeneas' *pietas*, die sich gerade im Angesicht der Götter bewähre, ist es nicht weit her: sein Verrat an Dido disqualifiziert ihn als Hohenpriester seines Volkes. Das zweite Distichon bietet dabei mitnichten einen matten Aufguß des ersten⁷¹ – stilistisch raffiniert verpackt, serviert es einen so witzigen wie hintersinnigen Scherz: witzig, weil die Stammgötter Roms lieber sterben wollen als von einem Taugenichts wie Aeneas umsorgt werden; hintersinnig, weil Götter *per definitionem* eher selten zu Tode kommen – und hier zudem durchklingt, im Falle des Aeneas habe es ihnen an der nötigen Weitsicht gemangelt. – Verschlagener könnte ein Angriff auf die programmatische Kardinaltugend des *pius Aeneas* kaum ausfallen.

Sein ärgstes Vergehen gegen die *pietas* ist ihm dabei womöglich nicht einmal bewußt. Abrupt wechselt Dido vom Höchsten, dem Reich der Himmlischen, zum Intimsten (133–138):⁷²

> «Vielleicht läßt du sogar eine schwangere Dido sitzen, du Unmensch,
> und ein Teil von dir lebt tief verborgen in meinem Leib. (…)»

Dido ist womöglich guter Hoffnung; dann aber wäre ihr gemeinsames Kind ebenso dem Untergang geweiht wie die Mutter (einen Gedanken, den sie in zwei weiteren Distichen rhetorisch eskalieren läßt). Im Epos träumt Dido einen zärtlichen Augenblick lang davon, als süße Erinnerung bliebe ihr «ein kleiner Aeneas» (*Aen.* 4,327–330).⁷³ Ovids Dido schmiedet diesen Traum zur Waffe um: sie könnte sehr wohl schwanger sein – und würde das Ungeborene unausweichlich mit in den Tod nehmen, in den Aeneas sie treibt. Nicht *ein* Mord beflecke dann sein Gewissen, sondern gleich ein Doppelmord – noch dazu am eigenen Blut.⁷⁴

Wie aber steht es mit der angeblichen göttlichen Mission, mit der Aeneas seinen Verrat entschuldigt (139–142)?:⁷⁵

> «‹Doch ein Gott mahnt zum Aufbruch!› – Hätte er dir doch verboten zu kommen!
> Hätten niemals Teukrer punischen Boden betreten!
> Ja: während dieser Gott dich führt, wirst du zum Spielball widriger Winde,
> und vergeudest endlose Zeit auf stürmischer See?»

---

⁷⁰ 129–132 *pone deos et quae tangendo sacra profanas: / non bene caelestes impia dextra colit. / si tu cultor eras elapsis igne futurus, / paenitet elapsos ignibus esse deos.*
⁷¹ So quasi alle Interpreten; zuletzt KNOX *ad loc.*
⁷² 133 f. *forsitan et grauidam Dido, scelerate, relinquas, / parsque tui lateat corpore clausa meo.*
⁷³ Bald nach Aeneas' Ankunft fragt Anna ihre Schwester in einem sinnigen Hysteron-Proteron, ob sie allezeit auf «süße Kinder» und «die Freuden der Venus» verzichten wolle (4,33 *nec dulcis natos Veneris nec praemia noris?*).
⁷⁴ Vgl. DÖPP 43; ANDERSON 63; VOIT 346 f. (der Didos Mutmaßung freilich für bare Münze nimmt).
⁷⁵ 139–142 ‹*sed iubet ire deus.*› *uellem uetuisset adire, / Punica nec Teucris pressa fuisset humus! / hoc duce nempe deo uentis agitaris iniquis / et teris in rabido tempora longa freto.*

Dies ist das einzige Mal in der gesamten Epistel, daß Dido nach bewährtem rhetorischen Muster Aeneas zu Wort kommen läßt.[76] Doch die vier Worte, die sie ihm als Stenogramm seiner langen Rede im Epos[77] zugesteht, zeitigen eine unerwartete Wirkung: das Gefühl, seinen faulen Ausreden schon viel zu lange gelauscht zu haben; bessere Gründe wisse der Schelm nicht vorzubringen. Vor allem aber trägt sie seine Entschuldigung – den angeblichen göttlichen Auftrag – nur vor, um sie sogleich vom Tisch zu fegen, rhetorisch (hätten seine Götter ihn doch von Karthago ferngehalten!),[78] vor allem aber theologisch. Die Endlosigkeit seiner Sendung spreche dem Segen hohn, unter dem die troische Mission ihm zufolge stehe. Damit variiert und erweitert Dido ihren Einfall, die siebenjährige Irrfahrt zur göttlichen Strafe für Kreusas Tod umzudeuten (87f.). Nie stand der Heros den Göttern ferner (vgl. 129–132); die Ironie seiner Geschichte sucht ihresgleichen.

Eine solche Odyssee würde Aeneas nicht einmal auf sich nehmen, stünde ihm die Heimkehr in ein unversehrtes Troja offen (143f.).[79] So aber jage er einem Phantom nach, statt die Größe ihres Geschenks zu begreifen und Karthago zur Heimat zu erwählen. Warum in die Ferne schweifen, wenn das Gute liegt so nah: eine herrliche Stadt, Reichtümer, Macht, und Raum genug für heroische Taten – auch für Ascanius (145–156).[80]

Nun kommt ein großer Moment in ihrem Brief – der sich nach den bösen Angriffen um so lichter abhebt. Besiegelt von Gelübde und Gebet im Namen der Venus, des Eros und der troischen Hausgötter, spricht Dido eine feierliche Beschwörung (157–168): Aeneas' Volk und Familie mögen in Friede und Glück leben. Nur ihr Haus soll er verschonen! Denn welchen Vergehens zeihe er sie – es sei denn ihrer Liebe? (164 *quod crimen dicis praeter amasse meum?*) Didos Logik ist kaum zu erschüttern: sie hat Aeneas nichts Böses getan; sie entstammt auch nicht wie Achill oder Agamemnon dem Volk seiner Erzfeinde.[81] Sie hat ihn nur geliebt.

Diese in der Sekundärliteratur bislang kaum beachtete Passage ist bedeutsam, denn in ihr findet Didos fataler Fluch in der *Aeneis* (4,607–629) sein genaues Gegenstück. Bei Vergil wünscht die Königin Aeneas den baldigen Tod und beschwört ewige Feindschaft zwischen beiden Völkern herauf. Bei Ovid überhäuft sie ihn und sein Volk mit Segenswünschen – im Namen seiner huldvollen Götter (129ff. scheinen vergessen). Im Gegenzug erbittet sie nur eines: ‹Verschone mein Haus – das ohnehin dir gehört!› Doch der Sinn dieses unschuldigen (und dezent vorgetragenen) Wunsches tritt in den folgenden Versen nach und nach zutage. Sie habe sich nur *ein* Vergehen vorzuwerfen: ihre Liebe.[82] Und die sei mehr als genügsam. Sie muß nicht seine Gattin sein; sie bescheide sich mit der Rolle der Gastgeberin – solange sie die seine ist.[83]

---

[76] Zuvor legt Dido ihm einmal ein fiktives Zitat in den Mund (71).
[77] *Aen.* 4,333ff., bes. 356–359. – Vers 139 faßt ironisch-höhnisch die ganze Szene Iuppiter – Merkur – Aeneas zusammen (Döpp 25; vgl. ebd. 43f.).
[78] Bereits in der *Aeneis* greift Dido dieses Argument sarkastisch an: ‹Aber ja – Götterboten!› (4,376–380).
[79] Das gleiche Argument, jedoch stumpfer, findet sich bereits *Aen.* 4,311–313. – Lt. ADAMIETZ 130 beginnt mit Vers 143 der Schlußteil des Briefes – eine Art *peroratio*, die noch einmal wesentliche Argumente bündelt.
[80] Vgl. JACOBSON 88f.
[81] Von solcher ‹Sippenhaft› spricht sich bereits die Dido des Epos frei (*Aen.* 4,425–427).
[82] Vgl. DÖPP 51ff. – Zu Didos Fluch vgl. jetzt auch SCHMIDT 131f.
[83] Ein merklicher Bruch mit der Dido der *Aeneis*, die am Scheitern ihrer ‹Ehe› verzweifelt (*Aen.* 4,323f. 431), aber auch jeden Gedanken an eine ‹Nebenrolle› bitter von sich weist (4,537–539: sie will Aeneas nicht als Kebse folgen). Vgl. DÖPP 46–49; JACOBSON 81; 89.

Ungeachtet der harmlosen Rhetorik will Dido nur eines – daß Aeneas bleibt, mit anderen Worten: der ihre bleibt.

Doch wo sie eben noch davon zu träumen scheint, Aeneas könne auf immer ihr Leben teilen, findet Dido nun fast übergangslos zur Nüchternheit zurück. Als wisse sie um die Vergeblichkeit ihrer Beschwörung, bittet sie im folgenden Passus nur noch um einen Aufschub der Abreise (169–180; der wäre immerhin ein erster Schritt zu ihrem Herzenswunsch).[84] Ohnehin hielten die Winterstürme die Schiffe am Strand fest (vgl. 41 ff.);[85] sobald der Frühling nahe (vgl. 49 f.), werde Aeneas auslaufen (173 f.):[86]

«Laß es meine Sache sein, auf das Wetter zu achten! Sicherer wirst du reisen.
Und auch wenn du es wolltest – ich selbst werde dir nicht gestatten zu bleiben!»

Er möge also noch bleiben (179 f.),[87]

«bis das Meer sich beruhigt – und meine Liebe; bis ich durch Zeit und
Gewöhnung es tapfer erlerne, das Traurige zu ertragen.»

Schon vorher hat Dido Aeneas aufgefordert, nicht den Winterstürmen zu trotzen:
«Gönne der Wut des Meeres ein wenig Zeit – und deiner!»[88]

Dieser Vers kehrt nun in aufschlußreicher *variatio* wieder. Wo zunächst die Hoffnung regiert, mit dem wiederkehrenden Frühling werde auch Aeneas zu sanfter Sinnesart zurückfinden (mit anderen Worten: sich der Liebe ergeben), bleibt hier nur noch die bescheidene Bitte, er möge ihr Zeit lassen, damit *sie* sich an den Verlust gewöhne.

Dido drängt zum Ende (181 ff.). Sollte Aeneas ihr selbst diese bescheidene letzte Bitte abschlagen, sei sie willens zu sterben (183–186):[89]

«Könntest du doch sehen, was für ein Bild die Schreiberin bietet!
Ich schreibe, und in meinem Schoß liegt das troische Schwert,
und über die Wangen rollen meine Tränen auf die entblößte Klinge,
die statt Tränen bald – Blut tränken wird.»

Ein pathetisches Szenario: Dido in Tränen aufgelöst am Schreibtisch, in der Hand den Federkiel, im Schoß Aeneas' Waffe,[90] mit der sie – sollte sein erlösendes Wort ausbleiben –

---

[84] Vgl. Döpp 47–49.
[85] Dabei sind die Schiffe längst repariert, und die Mannschaft ersehnt die Abfahrt (vgl. Jacobson 78).
[86] 173 f. *tempus ut obseruem, manda mihi: certior ibis, / nec te, si cupies, ipsa manere sinam.* – Sollen wir sie hier ernstnehmen?
[87] 179 f. *dum freta mitescunt et amor, dum tempore et usu / fortiter edisco tristia posse pati.*
[88] 73 *da breue saeuitiae spatium pelagique tuaeque.*
[89] 183–186 *aspicias utinam quae sit scribentis imago! / scribimus, et gremio Troicus ensis adest, / perque genas lacrimae strictum labuntur in ensem, / qui iam pro lacrimis sanguine tinctus erit.* – Vgl. Döpp 49 f.
[90] Mit einem ähnlichen Szenario beginnt Canaces Brief (*her.* 11,3–6). – Daß ausgerechnet Aeneas' Schwert ihr Leben beendet, macht Sinn: es stellt (vielleicht auch in der latent sexuellen Metaphorik der Waffe) eine letzte, endgültige Verbindung zwischen den beiden her; zugleich ist das Schwert «a concrete symbol of the failure of their love and of the future enmity between their descendants» (Jacobson 82); und es unterstreicht Aeneas' Schuld an Didos Ende. – Dido stürzt sich nicht in die punische Prunkwaffe, die sie Aeneas schenkt (*Aen.* 4,261–264; so e. g. Quinn 148), sondern in sein altes trojanisches Schwert, um das sie ihn im Gegenzug bittet und das er bei der Abfahrt in ihrem Schlafgemach zurückläßt (4,495 *arma uiri thalamo quae fixa reliquit*; 4,507; 4,646 f. *ensemque recludit / Dardanium, non hos quaesitum munus in usus*; vgl. Heinze 143 Anm. 3). Für eine eindringliche Deutung dieses Waffentausches vgl. Schmidt 128–131.

ihrem Leben ein Ende setzen, oder (modern formuliert) einen anderen, tödlichen Text schreiben will – in ihrem Leib.[91] Wie, erfahren wir im übernächsten Distichon (189f.):[92]

> «Und nicht zum ersten Mal trifft jetzt eine Waffe meine Brust –
> längst klafft dort die Wunde rasender Liebe.»

Diese «Wunde» hat Dido sich bewußt für das Ende aufgespart. In der *Aeneis* erscheint sie gleich zu Beginn von Buch IV, als Metapher für die jäh über Dido hereinbrechende Leidenschaft (die erste Waffe war Amors Pfeil)[93] – um ganz am Ende des Buchs wiederzukehren, Fleisch geworden in Didos tödlicher Verletzung, die Aeneas' Schwert schlägt (4,689 *infixum stridit sub pectore uulnus*).

Das ist nun weder ein «trivialer, wahrscheinlich interpolierter Gemeinplatz», noch «einer der niveaulosesten Verse in Ovids gesamtem Werk», wie zwei wohlmeinende Exegeten urteilen.[94] Indem Ovid beide Passagen verschmilzt, tritt bei ihm zutage, was deren großer Abstand bei Vergil subtil verbirgt: daß metaphorische und physische Wunde am selben Ort sitzen – «*sub pectore*». Dank dieser (zugegebenermaßen expliziten) Figur bringt Dido beide Ebenen bewußt zur Deckung und verhilft der Metapher zur Materialität – das Bild wird gleichsam lebendig und tritt aus dem Text heraus. In diese «rasende Leidenschaft» (190 *saeui ... amoris*) war die tödliche Verletzung von Anfang an eingeschrieben – Dido konnte sie nicht überleben.[95]

Der eigentliche Selbstmord bleibt in der *Aeneis* ausgespart. Wir hören Didos letzte Worte – und sehen sie dann (durch die Augen ihrer Dienerinnen) ins blutige Schwert sinken.[96] Ähnliches geschieht hier; wieder spart der Text den tödlichen Augenblick aus. Wir sehen Dido todeswillig am Schreibtisch, die Waffe zur Hand – um als nächstes (und zugleich letztes) ihre Worte an ihre Schwester Anna zu hören,[97] der sie ihre Bestattung ans Herz legt, und das abschließende Urteil über ihr Schicksal (191–196). Auf dem marmornen Grabmal, das ihre Asche bergen wird, soll die Nachwelt nicht lesen «Elissa, Sychaeus' Frau» (193 *Elissa Sychaei*), sondern jenes «Epigramm» (194 *carmen*), das Didos Leben wie Didos Brief beschließt:[98]

> «Den Todesgrund und das Schwert gab Aeneas;
> zu Tode kam Dido durch eigene Hand.»

---

[91] Ähnlich FARRELL 335f., der auf die symbolischen Entsprechungen von Schreiben und Bluten, von Feder und Schwert in der Schlußpassage verweist. Fließend geht der Akt des Schreibens in den Freitod über.

[92] 189f. *nec mea nunc primum feriuntur pectora telo; / ille locus saeui uulnus amoris habet* (eine verwandte Formel Ps.-Sen. *Oct.* 651f. *non hoc primum pectora vulnus / mea senserunt: graviora tuli*; s. auch Sen. *dial.* 11,15,4 *graviore multo animi vulnere quam postea corporis ictus est*).

[93] *Aen.* 4,1f. *At regina graui iamdudum saucia cura / uulnus alit uenis et caeco carpitur igni*; 4,67 *tacitum uiuit sub pectore uulnus*; vgl. das Hindinnen-Gleichnis 4,68–73, in dem ein «tödlicher Pfeil» (4,73 *letalis harundo*) die Hindin trifft.

[94] PALMER *ad* 189f.: «a trivial and commonplace distich, which interrupts the thought: probably spurious»; JACOBSON 82: «one of the most bathetic lines in all his work».

[95] Vgl. DESMOND 64. – Bereits Vergil deutet im Hindinnen-Gleichnis das tödliche Ende der Geschichte an (vgl. Anm. 93).

[96] *Aen.* 4,663ff. Vgl. HEINZE 143f.

[97] Didos Anrede (191 *meae male conscia culpae*) macht deutlich, daß sie Annas Verstrickung in ihren Untergang weit klarer sieht als im Epos.

[98] 195f. *praebuit Aeneas et causam mortis et ensem / ipsa sua Dido concidit usa manu* (Ovid zitiert dieses Distichon erneut *Fasti* 3,549f.; vgl. das Grabepigramm der Phyllis *her.* 2,147f. *Phyllida Demophoon leto dedit hospes amantem; / ille necis causam praebuit, ipsa manum*). – In der Unterwelt fragt Aeneas ungläubig Didos Schatten (*Aen.* 6,458): *funeris heu tibi causa fui?* Hier liest er die Antwort (KNOX *ad* 195).

Der letzte Adressatenwechsel des Briefs schließt Aeneas bewußt aus; nur noch gebrochen bekommt er mit, wie Dido sich auf ihr Ende vorbereitet (das unerbittlich kommen wird, wenn nicht er dem Verhängnis ins Rad greift), und was ihr Grabmal künftigen Geschlechtern über ihn verraten wird: Dido starb den Freitod (ein Zeugnis ihres Mutes wie ihrer Verzweiflung), in den Aeneas sie trieb.[99]

Schon die flüchtige Lektüre läßt ahnen, wie eng Didos Brief an die *Aeneis* anschließt – so eng, daß er ohne *Aeneis* schlechterdings unverständlich bleiben muß.[100] Er bringt aber genug Neues ins Spiel, daß klar wird: es geht um anderes, um mehr als simple *imitatio* oder einen Wettstreit um die überzeugendere Dido. Ovid setzt sich mit Vergil ernsthaft auseinander.

Wie läßt dieser Brief sich nun lesen?[101] Beginnen wir mit einer Äußerlichkeit – der Chronologie. Wann entsteht er? Wo genau im 4. Buch der *Aeneis* ist er anzusiedeln? Fast alle Interpreten denken an die Szene, in der Dido den zur Abfahrt rüstenden Troern zuschaut und verzweifelt Anna zu Aeneas schickt, um eine letzte kleine Frist zu erwirken.[102] Das ist richtig. Wir können aber noch präziser werden. Denn offenbar hat Ovid einen ganz bestimmten Augenblick im Sinn – jene Stelle, an der Vergil (was äußerst selten geschieht) eine seiner Figuren in einer Apostrophe unmittelbar anspricht: «Was hast du da empfunden, Dido, als du dies bemerktest, wie hast du geseufzt, als du von der Höhe deiner Burg aus erkanntest, wie es die ganze Küste entlang wimmelte, als du mit deinen Augen sahst, wie unter heftigem Lärmen die Fläche des Meeres sich füllte! *usw.*»[103] An dieser Frage des epischen Erzählers bleibt Ovid hängen, in eben diesem Augenblick sieht er in Dido den Brief Gestalt gewinnen, der sich alsbald im Wachs niederschlagen wird.

Bei der ersten Lektüre wirkt ihr Brief tatsächlich wie eine spontane Ausgeburt jener Stunde, in der (wie bei der epischen Dido) Gedanken, Gründe, Vorwürfe in ihrem gequälten Sinn einander jagen.[104] Je genauer wir Didos Verse jedoch lesen (und das heißt vor allem: zwischen ihren Versen lesen), desto überlegter wirken sie. Ein wohldurchdachter Aufbau tritt zutage, der Argument, Appell, Polemik gekonnt plaziert und dosiert, wohleingebettet in eine üppige Vielfalt sprachlicher und stilistischer Mittel, wie den steten Wechsel zwischen dialogischen und monologischen Partien, oder die Anrede Dritter (Venus, Amor, Anna, Sychaeus), und insgesamt die reiche *variatio* in Tonfall und Stimmung, die Klage und Anklage, Vorwurf und Flehen, Dur und Moll geschickt ver-

---

[99] Daß nichts an die alte Ehe erinnern soll, ist wohl auch ihrer Scham geschuldet; doch vor allem soll nichts ablenken von der entscheidenden Botschaft.
[100] Diese Voraussetzung verkennen etliche ältere Deutungen. – An manchen Stellen kommt hinter *Aeneis* IV wie in einem Palimpsest ein anderes Modell zum Vorschein: das bereits für Vergil wichtige Epyllion Catull 64 (ein sprechendes Beispiel: Catull 64,171–176 ~ *Aen.* 4,657 f. ~ *her.* 7,139 f.); vgl. DÖPP 18–20.
[101] Ein eigenes Kapitel verdiente die wissenschaftliche Rezeption, in der bis in die 70er Jahre Unverständnis, ja vernichtende Kritik dominierten, e. g. bei WILKINSON (93 «argument after weary argument, conceit after strained conceit», usw.), JACOBSON (*passim*, e. g. 91 «tedious and shallow»), O.S. DUE (Ulysses and Aeneas in Ovid: C&M 48, 1997, 347–358; e. g. 352 «a disastrous failure» – ein Urteil, das freilich auf den Aufsatz zurückfällt). DRYDENS böses Urteil (zit. ANDERSON 56 f.) wirkte gerade im angelsächsischen Raum lange nach.
[102] Vgl. e. g. PALMER 339; ANDERSON 52 f. – Abwegig DESMOND 59: Dido schreibe unmittelbar vor ihrem Selbstmord. Da segeln die troischen Schiffe längst gen Italien.
[103] *Aen.* 4,408–415 *quis tibi tum, Dido, cernenti talia sensus, / quosue dabas gemitus?* eqs. Die Übersetzung stammt von V. EBERSBACH (P. Vergilius Maro, Aeneis. Aus dem Lateinischen von V. E., Leipzig 1982).
[104] E. g. VOIT 348: «ihre Rede (…), die ohne Plan assoziativ einen Gedanken an den anderen reiht».

webt – schwarz gerahmt, in klassischer Ringkomposition, vom Bild todesbereiter Verzweiflung.[105]

Bei alledem fällt auf, daß die Schreiberin zugleich eine bestimmte Grenze nie überschreitet: die zum Unkontrollierten, wo die Emotionen (gerade die dunklen) sich verselbständigen und ihren unbestechlich klaren Blick trüben. Dido bleibt stets Herrin ihrer selbst – ihrer Gefühle und ihrer Äußerungen.

Dieses Bild stören auch jene Passagen des Briefes nicht, in denen Dido sich selbst zu widersprechen scheint – wenn sie z.B. Aeneas erst als Ausgeburt wilder Naturgewalten schmäht, dann aber als Sohn der Venus umwirbt.[106] Denn diese inneren Widersprüche lassen sich auflösen. Weniger durch den Hinweis, daß sie sich bereits im Epos finden; denn dort entspringen sie unterschiedlichen Situationen und sind Indiz einer inneren Entwicklung Didos. Im Brief, der ein statisches Stimmungsbild einfängt, könnten sie allenfalls den Umstand spiegeln, daß auch in Didos Brust zwei Seelen wohnen. Wer freilich im Auge behält, wie sorgfältig sie ihren Brief entwirft, auf eine größtmögliche Wirkung bedacht, gelangt von der psychologischen unweigerlich zu einer rhetorischen Erklärung: solche ‹Widersprüche› sind nichts anderes als verborgene Appelle, die den Leser (Aeneas) beeinflussen, oder besser: lenken sollen. Im zitierten Beispiel hieße das: die wenig schmeichelhafte Naturgenealogie soll ihn anstacheln, ihr das Gegenteil zu beweisen; die göttliche Abstammung – noch dazu von Venus – soll ihn zu einer Sinnesart beflügeln, die der Göttin der Liebe alle Ehre macht.

So prägt den ganzen Brief rhetorische Kunstfertigkeit, die mitunter ans Kunststück rührt und die sich wappnet mit überzeugenden Argumenten; beides, Kunst wie Vernunft, zielt auf die überlegene Wirkung auf ein Gegenüber.[107] Wie verträgt sich aber ein solcher Befund mit der Lesart, der sich so gut wie alle Interpreten verschrieben haben: daß wir hier wirklich (wie der ‹Buchstabe› es will) der Königin Nacht- und Schwanensang lesen, ihr Testament und Epitaph, in dessen todesschwangere Finsternis sich nur ab und an ein Strahl der Hoffnung verirre? Anders gefragt: ist Dido wirklich vom ersten Distichon an ihres Endes gewiß, zum Sterben fest entschlossen?[108]

---

[105] Vgl. Döpp 22; Adamietz 132f.: die Gedankenführung des Briefes zeige ein bewußtes Vorgehen im Detail wie in der Gesamtanlage und suche eine intensive Wirkung beim Leser; Argumente, die auf Aeneas' eigene Interessen zielen, lösen sich ab mit moralisch-emotionalen Gründen. Ein insgesamt stimmiges Schema des Briefs bietet Kuhlmann 259.

[106] Bei drei Themen v.a. handhabt Ovids Dido ihre Argumente mit fast sophistischer Mundfertigkeit: bei Aeneas' Abstammung (von rohen Naturmächten 37–39; von Venus 31f. 157), seinem Verhältnis zu den Göttern (als Privileg 77f. 107. 157ff.; als Katastrophe 79ff. 129ff.) und ihren kriegerischen Nachbarn (als Heimsuchung 121ff.; als ‹Heldenfutter› 153ff.).

[107] Vgl. Anderson 53. So *malgré lui* auch Jacobson 89: Was die Qualität der Argumente angehe, übertreffe dieser Brief Didos Reden im Epos; *her.* 7 sei am ehesten eine Suasorie in Versen, denn von Anfang bis Ende suche Dido Aeneas mit einer endlosen Folge von Argumenten zu überzeugen. – Diesen Eindruck unterstreicht auch die Beobachtung von Farrell 311–317 (vgl. Knox 25), der gewissermaßen ovidische Theorie und Praxis miteinander vergleicht und die *Heroides* im Licht der Ratschläge liest, die Ovid in der *Ars* zum Abfassen von Liebesbriefen gibt. In der Tat erachtet Ovid es für rechtens, ja notwendig, das im Brief umworbene Gegenüber mit aller Macht der Rhetorik für sich einzunehmen – auch mit unlauteren Mitteln wie Lügen oder falschen Versprechungen. Die Polarität eines ‹verlogenen männlichen› und eines ‹aufrichtigen weiblichen› Schreibens, die Farrell aus der *Ars* herausdestilliert und auf die *Heroides* projiziert, findet dort m.E. freilich kein Fundament.

[108] So e.g. Döpp 21; Knox 202f. Eine optimistische Position vertritt nur Anderson (bes. 55: «She does not die in Ovid's drama»). Das offene Ende des Dido-Briefes betont zurecht Walde 131.

Zugunsten dieser Lesart wird vor allem Didos leitmotivische Todesbeschwörung ins Feld geführt, die sich vom Schwanensang der ersten Verse bis zum Abschied von Anna spannt und gerade im Grabepigramm des letzten Distichons den Ton bestimmt (in diesen Versen finden etliche Interpreten den Schlüssel zu Didos späterem Schicksal). Doch just auf diese Wirkung hin ist der Brief samt Epilog ja kalkuliert und komponiert: er soll den Leser (Aeneas) überzeugen von Didos Bereitschaft, ihr Leben zu opfern. Denn das Pathos des überhitzten Schlußbildes wird der Situation nur bedingt gerecht: noch weilt Aeneas ja in Karthago – und hat den Brief nicht einmal gelesen.

Aufschlußreich ist nicht zuletzt der hoch-reflektierte Blick in den Spiegel, in dem Dido aus der Rolle der epischen Tragödin heraustritt und sich im Akt des Schreibens präsentiert. Diese Inszenierung einer *scribentis imago* (183)[109] läßt uns (ungewollt? oder mit Bedacht?) ahnen, daß Ovids Dido das Rührstück in ihren Worten erschafft, indem sie (sich ihrer Wirkung wohl bewußt) sich selbst dramatisiert – im Gegensatz zur Dido Vergils, die eine genuin tragische Situation durchlebt und ihren Entschluß zum Freitod allen verheimlicht (insbesondere Anna) – um ihn desto entschiedener in die Tat umzusetzen.[110]

Gerade auf dieses Ende des vierten *Aeneis*-Buches freilich beruft sich die pessimistische Lesart und führt an, im Epos sterbe Dido ja wirklich – was der Leser der *Siebten Heroide* wisse und erwarte. Ja just auf diesem Spiel beruhe zu einem Gutteil die dramatische Wirkung des Briefes: daß Dido ein letztes Mal alle Höhen und Tiefen des Liebens koste – um sich schlußendlich ihre völlige Desillusionierung einzugestehen und den Schlußstrich zu ziehen.[111]

Doch ist diese Deutung zwingend? Der Leser weiß es in der Tat – nämlich der reale Leser, der die *Heroides* (und die *Aeneis*) in Händen hält. Aber weiß es auch der seinen Seesack schnürende Aeneas, für den der Brief bestimmt ist? Oder, um das Argument weniger sophistisch zu formulieren: Anders als das Epos erzählt der Brief keine Geschichte; er läßt uns nicht wissen, was sich zutragen wird. Vom ersten bis zum Schlußvers führt Dido Regie; sie bestimmt ebenso das Geschehen wie den Text – dem wir als Leser auf Treu und Glauben ausgeliefert sind. Sie hat das letzte Wort.

Eines aber wissen wir: daß die schreibende Dido eindeutig lebt.[112] Und im Akt des Schreibens wendet sie sich stets aufs Neue an ihren Adressaten, als setze sie auf die Wirkung vernünftiger Argumente (selbst hartgesottene Skeptiker räumen dies ein).[113]

Wagen wir also den kleinen Schritt von der Annahme, Verzweiflung und Todesgewißheit seien die wahre Grundstimme, alles Hoffen und Werben nur ein trügerisches Interludium, zu der Mutmaßung, der entscheidende Tenor der Epistel sei der heilige Dreiklang Glaube, Hoffnung, Liebe, die tragische Koloratur hingegen nur manipulatorisches Instrument – insbesondere die Todesbilder am Beginn wie am Ende des Briefes, die signalisieren sollen, daß Höchstes auf dem Spiel stehe, die aber vor allem als warnende Geste gedacht

---

[109] Die Junktur ist quasi singulär. In der römischen Literatur erscheint sie nur noch einmal, bezeichnenderweise gleichfalls in den *Heroides* (11,5 *haec est Aeolidos fratri scribentis imago*; vgl. Anm. 90).

[110] Vgl. ANDERSON 55. – Auch zwei andere Heroinen Ovids lenken die Aufmerksamkeit auf ihr ‹Schreiben›: Canace (*her.* 11,1 ff.; vgl. Anm. 109) und Sappho (*her.* 15,1 ff.).

[111] Zugespitzt JACOBSON 84: Von Anfang an sei Dido zum Selbstmord entschlossen – und untergrabe schon deshalb ihre rhetorische Wirkung. Vgl. ADAMIETZ 132 f.: Nur deshalb gebe es im Brief immer wieder Momente der Hoffnung, damit Didos schlußendliche Desillusionierung um so plastischer zutage trete.

[112] Zudem vergeht zwischen dem dramatischen Zeitpunkt des Briefs (vgl. oben S. 87) und der Katastrophe im Epos noch eine gute Weile. Was geschieht in jenen Stunden, wenn Dido wirklich sterben will und soll?

[113] Vgl. Anm. 107.

sind.¹¹⁴ Anders gesagt: wir lesen ein Dokument, mit dem Dido überzeugen und gewinnen will – und überzeugen und gewinnen zu können glaubt. Warum aber sollte es ihrem Brief nicht gelingen, die Geschichte in ihrem Sinne um- und zuende zu schreiben?

Dieser Befund verträgt sich im Übrigen mit Ovids anderen Dido-Zeugnissen. Denn wo er festhält, daß die Königin zu Tode kommt, ist stets eindeutig von der Protagonistin des Epos die Rede (*rem.* 57f.; *met.* 14,78–81).¹¹⁵ Das gilt insbesondere für zwei aufschlußreiche Passagen, in denen er das Schlußepigramm von *her.* 7 zitiert, *verbatim* (*fast.* 3,545ff.), oder als gebrochenes Echo (*ars* 3,39f.).¹¹⁶ Denn auch diese beiden Passagen handeln von der epischen Figur, signalisieren aber zugleich Ovids Auffassung der Geschichte. Für deren fatalen Ausgang zieht er unmißverständlich Aeneas zur Rechenschaft.

Ein einziges Zeugnis scheint in die andere Richtung zu weisen, Ovids ‹Werkkatalog› in *Amores* 2,18, der den *Heroides* den Ehrenplatz zuweist (21–26). Dort spielt Ovid auch auf *her.* 7 an: er schreibe, «was, das gezückte Schwert in Händen, die arme Dido sagt» (25f. *quodque tenens strictum Dido miserabilis ensem / dicat*) – ein ernstes Bild, das unweigerlich den königlichen Freitod im Epos heraufbeschwört.¹¹⁷ Doch dieser erste Eindruck könnte täuschen – zumal Ovid wenige Zeilen zuvor diskret darauf hinweist, daß seine *Ars* und die *Heroides* unter dem Zeichen des heiteren Liebesgottes stehen (15 *risit Amor*). Zu fragen ist also, ob hier der reale Autor Auskunft gibt (vgl. 22 *scribimus*), oder ob er als Mundstück seiner fiktiven Autorin agiert (vgl. 26 *dicat*)? Die zweite Lesart besitzt unbestreitbare Vorzüge.

Damit sind wir bei einer Frage angelangt, die sich im Hintergrund schon lange aufdrängt: schreibt diesen Brief noch die Dido des Epos, oder führt eine andere Person die Feder? Die Frage ist fast rhetorisch – denn die Unterschiede zwischen den beiden Frauen springen dem Betrachter unweigerlich ins Auge. Die Dido Ovids ist lichter, heller charakterisiert als ihr epischer Zwilling. Sie ist klug und wohlartikuliert, ja eine meisterliche Rhetorikerin (was nebenbei die spannende Frage nach ihrem Bildungsweg in Tyros aufwirft),¹¹⁸ die das Wort bewußt als Werkzeug einsetzt (anders als die Dido des Epos, die die Wirkung ihrer Worte oder Taten nie kalkuliert).

---

[114] In diese Richtung weist bereits ADAMIETZ 131 (vgl. DÖPP 50): Das Schlußbild soll Aeneas rühren und sein Gewissen belasten, um eine Änderung seines Entschlusses zu bewirken.

[115] *Trist.* 2,533–536 spart Didos Ende aus und unterstreicht statt dessen die Verantwortung des Epikers für die tödliche Mesalliance: Vergil «legte in tyrische Pfühle Waffen und Mann» (2,534 *contulit in Tyrios arma uirumque toros*).

[116] *Ars* 3,39f. *et famam pietatis habet, tamen hospes et ensem / praebuit et causam mortis, Elissa, tuae*. Von Aeneas' Kardinaltugend bleibt allenfalls die *fama* übrig.

[117] So versteht es HELDMANN 202, der aus *am.* 2,18 so geistreiche wie spekulative Schlüsse zu den *Heroides* zieht. Den Phyllis- und den Didobrief betrachtet er als thematisches Paar: beide entstünden in ausweisloser Lage; zumal die beiden verwandten Grabepigramme an den Briefenden kündigten den bevorstehenden Freitod an. Und Sabinus' Antwortbriefe (als erste Stimme einer langen Wirkungsgeschichte läßt Ovids Freund den «lauteren Aeneas» zurückschreiben: 31 *iam pius Aeneas miserae rescripsit Elissae*) seien an zwei Tote gerichtet; dies belege für Phyllis Vers 32 *quodque legat Phyllis, si modo uiuit, adest*. Doch genau das bleibt in der Schwebe: «wenn sie denn lebt» (vgl. *her.* 10,75; *trist.* 4,3,20; die Junktur erscheint in der römischen Literatur nur an diesen drei Stellen). Ovid *weiß* es nicht.

[118] Einen nicht geringen Teil seines Humors gewinnt dieser Brief aus dem Antagonismus seiner ‹realistischen› Botschaft (Didos Liebesleid) und bewußter Verfremdungen (war eine punische Königin zehn Jahrhunderte vor Ovids Zeit überhaupt des Schreibens mächtig? und zudem eines so eleganten Lateins – in Versen statt in Prosa?). Sie erhöhen nicht nur den Reiz der Sache; sie warnen auch vor einer allzu ‹wörtlichen› Lektüre.

In einem losen Scherz in seiner *Ars* nennt Ovid vier Heroinen, die an ihrer arglosen Liebe zugrunde gingen – unter ihnen Dido. Ihnen fehlte, so seine Quintessenz, die ‹Kunst der Liebe› – wie eben er sie lehrt.[119] Von der Dido dieses Briefs gilt dies nicht mehr: sie hat die *Ars* gleichsam verinnerlicht. Sie zeigt sich reflektiert, ist sich ihres Denkens und Handelns bewußt, voller Einsicht in ihr Herz und ihren Passionsweg – anders als die impulsive, in ihren spontanen Ausbrüchen so ‹authentische› Dido Vergils. Sie sieht und begreift, was um sie herum, und vor allem, was mit ihr selbst geschieht – und beides beurteilt sie so eigenständig wie unbestechlich.

Der Energiequell, der Sinn ihres Daseins aber liegt in ihrer Hingabe an die Liebe. Sie bedeutet ihr mehr als ihr Ruf, ihre königliche Würde – oder die Treue dem verstorbenen Gemahl gegenüber.[120] Und zu dieser Liebe bekennt sie sich freimütig (anders als in der *Aeneis*, wo Dido ihr Herz nur der Schwester öffnet, und Aeneas gegenüber nur die winzigste Andeutung wagt, *Aen.* 4,429 *miserae ... amanti*).[121] Diese Liebe brennt mächtig – auch wenn ihr, wie sie selbst erkennt, deren dunkler Wiedergänger, der Haß, unbekannt bleibt (anders wieder die Dido des Epos, die alle Extreme des Gefühls auslotet).[122] Und Aeneas' Unvermögen zur Liebe bewirkt nur eines: daß *ihr* Lieben erstarkt, und sie für ihn gleichsam mitlieben will – ein Topos der erotischen Elegie, wie wir gesehen haben.

Jede Idee einer Schuld (etwa Sychaeus gegenüber), die sie im Epos in die Tiefe zieht wie ein Mühlstein, weist sie jetzt freimütig von sich. Eine so mächtige Liebe schafft ihr eigenes Gesetz – und kennt keine Reue. Schuldig (und töricht) ist einzig Aeneas, der eine solche Liebe in den Wind schlägt.

Diese neue Dido (die schreibt und denkt, als gehörten Ovids *Amores* zu ihrer bevorzugten Nachttischlektüre) löst die Geschichte unmerklich aus der Welt (und Weltsicht) der *Aeneis* heraus und läßt sie hinübergleiten in die Ära des frühen Prinzipats und den Kosmos der zeitgenössischen Elegie. Wie im Brennglas verdichtet das Drama sich ganz auf eine Frau, die liebt, und ihren kleinmütigen Geliebten.[123]

Dieser Kulissenwechsel erklärt manche markanten Züge des Briefes, die neues Licht auf die Geschichte fallen lassen. Denn während im Epos dieser ganze *amour fou* verdächtig körperlos bleibt, beinahe ätherisch, holt Ovids Dido ihn auf den Boden harter Tatsachen zurück. So klärt sie Aeneas (und uns) in klaren Worten darüber auf, was in jener ominösen Höhle vonstatten ging. Wo die *Aeneis* alles Augenmerk auf das symbolträchtige Naturschauspiel lenkt und Dido verschämt von «heimlicher Liebschaft» (4,171 *furtiuum ... amorem*) und «Ehe» (4,172 *coniugium*) murmelt, spricht sie im Brief freimütig von «Beischlaf»

---

[119] *Ars* 3,33–42, bes. 41 f. *quid uos perdiderit, dicam: nescistis amare; / defuit ars uobis: arte perennat amor* (vgl. *rem.* 55 ff.). Die anderen Heroinen sind Medea, Ariadne und Phyllis (sie alle figurieren auch in den *Heroides*).
[120] Hier freilich mit ADAMIETZ 134 von *insanus amor* zu sprechen, heißt den Bogen überspannen.
[121] Vgl. DÖPP 23.
[122] Das ist kaum der berechnende Akt, den ADAMIETZ 134 ihr unterstellt (Dido verzichte nur deshalb auf Haßgefühle, weil die «kontraproduktiv» seien). Verwandt ist eher die in den *Amores* beschriebene Geisteshaltung (3,11,33–35): *luctantur pectusque leue in contraria tendunt / hac amor, hac odium; sed, puto, uincit amor. / odero, si potero; si non, inuitus amabo.*
[123] Vgl. etwa ANDERSON 61 (deshalb wird Dido aber nicht notwendig zur «charmanten Kokotte»). – Die ‹Verfremdung der Form› kommt hinzu: das elegische Metrum markiert den Abstand zum epischen ‹Urtext› (vgl. DESMOND 59). WALDE 135 betont die Distanz der *Heroides* zur Elegie. Sie zeichneten ein Frauenbild, «das zwar Impulse aus der römischen Liebeselegie empfangen hat, das aber die Frauen aus deren Schematismus befreit und ihnen im Gegensatz zu den elegischen Geliebten Individualität und Tiefenschärfe, ja eine eigene Biographie gibt».

(92 *concubitu*).[124] Gleiches gilt für die Passage, in der sie, zum Entsetzen ganzer Philologengenerationen, Aeneas an seine mögliche Vaterschaft erinnert (133–138). Für die Dido Ovids ist Liebe auch etwas sehr Physisches – und mitunter hat sie Folgen.[125]

Die ihr eigene Tiefe gewinnt die neue Position aber dadurch, daß der Brief bewußt vor dem Hintergrund der *Aeneis* steht – und zu dieser bewußt Stellung bezieht. Manche Passagen wirken, als habe Dido das Epos mit dem *stilus* in der Hand gelesen und die wunden Punkte in Aeneas' und ihrem eigenen (alten) Denken und Handeln markiert.[126] Die (selten harmonische) Polyphonie der epischen Dido bündelt sie zu *einer* Stimme, die auch andere stichhaltige Argumente ins Feld führt, die sich aus der epischen Erzählung herausfiltern lassen, und die der latenten Misogynie, die in der *Aeneis* gelegentlich Laut gibt (zum Klassiker brachte es das bereits erwähnte Götterwort *uarium et mutabile semper femina*), eine betont weibliche Sicht der Dinge entgegensetzt.[127]

So geißelt sie die eigene Kurzsichtigkeit, die sie etwa das mahnende Beispiel Kreusas verkennen ließ, Aeneas' erstem Damenopfer zum Heile Roms (83–85).[128] Pikant ist gerade diese Episode, weil bereits Vergils Schilderung zarte Zweifel an Aeneas' Rolle durchschimmern läßt. Im Brief denkt Dido die Sache konsequent zu Ende: Aeneas hat Kreusa im brennenden Troja nicht einfach verloren – er hat sie feige im Stich gelassen.[129]

Vor allem aber kritisiert sie in immer neuen Volten den Standpunkt des Heroen. Denn da alles, was zwischen ihr und ihm geschehen ist, allein die private Sphäre berührt (in *ihren* Augen), kann sie Aeneas persönlich zur Rechenschaft ziehen. Und keine Entschuldigung läßt sie ihm durchgehen; sein göttlicher Auftrag, und damit seine Weltsicht, hinter denen er sich (in *ihren* Augen) versteckt, sind wenig mehr als das trügerische Hirngespinst eines Träumers.[130] Kurzum: Aeneas verhält sich verantwortungslos (seinem Sohn gegenüber), widerrechtlich (ihr gegenüber), unvernünftig (sich selbst gegenüber).[131]

---

[124] Vgl. KNOX 22.
[125] Vgl. KNOX ebd. (und zur Höhlenszene der *Aen.* jetzt auch SCHMIDT 122–124). – Für das ‹Entsetzen› der Philologen vgl. e. g. AUSTIN *ad Aen.* 4,329. – Das gleiche Motiv kehrt wieder *her.* 6,61 f. 119–122; 11,37–64.
[126] Von der die *Aeneis* ‹lesenden› Dido spricht DESMOND (vgl. KNOX 19). *In nuce* findet die Idee sich bereits bei DÖPP 25: Dido meine «den Aeneas des Epos – auf den sie sich mit Spott, Ironie, Verachtung bezieht». Diese kritische Dido sei im Grunde bereits im Epos angelegt, sympathetisch begleitet und zugleich bevormundet von der auktorialen Stimme des olympischen Erzählers. – In gewisser Weise trifft hier zu, was der Rhetoriker Gallio zu Ovids ostentativer Aneignung Vergils vermerkt: *Hoc autem dicebat Gallio Nasoni suo ualde placuisse; itaque fecisse illum quod in multis aliis uersibus Vergilii fecerat, non subripiendi causa, sed palam mutuandi, hoc animo ut uellet agnosci* (Sen. *suas.* 3,7).
[127] Vgl. oben S. 91. – Merkurs vielzitierte Definition des weiblichen Charakters unterstreicht seine Warnung vor Didos Tücke (*Aen.* 4,569 f.). Zu Ovids Antwort auf die latente Misogynie der *Aeneis* vgl. DESMOND 65.
[128] Für DESMOND 58 f. ist die Dido der *Aeneis* eine schlechte ‹Leserin›. Sie höre Aeneas' lange Erzählung (*Aen.* II/III), ohne deren Botschaft zu begreifen – Aeneas' göttliche Mission und historische Bestimmung: Italien. Ihr Blick verenge sich ganz auf ein ihr wohlvertrautes Leitmotiv: Aeneas' Leiden am Schicksal (*Aen.* 4,13 f. *heu, quibus ille / iactatus fatis!*).
[129] KNOX 21 f.
[130] Strenger geht nur noch Purcells Dido mit dem Heroen ins Gericht (*Thus on the fatal banks of Nile / weeps the deceitful crocodile*). – Eindeutig falsch ist das oft zu lesende Urteil, Dido *begreife* Aeneas' Mission nicht (e. g. JACOBSON 90 f.). Das gilt nur für die Dido des Epos, oder in den *Heroides* etwa für Briseis, die «keinerlei Verständnis für das Wertesystem Homers zeigt» (S. DÖPP, Werke Ovids, München 1992, 89).
[131] Vgl. DÖPP 25. – Das ist letztlich auch die Essenz der kameenhaften Skizze von *Aeneis IV* in *met.* 14,78–81: *excipit Aenean illic animoque domoque / non bene discidium Phrygii latura mariti / Sidonis inque pyra sacri sub imagine facta / incubuit ferro deceptaque decipit omnes.*

Diese Umdeutung der *Aeneis* aus dem Geiste des Eros fordert die Werte des Epos, wie *patria* und *pietas*, wie *fata* und *fides*, bewußt heraus. Aeneas' höchstes Gesetz, *ROMA*, kollidiert spiegelbildlich mit Didos höchstem Gesetz (und Schutzpatron), *AMOR*.[132] In letzter Konsequenz stellt sie damit das römische Reich in Frage. Denn – und das ist die Utopie, auf die ihr Brief im Verborgenen zielt: wäre Aeneas nur so vernünftig wie sie, teilte er ihren lebensklugen, weiblichen Blick auf die Welt, der seine Erfüllung im Eros findet – dann könnten beide leben, glücklich vereint für immer, in Karthago – und Rom wäre nie gegründet worden.[133]

Ob dies bereits die «pessimistische Lektüre» der *Aeneis* ist, die einem Interpreten zufolge mit Ovids *Siebter Heroide* beginnt, wäre zu diskutieren.[134] Auf alle Fälle aber wirft Didos Brief einen gewagt respektlosen Blick auf das Hohelied des neuen Prinzipats, und treibt ein so kühnes wie intelligentes Spiel mit der jungen Sonne am literarischen Himmel Roms.[135] Vergil hätte es vielleicht sogar goutiert. Im Fall des Augustus scheinen Zweifel angebracht.

Literatur (in Auswahl)

ADAMIETZ, J., Zu Ovids Dido-Brief: WJA 10, 1984, 121–134.
ANDERSON, W. S., The Heroides, in: J.W. Binns (Hrsg.), Ovid, London 1973, 49–83.
AUSTIN, R. G., P. Vergili Maronis Aeneidos Liber Quartus, Oxford 1955.
CAMPS, W. A., An introduction to Virgil's Aeneid, Oxford 1969.
DESMOND, M., When Dido reads Vergil. Gender and intertextuality in Ovid's Heroides 7: Helios 20, 1993, 56–68.
DÖPP, S., Virgilischer Einfluß im Werk Ovids, Diss. Universität München 1968, 17–55.
FARRELL, J., Reading and writing the Heroides: HSCP 98, 1998, 307–338.
HEINZE, R., Virgils epische Technik, Leipzig ³1915.
HELDMANN, K., Ovids Sabinus-Gedicht (*am.* 2,18) und die *Epistulae Heroidum* : *Hermes* 122, 1994, 188–219.
JACOBSON, H., Ovid's Heroides, Princeton 1974, 76–93.
KLINGNER, F., Virgil. Bucolica - Georgica - Aeneis, Zürich 1967.
KNOX, P. E., Ovid, Heroides. Select Epistles, Cambridge 1995.

---

[132] Vgl. auch KNOX 202.
[133] Es ist mehr ein geistreiches als ein abgründiges Spiel mit dem erlauchten Ahnherrn des julischen Herrscherhauses. Auch hier trifft zu, was DÖPP [Anm. 130] 115f. zur ovidischen *Ars* festhält, nämlich «wie respektlos Ovid nicht allein mit der literarischen Tradition umgeht, sondern auch mit Dingen, die der offiziellen Politik wichtig waren. Wenn solch souveräne Spottlust, solches Spiel der Ironie ein ‹Verbrechen› (*crimen*) ist – dann allerdings hat sich Ovid mit der *Ars* eines Vergehens schuldig gemacht.» – Wie leichtfüßig Ovid seine Position wechseln kann, zeigt etwa die *Ars*. Dort preist er Rom als Stadt der Venus, der göttlichen Mutter ihres Ahnherrn – und eben deshalb als Kapitale der Sinneslust (1,55–60).
[134] KNOX 202. – Erst in den letzten Jahren nimmt die Kritik Ovids bewußte Distanz zur *Aeneis* ohne mißbilligenden Unterton zur Kenntnis. Noch 1975 bricht eine so feinsinnige Philologin wie E. FANTHAM über Ovids Heroinen den Stab (Virgil's Dido and Seneca's tragic heroines: Greece & Rome 22, 1975, 1–10, hier 1): «the lovesick heroines of Ovid's Heroides are rhetorically versatile but without the moral stature to give value to their sufferings».
[135] Zu diesem reizvollen Spiel gehört nicht zuletzt, daß Ovid als Autor in die Rolle Didos schlüpft – und seinem Leser damit notwendig den mißlichen Konterpart zumutet – die Rolle des Aeneas. – Vgl. zu diesem Punkt auch WALDE 130f. Ihre Deutung des Dido-Briefes (ebd. 136f.) gelangt auf anderem Wege zu ähnlichen Einsichten.

Krummen, E., Dido als Mänade und tragische Heroine. Dionysische Thematik und Tragödientradition in Vergils Didoerzählung: Poetica 36, 2004, 25–69.

Kuhlmann, P., *Sed iubet ire deus*. Argumentation und poetologische Kritik in Ovids Dido-Brief: Philologus 147, 2003, 254–269.

Miller, P. A., The parodic sublime. Ovid's reception of Virgil in Heroides 7: MD 52, 2004, 57–72.

Palmer, A., P. Ovidi Nasonis Heroides, Oxford 1898, 339–350.

Pease, A. S., P. Vergili Maronis Aeneidos Liber Quartus, Cambridge/Mass. 1935.

Quinn, K., Virgil's Aeneid. A critical description, Ann Arbour ²1969.

Schmidt, E. A., Vergil. Die Tragödie der karthagischen Königin Dido als Anfrage an den Sinn der römischen Geschichte, in: ders., Musen in Rom. Deutung von Welt und Geschichte in großen Texten der römischen Literatur, Tübingen 2001, 119–132.

Vessey, D. W. T., Humor and humanity in Ovid's Heroides: Arethusa 9, 1976, 91–110.

Voit, L., Dido bei Ovid (*epist.* 7): Gymnasium 101, 1994, 338–348.

Walde, C., Literatur als Experiment? Zur Erzähltechnik in Ovids Heroides: A&A 46, 2000, 124–138.

Wilkinson, L. P., Ovid recalled, Cambridge 1955.

BEATE CZAPLA

Die Wandlung der Nereide Galatea von einer Kokotte zur Heiligen oder die Usurpation eines griechischen Mythos durch den Petrarkismus*

I. Die berühmte Galatea

Gleich bei ihrem ersten Auftritt auf der literarischen Bühne als Mitglied des Nereiden-Chores in Homers *Ilias* (18,45) wird Galatea durch das Epitethon ἀγακλειτή (hochberühmt) aus der Schar ihrer Schwestern herausgehoben. Von den 33 Nereustöchtern seines Katalogs hat Homer nur noch Halie (18,40) und Amathia (18,48) jeweils mit einem Epitheton versehen, jedoch handelt es sich mit βοῶπις und ἐυπλόκαμος um konventionelle, auf das Äußere zielende Attribute, wie er sie sonst der Eos oder der Artemis beilegt. Worin allerdings die Berühmtheit Galateas bestehen soll, sagt er nicht. Doch Bekanntheit erlangt sie eigentlich erst später, als sie die Rolle der Geliebten einer wirklich prominenten mythischen Figur übernimmt, des Kyklopen Polyphem, dem Homer fast einen ganzen Gesang widmet (Od. 9). Die Frage, weshalb Homer das im vorliegenden Zusammenhang erstaunliche Adjektiv ἀγακλειτή verwendet haben mag, soll aber erst am Ende dieses Beitrags beantwortet werden.

Hesiod, der immerhin 12 seiner 53 Nereiden ein Epitheton zubilligt, gibt Galatea (theog. 250) das Attribut εὐηδής (wohlgestaltet, schön), und Schönheit, der Männer rettungslos verfallen, wird in der Folge zu ihrem Markenzeichen. Ganz das Gegenteil ist der Fall bei ihrem Liebhaber, der berühmt für seine struppige Häßlichkeit mit dem einen riesigen Auge mitten auf der Stirn ist. Diese archetypische Konstellation eines häßlichen Mannes und einer schönen Frau wird nun in Literatur und bildender Kunst in allen Möglichkeiten durchgespielt: 1) Sie erwidert seine Liebe; 2) sie weist seine Liebe schnöde ab; 3) sie weist seine Liebe ab, weil sie einen anderen, einen Schönen liebt. Erst in der späteren Rezeption wird die Struktur des Kontrastes insoweit aufgegeben, als der Kyklop durch ästhetisch indifferente Männer substituiert wird.

Da durch die Untersuchungen von Georg Richard Holland und Heinrich Dörrie[1] die grundlegende Arbeit bereits geleistet wurde, ist es an dieser Stelle nicht nötig, einen vollständigen Überblick über die Bearbeitungen dieser Geschichte zu geben, die über die Jahrhunderte hinweg hervorgebracht worden sind. Deshalb sollen nur die wesentlichen Stationen in der antiken Entwicklung des Mythos unter bestimmten Aspekten skizziert und aus der rinascimentalen Rezeption vor allem solche Texte vorgestellt werden, die von Dörrie unberücksichtigt

---

* Dieser Beitrag stellt eine erweiterte und überarbeitete Fassung eines Vortrags dar, den ich beim Kolloquium der Mommsen-Gesellschaft *Mythos und Identität*, Bonn 04.–05. 06. 04 (Galateia als Chiffre für die unerreichbare Schöne) und vor der Petronian Society, Munich Section, 09.02.06 (Galatea als Kokotte oder Heilige. Literarische und ikonographische Aspekte einer mythischen Figur im Wandel der Zeiten) gehalten habe. Ich danke allen, die sich an den Diskussionen beteiligt haben, für wertvolle und weiterführende Hinweise.
[1] Holland 1884; Dörrie 1968.

blieben, und zwar vor allem aus eben jenem Genus, in dem Galatea für uns prominent, ἀγακλειτή wurde, d.h. aus der Bukolik. Überdies werden die Textinterpretationen durch die Betrachtung von Umsetzungen der bildenden Kunst aus verschiedenen Epochen ergänzt.

II. Die schöne milchweiße Galatea

Auf einen ursprünglichen Galatea-Kult gibt es keine archäologischen Hinweise, in den Texten ist er nur schwach bezeugt. Der Historiker Duris auf der Schwelle vom 4. zum 3. Jahrhundert leitet den Namen Γαλάτεια offensichtlich von γάλα ab und behauptet, Polyphem habe wegen der prächtigen Verfassung seiner Lämmer und des Überflusses an Milch ein Heiligtum der Galatea, der Milchweißen, am Ätna gebaut und Philoxenos, d.h. der Tragödien- und Dithyrambendichter Philoxenos von Kythera auf der Wende vom 5. zum 4. Jahrhundert, der Verfasser eines Dithyrambos Κύκλωψ ἢ Γαλάτεια, habe, als er dort war, den Grund nicht erfassen können und die Geschichte erfunden, Polyphem habe die Galatea geliebt (PMG 817 = FGrH 76,58 = Schol. Theocr. 6 init., p. 189 Wendel: Δοῦρίς φησι διὰ τὴν εὐβοσίαν τῶν θρεμμάτων καὶ τοῦ γάλακτος πολυπλήθειαν τὸν Πολύφημον ἱδρύσασθαι ἱερὸν παρὰ τῇ Αἴτνῃ Γαλατείας· Φιλόξενον δὲ τὸν Κυθήριον ἐπιδημήσαντα καὶ μὴ δυνάμενον ἐπινοῆσαι τὴν αἰτίαν ἀναπλάσαι ὡς ὅτι Πολύφημος ἤρα τῆς Γαλατείας.).[2] Ihm folgt im 2. Jahrhundert n. Chr. Lukian mit seiner *Wahren Geschichte* vom Heiligtum der Nereide Galatea auf der Käseinsel, auf der Weinstöcke wachsen, deren Trauben nicht Saft, sondern Milch enthalten (Ver. hist. 2,3),[3] sowie mit dem 1. Meergöttergespräch, in dem Doris an der Weiße ihrer Schwester das fehlende Rot moniert (Dial. Marini 1,3).[4] Da wir davon ausgehen können, daß Lukian seine *Wahre Geschichte* aus früherer Literatur, möglicherweise aus Duris herausgesponnen hat, bleibt uns nur die Behauptung des Duris, und auch diese steht auf wackeligen Füßen. Der hellenistische Dichter Hermesianax spricht nämlich zum einen von der großen Liebe des Philoxenos, den er implizit mit Polyphem identifiziert, zu Galatea, zum anderen – offensichtlich ausgehend von dessen Text – von dem großen Liebesverlangen, das Galatea den erwachsenen Schafen einflößte (PMG 815 = Athen. 13,598e = Coll. Alex. p. 100 Powell, 69-74: μέγαν πόθον, ὃν Γαλατείη / αὐτοῖς μηλείοις θῆκαθ' ὑπὸ προγόνοις). Es besteht also durchaus die Möglichkeit, daß der prächtige Zustand von Polyphems Herden und die Gründung des Heiligtums der Interpretation von Philoxenos' Dithyrambos in Verbindung mit dem Namen Galatea entspringen.[5] In jedem Fall aber erfahren wir bei Hermesianax

---

[2] Cf. Eust. in Od. 331,25sq.: Διόπερ ὁ μῦθος Γαλατείας αὐτὸν ἐραστὴν τῆς Νερηΐδος εἶναι πλάττει πιθανῶς διὰ τὴν ῥηθησομένην ἐν γάλατι περιουσίαν.

[3] Während Holland (cf. 186; außerdem Anello, 24sq.) die Lukian-Stelle für insofern als Bestätigung von Duris ansieht, als sie die Nachricht von einem Galatea-Heiligtum auf Sizilien bezeuge, will Dörrie (cf. Dörrie 1968, 26) sie nicht «als dokumentarisches Zeugnis mißverstehen». Zur identischen (inkorrekten?) Etymologie von Duris und Lukian cf. Hordern, 447.

[4] [...] ἰδὲ σεαυτὴν οὐδὲν ἄλλο ἢ χροιὰν λευκὴν ἀκριβῶς· οὐκ ἐπαινεῖται δὲ τοῦτο, ἢν μὴ ἐπιπρέπῃ αὐτῷ καὶ τὸ ἐρύθημα [Sieh dich an, nichts als weiße Farbe; das gilt nicht als schön, wenn nicht auch das Rote hinzukommt].

[5] Cf. Jacobi, 2c, 126 und Gattinoni, 164, die Duris' Aussage als rationalistische Mythos- und Literatur-Erklärung verstehen. Gattinoni (165) sieht überdies grundsätzlich ein lebhaftes Interesse des Duris an den Autoren der Zeit des Dionysios. Zur eingeschränkten Glaubwürdigkeit und der am Sensationellen orientierten Darstellungsweise des Duris cf. überdies Meister, 96–100.

zum ersten Mal, welche außerordentlichen Wirkungen die Schönheit der Galatea zeitigte, die sie in die Nähe der Aphrodite rückt.[6] Schließlich teilt sie mit ihr möglicherweise einen ähnlichen Ursprung. Denn wie Aphrodite aus dem Schaum des Meeres geboren wurde, ist der Name Galatea nach Eustathios vom milchweißen Meerschaum, von den γαλατάχροοι ἄφροι (Eust. Commentarii ad Homeri Iliadem pertinentes 1131,7sq., Vol. 4,135,14sq. van der Valk: αὕτη δὲ καὶ διὰ τοὺς τῶν κυμάτων γαλαταχρόους ἀφροὺς οὕτω καλεῖται), abzuleiten.[7] So sind drei Epigramme der *Anthologia Latina* ausschließlich ihrer entflammenden Schönheit gewidmet (141–143 Shackleton Baily), die – zumindest in der Fiktion – Galatea-Darstellungen im Inneren von Tonschüsseln beigegeben waren.[8] Hier sollen zwei Verse genügen:

De Galatea in vase
Fulget et in patinis ludens pulcherrima Nais,
prandentum inflammans ‹c›or‹d›a decore suo. (Anth. Lat. 141,1 sq.)
Galatea in einer Schüssel
Es glänzt auch in Schüsseln tändelnd die überaus schöne Najade und entflammt die Herzen der Männer beim Essen durch ihre Schönheit.

III. Die schöne Galatea, die den Kyklopen liebt

In Zusammenhang mit dem Kult wird diejenige Version des Mythos gebracht, die besonders in der älteren Forschungsliteratur als ursprüngliche angesehen wird,[9] daß nämlich Polyphems Liebe von Galatea erwidert wurde. Die beiden werden sogar zu Eltern eines

---

[6] Zu dem Phänomen, daß in der Antike seit Sappho 31 Lobel/Page Schönheit meist nicht durch positive Beschreibung, sondern durch ihre Wirkung e.a. beschrieben wird, cf. Funke, 53–57.

[7] Cf. Weicker, 517. Zur Form des Adjektivs cf. van der Valk im Apparat ad loc.: *Adiect. γαλακτόχρως apud auctores interdum reperitur*, cf. LSJ, s.v. Eust. scribit γαλακτόχρως, cf. ad Eust. 620,3.

[8] Die Epigramme 140–143 der Anth. Lat. bilden einen kleinen Zyklus von Galatea-Gedichten, von denen epigr. 140 Ovid folgt, die Gedichte 141–143 die Schönheit der Galatea in teilweise witziger Weise thematisieren. Zu diesem Zyklus cf. Paolucci, die zum einen an mehreren Stellen mit einleuchtenden Argumenten für die Bewahrung des überlieferten Textes und gegen die Textherstellung von Shackleton Baily argumentiert, zum anderen in den Epigrammen 141–143 nicht fiktive, sondern reale Ekphraseis sieht. Obwohl an zwei Stellen explizit vom Schwimmen der Nereide die Rede ist (142,1; 143,4) und einmal davon, daß sie ihre *membra venusta* bewege (142,2), was ebenfalls nur auf eine Schwimmbewegung deuten kann, wie Galatea auch sonst in der Literatur mehrmals schwimmend dargestellt wird (Verg. Aen. 9,102; Val. Flacc. 1,135sq.; Claud. rapt. Pros. 3,333), soll als Vorbild für die der zahlreichen Darstellungen gedient haben, auf denen Galatea auf einem Meerestier reitet (Zur Galatea-Ikonographie cf. zusammenfassend Montón). Das Verbindungsglied zu diesen Darstellungen bildet für Paolucci das Verb *ludere* (141,1; 142,1), da auch Philostrats Galatea (imag. 2,18,4, zur Galatea Philostrats v.i.) spiele (cf. 122). Allerdings steht bei Philostrat das παίζειν zu Beginn der Bildbeschreibung im Kontrast zur eifrigen Werbung des zuvor beschriebenen Polyphem, überdies reitet Galatea bei Philostrat nicht, sondern fährt im Wagen (weitere Belege für die reitende oder fahrende Galatea in der Literatur: Prop. 3,2,7sq.; Claud. carm. 10,159–168; Drac. Romul. 7,151; Lux. anth. 18,40sq Riese). Ohne zu spezifizieren, ob sie schwimmt, reitet oder fährt, bezeichnet Vergils Moeris den Aufenthalt Galateas im Wasser (ecl. 9,39: *quis est nam lusus in undis?*). Ein weiterer Beleg für die Schönheit Galateas ist das Hochzeitsgedicht Lux. anth. 18,40sq. Riese, in dem die Schönheit der Braut mit derjenigen der Nereiden Doto und Galatea verglichen wird, Galatea also wie konventionellerweise Venus, Diana oder andere Göttinnen des Pantheon zum Maßstab von Schönheit wird.

[9] Cf. Weicker, 517sq.; Anello, 22–29, die den γάμος zweier indigener sizilischer Gottheiten annimmt, die später mit den Figuren aus dem griechischen Mythos identifiziert wurden; Harder; unbestimmt: Weizsäcker, 1587sq.

Galas, Galates oder Galatos und Stammeltern der Galater gemacht.[10] Die literarische Bezeugung dieses Stammes-Mythos ist allerdings ebenfalls ausgesprochen schütter. Wir haben eine diesbezügliche Aussage des Historikers Timaios (FGrH 566F69 = Et. M. p. 220,5: Γαλατία. χώρα· ὠνομάσθη, ὥς φησι Τίμαιος, ἀπὸ Γαλάτου, Κύκλωπος καὶ Γαλατείας υἱοῦ), der danach strebte, griechische Mythologie im Westen zu verankern,[11] und dürftige Fragmente eines Galatea-Epyllions von Kallimachos (Call. fr. 378 sq. Pfeiffer), aus denen man bestenfalls vermuten kann, Kallimachos habe darin die Abstammung der Galater von Galatea bzw. ihrem Sohn hergeleitet.[12] Andere Quellen nennen sowohl andere Väter als auch andere Mütter der Galater bzw. Kelten.[13] Eine Anspielung des Properz (3,2,7sqq.: «quin etiam, Polypheme, fera Galatea sub Aetna / ad tua rorantis carmina flexit equos» [ja, Polyphem, auch Galatea lenkte am wilden Ätna die triefenden Pferde auf seinen Gesang hin um]) und das Verhalten der Galatea in Nonnos' *Dionysiaka* bezeugen tatsächlich ihre Liebe zum Kyklopen (esp. 39,257–266; 40,553–557).[14] Nicht als Beleg für eine Zuneigung Galateas zu Polyphem kann wohl Lukians erwähntes 1. *Meergöttergespräch* zwischen ihr und ihrer Schwester Doris gelten. Sie verteidigt ihn und seinen Gesang zwar gegenüber den Herabsetzungen der Schwester und fühlt sich ihr dadurch überlegen, daß sie einen Verehrer hat, äußert aber kein wirkliches Wort der Zuneigung oder gar Liebe. In der bildenden Kunst der Antike aber finden sich immerhin zwei pompejanische Wandgemälde und ein Relief, die das Liebespaar Polyphem und Galatea in inniger Umarmung zeigen.[15] Trotz des traurigen Erhaltungszustandes läßt m.E. das Wandgemälde

---

[10] Cf. Appian Illyr. 2: Πολυφήμῳ ... τῷ Κύκλωπι καὶ Γαλατείᾳ Κελτὸν καὶ Ἰλλυριὸν καὶ Γάλαν παῖδας ὄντας ἐξορμῆσαι Σικελίας καὶ ἄρξαι τῶν δι' αὐτοὺς Κελτῶν καὶ Ἰλλυριῶν καὶ Γαλατῶν λεγομένων. Jacoby hält diese Genealogie für die Erfindung eines Dichters am Hof des Dionysios von Syrakus (cf. Jacoby 3b, 335). Auf Natale Contis Zuschreibung einer ähnlichen Aussage, aus der Liebe zwischen Polyphem und Galatea sei ein Sohn Galatos hervorgegangen, an Bakchylides (Bacchylides fr. 59 Snell/Maehler), i. e. an einen frühen Gewährsmann zu vertrauen, bedeutet jedenfalls angesichts der häufig unzuverlässigen Zuschreibungen und Stellenangaben der Frühen Neuzeit und insbesondere Contis überaus dünnes Eis zu betreten (Conti weist auch die zitierte Mythenerklärung des Duris mit Stellenangabe [3. Buch] dem älteren Alkidamas zu [FGrHist 506F10], wobei er auf das Theokrit-Scholion verweist und dieses wörtlich übersetzt; zu Contis Unzuverlässigkeit cf. Pfeiffer, 304sq.; cf. für die Authentizität der Alkidamas-Zuschreibung Anello, 20). In die Bacchylides-Ausgabe von Jean Irigoin/Jacqueline Duchemin/Louis Bardollet (Paris 1993) ist Contis ‹Testimonium› nicht aufgenommen. Ausgehend von der Authentizität des Bakchylides-Fragments hingegen interpretiert es Anello (cf. 22–29.35) als Identifikation einer indigenen Herdengöttin mit der Nereide Galatea aus dem griechischen Mythos, die sich mit einem indigenen Polyphem vereinigt und die Politik des Hieron einer vorsichtigen Öffnung zu den einheimischen Nicht-Griechen symbolisiert (v. s. No. 9).

[11] Cf. Jacobi, 3b, zu 566F85–88, 576sq.; zum Verfahren des Timaios cf. Pearson, 53–90.260, zur Stelle esp. 72sq.; Walbank, 14. Timaios' Genealogie ist unter Umständen auch durch die Propaganda des Dionysius I. geprägt, der die Verbindungen zwischen Sizilien und den Galatern/Kelten (und Illyrern), seinen Verbündeten, möglichst prominent und alt erscheinen lassen wollte (cf. Caven, 152sq.; Gattinoni, 164).

[12] Cf. Pfeiffer, 305sq.; Frazer, Vol. 1, 659 mit No. 352 (Vol. 2, 925); Herter, 209; Nachtergael, 184sq.; Meillier, 55; Mommigliano, 78; Petzl, 144; Rankin, 81.

[13] Diodor (5,24,1) nennt nach einer anderen Quelle als Timaios den Herakles und eine ungenannte Tochter eines ungenannten Keltenkönigs als Eltern des Galates; zu weiteren Quellen und Genealogien cf. Pfeiffer, 304–306.

[14] Holland (cf. 285) vermutet die Quelle in verlorener hellenistischer Dichtung.

[15] Zum ersten Wandgemälde cf. Helbig, 211, No. 1052 (= Dörrie 1968, Tab. 4; Montón, No. 37); das zweite (cf. Sogliano, No. 475 = Montón, Nr 38) bezeichnet Schefold (cf. 241 [IX 2,10 g]) als Replik dieses Bildes; zum Relief cf. Monton, No. 39; ein weiteres (verlorenes) Gemälde (Sogliano, No. 474; Schefold, 8 [I 2,3 c] = Montón, No. 31) zeigt Galatea auf Polyphems Knien (cf. Weicker, 518); nicht eindeutig bewiesen wird die

(p. 117), das eine helle stehende Galatea in Rückansicht in den Armen eines dunklen sitzenden Kyklopen zeigt, besser als die literarischen Quellen den Kern erkennen, der diese Liebe ausmacht: die Vereinigung der Gegensätze schön und häßlich, hell und dunkel,[16] die wir nicht nur in dem bekannten aufklärerischen Märchen von der Schönen und dem Biest wiederfinden,[17] sondern bereits in der Verbindung zweier Götter im griechischen Mythos der Archaik: Ausgerechnet der physisch defektive Schmiedegott Hephaistos ist bei Homer der Gemahl der Aphrodite (Hom. Od. 8,266–366) bzw. der Charis (Hom. Il. 18,382sq.). Die Renaissance hat sich für diese Version des Galatea-Mythos nicht interessiert, obwohl e. g. der italienische Humanist Angelo Poliziano die *Dionysiaka* nachweislich gekannt hat.

IV. Die widerspenstige und kokette Galatea

In der ersten uns bekannten Literarisierung von Polyphems Liebe zu Galatea, in dem genannten Dithyrambus des Philoxenos, hat der Kyklop hingegen wahrscheinlich keine Chance, die Liebe der Nereide zu erringen. Leider ist uns von diesem Text so wenig erhalten, daß wir im wesentlichen auf Spekulationen angewiesen sind, und wir wissen auch nicht, ob die Verbindung des Riesen und der Nymphe eine Erfindung des Philoxenos ist oder dieser einen existierenden Mythos aufgegriffen hat.[18] Faßbar ist von ihrer Liebesgeschichte aus einem Zitat des Athenaios zunächt Polyphems Lob für Galateas Schönheit: ὦ καλλιπρόσωπε χρυσεοβόστρυχε [Γαλάτεια] χαριτόφωνε θάλος Ἐρώτων [oh du Kind der Eroten mit schönem Gesicht, goldenen Locken und lieblicher Stimme] (PMG 821 = Athen. 13,564e), eine Trias von exquisiten Attributen, die zwar nach dem Muster der zusammengesetzten Epitheta wie γλαυκῶπις, βοῶπις, λευκώλενος, ἀργυρόπεζα, χρυσοπέδιλος, ἠύκομος, καλλιπλόκαμος etc. gebildet sind, die Homer der Athene, Hera, Thetis, Helena e.a. beizulegen pflegt, von denen χαριτόφωνος aber vor Philoxenos nicht belegt ist, χρυσεοβόστρυχος nur einmal als Epitheton der Artemis in einer lyrischen Partie in den ca. 411 aufgeführten Phönissen des Euripides[19] und καλλιπρόσωπος ebenfalls einmal, und zwar ebenfalls im Vokativ, möglicherweise in einem Liebesgedicht, bei Anakreon: ὦ καλλιπρόσωπε παίδων (fr. 1,3 Page). Weiterhin können wir Aristophanes' Parodie des Dithyrambos im *Plutos* (290–301 mit PMG 819 = Schol. Ar. Plut. Dübner 290; Suda θ 475) entnehmen, daß Philoxenos den Polyphem sich als Sänger bzw. Dichter

---

Liebe Galateas zu Polyphem durch Bilder, auf denen sie mit oder ohne Unterhändlerin vor Polyphem steht (cf. Helbig, No. 1050 = Montón, No. 20; gegen Weicker, 518), Polyphem vor ihr kniet (Helbig, No. 1053 = Montón, No. 21; gegen Weicker, 518) oder Polyphem einen Brief bzw. ein Diptychon (durch Eros) erhält bzw. liest (Schefold, 74 [V 2,Mau9 m] = Montón, No. 43; Schefold, 134 [VI 14,28] = Sogliano, No. 472 = Dörrie 1968, Tab. 3; 247 [IX 3,5,7] = Montón, No. 45; Schefold, 247 [IX 3,5] = Helbig, No. 1049 = Montón, No. 44; Helbig, No. 1048 = Montón, No. 46).

[16] Reduziert ist auf dem Bild der Gegensatz von groß und klein. Zwar ist Galatea deutlich kleiner als der Kyklop, doch handelt es sich nicht um Größenverhältnisse, wie sie der Homerischen Beschreibung entsprechen, daß nämlich Polyphem in der Lage ist, zwei Gefährten des Odysseus auf einmal wie Hunde zu packen (Od. 9,288sq.).

[17] Cf. Scherfer, 1056–1059; sonst entspricht im Märchen der ästhetische Kontrast oft einem ethischen, in dem am Ende der/die Schöne/Gute über den/die Häßliche(n)/Schlechte(n) siegt (cf. Uther, 13–16.).

[18] Für die Existenz eines entsprechenden Mythos vor Philoxenos votieren Holland, 186, Weizsäcker, 1586, Weicker, 517, Anello, 22–24.

[19] Zur Datierung von Philoxenos' Kyklops zwischen 406 und 388 v. Chr. cf. Hordern, 445.

betätigen und entweder Kithara spielen oder den Klang der Kithara mit der Stimme durch das lautmalerische θρεττανελό hat nachahmen lassen sowie daß die Schafe eine Rolle spielten, was, wie gesehen, auch aus den Worten des Duris und des Hermesianax zu folgern ist. Mit folgenden Worten schlüpft nämlich die Figur Karion in die Rolle des Kyklopen und fordert die Choreuten auf, die der Schafe und Ziegen zu übernehmen (Aristoph. Plut. 292-294):

> Καὶ μὴν ἐγὼ βουλήσομαι θρεττανελὸ τὸν Κύκλοπα
> μιμούμενος καὶ τοῖν ποδοῖν ὡδὶ παρενσαλεύων
> ὑμᾶς ἄγειν. Ἀλλ' εἶα τέκεα θαμίν' ἐπαναβοῶντες
> βληχώμενοί τε προβατίων
> αἰγῶν τε κιναβρώντων μέλη
> ἕπεσθ' ἀπεψωλημένοι [...].

Und wahrlich, ich will – threttanelo – den Kyklopen nachahmen und das Tanzbein schwingend euch führen. Wohlan Kinder, rufet rasch und blökt die Lieder der Schafe und der stinkenden Ziegen und folgt mit erhobenem Schwanz!

Mag das sexuelle Element auch sonst konstitutiv für die Alte Komödie sein, so ist hier doch die Parallele zu den erotisch stimulierten Schafen bei Hermesianax bemerkenswert. Schließlich ist in einem Theokrit-Scholion (11,1, p. 241 Wendel) und bei Plutarch (quaest. conv. 1,5, 622c; PMG = 822 amator. 18, 762f) die Nachricht überliefert, Philoxenos habe den Polyphem Heilung von seiner Liebe in der Dichtung bzw. Musik finden lassen, was dieser der Galatea durch Delphine übermitteln ließ (Schol. Theocr. 11,1, p. 241 Wendel) und was dafür spricht, daß sie ihn nicht erhört hat. Hinzu kommen noch zwei kurze Textstücke, die sinnvollerweise nur aus einem Dialog zwischen Polyphem und dem in seiner Höhle eingesperrten Odysseus stammen können (PMG 823 = Suda α 336, II 211 Adler; PMG 824 = Zenob. cent. 5,45, I 139 Leutsch/Schneidewin).[20]

Nicht nur eine inhaltliche Rekonstruktion aus diesen geringen Bruchstücken, sondern auch die Form von Philoxenos' *Kyklops* hat der Forschung einige Schwierigkeiten bereitet. Denn i.a. deswegen, weil er bereits in der Antike als δρᾶμα bezeichnet wird (PMG 819 = Schol. Ar. Plut. Dübner 290; PMG 824 = Zenob. cent. 5,45 [1,139 Leutsch/Schneidewin]), wird er von einigen Wissenschaftlern als moderner Dithyrambos mit monodischen und dialogischen Partien interpretiert, in dem ein Solist die Rolle des Odysseus oder der Chor die Rolle des Odysseus und seiner Gefährten singt, ein (zweiter) Solist diejenige des Polyphem, und dieser auch mit seiner Stimme den Klang der Kithara nachahmt.[21] Sie stützen sich neben der Bezeichnung als Drama auf seine Auslegung als Allegorie einer Affäre des Dichters mit einer Favoritin des Tyrannen Dionysios I. von Syrakus, an dessen Hof er weilte (PMG 816 = Athen. 1,6e-7a; PMG 819 = Schol. Ar. Plut. Dübner 290; Suda θ 475, II 727 Adler): Er sei zur Strafe in die Steinbrüche geworfen worden und habe entweder dort (PMG 816 = Athen. 1,6e-7a) oder, nach seiner Flucht, auf Kythera (PMG 819 = Schol. Ar. Plut. Dübner 290) den Dithyrambus verfaßt, in dem der musikalisch dilettierende Dionysios durch den ungeschickt werbenden Kyklopen, die Favoritin durch Galatea und der Dichter selbst durch den gewitzten Odysseus dargestellt wurden. Zum einen ist allerdings

---

[20] Cf. Hordern, 450; Casolari, 129sq.
[21] Cf. Gomperz; Sutton; Anello, 19; Zimmermann, 125; Casolari, 129sq., No. 8. Einen ausführlichen Versuch, die Handlung einschließlich eines Auftrittes der Galatea zu rekonstruieren, bietet Holland (cf. 191-209).

die Authentizität der Allegorese nicht gesichert,[22] zum anderen belegt sie weniger den dramatischen Charakter der Dichtung als ihre Offenheit für eine satirische Leseweise und gewisse komische Elemente,[23] die sich allein aus der Diskrepanz zwischen der Homerischen Darstellung des Kyklopen als ungeschlachtes, gemeinschaftsunfähiges, menschenfressendes Ungeheuer, das keine Ehrfurcht vor Göttern kennt (Od. 9,187-192.274-278), und seiner Rolle als Liebhaber ergeben. Dementsprechend wird auch unabhängig von der Frage, ob die allegorische Interpretation tatsächlich auf eine autobiographische Intention des Philoxenos zurückgeht, die entgegengesetzte Ansicht vertreten, der *Kyklops* sei kein Drama, sondern ein konventioneller Dithyrambus – möglicherweise mit einem hohen Anteil an (berichtetem?) Dialog – gewesen.[24] Hinsichtlich des Inhalts werden hierbei jedoch wiederum einander diametral entgegengesetzte Vermutungen geäußert: 1) In Philoxenos' Dithyrambos sei von der Liebe des Kyklopen die Rede gewesen, von den Wirkungen der Schönheit Galateas auf ihn selbst und auf die Schafe, wie es sich in dem Zeugnis des Hermesianax spiegelt, die Hinzufügung der Figur des Odysseus aber sei wie diejenige anderer Handlungselemente eine Zutat der Mittleren Komödie, die mehrere Kyklops- bzw. Galatea-Stücke hervorgebracht hat, von denen jedoch leider nur wenig erhalten ist.[25] 2) Der Dithyrambos habe weitgehend aus einem Dialog zwischen Polyphem und Odysseus bestanden, die Liebe des Kyklopen zu Galatea sei nur ein Randmotiv gewesen, etwa in der Weise, wie Synesius in seinem 121. Brief (PMG 818 = Synes. epist. 121, Patr. Graec. 66, 1500B-D Migne) einen eingekerkerten Athanasios mit dem in der Höhle eingeschlossenen Odysseus vergleicht, der Polyphem anbietet, ihm bei der Gewinnung der Galatea behilflich zu sein. In der Mittleren Komödie sei Odysseus, der in den erhaltenen Fragmenten nicht erwähnt

---

[22] Andere Quellen (Diod. Sic. 15,6,2; Lucian. adv. indoct. 15; Plut. de Alex. fort. 2,334c; Suda ϑ 397, IV 729sq. Adler; Tzetzes, Commentarii in Aristophanem I 83sq. [V. 290] Positano; historiae V: 159sqq. [p. 173]; X: 838sqq. [p. 423] Leone) nennen Kritik an Dionysios' poetischen Versuchen als Grund dafür, daß Philoxenos in die Steinbrüche geworfen wurde, wobei selbst die Verbannung in die Steinbrüche nicht zweifelsfrei ist. So hält Caven (223sq.) sie für das Ergebnis biographischer Literaturinterpretation, deren Ursprung in der Bezeichnung der Kyklopen-Höhle in der literarischen Kyklops-Produktion als λατομίαι zu suchen sei, mit der auf die Gefangenschaft der 7000 Athener in den Steinbrüchen von Syrakus während der sizilischen Katastrophe angespielt werden sollte. Nur scheinbar ist die Allegorese durch das Alter der Quelle gesichert, indem Athenaios, bevor er zwei Anekdoten über Philoxenos erzählt, von denen die Allegorese des *Kyklops* die zweite ist, als Gewährsmann den Peripatetiker Phainias nennt, einen Zeitgenossen Theophrasts (1,6e). Denn diese Quellenangabe ist wohl nur auf die erste der beiden Anekdoten zu beziehen, derzufolge Philoxenos bei einem Bankett, nachdem er gesehen hatte, daß dem Dionysios eine große, ihm aber nur eine kleine Barbe serviert worden war, seine an sein Ohr hielt. Auf die Frage des Dionysios, warum er das tue, antwortete Philoxenos, er habe die Barbe über Galatea befragt, über die er schreiben wolle, die Barbe habe ihm aber geantwortet, sie sei zu jung gefangen worden, um hierüber Auskunft geben zu können, er möge die ältere des Dionysios befragen. Dionysios habe ihm daraufhin seine Barbe geben lassen. Da zum einen diese Anekdote im Widerspruch zur Allegorie des *Kyklops* steht, zum anderen Athenaios mit ihr von der indirekten Rede zur direkten übergeht, hat er vermutlich, ohne es anzuzeigen, an dieser Stelle die Quelle gewechselt (cf. Holland, 188; Casolari, 128, No. 3; dagegen Hordern, 446). Zur Allegorie vgl. v. i. [63] eine ähnliche Auslegung der Ovidischen Version von Galatea, Polyphem und Acis. Zu einer modernen allegorischen Auslegung des Dithyrambos cf. Anello, 47-50, die in der Hinwendung der Galatea, einer Figur des griechischen Mythos und Symbol für das Griechentum, zu dem Griechen Odysseus und ihrer Ablehnung des Barbaren Polyphem eine Kritik des Philoxenos aus griechischer, esp. attischer Sicht an der barbarenfreundlichen Politik des Polyphem/Dionysios sieht.
[23] Cf. Hordern, 448.
[24] Cf. Webster, 21sq.; Hordern, 451-455.
[25] Cf. Arnott, 140; Caspers, 35-39. Zu den Rollen von Kyklop und Galatea bei Nikochares, Antiphanes und Alexis cf. Casolari, 138-143.

werde, aus der Geschichte eliminiert worden und finde sich dementsprechend auch nicht in den hellenistischen Versionen.[26] Während die erste Vermutung die Fragmente PMG 823.824 außer acht läßt, berücksichtigt die zweite nicht die Möglichkeit, daß Odysseus in den weitaus größeren Teilen der Komödien seinen Auftritt gehabt haben könnte, die uns verloren sind. Wenn man also von allen hochspekulativen Rekonstruktionsversuchen absieht, bleibt für den vorliegenden Zusammenhang Polyphems Verwandlung in einen Dichter und Sänger, das Lob von Galateas Schönheit im *genus grande*, ihre wahrscheinlich abweisende Haltung, die erotische Stimulierung der Schafe und die Möglichkeit, daß der Kyklop in Odysseus einen Nebenbuhler gehabt haben könnte.

Bei Theokrit endlich können wir in Idyll 6 und 11 auf einer sicheren Textbasis die Liebeswirkung der Galatea auf einen als liebenswerten jugendlichen Tolpatsch gezeichneten Polyphem beobachten, der wiederum in der Rolle des Liebhabers und Dichters zugleich Galatea nicht gewinnen kann, in die er sich unheilbar verliebte,[27] als er sie und ihre Mutter zum Blumenpflücken in die Berge führte (11,25–26). Außer einigen kurzen Bemerkungen des Dichters zu Beginn und am Schluß, in denen er den Kyklopen zum Beispiel für die heilsame Wirkung der Musik im Fall einer Liebeskrankheit erklärt, besteht das 11. Idyll aus einem sicherlich auf komische Effekte abzielenden Werbelied, in dem der Riese seine Liebes-Pathologie mit den Symptomen Gewichtsverlust und Pulsieren in Kopf und Füßen beschreibt (11,69–71). Natürlich preist er die Schöne auch, und zwar als: λευκοτέρα πακτᾶς ποτιδεῖν, ἁπαλωτέρα ἀρνὸς,/ μόσχω γαυροτέρα, φιαρωτέρα ὄμφακος ὠμᾶς [weißer als Quark anzuschauen, zarter als ein Lamm, munterer als ein Kälbchen, glänzender als eine unreife Traube] (Id. 11,20sq.). Von den vier Vergleichen, die der Komik halber alle seiner derb-bäurischen Lebenswelt entnommen sind, verweist der erste sowohl auf den Namen Galatea als auch auf die besondere Art ihrer milchweißen Schönheit. Aus dem dritten und vierten Vergleich hingegen können auch Eigenschaften herausgelesen werden, die dem Kyklopen weit weniger gefallen. So bedeutet γαυρός auch bockig, und ebenso deutet die ὠμότης der Weintraube auf die Herbheit der sich verweigernden Nymphe.[28] Ovid hat

---

[26] Cf. Hordern, 450sq. Die direkte oder indirekte Abhängigkeit des Synesios von Philoxenos ist umstritten. Während Ribbeck i.a. den Dithyrambus für die Quelle des Synesios hält (bestätigt von Sutton, 41; cf. auch Anello, 18), sieht Holland die von ihm benutzten Handlungselemente eher in der Nähe der Komödie (ibid. 193–196). Synesios hat seinerseits die weitere Rezeption des Galatea-Mythos nicht beeinflußt. Eine Dichtung, die seiner Konstellation recht nahekommt, ist der derb-komische Brief des Polyphem an Galatea, den Luca Pulci, ein Dichter aus dem Kreis um Lorenzo de' Medici in Florenz, in toskanischem Terzinen in *verse sdrucciole* verfaßte (Pulci, 106sq.): Polyphem schreibt an Galatea auf eine Steintafel, nachdem er dies von dem bei ihm eingekerkerten Odysseus gelernt hat, und wirft am Ende diese Tafel auf die Insel, auf der er Galatea vermutet. Da es unwahrscheinlich ist, daß die humanistische Bildung der Pulci-Brüder das Griechische einschloß (zur eher beschränkten humanistischen Bildung Luigi Pulcis cf. Walter, 92), wird Luca Pulci Synesios schwerlich selbst gekannt haben. Allenfalls könnte die Kenntnis durch den ebenfalls zum Kreis Lorenzos gehörenden Poliziano vermittelt worden sein.

[27] Über die Frage, ob Polyphem sich durch sein Lied an Galatea heile, wie Theokrit behauptet, hat die Forschung lange gestritten, ohne daß die Frage letztgültig geklärt worden ist. Zu einer kurzen Zusammenfassung der Diskussion mit Literaturhinweisen cf. Hunter, 220–223. Als kaum beachtetes Zeugnis für die Unheilbarkeit der Liebe zu Galatea kann ein Epigramm des Paulos Silentiarios gelten (Anth. Graec. 5,256), in dem Galatea dem Dichter-Ich die Tür vor der Nase zuschlägt und Heilung von der Liebe durch diese ὕβρις verspricht. Allerdings schlägt auch dieses rüde Mittel fehl.

[28] Cf. Hunter, 230sq.; zur Konjektur φιαλωτέρα [saurer] statt φιαρωτέρα cf. Ribbeck, 565–569; bei Ovid ist die Traube hingegen reif und süß, und der Vergleich mit ihr gehört zu den guten Eigenschaften: *matura dulcior uva* (795). Zum Schönheitsideal der weißen Haut (in Verbindung mit roter Farbe) cf. Bömer, Vol. 1, 420–422.

jedenfalls in seinem Polyphemlied (met. 13,789–869) diese vier, über zwei Verse reichenden Vergleiche zu einer langen Reihe von 19 Versen amplifiziert (789–807) und in zwei Abschnitte auseinandergelegt, von denen der erste ihre ‹guten› Eigenschaften, insbesondere ihre Schönheit beschreibt, der zweite, um einen Vers längere ihre ‹schlechten› Eigenschaften, die sich in ihrer Verweigerung manifestieren. Diese ist, wie wir Theokrits 6. Idyll entnehmen können, überdies gepaart mit einer gewissen herzlosen Koketterie. Denn durch das bekannte Liebesspiel des Äpfelwerfens suggeriert sie Zuneigung (6). Wie ernst sie es aber meint und ob diese vorgebliche Zuneigung von Dauer sein wird, ist zumindest zweifelhaft.[29] Als kokettes Spiel interpretiert Galateas Verhalten jedenfalls Claudian in seinem Brief an Serena, die Nichte und Adoptivtochter des Kaisers Theodosius, Tochter von dessen Bruder Honorius und Ehefrau des Feldherrn Stilicho. Um ein unübliches, i. e. in diesem Falle ehrerbietiges Verhalten der Meeresbewohner zu beschreiben, während die Honoriustöchter Thermantia und Serena zu Schiff passieren, formuliert er i.a.: *non ludit Galatea procax* [nicht treibt die freche Galatea ihr Spiel] (carm. min. 30,125).[30] Daher ist es nicht verwunderlich, daß der späthellenistische Dichter Bion, der Theokrit in mancher Hinsicht verpflichtet ist, sie mit dem Epitheton ἀπηνής [hart] versieht (Aposp. 16,3), verwunderlich ist nur, daß er nichtsdestoweniger, und zwar mit seinem lyrischen Ich, nicht unter der Maske des Polyphem, ein Lied an sie richtet. Leider ist es uns wohl nicht vollständig erhalten, und wir wissen nicht, ob er es als erfolgreiche Werbung gestaltete oder ob ihre Freude an seinen Liedern und ihre Trauer über seinen Tod, von der wir im ἐπιτάφιος Βίωνος lesen ([Mosch.] 3,58–64), ausschließlich dazu dient, seine Dichtung zu glorifizieren. Kennzeichen der Beziehung zwischen Polyphem und Galatea ist also neben dem Gegensatz schön-häßlich derjenige zwischen dem Verliebten, der seine Souveränität verliert, und dem Nicht-Verliebten, der nicht nur seine eigene Souveränität behält, sondern zusätzlich Macht über den Verliebten gewinnt. Daß der Mächtige in diesem Spiel physisch weit unterlegen, der Ohnmächtige aber über die Maßen groß und stark ist, gibt der Sache eine komische Note und hat sicherlich für die hellenistischen Dichter den Reiz erhöht, sich mit dem Stoff zu beschäftigen. Daß aber ein Verliebter dichtet, scheint früh topisch geworden zu sein.[31]

Auf bildlichen Darstellungen der Antike dokumentiert sich Galateas Abwendung von Polyphem in der Regel darin, daß sie auf einem Delphin oder einem Hippokampen über

---

[29] Cf. Hunter, 244.
[30] Das kokette, i. e. mal lockende, mal spröde Verhalten der Galatea, die den Polyphem abweist, wenn er um sie wirbt, ihn aber lockt, wenn sie ihn nicht beachtet, sieht Betts sehr passend illustriert durch den Vergleich mit der leichten Distelwolle (Theocr. 6,15–17), die sich gegen unseren Willen an Haare und Kleider heftet, aber durch den Luftzug unserer Bewegung davonfliegt, wenn wir nach ihr schnappen wollen. Interessant ist in diesem Zusammenhang auch die Funktionalisierung der Galatea-Geschichte in der erfolglosen Liebeswerbung des Kallidemos um die schöne Drosilla in Niketas Eugenianos' Versroman *Drosilla und Charikles* aus dem 12. Jahrhundert (6,503–534). Auf der einen Seite nämlich vergleicht Kallidemos Drosillas abweisende Haltung mit der Galateas in Theokrits 11. Idyll, auf der anderen interpretiert er das Werfen der Äpfel in Idyll 6,6sq. als tatsächliche Liebesbezeugung. Besonders erfolgreich scheint Kallidemos jedoch in der Einschätzung non-verbaler Signale von Frauen nicht zu sein. Denn er hält auch im folgenden ein Lächeln Drosillas, das wahrscheinlich spöttisch gemeint ist, für eine Gunstbezeugung (Cf. Plepelits, 95sq. mit No. 129, 166sq.).
[31] Cf. e. g. Eur. fr. 663 Kannicht = Nauck: ποιητὴν δ'ἄρα / Ἔρως διδάσκει, κἂν ἄμουσος ᾖ τὸ πρίν. Zum Zitat dieses Topos in der möglichen Antwort des Adressaten Nikias auf Theocr. 11 in Schol Theocr. 11 arg. c, p. 240 Wendel cf. Hunter, 221.

das Meer reitet, während der Kyklop sich an Land befindet.³² Es lassen sich wenigstens 16 solche Darstellungen nachweisen, auf einigen geben Eroten zusätzliche Interpretationshilfen. So führt auf einem Gemälde, das sich im Tablinum des Hauses der Kaiserin Livia auf dem Palatin in Rom an der Rückwand befindet und Ende des 1. Jh. v. Chr. entstanden ist (p. 118),³³ ein winziger Eros den riesigen Polyphem am Zügel, während Galatea nicht unter seiner Herrschaft steht. Polphem befindet sich an der rechten Bildseite etwa in der vertikalen Mitte bis zur Brust im Wasser und hält sich an einem Felsen fest. Galatea sitzt in der unteren Bildhälfte an der linken Seite auf einem Hippokampen, der sich von Polyphem wegbewegt, und zeigt dem Betrachter den Rücken. Der Bewegung von Galatea und dem Hippokampen entgegengesetzt sind die Fingerzeige zweier anderer Nereiden, die auf Polyphem weisen. Auf einem anderen Bild scheint es zwar umgekehrt zu sein (p. 119), da ein Eros einen Schirm über Galatea hält, die auf der rechten Bildhälfte auf einem Delphin über das Meer reitet, während Polyphem auf der linken Bildhälfte an Land steht, aber in Wahrheit wird wohl Galatea von Eros gegen Polyphems Liebe beschirmt.³⁴ Für wie schwierig der Fall Galatea in Sachen Liebe gehalten wurde, wird endlich in Drac. Romul. 2,34 deutlich, wo Amor, um seine außerordentliche Macht zu illustrieren, in einer längeren Rede aufgelistet hat, wen er alle in Liebe entbrennen lassen könne, nach einigen leichten Fällen wie Jupiter zu schwierigeren wie Minerva und schließlich zu den Meeresbewohnern gelangt ist, die im Wasser nur schwer zu entflammen sind, und sogar verspricht Galatea, zur Liebe zu den Tritonen zu bewegen.

In der zweiten Hälfte des 15. Jahrhunderts wird die hellenistische Dichtung, nicht zuletzt Theokrits 11. Idyll von den italienischen Humanisten begeistert rezipiert. Das gilt nicht für das 6. Idyll, obgleich auch dieses bereits in der *Editio princeps* (Mailand 1480) enthalten

---

[32] Cf. Pompeji: Schefold, 31 [I 7,7] (= Dawson, 99, No. 40, Tab. 15; Montón, No. 13), 65 [V 1,18] (= Dawson 106, No. 50), 97 [VI 5,5] (= Helbig, No. 1047; Montón, No. 15); 122 [VI 10,1] (= Helbig, No. 1044; Montón, No. 16), 159 [VI 16,32] (= Montón, No. 17), 182 [VII 4,48] (= Zahn, Vol. 3, Tab. 48; Helbig, No. 1043; Dawson, 111, No. 64, Tab. 24; Montón, No. 14), 184 [VII 4,51 resp. 31] (= Zahn, Vol. 2, 1841, Tab. 30; Helbig, No. 1042; Dawson, 110, No. 62, Tab. 23; Montón, No. 9), 187 [VII 4,59] (= Helbig, No. 1045; Dawson, 107, No. 53; Montón, No. 10), 206 [VII 15,2] (= Sogliano, No. 470; Dawson, 91, No. 26; Montón, No. 11), 244, [IX 2,18] (= Sogliano, No. 471; Dawson, 87, No. 16; Montón, No. 12), 268 [IX 7,12] (= Sogliano, No. 688; Dawson, 83, No. 6; Montón, No. 32); Herculaneum: Helbig, No. 1046 (=Montón, No. 19); Boscotrecase: Dawson, 100, No. 42, Tab. 16 + 17 (= Montón, No. 22); Antiochia: Montón, No. 23; Thysdrus: Montón, No. 25; Berlin: Montón, No. 30. Hinzu kommen die Darstellung des vom Eros beherrschten Polyphem und der ungerührten Galatea im Wasser in Rom (v.i. No. 34) und das Mosaik in Cordoba, das Galatea und Polyphem unbeteiligt nebeneinandersitzend zeigt (cf. Dörrie 1968, Tab. 5 = Montón, No. 24). In diesem Sinne läßt sich auch die Anspielung in Val. Flacc. 1,135sq. verstehen, wo in der Beschreibung eines Bildes auf der Argo Galatea zusammen mit Panope und Doto als ‹Brautjungfer› der Thetis auf dem Weg zum Brautgemach, den *antra*, ist, während der Kyklop sie (offensichtlich vergeblich) vom sizilischen Gestade zu sich ruft: «Prosequitur nudis pariter Galatea lacertis / antra petens; Siculo revocat de litore Cyclops» [Es folgt ebenso Galatea, mit nackten Armen der Höhle zustrebend, während sie der Kyklop vom sizilischen Gestade aus zurückruft].

[33] Cf. Dörrie 1968, Tab. 1 = Montón, No. 8.

[34] Cf. Zahn, Vol. 3, Tab. 4; Helbig, No. 1042; Dawson, 110, No. 42, Tab. 18; Schefold, 184 [VII 4,51 + 31]; Montón, No. 9. Außerdem gestaltet sich der Einfluß des Eros auf Polyphem auf einem römischen Relief in der Weise, daß Eros dem Kyklopen die – nicht dargestellte – Galatea zeigt (cf. Bieber, 153, Tab. 649; Montón, No. 28). Bei einer explizit namentlich bezeichneten Galatea befindet sich ein Eros auf einem tunesischen Mosaik (cf. Montón, No. 26), dessen Gestik allerdings schwer zu deuten ist. Sie kann ebenso deiktische Funktion haben wie Hilf- und Machtlosigkeit ausdrücken. Möglicherweise zeigte das Mosaik ursprünglich auch einen Polyphem. Es sind allerdings nur Reste erhalten.

ist.³⁵ So wirbt der Leiter der Neapolitanischen Akademie Giovanni Pontano (7. 5. 1429–9.1503) in sapphischen Strophen erfolglos als *Polyphemus* (Lyra 13) um die *dura Galatea* und klagt desweiteren als *Polyphemus a Galatea spretus* am Strand (Lyra 16).³⁶ Einen Schritt weiter geht sein Nachfolger Jacopo Sannazaro (28. 7. 1458–8.1530), dessen 2., *Galatea* betitelte *Ecloga piscatoria* sich als Klage über die Abweisung durch die Nymphe gestaltet, die als *immitis* (8), *crudelis* (28) und *dura* (48) bezeichnet wird.³⁷ Wie es sich in Bions Gedicht anbahnte, das Sannazaro aller Wahrscheinlichkeit nach nicht gekannt hat, ist der Mythos reduziert, der Gegensatz schön-häßlich aufgegeben und der Kyklop anscheinend völlig vergessen, in Wirklichkeit jedoch wohl nur als Identifikationsangebot an den notorisch abgewiesenen Liebhaber und Dichter verstanden worden. Vorbereitet hatte die Abkoppelung der Galatea von Polyphem für den lateinischen Westen freilich schon Vergil. Er hatte die aus Theokrit übersetzte Bitte an die Nereide, das Meer zu verlassen und zu ihm an Land zu kommen, seiner Figur Moeris als *non ignobile carmen* in den Mund gelegt (ecl. 9,37–43) sowie den Preis ihrer hellglänzenden Schönheit seinem Corydon (ecl. 7,37sq.). Überdies hatte er Hirtinnen ihren Namen gegeben (ecl. 1,30 f.; 3,64.72).³⁸ Nun aber wird Galatea zum Synonym für die topisch Unerreichbare, die *dura puella* des petrarkistischen Dichters, der, bei Sannazaro in der Maske eines Lycon, an die Stelle des Kyklopen tritt. War schon Pontanos *Polyphemus* nur noch bedingt komisch, so zeigt sich dieser Dichter in ernsthaftem Leid, indem er nicht wie Theokrits Polyphem am Ende zu seiner Arbeit zurückkehrt, sondern sich vom Felsen stürzen will (73–82). Noch einmal versucht Sannazaro in der 5. Ekloge als Thelgon vergeblich die *dura Galatea* (117) zu erweichen. Diese Dichtung ist Cassandra Marchese gewidmet, einer unglücklich verheirateten Adligen, zu der Sannazaro ein zumindest enges Verhältnis hatte, und es liegt wohl nicht allzu fern, sie mit Galatea zu identifizieren. Sicher identifizierbar ist die Galatea, die Lorenzo de' Medici (1. 1. 1449–8. 4. 1492) unter der Maske des Hirten Corintho in einer im toskanischen Volgare verfaßten Ekloge besang, die den Titel *Innamoramento di Lorenzo* trägt.³⁹ Es handelt

---

³⁵ Cf. Gow, XIV.
³⁶ Zum Text der Gedichte cf. Pontano 1948, 371–374.376–378. Ein weiteres Gedicht, in dem Polyphem Galatea im Meer verfolgt und ihr gegen ihren Willen einen Kuß raubt, findet sich nicht unter den Carmina des Pontano, sondern als Beispiel für «Leichtigkeit» (*facilitas*) in seinem Dialog *Actius* (cf. Pontano 1984, 238sq.).
³⁷ Zum Text der 2. und der im folgenden genannten 5. Ekloge Sannazaros cf. Sannazaro, 61–63.71–74; zu Text, Textgenese, Übersetzung und Interpretation der 2. Ekloge außerdem Czapla.
³⁸ Entsprechend begegnet man im Mittelalter Galateen, die sich als typisches bukolisches Personal in der Nachfolge Vergils erklären. Hierzu gehören diejenigen des Walther von Speyer (* 963), Scholasticus 82, des Hugo von Maçon, de militum gestis memorabilibus 5,197 (um 1250), des Giovanni Boccaccio, ecl. 1,34 (an dieser Stelle teilweise als Pseudonym einer nicht mehr identifizierbaren früheren Geliebten gedeutet, cf. Pier Giorgio Ricci, in: Boccaccio, 655); 4,31.152; 12,39; 16,68 (cf. Branca, 921) und vordergründig auch die des Radbert von Corbie (* ca. 790; Abt von Corbie 843/4–851), Ecloga duarum sanctimonialium (= carm. 1), 141.175; allerdings ist letztere in Analogie zur Erläuterung des Servius zu Verg. ecl. 1,30 (Galatea bedeutet Mantua, Amaryllis Rom) als Tochter des Menalcas, i. e. des Abtes Adalhard, allegorisch zu deuten als die von ihm neugegründete Abtei Nova Corbeia, die zusammen mit seiner Braut Philis, i. e. der alten Abtei Corbie, diesen nach seinem Tod beweint (cf. Berghoff-Bührer, 302). Wohl ohne Bedeutung dürfte die Wahl des Namens Galatea für die Protagonistin der anonymen, Ovid verpflichteten *Comoedia elegiaca* (rezipiert Ende des 11. Jh.) sein, in der die Vermittlung einer alten Frau der Liebe eines Pamphilus zu Galatea zur Erfüllung verhilft.
³⁹ Cf. de' Medici, 863–871. Im Gegensatz zu Sannazaros Figur Lycon, über deren Äußeres nichts mitgeteilt wird, überträgt Lorenzo äußere Merkmale des Kyklopen wie dunkle Haut, Körperbehaarung etc. auf seinen Corintho (112–117) und bezeichnet seine Verse explizit als «rozzi ... e poco ornati» [roh und wenig gefeilt] (43).

sich um die florentinische Patrizierin Lucretia Donati, die Lorenzo bereits im Alter von etwa fünfzehn Jahren in der Manier der Troubadours und Stilnovisten, sicherlich auch nach dem Beispiel Petrarcas mit einer angeblich keuschen Liebe als seine ‹donna› verehrte. Jedenfalls wurden sowohl Lorenzo als auch Lucretia mit anderen Partnern verheiratet.[40] Auch dort ist ebenso viel von der «belleza» (75.81.102.118.160.162) wie von der «durezza» und «crudeltate» (50.79.160) Galateas die Rede.

Auf dem berühmtesten Bild Galateas aus der italienischen Renaissance (p. 120), dem unter dem Titel *Triumph der Galatea* bekannten Werk Raffaele Santis (1483–1530), reitet Galatea nicht auf einem Delphin, sondern fährt in einem von zwei Delphinen gezogenen Muschelwagen inmitten einer Schar von Tritonen und Nereiden. Scheinen diese auf den ersten Blick einen ungeordneten Kreis um Galatea zu bilden, erweist sich ihre Anordnung doch als völlig symmetrisch. Einander schräg gegenüber finden sich zwei Paare: Links vorn umarmt ein Tritone eine Nereide von vorn, rechts hinten eine Nereide einen Tritonen von hinten. Hinter dem linken und vor dem rechten Paar befinden sich ebenfalls einander schräg gegenüber zwei einzelne Tritonen. Jeder von ihnen bläst zum seitlichen Bildrand gewandt auf einem Muschelhorn. Ein Eros ohne Waffen läßt sich am unteren Bildrand vom vorderen der Delphine ziehen, drei weitere, im oberen Bilddrittel im Dreieck angeordete Eroten zielen mit Pfeil und Bogen auf Galatea resp. auf die sie umgebende Schar, ein fünfter in der linken oberen Ecke halb von einer Wolke verdeckter hält seinen Köcher aufrecht und betrachtet das Geschehen. Dieses Bild befindet sich im Gartensaal der Villa Farnesina in Rom, und zwar neben einem *Polyphem* des Sebastino Piombo, der wohl – die Forschung hat lange über diese Frage gestritten – kurz vor Raffaels Galatea entstand. Beide Bilder sind etwa in den Jahren 1511/12 gemalt worden. Da bereits 1503 eine gedruckte Edition des Philostrat (Aldus) vorlag und noch zuvor Antonio Bonfini (1487) zumindest eine handschriftliche lateinische Übersetzung vorgelegt hatte, haben viele gern und lange geglaubt, daß Raffael seine Galatea nach der Beschreibung des Philostrat (imag. 2,18,4)[41] geschaffen habe:

> Ἡ δὲ ἐν ἁπαλῇ τῇ θαλάσσῃ παίζει τέτρωρον δελφίνων ξυνάγουσα ὁμοζυγούντων καὶ ταὐτὸν πνεόντων, παρθένοι δ' αὐτοὺς ἄγουσι Τρίτωνος, αἱ δμωαὶ τῆς Γαλατείας, ἐπιστομίζουσαι σφᾶς, εἴ τι ἀγέρωχόν τε καὶ παρὰ τὴν ἡνίαν πράττοιεν. ἡ δ' ὑπὲρ κεφαλῆς ἁλιπόρφυρον μὲν λῄδιον ἐς τὸν ζέφυρον αἴρει σκιὰν ἑαυτῇ εἶναι καὶ ἱστίον τῷ ἅρματι, ἀφ' οὗ καὶ αὐγή τις ἐπὶ τὸ μέτωπον καὶ τὴν κεφαλὴν ἥκει οὔπω ἡδίων τοῦ τῆς παρειᾶς ἄνθους, αἱ κόμαι δ' αὐτῆς οὐκ ἀνεῖται τῷ ζεφύρῳ· διάβροχοι γὰρ δή εἰσι καὶ κρείττους τοῦ ἀνέμου. καὶ μὴν καὶ ἀγκὼν δεξιὸς ἔκκειται λευκὸν διακλίνων πῆχυν καὶ ἀναπαύων τοὺς δακτύλους πρὸς ἁπαλῷ τῷ ὤμῳ καὶ ὠλέναι ὑποκυμαίνουσι καὶ μαζὸς ὑπανίσταται καὶ οὐδὲ τὴν ἐπιγουνίδα ἐκλείπει ἡ ὥρα. ὁ ταρσὸς δὲ καὶ ἡ συναπολήγουσα αὐτῷ χάρις ἔφαλος [...] γέγραπται καὶ ἐπιψαύει τῆς θαλάττης οἷον κυβερνῶν τὸ ἅρμα. θαῦμα οἱ ὀφθαλμοί· βλέπουσι γὰρ ὑπερόριόν τι καὶ συναπιὸν τῷ μήκει τοῦ πελάγους. (imag. 2,18,4)

> Sie aber spielt in der stillen See, indem sie zugleich vier Delphine antreibt, die einmütig ziehen und im Gleichtakt atmen; Töchter Tritons, Dienerinnen Galateas, führen sie und

---

[40] Cf. zu diesem Liebesspiel Orvieto, in: de' Medici, 857; Walter, 72–80.
[41] Die Forschungsgeschichte zur vieldiskutierten Frage, ob Philostrat tatsächlich Beschreibungen von real existierenden Bildern verfaßte, ist aufgearbeitet von Schönberger, 26–37; als weiteres Argument für die Authentizität der Beschreibungen kann der über den Kopf flatternde Schleier herangezogen werden der sich so tatsächlich auf Gemälden wiederfindet (cf. Helbig, No. 1045, Dawson, 107, No. 53; Montón, No. 10).

halten sie im Zaum, wenn sie übermütig werden und dem Zügel nicht gehorchen. Sie aber hebt über ihrem Kopf einen purpurnen Schleier gegen den Westwind, als Schattenspender für sich selbst und als Segel für ihr Gefährt, von dem zwar ein Abglanz auf Stirn und Antlitz fällt, der jedoch nicht lieblicher ist als die Farbe ihrer Wange. Ihre Haare sind dem Wind nicht preisgegeben, denn sie sind ganz feucht und für den Wind zu schwer. Ihr rechter Ellenbogen aber steht heraus in entgegengesetzter Richtung zum weißen Unterarm und läßt die Finger auf der zarten Schulter ruhen, die Arme sind wohlgerundet, die Brust ist aufgerichtet und auch der Oberschenkel nicht ohne Reiz. Die Fußsohle, bis zu der ihre Anmut reicht, [...] ist auf das Meer gemalt und berührt die See, als ob sie dem Wagen als Steuerruder diente. Ein Wunder sind ihre Augen; denn ihr Blick geht über den Horizont und mit der Weite des Meeres hinfort.

Doch Ende des 19. Jahrhunderts wies der Kunsthistoriker Richard Förster auf deutliche Unterschiede zwischen Raffael und Philostrat hin – auf dem Bild sind die Haare nicht naß, sondern flatten im Wind, die Haltung der Arme ist anders als in der Beschreibung, und die Delphine werden nicht von Tritonstöchtern geführt, um nur einiges zu erwähnen. Förster identifizierte die Raffael sicher leichter zugängliche und e. g. auch von Botticelli für seine *Geburt der Venus* benutzte volkssprachliche Dichtung des erwähnten Angelo Poliziano *Stanze comminciate per la giostra di Giuliano de' Medici* [Strophen, begonnen anläßlich des Turniersiegs des Giuliano de' Medici], genauer gesagt die 118. Strophe, als literarische Vorlage, die natürlich ihrerseits Philostrat folgt:

Due formosi delfini un carro tirono:
sovr'esso è Galatea che 'l fren correge;
e quei notando parimente spirono:
ruotasi attorno più lasciva gregge.
Qual le salse onde sputa, e quai s'aggirono;
qual per che per amor giuochi e vanegge.
La bella ninfa con le suore fide
di sí rozo cantar vezzosa ride.
Zwei schöne Delphine ziehen einen Wagen; auf diesem steht Galatea, die am Zügel zieht. Beim Schwimmen atmen beide im Gleichtakt. Herum kreist eine recht ausgelassene/lüsterne Schar. Einer speit die Salzflut aus, einige tummeln sich, ein anderer spielt liebestrunken und scherzt. Die schöne Nymphe und ihre treuen Schwestern lächeln lieblich über den so rohen Gesang.

Bereits zu Beginn des 19. Jahrhunderts war, insbesondere für das Gefolge muschelblasender Tritonen, als literarische Vorlage überdies Apuleius' Schilderung der über das Meer ziehenden Venus (met. 4,31,4–7) genannt worden[42] und wurde 1986 ebenso wie Philostrat von Klaus Heinrich erneut in die Diskussion gebracht.[43] Diese Vorlagendiskussion entspringt weniger der philologischen Freude an Abhängigkeitsforschung, sondern ist verknüpft mit

---

[42] Jacques Joseph J. Haus, Karl Friedrich von Ruhmor, Hermann Grimm; cf. Förster, 48; Thoenes 2002a, 67.
[43] Cf. Heinrich, 164sq. Völlig unhaltbar ist freilich seine Identifizierung des unbewaffneten Eros am unteren Bildrand mit Palaemon, dem Wagenlenker (*auriga*) der Venus bei Apuleius (4,31), da Galatea selbst den Wagen lenkt, der Eros hingegen sich nur mitziehen läßt. Sie steht auch im Widerspruch zu der ebenfalls von Heinrich vertretenen christlichen Entsprechung im Werk Raffaels, die dieser Eros im Jesuskind der Bridewater-Madonna habe (cf. 164). Auch rechtfertigt das im Wind flatternde Gewand durchaus nicht den erneuten Rückgriff auf Philostrat, da es sich nicht über ihrem Kopf zu einem Segel bauscht, wie es Philostrat beschreibt, wie es tatsächlich auf antiken Bildern zu sehen ist (v. s. No. 41) und wie es auch spätere Künstler gemalt haben (e. g. Jacques Stella, Jean Baptiste van Loo).

einer überaus kontrovers geführten Debatte über die Interpretation von Raffaels Galatea. Die von Christof Thoenes nachgezeichnete Forschungsgeschichte kann hier allerdings nur stark vereinfacht und gerafft wiedergegeben werden. Die Apuleius-Anhänger vertreten – unter Ausblendung des Polyphem – die von Förster e.a. relativ rasch widerlegte These, es handle sich nicht um eine Darstellung der Galatea, sondern der Venus. Doch nachdem schon in der deutschen Romantik die erotischen Aspekte des Bildes besonderen Widerhall fanden, Galatea als Inkarnation der Liebe und des Lebens, als Bekenntnis einer durch keine christliche Moral mehr eingeschränkte Sinnenfreude gefeiert worden war,[44] wurde in der Wissenschaft ebenfalls eine Verschmelzung von Galatea und Venus vertreten, wie sie sich auch uns an manchen Punkten andeutete.[45] Tatsächlich weisen die beiden Göttinnen ikonographisch große Ähnlichkeit auf, wie sich e. g. am Vergleich von Giuseppe Bezzuolis 1818–9 gemalter Galatea (Öl auf Leinwand, Brescia, Musei Civici d' Arte e Storia) und einem antiken Bild von Venus auf einem Seekentauren illustrieren läßt, das 1833 in Pompeji ausgegraben wurde (p. 121, 122).[46] Beide Göttinnen sind sowohl von Eroten als auch von Meerwesen umgeben. Auch die Darstellung der Galatea auf einem Muschelwagen bzw. auf einer Muschel rückt sie in die Nähe der Venus Anadyomene, wie sie von Botticelli e.a. gemalt wurde. Demgegenüber steht die Erkenntnis, daß Raffaels Galatea am lustvollen Treiben der um sie versammelten Wasserwesen nicht teilnimmt und daß die Pfeile der Eroten bei genauer Betrachtung nicht auf sie zielen. Vielmehr geht der Pfeil des mittleren Eros recht deutlich vom Betrachter aus gesehen links an ihr vorbei und dürfte das Paar links vorn treffen. Nicht ganz so eindeutig ist der Pfeil des rechten Eros auf dasselbe Paar gerichtet, während derjenige des linken Eros auf die rechte Gruppe zielt. Galateas Liebe wird dementspreched als eine geistige interpretiert und das Fresko als Synthese von Antike und Christentum.[47] Thoenes selbst deutet es in ähnlicher Weise als Ausdruck der von Marsilio Ficino propagierten neoplatonischen Liebeslehre der zwei Eroten und zwei Aphroditen, des himmlischen Eros und der himmlischen Aphrodite, die zur geistigen, und des gemeinen Eros und der gemeinen Aphrodite, die zur irdischen, leiblichen Liebe führen. Während Galateas Gefolge noch der irdischen Liebe verhaftet bleibe, folge sie selbst, die ein wenig über die anderen Figuren hervorragt und anscheinend aus der Gruppe der Meerwesen herausfährt, den himmlischen, da (im Gegensatz e. g. zum Eros in Botticellis *La Prima Vere*) ohne Augenbinde dargestellten Eroten. Die Pfeile dienten vornehmlich der diagonalen Linienführung, die Galatea heraushebt. Dieser Hervorhebung diene auch die Teilung nach dem goldenen Schnitt. Ihre Kopfhaltung deute auf eine entsprechende Entrückung.[48] Da die drei bewaffneten Eroten jedoch, wie gesehen, nicht Galatea, sondern ihr offensichtlich irdischer Liebe hingegebenes Gefolge zu treffen suchen, können himmlische Eroten nur in den beiden anderen zu suchen sein, die auf der Diagonale von links oben nach rechts unten angeordnet sind und von denen der eine von seinen Waffen keinen Gebrauch macht, der andere keine besitzt und überdies eine ähnliche Kopfhaltung zeigt wie Galatea und einen

---

[44] Wilhelm Heinse, Ludwig Tieck, Franz Kugler, Jacob Burckhart; cf. Thoenes 2002a, 60.
[45] A. v. Salis, W. Schöne; cf. Thoenes 2002a, 70–72.
[46] Cf. Zahn, Vol. 3, Tab. 4; Schefold, 183; Helbig, 308.
[47] Johann David Passavant, F. A. Gruyer, Ernst Förster; cf. Thoenes 2002a, 61sq.; 87, No. 125.
[48] Cf. Thoenes 2002a, 95–100, der sich allerdings später von dieser philosophischen Deutung hin zu einer ästhetischen distanziert, die Vorbilder von Teilen des Bildes in antiken Reliefs und Ausschnitten aus zeitgenössischer Malerei sucht (Cf. Thoenes 2002b), zur philosophischen jedoch nicht im Widerspruch steht.

vergleichbaren entrückten Blick. Eine Antithese zwischen Galatea und dem unbewaffneten Eros auf der einen und dem liebestrunkenen Gefolge auf der anderen Seite wird überdies gestützt durch Entsprechungen der Galatea und des Eros in Physiognomie und Körperhaltung mit christlichen Figuren des Raffael, nämlich der Galatea mit der heiligen Katharina von Alexandrien (p. 123) und des Eros mit dem Christuskind der Bridgewater-Madonna (p. 124), sowie der Entsprechung der Nereide links mit der Eva Michelangelos beim Sündenfall (p. 125).[49]

V. Die tugendhafte Galatea

Hier stellt sich natürlich die Frage, wie die kokette Nymphe Theokrits zu einem Symbol der Tugend und der geistigen Liebe, wie die Anrede als Galatea zu einem Kompliment für adlige Damen, wie neben herausragender Schönheit die Ehrbarkeit («honestidad», «honroso recato», «honra y honestidad»)[50] zur kennzeichnenden Eigenschaft der Galatea des spanischen Romanciers Miguel de Cervantes werden konnte. Die Antwort besteht in einem mehrfachen Läuterungsprozeß, dessen ersten Schritt der römische Dichter Ovid mit seiner Geschichte von Galatea und Polyphem vollzogen hat (met. 13,740–897). Er hat sie zunächst amplifiziert, und zwar einerseits durch rhetorische Mittel wie die beschriebene Ausweitung des Polyphem-Liedes, andererseits durch die Erweiterung von einer Zweier- auf eine Dreiecksbeziehung. Außerdem hat er sie erzähltechnisch im Zusammenhang seiner Metamorphosen funktionalisiert und für seinen Zweck die moralischen Positionen verschoben. Liegt die Sympathie des Lesers bei Theokrit, Pontano, Sannazaro und Lorenzo auf Seiten des von der *dura Galatea* abgewiesenen Polyphem bzw. Dichters, entlarvt Ovid Polyphems Freundlichkeit als Maske und zeigt ihn als blutrünstiges Monster, wie wir ihn aus Homer kennen (759–761: «ille immitis et ipsis / horrendus silvis et visus ab hospite nullo / impune et magni cum dis contemptor Olympi» [jener Grausame, vor dem selbst die Wälder erschrecken, den kein Gast je ungestraft erblickte und der den hohen Olymp und die Götter verachtet]; 773: «terribilem Polyphemum» [den schrecklichen Polyphem]).[51] Im Gegenzug wird – zumindest vordergründig – Galatea moralisch aufgewertet, i. e. ihre abweisende Haltung über die nachvollziehbare Abneigung gegen den riesigen häßlichen und grausamen Zausel hinaus motiviert. Sie tritt in Gegensatz zu Scylla, die ihr erzählte, wie sie die verliebten jungen Männern verspottet habe (737: «elusos iuvenum narrabat amores»), indem sie kein Spiel mit Polyphem treibt. Ihre Haltung ihm gegenüber ist vielmehr ein in jeder Hinsicht gerechtfertigtes, veritables und explizites *odium*, dem ein gleichstarker *amor* zu einem anderen entgegengesetzt ist (756–758: «nec, si quaesieris, odium Cyclopis amorne Acidis in nobis fuerit praesentior, edam: / par utrumque fuit» [und, wenn du mich fragst, ob der Abscheu vor dem Kyklopen oder die Liebe zu Acis stärker in mir war, werde

---

[49] Cf. Heinrich, 164sq. 171sq. Diese Überlegung gilt freilich mit der Einschränkung, daß Maler der Renaissance pagane Göttinnen und christliche Heilige oder Madonnen nicht grundsätzlich anders malten. So bediente sich e. g. Botticelli desselben Typus weiblicher Köpfe für Madonnen- und Venusbilder (Cf. Vasari, 238, No. 9).

[50] Cervantes, 39sq.

[51] Zu dieser Veränderung gegenüber Theokrit cf. Bömer, Vol. 6, 413.416. Weiter noch geht Dante in einer Anspielung auf Ovid (ecl. 2,76–80), der den Polyphem sogar die Eingeweide des Acis zerfleischen und seine Zähne in Blut tauchen läßt (Zur allegorischen Deutung der Stelle cf. Krautter, 46–51).

ich sagen: beides war gleich stark]).⁵² Dieser andere ist aber nicht, wie möglicherweise in älterer griechischer Literatur, Odysseus, ein moralisch ebenfalls fragwürdiger Mann in den mittleren Jahren, den Athene erst einmal verjüngen und mit κάλλος und χάρις ausrüsten muß, damit er stattlich aussieht (Hom. Od. 16,172–176; 23,156–163), sondern ein echter Anti-Polyphem, der bis dahin im Mythos nicht bekannte Acis, ein hübscher Sechzehnjähriger von appetitlicher pfirsichartiger Schönheit (Ov. met. 13,753: «pulcher et octonis iterum natalibus actis / signarat dubia lanugine malas» [schön und hatte, sechzehn Jahre alt geworden, die Wangen mit kaum wahrnehmbarem Flaum gezeichnet]).⁵³ Einen hübschen Knaben zu lieben ist sicherlich einfacher, als zu einem Monster Zuneigung zu entwickeln, doch immerhin ist Galateas Liebe zu Acis exklusiv (752: «nam me sibi iunxerat uni» [denn an sich ausschließlich hatte er mich gebunden]), und diese Haltung läßt sich durchaus als Treue interpretieren, wie es in der mittelalterlichen Ovid-Allegorese geschehen ist.⁵⁴ Nachdem man die Einführung des Acis lange Zeit einer hellenistischen Quelle zugeschrieben hat,⁵⁵ nimmt man heute eher an, Ovid habe diese Figur aus dem gegebenen Flußnamen selbst entwickelt.⁵⁶ Dies ist um so wahrscheinlicher, als das Motiv der Liebe und Treue der Galatea die notwendige moralische Autorität verleiht, Scyllas Verhalten implizit zu tadeln, indem sie ihrem Schmerz darüber Ausdruck verleiht, daß Scylla – jedenfalls bis zu diesem Zeitpunkt – sich dem «genus haud immite virorum» ungestraft versagen darf, während sie für die verständliche Abweisung des Kyklopen einen so hohen Preis zahlen mußte (740–745). Gleichwertig wäre das der Daphne vorbehaltene Motiv der beschworenen Jungfräulichkeit gewesen,⁵⁷ das im Werbelied des Kyklopen anklingt (859sq.: «atque ego contemptus essem patientior huius, / si fugeres omnes» [und ich ertrüge es leichter, verschmäht zu sein, wenn du auch die anderen miedest]), aber in diesem Fall hätte der Nebenbuhler gefehlt, an dem sich die Wut des Kyklopen noch mehr entzündete, und das unschuldige Opfer, an dem Ovid ihn seine blutrünstige Grausamkeit demonstrieren, i. e. es durch einen Steinwurf töten ließ.

---

⁵² Daß der Verbindung der Galatea mit Acis eine Tochter namens Catena entsprungen sein soll, wie Montón (cf. 1000) ohne Quellenangabe behauptet, läßt sich aus der antiken Literatur nicht belegen.
⁵³ Zu Ähnlichkeit und Gegensatz zwischen Polyphem und Acis, den Ovid mit beinahe denselben Worten beschreibt wie Theokrit seinen jugendlichen Kyklopen (11,9: ἄρτι γενειάσδων περὶ τὸ στόμα τὼς κροτάφως τε), aber durch die Attribute *tener* und *dubius* eher an jugendliche Schönheit als an unregelmäßige Bartstoppeln denken läßt, cf. Griffin, 192; Farrell, 243; Hopkinson, 212.
⁵⁴ Mit Recht hat bereits Dörrie (cf. 1969, 83sq.98) darauf hingewiesen, daß sich Galateas Unschuld auch aus dem Umstand ergebe, daß die Geschichte aus ihrer Perspektive erzählt wird, und daß sie in keinem Augenblick vor einer Entscheidung gegen Acis stehe, ihre Zurückhaltung insofern nicht keusch und verdienstlich sei. Zu einer negativen Auslegung von Galateas Härte, die Ovid dem Polyphem in den Mund legt (v. s.) und die sich auch darin äußert, daß sie zusammen mit Acis aus einem Versteck heraus anscheinend ungerührt den Kyklopen bei seiner Werbung beobachtet, cf. Griffin, 195sq. Dafür, daß der Dichter angesichts des «Voyeurismus» von Acis und Galatea mit dem Underdog Polyphem Mitleid empfinde, scheint mir jedoch keinen Beleg zu geben.
⁵⁵ Holland, Weicker, Haupt-Ehwald: Kallimachos, Preller-Robert, Scherling, Hunger: Sizilische Hirtendichtung (cf. Bömer, Vol. 6, 410).
⁵⁶ Cf. Dörrie 1968, 55sq.; Bömer, Vol. 6, 410; Griffin, 192; Irving, 302.
⁵⁷ Auch vom Daphne-Mythos existierte eine – offensichtlich ältere – Version, daß die Jägerin Daphne Zuneigung zu einem Leukippos gefaßt habe, der in Frauenverkleidung mit ihr jagte. Erst nach Entdeckung und Entrückung des Leukippos habe der verliebte Apoll Daphne verfolgt, die von Zeus auf ihre Bitte um Entrückung hin in den Lorbeer verwandelt worden sei (Parthenios, Erotica Pathemata 15; cf. Bömer, Vol. 1, 144).

Nachdem die Antike dem Stoff in der Ovidischen Fassung literarisch offenbar wenig abzugewinnen wußte,[58] ist er, wie Dörrie und Hunger gezeigt haben,[59] etwa vom Ende des 16. bis zur Mitte des 20. Jahrhunderts in zahlreichen Musikdramen und Balletten bearbeitet worden. Auch bildliche Darstellungen der treuen Galatea gibt es in der Antike kaum. Es läßt sich eine einzige ausmachen, auf der ein Hirte, vermutlich Acis, vor Polyphem flieht.[60] Dieser Armut steht wiederum die Fülle von Zeichnungen, Gemälden usw. aus Renaissance und Barock gegenüber.[61]

Thoenes entwickelt seine Deutung der tugendhaften Galatea nun aus der mittelalterlichen Ovid-Allegorese, dem zweiten Schritt des Läuterungsprozesses. Im *Ovidius moralizatus* des Petrus Berchorius (1290–1362) wird Gala-thea als *candida* oder *alba dea* erklärt, die sich für Acis, d.h. für die Tugend, gegen Polyphem, d.h. gegen die Verderbtheit, entscheidet:[62]

> Vel dic q(uod) p(er) Galathea(m) potes i(n)tellegere alba(m) deam: & dicitur a *gala* quod e(st) lac & *theos* quod est deus vel dea: quasi dea lactea id est alba: per acim intellege castitatem per polyphemum intellige plurimum corruptum: vel foemineu(m). Et dicitur a *poly* quod est pluritas & *phoemos* q(uo)d est foemina quasi plurimus foemineus. quia tunc dicit(ur) polyphemus acim. id est corruptio castitate(m) interficere: quando corruptio praedominatur castitati.[63]
>
> [Oder sage, daß man Galathea als weiße Göttin deuten kann und daß sie nach *gala* benannt ist, was Milch bedeutet, und von *theos*, was Gott oder Göttin bedeutet, gewissermaßen als milchige, d.h. weiße Göttin. Acis verstehe als Keuschheit und Polyphem als sehr viel Verderbtes oder Weibisches. Er wird nach *poly* benannt, was Vielheit bedeutet, und nach *phoemos*, was Weib oder weibisch bedeutet, gewissermaßen als reichlich Weibischer. Daher sagt man, daß Polyphem den Acis tötet, d.h. die Verderbtheit die Keuschheit, weil die Verderbtheit über die Keuschheit herrscht.].

Eine späte poetische Umsetzung dieser mittelalterlichen Sicht der Galatea bietet der Begründer des Petrarkismus Pietro Bembo in einem 35 Distichen umfassenden lateinischen Gedicht *Galatea*. Darin erwehrt sich sie sich erfolgreich der Nachstellungen des bocksfüßigen Pan, der ohnehin gern mit dem Teufel identifiziert wird und in dessen Gefolge sich

---

[58] Es finden sich eine kurze Anspielung bei Silius Italicus (14,221-26: Der durch die Grausamkeit des Polyphem in einen Fluß verwandelte Acis spült mit seiner *dulcis unda* die Galatea und vermischt sich mit ihr bzw. dem Meer; cf. die entsprechende Allegorese Boccaccios, Genealogiae deorum gentilium libri XV, 7,17, v.i. No. 62) und ein Epigramm in der *Anthologia Latina* (140 S.B.), das von der verzehrenden Liebe Galateas zu Acis handelt (v. s. No. 8).

[59] Dörrie 1968, 88-92; Hunger, 433sq. Zur Rezeption Ovids in Händels Oper *Acis und Galatea* cf. esp. Mack.

[60] Cf. Sogliano, No. 473; Schefold, 266 [I 6]; Dawson, 81, No. 2; Montón, 47. Möglicherweise der Ovidschen Tradition zuzurechnen ist noch ein römischer Sarkophag, der zum einen die konventionelle Anordnung von Polyphem, der auf einem Felsen sitzt, und Galatea rittlings auf einem Delphin zeigt, darüber hinaus aber über ihr im Gebirge einen jungen Flußgott (cf. Montón, No. 29).

[61] Cf. Hunger, 433.

[62] Cf. Thoenes 2002a, 90-95.

[63] Berchorius, 170 (fol. XCII); rationalistisch hingegen deutet Boccaccio (Genealogiae deorum gentilium libri XV, 7,17) zwar Galatea auch als *albedinis dea*, versteht das Weiß aber als *albedo undarum sese frangentium* und interpretiert die Liebe des Acis zu Galatea als die Vereinigung von Süß- und Salzwasser resp. den Polyphem nach einem mittelalterlichen Kompilator namens Theodontius als sizilischen Tyrannen, der Galatea vergewaltigte und anschließend ihren Liebhaber Acis in einen Fluß werfen ließ, den dann die Anwohner nach diesem benannten. Als Teil des Meeres erschien Galatea bereits bei Dracontius (Romul. 7,151sq.).

explizit der Inkubus befindet, der sich immer für Liebesaffären mit den Nymphen und die rauhe Flöte mit ihrem klagenden Klang interessiert (35-37: «[...] cordi cui semper amores / Nympharum, et querulo tibia rauca sono, / Incubus [...]»).[64]

Noch einmal geadelt wurde Galatea durch keinen geringeren als den «Vater des Humanismus» Francesco Petrarca (1304-1374) selbst in seiner *Galathea* betitelten 11. Ekloge, die etwa im gleichen Zeitraum entstanden ist wie der *Ovidius moralizatus* seines Freundes Berchorius.[65] Sie ist wie auch die anderen Stücke von Petrarcas *Bucolicum Carmen* in jedem Fall allegorisch zu lesen, und hinter der *alba dea* verbirgt sich keine geringere als seine berühmte Geliebte Laura.[66] Ihren Tod beklagt Petrarca in Gestalt von drei Frauen, die seine verschiedenen Seelenzustände symbolisieren, im gleichen Maße, wie er ihre christliche Apotheose feiert. Es ist der einzige Text, in dem er Laura, die er sonst mit dem Lorbeer, i. e. mit Daphne, i. e. wiederum mit seinem Dichterruhm identifiziert, diesen Namen gibt. Die Benennung ist insofern konsequent, als die schon im Leben als schön, keusch und unerreichbar besungene Geliebte nun als reine Tugend sublimiert und transzendiert wird. Hatte sich bei Ovid bereits die Nähe der moralisch erhöhten Galatea zu Daphne angedeutet, konvergieren die beiden Gestalten in Laura. Galatea aber ist von der paganen Göttin niederen Ranges mit überaus menschlichen Verhaltensweisen zur christlichen ‹donna angelica› oder himmlischen Aphrodite aufgestiegen. Wenn also in der Folgezeit Dichter wie Sannazaro oder Lorenzo de' Medici adlige oder bürgerliche ‹donne› unter ihrem Namen besingen, wird dies ohne Zweifel als Kompliment ebenso für die äußeren Reize der Damen wie für ihre als Härte und Grausamkeit maskierte Tugendhaftigkeit verstanden. Denn Petrarca, der wie die meisten seiner Zeitgenossen die griechische Sprache nicht beherrschte, kannte nur die treue Ovidische Galatea, Sannazaro aber und alle anderen, welche auch die freche Galatea Theokrits kannten, übernahmen zwar die poetische Situation des 11. Idylls, in der nur der Liebhaber spricht, Galatea aber ebenso stumm bleibt wie Petrarcas Laura im *Canzoniere*, führten aber auf der Grundlage ihrer intensiven Lektüre der römischen Klassiker und Petrarcas als Vorbild der volkssprachigen Dichtung die Tradition der tugendhaften Galatea fort.[67] Als Inbegriff der keuschen Schönheit eignet sich Galatea dann in der Tat als Namensgeberin für die zum Leben erweckte Statue Pygmalions (in Rousseaus *Pigmalion, scène lyrique* von 1770),[68] wobei natürlich die weiße Farbe einer solchen Statue nicht vergessen werden darf, die nach einem entsprechend konnotierten Namen verlangt. Doch

---

[64] Bembo, 343sq., esp. 344.
[65] Zur Freundschaft zwischen Berchorius und Petrarca schon zu ihrer Zeit in Avignon cf. Wilkins, 513; Samaran/Monfrin, 9: Diese Freundschaft bezeugt Petrarcas Brief Ep. sen. 16,7; überdies bekennt Berchorius im Prolog zu seinem *Ovidius moralizatus*, zur Darstellung antiker Götter Petrarca zu Rate gezogen zu haben (cf. Wilkins, 515; Samaran/Monfrin, 81).
[66] Nicht von Berchorius ausgehend, sondern von Petrarcas Erklärer Piendibeni, der Galathea von einem imaginierten, angeblich nach Milch und *theos* bzw. ‹Gott› klingenden griechischen Wort *Calathyn* herleitet (cf. Avena, 285), erklären auch Berghoff-Bührer (cf. 301) und Branca (cf. 921) den Namen Galathea als *candida dea*; letzterer identifiziert auf dieser Grundlage die Galatea in Boccaccios ecl. 7,21.38.43 mit der Stadt Rom im Gegensatz zu der *lusca* (21), i. e. Florenz (cf. 972).
[67] Von der Überlagerung der Theokriteischen durch die Ovidische Galatea sowie von dem Hervortreten der Galatea und dem gleichzeitigen Zurücktreten des Kyklopen zeugen im Bereich der bildenden Kunst die drei Deckengemälde im Saal IV, der Galleria degli Imperatori, der Villa Borghese in Rom, die Domenico de Angelis Ende des 18. Jh. (ca. 1778-1780) geschaffen hat: Ein rechteckiger Triumph der Galatea in der Mitte wird gerahmt von zwei runden Gemälden, von denen das eine zeigt, wie Polyphem den Stein wirft und Acis und Galatea fliehen, das andere den Abschied der Galatea von Acis, der in die Quelle verwandelt wird.
[68] Cf. Dörrie 1968, 68-70.

Pygmalions Galathée gehört in einen anderen Mythos, der uns an dieser Stelle nicht beschäftigen soll.

Zurückzukommen ist nun, wie angekündigt, noch einmal auf Homers Wahl des inhaltlich nicht unmittelbar einsichtigen Epithetons ἀγακλειτή. Gerade bei Autoren wie Pontano und Sannazaro, die immensen Wert auf den Wohlklang ihrer Dichtungen gelegt haben,[69] ist die Überlegung nicht ganz von der Hand zu weisen, daß sich ihre Vorliebe für den Namen Galatea neben den inhaltlichen Konnotationen auch durch seinen schönen Klang erklärt.[70] Ebenso ist bei Cervantes nicht zu übersehen, daß die meisten Namen seiner Schäfer und Schäferinnen wie Artemidoro, Rosaura, Teolinda etc. dem Ohr schmeicheln. Nicht anders zeichnet sich Homers Nereiden-Katalog durch Euphonie aus, die sich i.a. in mehreren Homoioteleuta manifestiert, und ἀγακλειτή zeigt die gleiche Vokalfolge wie Γαλάτεια.[71] Weder müssen wir also befürchten, Homer habe einen nicht überlieferten Mythos gekannt, durch den Galatea berühmt war,[72] noch ihm wahrhaft seherische Fähigkeiten attestieren.

Literaturverzeichnis

ANELLO, Pietrina: Polifemo e Galatea, in: Seia 1 (1984), 11–51.
ARNOTT, W. Geoffrey: Alexis: The Fragments and a Commentary, Cambridge 1996 (Cambridge Classical Texts and Commentaries. 31).
AVENA, Antonio: Francesco Petrarca, Il Bucolicum Carmen e i suoi commenti inediti, Padua 1906.
BEMBO, Pietro: Galatea, in: Opere del Cardinale Pietro Bembo, ora per la prima volta tutte in un corpo unite, Vol. 4, Venedig 1729.
BERCHORIUS, Petrus: Reductorium morale, liber XV, cap. II–XV. «Ovidius moralizatus» naar de Parijse druk van 1509, Utrecht 1962.
BERGHOFF-BÜHRER, Margrith: Das Bucolicum Carmen des Petrarca. Ein Beitrag zur Wirkungsgeschichte von Vergils Eklogen, Bern e. a. 1991.
BETTS, John: Theocritus 6.16–17, in: Classical Philology 66 (1971), 252sq.
BIEBER, Margarete: The Sculpture of the Hellenistic Age, Columbia, New York ²1961.
BOCCACCIO, Giovanni: Opere in versi, Corbaccio, trattello in laude di Dante, prose latine, epistole, a cura di Pier Giorgio Ricci, Mailand/Neapel 1965.
BÖMER, Franz: P. Ovidius Naso, Metamorphosen. Kommentar, Vol. 1: Bücher 1–3, Heidelberg 1969; Vol. 6: Bücher 12–13, Heidelberg 1982.
Vittore Branca (Ed.): Tutte le opere di Giovanni Boccaccio, Mailand 1994.
CASOLARI, Federica: Die Mythentravestie in der griechischen Komödie, Münster 2003 (Orbis Antiquus. 37).
CASPERS, Christiaan: The Loves of the Greek Poets. Allusion in Hermesianax fr. 7 Powell, in: Annette Harder e. a. (Ed.): Hellenistica Groningana 7: Beyond the Canon, Leuwen 2006, 21–42.
CAVEN, Brian: Dionysius I. War-Lord of Sicely, New Haven/London 1990.

---

[69] Cf. die Überlegungen zur Euphonie, die Pontano dem Sannazaro bzw. der Figur Actius in seinem gleichnamigen Dialog in den Mund legt (Pontano, 1984, 333–415).
[70] Zur Verbreitung des Namens Galatea auf Grund seines Wohlklangs im lateinischen Westen cf. Bömer, Vol. 6, 409.
[71] Cf. Edwards, 148.
[72] Vgl. Holland, 185, der das Attribut für keinen hinreichenden Beleg dafür hält, daß Galatea vor Philoxenos in der Dichtung prominent erwähnt worden sei.

DE CERVANTES Saavedra, Miguel: Obras completas, ed. Florencio Sevilla Arroyo, Madrid 2000.
CZAPLA, Beate: Sannazaros zweite Ekloge *Galatea* als Neufassung eines *non ignobile carmen* (Verg. Ecl. 9,37-43), in: Eckart Schäfer (Ed.): Sannazaro und die Augusteische Dichtung, Tübingen 2006 (NeoLatina. 10), 69-86.
DAWSON, Christopher M.: Romano-Campanian Mythological Landscape Painting, New Haven 1944 (Yale Classical Studies. 9).
DÖRRIE, Heinrich: Die schöne Galatea, München 1968.
ID.: Der verliebte Kyklop. Interpretation von Ovid met. 13,750-897, in: Der altsprachliche Unterricht 12,3 (1969), 75-100.
EDWARDS, Mark W.: The Iliad: A Commentary, Volume V: books 17-20, Cambridge 1991.
FARRELL, Joseph: Dialogue of Genres in «Ovid's Lovesong» of Polyphemus (Metamorphoses 13.719-897), in: American Journal of Philology 113 (1992), 235-268.
FÖRSTER, Richard: Farnesina-Studien. Ein Beitrag zur Frage nach dem Verhältnis der Renaissance zur Antike, Rostock 1880.
FRAZER, Peter M.: Ptolemaic Alexandria, 3 Vol., Oxford 1972.
FUNKE, Hermann: *Urit me Glycerae nitor* ... Literarische Schönheitsbeschreibungen in der Antike, in: Theo Stemmler (Ed.): Schöne Frauen - schöne Männer. Literarische Schönheitsbeschreibungen. 2. Kolloquium der Forschungsstelle für europäische Literatur des Mittelalters, Mannheim 1988, 47-67.
GATTINONI Landiccu, Franca: Duride di Samo, Rom 1997.
GOMPERZ, Theodor: Skylla in der aristotelischen Poetik und die Kunstform des Dithyrambos, in id.: Hellenika. Eine Auswahl philologischer und philosophiegeschichtlicher Studien, Leipzig 1912, 85-92.
GOW, A. S. F. (Ed.): Bucolici Graeci, Oxford 1952.
GRIFFIN, Alan H. F.: Unrequitted love: Polyphemus and Galatea in Ovid's Metamorphoses, in: Greece & Rome 30 (1983), 190-197.
HARDER, Ruth E.: Galateia, in: NP 4 (1998), 741.
HEINRICH, Klaus: Götter und Halbgötter der Renaissance. Eine Betrachtung am Beispiel der Galatea, in: Richard Faber/ Renate Schlesier (Edd.): Die Restauration der Götter. Antike Religion und Neopaganismus, Würzburg 1986, 153-182.
HELBIG, Wolfgang: Wandgemälde der vom Vesuv verschütteten Städte Campaniens, Leipzig 1868.
HERTER, Hans: Kallimachos aus Kyrene, RE Suppl. 13 (1973), 184-260.
HOLLAND, Georg Richard: De Polyphemo et Galatea, in: Leipziger Studien zur Classischen Philologie 17 (1884), 139-312.
HOPKINSON, Neil (Ed.): Ovid: Metamorphoses Book XIII, Cambridge 2000.
HORDERN, James H.: The Cyclops of Philoxenos, in: Classical Quarterly 93 = N.S. 49 (1999), 445-455.
HUNGER, Herbert: Lexikon der griechischen und römischen Mythologie, s.v. Polyphem, Wien ^{8}1988.
HUNTER, Richard (Ed.): Theocritus, A Selection: Idylls 1, 3, 4, 6, 7, 10, 11 and 13, Cambridge 1999.
IRVING FORBES, P. M. C.: Metamorphosis in Greek Myths, Oxford 1990.
JACOBI, Felix: Die Fragmente der Griechischen Historiker, Vol. 2c, Berlin 1926; Vol. 3b, Leiden 1955.
KRAUTTER, Konrad: Die Renaissance der Bukolik in der lateinischen Literatur des XIV. Jahrhunderts: von Dante bis Petrarca, München 1983 (Theorie und Geschichte der Literatur und der schönen Künste. 65).
MACK, Sara: Acis and Galatea or the Metamorphosis of Tradition, in: Arion, 3. Series 6,3 (1999), 51-67.

DE' MEDICI, Lorenzo: Tutte le opere, a cura di Paolo Orvieto, Rom 1992, Vol. 2.
MEILLIER, Claude: Callimaque et son temps. Recherches sur la carrière et la condition d'un écrivain à l'époque des premiers Lagides, Lille 1979 (Publications de l'université de Lille. 3)
MEISTER, Klaus: Die griechische Geschichtsschreibung. Von den Anfängen bis zum Hellenismus, Stuttgart 1990.
MOMMIGLIANO, Arnaldo: Hochkulturen im Hellenismus. Die Begegnung der Griechen mit Kelten, Römern, Juden und Persern, München 1979.
MONTÓN SUBIAS, Sandra: Galateia, in: Lexicon Iconographicum Mythologiae Classicae, Vol. 5,1, Zürich/München 1990, 1000–1005.
NACHTERGAEL, Georges: Les Galates en Grece et les Sôtéria de Delphes. Recherches d'histoire et d'epigraphie hellenistiques, Brüssel 1977.
PAOLUCCI, Paola: Ciclo di Galatea, in: Bollettino di studi latini 32 (2002), 111–127.
PEARSON, Lionel: The Greek Historians of the West: Timaeus and his Predecessors, Atlanta 1987 (Philological Monographs of the American Philological Association. 35).
PETZL, Georg: Kein Umsturz beim Galater-Überfall auf Delphi, in: ZPE 56 (1984), 141–144.
PFEIFFER, Rudolf (Ed.): Callimachus, Vol. I: Fragmenta, Oxford 1949.
PLEPELITS, Karl: Niketas Eugenianos: Drosilla und Charikles, eingeleitet, übersetzt und erläutert von Karl Plepelits, Stuttgart 2003 (Bibliothek der griechischen Literatur. 61).
PONTANO, Giovanni G.: Carmina: Ecloghe – elegie – liriche Ioannis Ioviani Pontani, ed. Johannes Oeschger, Bari 1948 (Scrittori d'Italia. 198).
PONTANO, Giovanni G.: Dialoge, übersetzt von Hermann Kiefer unter Mitarbeit von Hanna-Barbara Gerl und Klaus Thieme, mit einer Einleitung von Ernesto Grassi, München 1984 (Humanistische Bibliothek. Texte und Abhandlungen, 2, 15).
PULCI, Luca: Polifemo a Galatea Ninfa Maritima. Epistola Ottava, in: Ciriffo Calvaneo di Luca Pulci Gentilhuomo Fiorentina. Con la Giostra del Magnifico Lorenzo de Medici. Insieme con Le Epistole Composte Dal Medesimo Pulci, Florenz 1572.
RANKIN, Herbert D.: Celts and the Classical World, London/Sidney 1987.
RIBBECK, Otto: Theokriteische Studien, in: Rheinisches Museum 17 (1862), 543–577.
SAMARAN, Charles/ Monfrin, Jacques: Pierre Bersuire. Prieur de Saint-Eloi de Paris (1290?–1362). Extrait de l'histoire litteraire de la France, Tome 39, Paris 1962.
SANNAZARO, Jacopo: The Piscatory Eclogues, ed., with introduction and notes, by Wilfred P. Mustard, Baltimore 1914.
SCHEFOLD, Karl: Die Wände Pompejis. Topographisches Verzeichnis der Bildmotive, Berlin 1957.
SCHERFER, Walter: Das Märchenlexikon, München 1995, Vol. 2.
SCHÖNBERGER, Otto: Philostratos, Die Bilder, Griech.-deutsch, nach Vorarbeiten von Ernst Kalinka, herausgegeben, übersetzt und erläutert von Otto Schönberger, München 1968.
SOGLIANO, Antonio: Le pitture murali campane scoverte degli anni 1867-79, Neapel 1880.
SUTTON, Dana F.: Dithyramb as δρᾶμα: Philoxenus of Cythera's Cyclops or Galatea, in: Quaderni urbinati di cultura classica N.S. 13 (1983), 37–43.
THOENES, Christof: Zu Raffaels Galatea, in: id.: Opus incertum. Italienische Studien aus drei Jahrzehnten, München/Berlin 2002, 51–116.
ID.: Galatea, tentativi di avvicinamento, ibid., 215–244
UTHER, Hans Jörg: Schönheit im Märchen, in: Lares. Rivista trimestrale di studi demo-etno-antropologici 52 (1986), 5–16.
VASARI, Giorgio: Leben der ausgezeichneten Maler, Bildhauer und Baumeister, von Cimabue bis zum Jahre 1567, aus dem Italienischen, mit einer Bearbeitung sämtlicher Anmerkungen der früheren Herausgeber, so wie mit eigenen Berichtigungen und Nachweisen von Ludwig Schorn, Vol. 2,2, Stuttgart/Tübingen 1839.
WALBANK, Frank W.: Timaios und die westgriechische Sicht der Vergangenheit, Konstanz 1992 (Konstanzer althistorische Vorträge und Forschungen. 29).

WALTER, Ingeborg: Der Prächtige. Lorenzo de' Medici und seine Zeit, München 2002.
WEBSTER, Thomas B. L.: Studies in Later Greek Comedy, New York ²1970.
WEICKER, Georg: Galateia, in: RE 6,1 (1910), 517–519.
WEIZSÄCKER, Karl: Galateia, in: Wilhelm H. Roscher: Ausführliches Lexikon der griechischen und römischen Mythologie, Leipzig 1886–1890, Vol. 1,2, 1586–1588.
WILKINS, Ernest H.: Descriptions of Pagan Divinities from Petrarch to Chaucer, in: Speculum. A Journal of Mediaeval Studies 32 (1957), 510–522.
ZAHN, Wilhelm: Die schönsten Ornamente und merkwürdigsten Gemälde aus Pompeji, Herkulaneum und Stabiae, nebst einigen Grundrissen und Ansichten nach den an Ort und Stelle gemachten Originalzeichnungen, Vol. 2, Berlin 1841, Vol. 3, 1849.
ZIMMERMANN, Bernhard: Dithyrambus. Geschichte einer Gattung, Göttingen 1992 (Hypomnemata. 98).

Die Wandlung der Nereide Galatea von einer Kokotte zur Heiligen

Galatea in den Armen des Kyklopen, Pompeji

Polyphem von Eros beherrscht, Galatea und andere Nymphen,
Rückwand im Tablinum des Hauses der Kaiserin Livia, Rom, Palatin

Landschaft mit Polyphem und Galatea, muschelblasendem Triton und Eros mit Sonnenschirm, Pompeji

Raffael, Galatea

Die Wandlung der Nereide Galatea von einer Kokotte zur Heiligen

Bezzuoli, Galatea

Venus auf einem Seekentauer, Pompeji

Die Wandlung der Nereide Galatea von einer Kokotte zur Heiligen

Raffael, Heilige Katharina von Alexandrien

Raffael, Bridgewater-Madonna

Michelangelo, Eva beim Sündenfall

Paul Barone

Herakles in der Moderne:
Zu Schillers Rezeption des antiken Mythos

I

Als Schiller am 30. November 1795 Humboldt seinen Plan mitteilte, eine Herakles-Idylle zu verfassen, hoffte er, durch diese Idylle mit der «sentimentalischen» über die «naive» Dichtung «triumphieren» zu können. Schiller stellte an sich selbst keinen geringeren Anspruch, als durch ein eigenes Werk die Überlegenheit der modernen Dichtung über die antike zu erweisen:

> Ich will eine *Idylle* schreiben, wie ich hier eine Elegie schrieb. Alle meine poetischen Kräfte spannen sich zu dieser Energie noch an – das Ideal der Schönheit objektiv zu individualisieren, und daraus eine Idylle in *meinem* Sinne zu bilden [...] Ich habe ernstlich im Sinn, da fortzufahren, wo das Reich der Schatten aufhört, aber darstellend und nicht lehrend. Herkules ist in den Olymp eingetreten, hier endigt letzteres Gedicht. Die Vermählung des Herkules mit der Hebe würde der Inhalt meiner Idylle seyn. Ueber diesen Stoff hinaus giebt es keinen mehr für den Poeten, denn dieser darf die menschliche Natur nicht verlassen, und eben von diesem Uebertritt des Menschen in den Gott würde diese Idylle handeln. Die Hauptfiguren wären zwar schon Götter, aber durch Herkules kann ich sie noch an die Menschheit anknüpfen und eine *Bewegung* in das Gemählde bringen. Gelänge mir dieses Unternehmen, so hoffte ich dadurch mit der sentimentalischen Poesie über die naive selbst triumphiert zu haben.[1]

Schillers Idyllenplan steht im Zusammenhang mit seinen Bemühungen um eine Standortbestimmung der Moderne im Verhältnis zur Antike. Mit seiner Schrift *Über naive und sentimentalische Dichtung*, die er wenige Tage zuvor fertiggestellt hatte, verfolgte Schiller nicht bloß das Ziel, seine eigene Art zu dichten gegenüber derjenigen Goethes zu rechtfertigen, sondern auch das Eigenrecht der modernen Dichtung gegenüber der antiken zu begründen. Die Wiederaufnahme der *Querelle des Anciens et des Modernes* führte Schiller dabei zur Überwindung des Klassizismus und dessen Nachahmungsästhetik, wie sie Winckelmann in seiner Frühschrift *Gedanken über die Nachahmung der griechischen Werke in der Malerei und Bildhauerkunst* (1755) gefordert hatte.[2] Denn durch die geschichtsphilosophische Situierung der modernen und antiken Dichtung gelangte Schiller zur Einsicht in die historische Eigenständigkeit beider Epochen. Den Vorzügen der antiken Dichtung ließen sich diejenigen der modernen entgegenhalten. In der Erstausgabe der Abhandlung *Über naive und sentimentalische Dichtung*, die 1795/1796 in den *Horen* erschien, heißt es:

---

[1] Schillers Werke. Nationalausgabe. Begr. von Julius Petersen, fortgef. von Lieselotte Blumenthal, Benno von Wiese und Siegfried Seidel, hrsg. von Norbert Oellers. Weimar 1943 ff., Band 28, S. 118 f. (=NA). Zu Schillers Plan einer Herakles-Idylle vgl.: Reinhardt Habel (1961), S. 265–294; Norbert Oellers (1996), S. 192–208; Volker Riedel (1996); Ursula Wertheim (1959).
[2] Vgl. Werner Frick (1998).

Individualität mit einem Wort ist der Charakter des Alten, und Idealität die Stärke des Modernen. Es ist also natürlich, daß in allem, was zur unmittelbaren sinnlichen Anschauung gelangen und als Individuum wirken muß, der erste über den zweyten den Sieg davon tragen wird. Eben so natürlich ist es auf der andern Seite, daß da wo es auf geistige Anschauungen ankommt und die Sinnenwelt überschritten werden soll und darf, der erste nothwendig durch die Schranken der Materie leiden, und eben weil er sich streng an diese bindet, hinter dem andern, der sich davon freyspricht, wird zurückbleiben müssen.[3]

Vor dem Hintergrund dieser Textstelle wird deutlich, inwiefern Schiller hoffte, mit der Herakles-Idylle die Überlegenheit der modernen, sentimentalischen über die antike, naive Dichtung aufzeigen zu können. In seinem Brief an Humboldt schrieb er, es sei sein selbstgesetztes Ziel, «das Ideal der Schönheit objektiv zu individualisieren». Der zitierte Passus aus der Schrift *Über naive und sentimentalische Dichtung* zeigt nun, daß Schiller damit nichts geringeres intendierte als die dialektische Synthese dessen, was er für das jeweilige Prinzip der Antike und der Moderne hielt, nämlich die Synthese von Individualität und Idealität. Die Vollendung der modernen, sentimentalischen Dichtung in der Herakles-Idylle stellte Schiller sich als Vereinigung der antiken und modernen Dichtung vor – als «Coalition des alten Dichtercharakters mit dem modernen», wie es in der Schrift *Über naive und sentimentalische Dichtung* heißt: «Nun entsteht natürlicherweise die Frage [...] ob und in wie fern in demselben Kunstwerke Individualität mit Idealität zu vereinigen sey – ob sich also (welches auf eins hinausläuft) eine Coalition des alten Dichtercharakters mit dem modernen gedenken lasse, welche, wenn sie wirklich statt fände, als der höchste Gipfel aller Kunst zu betrachten seyn würde.»[4] Die dialektische Synthese von Individualität und Idealität, die bewahrende Aufhebung der antiken in der modernen Dichtung wird für Schiller zum höchsten Ziel des modernen, sentimentalischen Dichters: «Es sey dieß aber nun erreichbar und erreicht oder nicht, so ist es wenigstens die Aufgabe auch in der Dichtkunst, das ideale zu individualisieren und das individuelle zu idealisieren. Der moderne Dichter *muß* sich diese Aufgabe machen, wenn er sich überall nur ein höchstes und letzes Ziel seines Strebens gedenken soll.»[5]

Es erscheint zunächst paradox, daß Schiller einen antiken Mythos, den Herakles-Mythos, zum Stoff seiner Idylle wählt, durch welche er die Überlegenheit der modernen Dichtung erweisen will. Dieses Paradox löst sich allerdings in der für Schiller typischen dialektischen Denkstruktur auf. Im antiken Mythos hofft Schiller, der sentimentalische Idealist, dasjenige zu finden, was ihm aus ihm selbst zur angestrebten «Coalition des alten Dichtercharakters mit dem modernen» mangelt, nämlich die seiner modernen Idealität entgegengesetzte Individualität. Dieses im antiken Mythos aufbewahrte Nicht-Moderne soll dann dialektisch mit dem entgegengesetzten Modernen synthetisiert werden – was nach Schiller die Dichtung zu ihrem unübertrefflichen Höhepunkt führen würde.

Der Idyllen-Plan wirft somit erstens die Frage auf, welche Funktion oder welcher Sinn, Schillers Dichtungstypologie zufolge, dem antiken Mythos in moderner, sentimentalischer Dichtung zukommt. Da Schiller in der Schrift *Über naive und sentimentalische Dichtung* das klassizistische Nachahmungspostulat überwunden hat, moderne Dichtung also nicht mehr die antike nachahmen, sondern vielmehr ihre Eigenständigkeit behaupten soll, muß der

---

[3] NA, Band 21, S. 278 (Lesarten).
[4] NA, Band 21, S. 288.
[5] NA, Band 21, S. 288.

Mythos, wenn er in moderne Dichtung eingeht, notwendigerweise neue Sinndimensionen gewinnen, die von seinen naiv-antiken prinzipiell verschieden sind. Dies bedeutet, daß der sentimentalische Dichter den antiken Mythos, wenn er ihn zum Stoff seiner Dichtung auswählt, in seiner Sinnstruktur umgestalten muß. Es ergibt sich damit als eine weitere Frage, welche Transformationen der antike Mythos nach Schillers Dichtungskonzeption erfahren muß, um in moderner Dichtung aktualisiert werden zu können.

Da Schiller seinen Plan einer Herakles-Idylle nie realisiert hat, werden wir im folgenden versuchen, seinen Mythosbegriff durch die Interpretation sowohl der Abhandlung *Über naive und sentimentalische Dichtung* als auch des Gedichts *Das Reich der Schatten* zu rekonstruieren. Denn zum einen kann der Idyllenplan als Versuch verstanden werden, die dichtungstheoretischen Grundsätze der Schrift *Über naive und sentimentalische Dichtung* unmittelbar in die dichterische Praxis umzusetzen. Und zum anderen wollte Schiller mit der Herakles-Idylle, seinem Brief an Humboldt zufolge, ja gerade dort fortfahren, wo *Das Reich der Schatten* aufhört – nämlich mit der Apotheose des Herakles, welche er bereits in der Schlußstrophe dieses Gedichts dargestellt hat.

Die Tatsache, daß die Herakles-Idylle, an die Schiller so hohe Erwartungen geknüpft hat, nie zustande kam, wirft freilich die Frage auf, aus welchen Gründen der Plan gescheitert ist. Es dürfte nicht verfehlt sein, den entscheidenden Grund hierfür in der spekulativen Abstraktheit des Idyllenplans zu erblicken, die den Anforderungen konkreter dichterischer Praxis offensichtlich nicht gerecht zu werden vermag. Wir werden daher in einem letzten Schritt versuchen, die Aporien und inneren Widersprüche von Schillers Idyllenplan aufzudecken. Dies wird uns die Möglichkeit geben, einen kritischen Blick auf Schillers Mythen- und Antikenrezeption zu werfen.

II

Schiller wählt aus dem komplexen, handlungs- und deutungsreichen Herakles-Mythos einen eng begrenzten Stoffkreis aus, der den Inhalt der Idylle bilden soll: die Vermählung des Herakles mit Hebe im Olymp.[6] Der vergöttlichte Herakles, der nach seiner Selbstverbrennung auf dem Öta-Gebirge in den Olymp aufgenommen wurde, nicht der irdische Held soll der Gegenstand der Idylle sein. Diese stoffliche Auswahl erfordert es, die Frage nach der Funktion oder dem Sinn des antiken Mythos, der sowohl Erzählung von Göttern als auch von Helden ist, zu spezifizieren: ausgehend vom Herakles-Plan können wir zunächst nur die Frage stellen, welcher Sinn dem antiken *Göttermythos* nach Schillers Dichtungskonzeption in der modernen Dichtung zukommen kann; erst in einem zweiten Schritt werden nach dem Sinn des *Heldenmythos* fragen können.

Die griechische «Götterlehre» hält Schiller für «die Eingebung eines naiven Gefühls, die Geburt einer fröhlichen Einbildungskraft, nicht der grübelnden Vernunft, wie der Kirchenglaube der neuern Nationen».[7] Der antike Göttermythos entspringt nach Schiller also der sinnlichen Vorstellungskraft, nicht der abstrakten Vernunft. Mit der Zuordnung des antiken Göttermythos und seiner frühen dichterischen Gestaltungen zur Kategorie des Naiven

---

[6] Zum Herakles-Mythos im allgemeinen vgl.: Ralph Kray et al. (1994); Bernd Effe (1980); G. Karl Galinsky (1972); Abraham J. Malherbe (1988).
[7] NA, Band 20, S. 431.

verbindet sich eine bestimmte Deutungsweise des Mythos, die bereits eine Vorentscheidung über seine Verwendungsmöglichkeiten in der modernen Dichtung impliziert.

Schillers Dichtungstypologie gründet im Versuch, die Dichtung insgesamt in ihrem Verhältnis zur «Natur» zu bestimmen, die für ihn «die einzige Flamme [ist], an der sich der Dichtergeist nähret»: aus der Natur «allein schöpft er seine ganze Macht, zu ihr allein spricht er».[8] Im Rahmen dieser Gattungsbestimmung der Dichtung unterscheidet Schiller zwischen zwei grundsätzlichen Arten, wie sich der Dichter zur Natur verhalten kann: «Der Dichter [...] *ist* entweder Natur, oder er wird sie *suchen*. Jenes macht den naiven, dieses den sentimentalischen Dichter.»[9] Der naive Dichter befindet sich in Einheit mit der Natur, der sentimentalische Dichter dagegen befindet sich in einem Zustand der Entfremdung von der Natur, das heißt im künstlichen Zustand der Kultur, und aus dem Gefühl der Entfremdung von der Natur stellt er diese als Ideal dar. Den Begriff der Natur gebraucht Schiller dabei als Chiffre für einen Zustand der Einheit, wobei er vor allem an den harmonischen Ausgleich von Sinnlichkeit und Vernunft denkt, der nach dem Humanitätsideal der Weimarer Klassik das Ziel menschlicher Vollendung ist.[10]

Schiller verbindet seine Dichtungstypologie mit einer geschichtsphilosophischen Konstruktion, nach welcher der Zustand der Natur mit der harmonischen Existenz der frühen Menschheit, besonders der griechischen, zusammenfällt und dem Zustand der modernen Kultur entgegengesetzt ist, deren Kennzeichen Entfremdung, Entzweiung und Zerrissenheit sind.[11] Unter dieser geschichtsphilosophischen Perspektive ergibt sich für ihn die Möglichkeit, den naiven Dichter (der Natur ist) der Antike, den sentimentalischen (der unter den Bedingungen der Kultur die Natur sucht) der Moderne zuzuordnen – ohne daß die beiden Begriffspaare *naiv – sentimentalisch* und *antik – modern* vollständig zur Deckung kämen.

Für den naiven Dichter ist die Natur *Wirklichkeit*, für den sentimentalischen Dichter wird sie zum *Ideal*. Da beide Dichtertypen die «*Bewahrer* der Natur»[12] sein sollen, d.h. da die Natur den letzten Bezugspunkt sowohl der naiven als auch der sentimentalischen Dichtung bilden soll, ergibt sich aus dem verschiedenen Verhältnis beider Dichtertypen zur Natur eine unterschiedliche Grundbestimmung der naiven und sentimentalischen Dichtung: Aufgabe der naiven Dichtung ist die *Nachahmung des Wirklichen*, die der sentimentalischen *Darstellung des Ideals*. Die moderne Ablösung der Nachahmungsästhetik durch eine Darstellungsästhetik findet hier ihre geschichtsphilosophische Begründung:

> Wendet man nun den Begriff der Poesie, der kein andrer ist, *als der Menschheit ihren möglichst vollständigen Ausdruck zu geben*, auf jene beyden Zustände an, so ergiebt sich, daß dort in dem Zustande natürlicher Einfalt, wo der Mensch noch, mit allen seinen Kräften zugleich, als harmonische Einheit wirkt, wo mithin das Ganze seiner Natur sich in der Wirklichkeit vollständig ausdrückt, die möglichst vollständige *Nachahmung des Wirklichen* – daß hingegen hier in dem Zustande der Kultur, wo jenes harmonische Zusammenwirken seiner ganzen Natur bloß eine Idee ist, die Erhebung der Wirklichkeit zum Ideal oder, was auf eins hinausläuft, *die Darstellung des Ideals den Dichter machen muß*.[13]

---

[8] NA, Band 20, S. 436.
[9] NA, Band 20, S. 436 (vgl. auch S. 432).
[10] In seinen philosophischen Schriften verwendet Schiller den Begriff der Natur freilich auch in anderen Bedeutungen, so vor allem zur Bezeichnung der Sphäre der Sinnlichkeit.
[11] Vgl. NA, Band 20, S. 436f.
[12] NA, Band 20, S. 432.
[13] NA, Band 20, S. 437.

Obwohl Schiller an dieser Stelle nicht explizit auf den antiken Mythos zu sprechen kommt, können wir von hier aus seinen Mythosbegriff rekonstruieren. Die zitierte Stelle läßt nämlich erkennen, daß Schiller im Rahmen seiner dichtungstheoretischen Prämissen dem Göttermythos – sowohl in naiver als auch in sentimentalischer Gestaltung – grundsätzlich keinen anderen wesentlichen Sinn zuschreiben kann als «*der Menschheit ihren möglichst vollständigen Ausdruck zu geben*», d.h. die Menschheit in ihrer Einheit und Ganzheit darzustellen. In Übereinstimmung hiermit heißt es in den *Briefen über die ästhetische Erziehung*, die Mythologie der Griechen habe «die menschliche Natur [...] in ihrem herrlichen Götterkreis vergrößert» auseinandergeworfen, so daß die «ganze Menschheit [...] in keinem einzelnen Gott» fehle.[14]

Die naive Dichtung realisiert die gemeinsame Funktion aller Dichtung, «*der Menschheit ihren möglichst vollständigen Ausdruck zu geben*», als *Nachahmung wirklicher*, in einem bestimmten Stadium der Menschheitsgeschichte sinnlich erfahrbarer *Einheit und Ganzheit* des Menschen. Der griechische Göttermythos muß für Schiller demnach in naiver Gestaltung die vollendete Einheit des griechischen Menschen nachahmen; er ist ein allerhöchstens imaginativ erhöhter Spiegel der wirklichen Ganzheit des griechischen Menschen. In moderner, sentimentalischer Realisierung dagegen kann der antike Göttermythos keine wirklich erfahrbare menschliche Harmonie nachahmen – denn unter den Grundbedingungen der Moderne ist diese verlorengegangen. Seine Funktion kann bloß in der *Darstellung des Ideals menschlicher Einheit und Ganzheit* bestehen.

Nach Schillers geschichtsphilosophischer Konzeption ist das Ziel der Geschichte die Wiederherstellung der ursprünglichen Ganzheit in einem idealen Endzustand – ohne die Vorzüge und Errungenschaften der Moderne, Vernunft und Freiheit, aufzugeben. Das Telos der Geschichte ist die dialektische Synthese der Antike und der Moderne. Das heißt: der Zustand kultureller Entfremdung soll nicht durch die Wiederherstellung der vorbewußten und auf Notwendigkeit beruhenden Harmonie des Naturzustandes überwunden werden, sondern es soll im Ideal eine aus vernünftigem Bewußtsein frei gewählte Harmonie realisiert werden, die die Vorzüge sowohl des Natur- als auch des Kulturzustandes bewahrt, ihre Defizite aber hinter sich läßt. Unter diesem eschatologischen Gesichtspunkt kann die Funktion des antiken Göttermythos in der sentimentalischen Dichtung nur darin bestehen, den idealen Endzustand der Menschheit in utopischer Vorwegnahme darzustellen.

Es stellt sich nun die Frage, wie der ursprünglich naive Göttermythos in seiner Sinnstruktur umgeformt werden muß, um in moderner Dichtung eine derartige Funktion übernehmen zu können. Wir werden diese Frage im folgenden konkret am Beispiel der sentimentalischen Gattung der Idylle erörtern. Im Unterschied zur Elegie, welche die Natur oder das Ideal als verloren oder unerreicht, als Gegenstand der Trauer darstellt, stellt die Idylle die Natur oder das Ideal als wirklich vor, als Gegenstand der Freude: «Die poetische Darstellung unschuldiger und glücklicher Menschheit ist der allgemeine Begriff dieser Dichtungsart [...] Der Zweck selbst ist überall nur der, den Menschen im Stand der Unschuld, d.h. in einem Zustand der Harmonie und des Friedens mit sich selbst und von aussen darzustellen»[15]. Von der arkadischen Idylle, deren Schauplatz der «einfache Hirtenstand» ist und die «*vor dem Anfange der Kultur* in dem kindlichen Alter der Menschheit»[16]

---

[14] NA, Band 20, S. 322 (6. Brief).
[15] NA, Band 20, S. 467.
[16] NA, Band 20, S. 467.

angesiedelt ist, unterscheidet Schiller die elysische Idylle, die das utopische Ziel der Menschheit, den letzten Zweck ihrer Geschichte als wirklich darstellt: «Der Begriff dieser Idylle ist der Begriff eines völlig aufgelösten Kampfes sowohl in dem einzelnen Menschen, als in der Gesellschaft, einer freyen Vereinigung der Neigungen mit dem Gesetze, einer zur höchsten sittlichen Würde hinaufgeläuterten Natur, kurz, er ist kein andrer als das Ideal der Schönheit auf das wirkliche Leben angewendet.»[17]

Das Ideal der Menschheit – welches in Schillers ästhetischem Humanismus mit dem Ideal der Schönheit identisch ist – besteht dem *Inhalt* nach in der dialektischen Synthese zweier Vorstellungen: erstens der *Einheit, Ganzheit und Harmonie*, welche bereits im anfänglichen Naturzustand der Menschheit realisiert waren, und zweitens der *Vernunft und Freiheit*, welche die Errungenschaften der Kultur sind. Der *Form* nach ist das Ideal der Menschheit als Idee allgemein, unendlich und unbegrenzt. Wenn dieses Ideal in der elysischen Idylle als *wirklich* dargestellt werden soll, muß der sentimentalische Dichter neben der bereits genannten eine zweite, diesmal die dichterische Form betreffende dialektische Synthese leisten: nämlich die Versöhnung von Idee und Wirklichkeit, von Allgemeinheit und Individualität, von Unendlichkeit und Begrenzung. Wenn demnach die elysische Idylle sowohl der Form als auch dem Inhalt nach aus der dialektischen Synthese gegensätzlicher Momente hervorgeht, können wir zwei Gegensatzpaare, also vier Momente unterscheiden, die für die elysische Idylle konstitutiv sind: erstens die Synthese von (1) Einheit, Ganzheit und Harmonie einerseits, (2) Freiheit und Vernunft andererseits; zweitens die Synthese von (3) Individualität und sinnlicher Begrenzung einerseits, (4) Allgemeinheit und Unendlichkeit der Idee anderseits.

Der antike Göttermythos trägt nun – im Horizont von Schillers geschichtsphilosophischer Deutung – aufgrund seines naiv-antiken Ursprungs das erste und dritte Moment von sich aus in sich. Damit wird aber zugleich deutlich, welche Transformation der antike Mythos in moderner, sentimentalischer Dichtung erfahren muß: im Fall der elysischen Idylle müssen in seiner dichterischen Umsetzung neben dem ersten und dritten Moment auch das zweite und vierte realisiert werden. Der antike Mythos muß also in der modernen Dichtung erstens auf Ideen in ihrer Allgemeinheit bezogen werden, d. h. er muß unter die Grundbedingungen der Reflexion gestellt werden. Zweitens müssen die Vorzüge der modernen Kultur, v. a. die Vorstellung der subjektiven Freiheit, in die Sinnstruktur des Mythos aufgenommen werden. Mit anderen Worten: der Mythos muß unter die Grundbedingungen der Moderne, Vernunft und Freiheit, gestellt werden, um in moderner Dichtung aktualisiert werden zu können.

III

Da Schiller seinen Idyllenplan nie umgesetzt hat, werden wir am Beispiel der beiden Schlußstrophen des Gedichts *Das Reich der Schatten*, an welches er mit der Herakles-Idylle anknüpfen wollte, aufzeigen, wie er versucht, den Herakles-Mythos den Grundbedingungen der Moderne entsprechend in seiner dichterischen Gestaltung umzuformen. Schiller greift in diesem Gedicht den Herakles-Mythos in der Absicht auf, das in den vorhergehenden Strophen entwickelte ästhetische und anthropologische Konzept anschaulich zu ex-

---

[17] NA, Band 20, S. 472.

emplifizieren.[18] *Das Reich der Schatten*, das in der Endfassung von 1804 den Titel *Das Ideal und das Leben* erhielt, entfaltet programmatisch ein dualistisches Welt- und Menschenbild, das durch die Polarität von «Leben» und «Ideal» bestimmt ist: dem «Leben», einer Chiffre für den Zustand menschlicher Realität, der Entzweiung von Natur und Geist, wird das «Ideal» entgegengesetzt, ein Zustand idealer menschlicher Vollkommenheit, der sich durch die vollendete Versöhnung von Natur und Geist im Individuum und in der Gesellschaft auszeichnet. Dieser Zustand idealer Humanität wird mit dem Reich der Schönheit und des schönen Scheins, dem «Reich der Schatten», gleichgesetzt (denn nach Schillers ästhetischem Humanismus ist es einzig die Schönheit, die den Menschen in einen Zustand der Harmonie von Natur und Geist versetzen kann und dem Menschen somit ermöglicht, ganz Mensch zu sein). In den beiden Schlußstrophen versinnbildlicht Schiller dann die Grundaussagen des Gedichts im mythischen Bild des irdischen und des vergöttlichten Herakles:

>   Tief erniedrigt zu des Feigen Knechte
>   Gieng in ewigem Gefechte
>   Einst Alcid des Lebens schwere Bahn,
>   Rang mit Hydern und umarmt' den Leuen,
> 165   Stürzte sich, die Freunde zu befreyen,
>   Lebend in den Acherontschen Kahn.
>   Alle Plagen, alle Erdenlasten
>   Wälzt der unversöhnten Göttin List
>   Auf die will'gen Schultern des Verhaßten,
> 170   Biß sein Lauf geendigt ist,
>   Biß der *Gott*, des Irrdischen entkleidet,
>   Flammend sich vom *Menschen* scheidet,
>   Und des Aethers leichte Lüfte trinkt.
>   Froh des neuen ungewohnten Schwebens
> 175   Fließt er aufwärts, und des Erdenlebens
>   Schweres Traumbild sinkt und sinkt und sinkt.
>   Des Olympus Harmonien empfangen
>   Den Verklärten in Kronions Saal,
>   Und die Göttin mit den Rosenwangen
> 180   Reicht ihm lächelnd den Pokal.[19]

Die beiden Schlußstrophen spiegeln die Doppelstruktur des Herakles-Mythos wider, der sowohl Götter- als auch Heldenmythos ist: der vorletzten Strophe des Gedichts liegen als mythischer Stoff die irdischen Taten des *Helden* Herakles, insbesondere die berühmten zwölf Arbeiten, der letzten Strophe dagegen seine *Apotheose* und Aufnahme in den Olymp zugrunde.

Ein Vergleich von Schillers dichterischer Gestaltung der Apotheose mit der antiken Überlieferung zeigt, wie Schiller den Mythos den Anforderungen moderner Dichtung entsprechend umsetzt. In der *Bibliothek* des Apollodoros, einem der wichtigsten erhaltenen mythographischen Werke der Antike, wird die Apotheose wie folgt erzählt:

---

[18] Zu Schillers Gedicht *Das Reich der Schatten* vgl.: Walter Hinderer (1996); Helmut Koopmann (1984); Norbert Oellers (1981).
[19] NA, Band 1, S. 251.

Herakles [...] begab [...] sich ins Oitagebirge, das im Gebiet von Trachis liegt, schichtete dort einen Scheiterhaufen auf und, indem er ihn bestieg, befahl er, ihn anzuzünden. Als sich niemand dazu bereit fand, kam auf der Suche nach Herdetieren Poias vorbei. Der zündete ihn an, und er war es auch, dem Herakles Bogen und Pfeile schenkte. Als der Scheiterhaufen brannte, nahm ihn – so erzählt man – eine Wolke auf und trug ihn unter Donner zum Himmel empor. Von da wurde ihm die Unsterblichkeit zuteil und, mit Hera ausgesöhnt, bekam er ihre Tochter Hebe zur Gattin, die ihm zwei Söhne gebar, Alexiares und Aniketos.[20]

Benjamin Hederich folgt in seinem *Gründlichen mythologischen Lexikon* (1770) der Erzählung des Apollodoros: «Als derselbe [Scheiterhaufen] brannte, soll sich ein Donnern erhoben, und eine Wolke den Herkules in den Himmel geführet haben, woselbst er nicht allein die Unsterblichkeit erlangete, sondern auch, nachdem er mit der Juno ausgesöhnet worden, deren Tochter, die Hebe, zur Gemahlinn, bekam.»[21]

Die mythographische Erzählung beschränkt sich darauf, die mythische Handlungsfolge bzw. das bloße Erzählgerüst wiederzugeben. Die vier Schlußverse des Gedichts unterscheiden sich nun in wesentlichen Punkten von einer einfachen Wiedergabe der mythischen Erzählung. In Schillers dichterischer Gestaltung wird das Motiv der Vermählung des Herakles mit Hebe zum Sinnbild des Ideals freier Harmonie. Es fällt zunächst auf, daß Schiller individuelle Götternamen vermeidet. Erinnern wir uns daran, daß Individualität für Schiller ein Spezifikum der naiven Dichtung ist. Wenn Schiller nun die individualisierenden Götternamen durch ein Abstraktum («Des Olympus Harmonien») oder durch eine Periphrase («die Göttin mit den Rosenwangen») ersetzt, bezieht er die sinnlich-individuelle Vorstellung des Mythos auf allgemeine Ideen. Indem er mittels der Wortverbindung «Des Olympus Harmonien» das mythische Bild der griechischen Götterwelt mit dem abstrakten Begriff der Harmonie verknüpft, evoziert er im mythischen Bild griechischer Götter das Ideal der Humanität, ganzheitliche Harmonie. Durch eine derartige Verknüpfung der individuellen mythischen Vorstellung mit dem Ideal der Harmonie versucht Schiller, seinem Begriff der Idylle entsprechend der abstrakten Idealität im mythischen Bild Individualität zu verleihen.

Die Periphrase «die Göttin mit den Rosenwangen», die für Hebe, die Göttin der jugendlichen Schönheit, steht, verbleibt zwar im Bereich der sinnlichen Vorstellung, stellt aber durch den Vorstellungsgehalt des Wortes «Rosenwangen» einen indirekten Bezug zur Idee der Schönheit her. Nach Schillers ästhetischem Humanismus kann der Mensch, wie gesagt, den Idealzustand ganzheitlicher Harmonie nur im Zeichen der Schönheit erreichen. Die Periphrase «die Göttin mit den Rosenwangen» erfüllt damit ebenfalls die Funktion, die mythische Vorstellung auf das sentimentalische Ideal schöner Humanität zu beziehen. Die moderne Reflexion durchdringt die mythische Erzählung bis ins kleinste sprachliche Element hinein.

Damit hat sich in ersten Konturen gezeigt, wie Schiller den antiken Mythos unter die erste der beiden Grundbedingungen der Moderne, die Rationalität oder Reflexion, stellt. An denselben vier Schlußversen läßt sich aber auch ablesen, wie er bestrebt ist, den Mythos unter die zweite Grundbedingung, die Freiheit, zu bringen. Besonderer Bedeutung kommt hierbei

---

[20] Griechische Sagen: Apollodoros, Parthenios, Antoninus Liberalis, Hyginus. Eingel. u. neu übertr. von Ludwig Mader [Aus. d. Nachlass hrsg. u. erg. von Liselotte Rüegg]. Zürich 1963, S. 72.
[21] Benjamin Hederich: Gründliches mythologisches Lexikon. Leipzig/ Gleditsch 1770 (ND Darmstadt 1996), Sp. 1252f.

dem Schlußbild des Gedichts zu, daß Hebe Herakles bei der Aufnahme in den Olymp einen Pokal reicht. Die Unsterblichkeit erscheint damit als Herakles' eigener Verdienst, als Belohnung für seinen tugendhaften Willensheroismus, für seine freie, willentliche Anstrengung (vgl. auch die vorletzte Strophe). Was Schiller in den Schlußversen des Gedichts nur andeutet, die Vorstellung, daß Herakles aus eigener Willenskraft die göttliche Unsterblichkeit errungen hat – ein mythisches Bild dafür, daß die Menschheit aus eigener Kraft nach ihrer utopischen Vollendung streben soll – hat er pointiert in seinem Epigramm *Zeus zu Herkules* zum Ausdruck gebracht: «Nicht aus meinem Nektar hast du dir Gottheit getrunken./ Deine Götterkraft wars, die dir den Nektar errang.»[22] Zwar gehört der Gedanke, daß Herakles die Unsterblichkeit als Lohn für seine Mühen und Arbeiten erhält, bereits zur antiken Überlieferung.[23] Dennoch berechtigt uns die spezifische Art und Weise, wie Schiller dieses Motiv gestaltet, dazu, hierin eine ‹sentimentalische Operation› zu erblicken: das mythische Bild soll auf den Gedanken der Willensfreiheit und -kraft hin geöffnet werden.

Der sentimentalische Gestaltungswille, den antiken Mythos unter die Bedingungen der Reflexion zu stellen, läßt sich auch an der ersten Versgruppe der Schlußstrophe ablesen. In der Wortverbindung «des Irrdischen entkleidet» wird in typisch Schillerscher Manier eine sinnliche Anschauung mit einem allgemeinen Begriff verknüpft. Durch den synekdochischen Gebrauch der Gattungsbezeichnung «Mensch» wird des weiteren die Apotheose des Herakles von der individuell-konkreten Ebene der mythischen Erzählung auf eine kollektiv-allgemeine gehoben und somit zum Sinnbild der Bestimmung des Menschen überhaupt. Die nach Schiller zur naiven Dichtung gehörende sinnliche Begrenzung wird damit in Richtung auf die Allgemeinheit des Begriffs aufgehoben.

Eine ähnliche sinnbildliche Funktion kommt dem Gegensatzpaar «leicht» (V. 173) – «schwer» (V. 176) zu, das Schiller im Gedicht *Das Reich der Schatten* leitmotivisch einsetzt: indem er die Eigenschaft «leicht» durchgehend mit der Sphäre des Ideals, «schwer» dagegen mit der entgegengesetzten Sphäre der Wirklichkeit im Zustand der Entfremdung assoziiert, werden die sinnlich-konkreten Qualitäten zum Träger allgemeiner Vorstellungen.[24] Auch das Bild des Schwebens (V. 174) erscheint im Kontext des ganzen Gedichts als Sinnbild des idealen Gleichgewichts von Sinnlichkeit und Vernunft, das mit dem Ideal der Menschheit identisch ist (vgl. z.B. V. 61 ff.: «Jugendlich, von allen Erdenmaalen/ Frey, in der Vollendung Strahlen/ Schwebe hier [im Reich des Ideals] der Menschheit Götterbild»).

Während Schiller in der Schlußstrophe des Gedichts das mythische Bild des vergöttlichten Herakles zum Symbol des utopischen Ideals der Menschheit umdeutet, liegt der vorletzten Strophe ein anderes Motiv aus dem Stoffkomplex des Herakles-Mythos zugrunde: nämlich der Dodekathlos, die zwölf Arbeiten des Herakles.[25] Dieser Motivzusammenhang

---

[22] NA, Band 1, S. 227.
[23] Vgl. z.B. Pindars *Erste Nemeische Ode*, V. 61–72.
[24] Schiller greift hier den philosophischen Gedanken der Erdenschwere auf, der seit Platon ein Topos abendländischen Denkens ist (vgl. z.B. Platon: *Phaidon* 81c-d und Boethius: *De consolatione philosophiae* 3,12c 3f.).
[25] Der Vers «Rang mit Hydern und umarmt' den Leuen» bezieht sich auf die beiden ersten der zwölf Aufgaben, die Tötung des Nemeischen Löwen und die Bezwingung der fünfköpfigen Hydra von Lerna. Die beiden folgenden Verse spielen auf die letzte der zwölf Arbeiten, die Entführung des Höllenhundes Kerberos, an, bei welcher Aufgabe Herakles seinen Freund Theseus aus der Unterwelt befreit hat. Daß Herakles «des Feigen Knechte» genannt wird, ist eine Anspielung darauf, daß er im Dienst des Eurystheus die zwölf Arbeiten verrichten mußte. «Alcid» ist ein Beiname des Herakles, des Enkels des Alkaios.

ist typologisch nicht dem Göttermythos, sondern dem Heldenmythos zuzuordnen. Der Heldenmythos gewinnt nun in Schillers dichterischer Umsetzung eine dem Göttermythos entgegengesetzte Funktion: die Heldentaten des Herakles werden zum Sinnbild der entfremdeten Wirklichkeit, die durch Antagonismen und Entzweiung bestimmt ist, zum Sinnbild für die Sphäre des «Lebens», für «des Lebens schwere Bahn» (V. 163). Der Herakles-Mythos dient hier also nicht mehr der Darstellung des Ideals bzw. des Naturzustandes, sondern der Darstellung der Wirklichkeit bzw. des Kulturzustandes. Dem Heldenmythos kommt also vorzugsweise eine elegische Funktion zu, im Unterschied zur idyllischen des Göttermythos. Dabei ist es das mythische Motiv des Kampfes – ein wichtiges Strukturprinzip antiker Mythen, besonders der sogenannten Kampferzählungen –, welches Schiller eine derartige Funktionalisierung des antiken Heldenmythos im Sinne seiner Geschichtsphilosophie ermöglicht. Denn der Kampf ist ein spezifisches Merkmal des Kulturzustandes. So ist auch im Gedicht *Das Reich der Schatten* das Kampfmotiv leitmotivisch mit der Sphäre der Wirklichkeit verbunden (vgl. V. 69–90).[26]

Die Antagonismen von Herrn und Knecht («Tief erniedrigt zu des Feigen Knechte/ Gieng in ewigem Gefechte»), von Mensch und Natur («Rang mit Hydern und umarmt' den Leuen»), von Leben und Tod («Stürzte sich, die Freunde zu befreien,/ Lebend in den Acherontschen Kahn»), die dem Herakles-Mythos strukturell zugrundeliegen, werden im Kontext von Schillers Gedicht zum Sinnbild der universalen Entzweiung des Menschen im Kulturzustand. Durch den Vers «Alle Plagen, alle Erdenlasten» stellt Schiller die individuell-konkrete mythische Erzählung in den Kontext der allgemeinen Situation des unter den Antagonismen der Wirklichkeit und der Kultur leidenden Menschen, die in den vorhergehenden Strophen breit geschildert wurden: Herakles wird damit zum Sinnbild *aller* Leiden des entfremdeten Menschen. Hierin darf man eine ‹sentimentalische Operation› erblicken, indem die Grenze des individuell bestimmten mythischen Gegenstandes auf eine allgemeinere und abstraktere Dimension hin überschritten wird.

Auch in dieser Strophe bringt Schiller den antiken Mythos nicht bloß unter die erste Bedingung sentimentalischer Dichtung, die Reflexion, sondern auch unter die zweite, die Freiheit. Denn durch die Wortverbindung «will'ge Schultern» stellt Schiller Herakles' Taten prägnant als einen Akt freien Wollens dar: Herakles vermag es, das furchtbare Verhängnis zu *wollen*, d.h. aus freiem Willen die schicksalshafte Notwendigkeit zu bejahen, sie in die eigene Willensbestimmung aufzunehmen und so seine Freiheit zu bewahren. Diese Deutung steht in der Tradition stoischer Herakles-Bilder, sie entspricht aber zugleich Schillers eigenem Freiheitsbegriff, wie er ihn vor allem in der Schrift *Über das Erhabene* entwickelt hat.[27]

Die beiden Schlußstrophen zeigen also, daß Schiller versucht, dem antiken Mythos in moderner, sentimentalischer Dichtung einen doppelten Sinngehalt zuzuordnen: den Göttermythos gestaltet er zur Darstellung des Ideals der Menschheit, den Helden-Mythos zur Darstellung der wirklichen Entfremdung des Menschen um. In beiden Fällen transformiert Schiller den antiken Mythos in doppelter Weise: erstens bezieht er die sinnlich-individuelle mythische Erzählung auf allgemeine Ideen, durch Verallgemeinerung stellt er sie unter Grundbedingungen der Reflexion; zweitens projiziert er die moderne Vorstellung der Willensfreiheit in die mythische Erzählung hinein.

---

[26] Vgl. auch die Schrift *Über naive und sentimentalische Dichtung*, bes. S. 471 ff. (NA, Band 20).
[27] Vgl. v.a. NA, Band 21, S. 51. Zu Schillers Freiheitskonzeption in der Schrift «Über das Erhabene»: Verf. (2004), S. 119–132.

IV

Schiller deutet den antiken Mythos allegorisch. Bereits in seiner ursprünglich naiven Form kommt dem Mythos in Schillers Lesart neben seiner wörtlichen oder besser: initialen Bedeutung noch eine zweite, allegorische zu: als Nachahmung menschlicher Einheit und Ganzheit weist er eine tiefere, über die initiale Bedeutung hinausgehende Sinndimension auf. Entsprechend gestaltet Schiller auch in seiner eigenen, sentimentalischen Dichtung den antiken Mythos allegorisch: die Sinndimension, die er dem Herakles-Mythos aus der Perspektive seines Humanitätsideals und seiner Erfahrung der Moderne zuschreibt, ist von der initialen Bedeutung der mythischen Erzählung eindeutig abgrenzbar. Der Mythos erscheint so als ein Text mit zwei Bedeutungen, d. h. als Allegorie.[28] Sofern die Allegorie, ihrer etymologischen Bedeutung nach, eine Strategie des Anders-Sagens ist (gr. ἄλλος: ‹anderer›; ἀγορεύειν: ‹offen, öffentlich sagen›), können wir dies auch so formulieren, daß der Mythos für Schiller zum Mittel wird, das Humanitätsideal der Klassik *anders auszusagen*, nämlich verhüllt und exemplifiziert im mythischen Bild.

Es scheint, daß der Ideendichter Schiller eine besondere Affinität zur literarischen Form der Allegorie hatte. So hat Goethe in den *Maximen und Reflexionen* Schillers dichterischen Stil grundsätzlich als allegorisch, seinen eigenen dagegen als symbolisch charakterisiert:

> Mein Verhältnis zu Schiller gründete sich auf die entschiedene Richtung beider auf *einen* Zweck, unsere gemeinsame Tätigkeit auf die Verschiedenheit der Mittel, wodurch wir jenen zu erreichen strebten.
> Bei einer zarten Differenz, die einst zwischen uns zur Sprache kam, und woran ich durch eine Stelle seines Briefs wieder erinnert werde, macht' ich folgende Betrachtungen.
> Es ist ein großer Unterschied, ob der Dichter zum Allgemeinen das Besondere sucht oder im Besondern das Allgemeine schaut. Aus jener Art entsteht Allegorie, wo das Besondere nur als Beispiel, als Exempel des Allgemeinen gilt; die letztere aber ist eigentlich die Natur der Poesie, sie spricht ein Besonderes aus, ohne ans Allgemeine zu denken oder darauf hinzuweisen. Wer nun dieses Besondere lebendig faßt, erhält zugleich das Allgemeine mit, ohne es gewahr zu werden, oder erst spät.[29]

Wenn es auch fragwürdig ist, ob Goethe mit dieser schematischen Gegenüberstellung Schillers Dichtung insgesamt gerecht wird, so sind seine Charakterisierungen doch im Hinblick auf Schillers Mythenrezeption aufschlußreich. Denn die Art und Weise, wie Schiller im *Reich der Schatten* den Herakles-Mythos allegorisiert, entspricht genau Goethes Allegoriebegriff: Schiller «sucht» in der Tat im Herakles-Mythos nichts anderes als das «Besondere», das als gleichnishaftes «Beispiel» dienen kann, ein «Allgemeines» zu veranschaulichen, nämlich das Humanitätsideal und die Erfahrung moderner Entfremdung.

Es ist zu beachten, daß Goethes wertender Allegoriebegriff nicht alle Formen allegorischer Dichtung trifft. Nach der traditionellen Allegorietheorie soll die zweite, allegorische Bedeutung aus der ersten, initialen konstruiert werden; diese soll dabei ihre Eigenbedeutung bewahren. Goethes Definition zielt dagegen gerade auf solche Formen der Allegorie, in welchen das Allgemeine *nicht* aus dem Besonderen heraus gewonnen wird, das Beson-

---

[28] Zum Begriff der Allegorie vgl.: Gerhard Kurz (⁴1997).
[29] Goethes Werke. Herausgegeben von Erich Trunz. Hamburger Ausgabe. München ¹⁵1993, Band 12, S. 471. Eine Zusammenstellung aller wichtigen Äußerungen Goethes zu den Begriffen der Allegorie und des Symbols findet sich in: Bengt Algot Sörensen (1972), S. 126–135.

dere vielmehr «nur» als Exempel des Allgemeinen dient und folglich seine Eigenbedeutung unter dem Übergewicht des Allgemeinen zu verlieren droht. Weil dieses spezifische Verhältnis von Allgemeinem und Besonderem aber nicht für alle Formen allegorischen Sprechens gelten kann, diskreditiert Goethes Kritik letztlich auch nur bestimmte Formen der Allegorie. Sie bringt aber Schillers allegorische Verfahrensweise im *Reich der Schatten* präzise auf den Punkt. In der Tat geht Schiller in der dichterischen Aktualisierung des Herakles-Mythos nicht vom initialen, besonderen Sinn der mythischen Erzählung aus, um die allgemeine Bedeutung aus diesem heraus zu konstruieren, er *projiziert* vielmehr moderne Vorstellungen und Ideale in den Mythos hinein. Die mythische Erzählung fungiert im *Reich der Schatten* «nur» noch als Beispiel der allgemeinen Lehre; ihre Eigenbedeutung droht sich aufzulösen.

Wenn Schiller in seinem Brief an Humboldt vom 30. November 1795 schreibt, es sei sein Ziel in der Herakles-Idylle «das Ideal der Schönheit objektiv zu individualisieren»[30], dann scheint er damit nichts anderes zu meinen als das von Goethe beschriebene allegorische Verfahren, zum Allgemeinen oder Idealen das Besondere oder Individuelle zu suchen. Macht man sich dies aber bewußt, wird deutlich, daß Schiller auf diesem Weg die von ihm mit der Herakles-Idylle angestrebte «Coalition des alten Dichtercharakters mit dem modernen»[31] von vornherein nicht erreichen kann. Denn die damit intendierte dialektische Synthese von Antike und Moderne, von Individualität und Idealität kann offenbar nicht in der Weise realisiert werden, daß moderne Ideale einseitig auf den antiken Mythos projiziert werden, daß der individuell-konkrete Mythos bloß als Exempel abstrakter Idealität gebraucht wird.

In der Abhandlung *Über naive und sentimentalische Dichtung* hatte Schiller dem modernen Dichter, der sich das Ziel einer «Coalition des alten Dichtercharakters mit dem modernen» setzt, die doppelte Aufgabe zugeschrieben, «das ideale zu individualisieren und das individuelle zu idealisieren»[32], d.h. er hat ihm erstens die Individualisierung des Idealen und zweitens die Idealisierung des Individuellen zur Aufgabe gemacht. Daraus ergibt sich für den Schaffensprozeß des modernen Dichters eine polare bzw. eine kreisförmige Bewegung: die Bewegung vom Idealen zum Individuellen soll durch die umgekehrte Bewegung vom Individuellen zum Idealen ergänzt werden. Mit anderen Worten: die Bewegung vom Modernen zum Antiken, vom Eigenen zum Anderen soll sich mit der Bewegung vom Antiken zum Modernen, vom Anderen zum Eigenen verbinden. Im Ansatz nimmt Schiller damit bereits die Struktur des hermeneutischen Zirkels vorweg: «eine Coalition des alten Dichtercharakters mit dem modernen» ist seiner eigenen Einsicht zufolge nur möglich, wenn der moderne Dichter sich auf das einläßt, was wir im Sinne der neueren Hermeneutik die Zirkelstruktur des Verstehens oder der Aneignung des Fremden nennen können: nämlich die doppelte Bewegung vom Eigenen zum Anderen und vom Anderen zum Eigenen. Bei Schiller bahnt sich bereits die Einsicht an, daß echte Antikenrezeption nur gelingen kann, wenn sie nicht bloß aus moderner Perspektive das Antike einseitig vereinnahmt, sondern auch umgekehrt vom Antiken aus sich das eigene Moderne neu erschließt.

Aber, so wird man kritisch fragen müssen, respektiert Schiller in seiner Rezeption des Herakles-Mythos diese methodologische Grundeinsicht? Bezeichnenderweise spricht er

---

[30] NA, Band 28, S. 118f.
[31] NA, Band 21, S. 288.
[32] NA, Band 21, S. 288.

im Brief an Humboldt nur noch davon, es sei sein Ziel in der Herakles-Idylle «das Ideal der Schönheit objektiv zu individualisieren» – und vergißt damit die zweite Aufgabe, die er selbst in der Schrift *Über naive und sentimentalische Dichtung* dem modernen Dichter vorgeschrieben hat, nämlich auch das Individuelle zu idealisieren. Und in der Tat scheint Schiller bei der dichterischen Umsetzung des Herakles-Mythos im *Reich der Schatten* nur eines zu tun: nämlich das eigene Ideal der Humanität und die eigene Erfahrung moderner Entfremdung im konkreten mythischen Bild zu ‹individualisieren›. Man gewinnt den Eindruck, daß Schiller das moderne Humanitätsideal in den Herakles-Mythos hinein projiziert, ohne zu versuchen, einen idealen Sinngehalt aus dem antiken Mythos *selbst*, aus dessen konkret-individueller Sinnstruktur zu gewinnen. Eben dadurch fällt er aber in die von Goethe kritisierte Art allegorischer Dichtung – und eben dadurch muß er auch von vornherein sein Ziel einer «Coalition des alten Dichtercharakters mit dem modernen» verfehlen. Durch die allegorisierende Projektion moderner Ideale auf den antiken Mythos kann eine echte Auseinandersetzung mit der Antike, die deren prinzipielles Anderssein respektiert, nicht stattfinden. Schiller bleibt mit seinem Herakles-Plan monologisch im Bannkreis seiner eigenen Ideale gefangen. Ein Dialog mit der Antike, der doch Voraussetzung jeder Synthese von Antike und Moderne sein müßte, läßt sich auf diesem Weg nicht realisieren.

Es spricht jedoch vieles dafür, daß Schiller sich selbst der Aporien seines Herakles-Plans bewußt geworden ist. Denn zwei Wochen später, am 17. November 1795, schreibt er an Goethe, es sei «hohe Zeit, […] für eine Weile die philosophische Bude»[33] zu schließen. Statt den Herakles-Plan auszuführen, in den er so hohe Erwartungen gesetzt hat, wendet er sich dem Wallenstein-Stoff zu. Im März 1796 teilt er Humboldt mit, er befinde sich auf einem «neuen und mir, nach allen vorhergegangenen Erfahrungen, fremden Wege»[34]. Der «anhaltendere Umgang mit Göthen und das Studium der Alten» habe ihn auf einen «realistischen» Weg gebracht.[35] Wie sein Brief an Körner vom 28. November 1796 zeigt, hat Schiller sich in zunehmendem Maße um ein «objectives Verfahren» bemüht, welches in erster Linie verlange, «die Handlung wie die Charactere aus ihrer Zeit, ihrem Lokal und dem ganzen Zusammenhang der Begebenheiten [zu] schöpfen». Das bedeutet, daß das Sinngefüge des Dramas, diesem objektiven Verfahren gemäß, aus dem historischen Stoff heraus gewonnen werden soll. Deshalb sei auch das «das weitläuftige und freudlose Studium der Quellen so unentbehrlich». In den historischen Quellen suche er «eine *Begrenzung*», um seine «Ideen durch die Umgebung der Umstände streng zu bestimmen und zu verwirklichen».[36] Keineswegs also sollen die besonderen Umstände bloß als Beispiel allgemeiner, a priori gegebener Ideen dienen, die Ideen sollen sich vielmehr erst im Kontext der historischen Zusammenhänge «bestimmen» und «verwirklichen», d. h. der ideale Sinngehalt soll sich erst im Horizont der besonderen geschichtlichen Zusammenhänge konstituieren und realisieren.

Durch dieses Bemühen um ein objektives und realistisches Verfahren, das nach Schillers eigenen Worten «die entscheidende Crise» in seinem «poetischen Character» hervorgerufen hat[37], will er offensichtlich seinen früheren Idealismus und Subjektivismus überwinden,

---

[33] NA, Band 28, S. 132.
[34] NA, Band 28, S. 204.
[35] NA, Band 28, S. 204f.
[36] NA, Band 29, S. 18.
[37] NA, Band 29, S. 18.

an deren Aporien er zuletzt mit seinem Herakles-Plan gescheitert ist. Es war dieser Idealismus, der ihn dazu verführte, subjektive Ideale einseitig auf fremde Stoffe zu projizieren und diese damit auf eine Weise zu allegorisieren, die Goethe nicht zu Unrecht kritisiert hat. Schiller wird sich nun selbst bewußt, daß es einen wesentlichen Unterschied zwischen der allegorisierenden Individualisierung des Idealen einerseits und der Idealisierung des Individuellen andererseits gibt. Am 5. Januar 1797 schreibt er an Goethe: «Ich werde es mir gesagt seyn laßen, keine andre als historische Stoffe zu wählen, frey erfundene würden meine Klippe seyn. Es ist eine ganz andere Operation das realistische zu idealisieren, als das ideale zu realisieren, und letzteres ist der eigentliche Fall bei freien Fictionen.»[38] Während er in der geplanten Herakles-Idylle, dem Brief an Humboldt vom 30. November 1795 zufolge, im wesentlichen eine allegorisierende Individualisierung des Idealen anstrebte, will Schiller jetzt seine Schaffensenergie überwiegend darin setzen, das Individuelle zu idealisieren.[39] Denn nur «die objective Bestimmtheit» des konkreten, individuellen Stoffes vermöge es, seine Phantasie zu zügeln, wie er im Anschluß an die zitierte Briefstelle schreibt: «Es steht in meinem Vermögen, eine gegebene bestimmte und beschränkte Materie zu beleben, zu erwärmen und gleichsam aufquellen zu machen, während daß die objective Bestimmtheit eines solchen Stofs meine Phantasie zügelt und meiner Willkühr widersteht.»[40]

Das «objective Verfahren», das Schiller sich seit der Arbeit am *Wallenstein* anzueignen versucht hat, eröffnete ihm aber nicht nur den Weg zu einer neuen dichterischen Gestaltungsweise, sondern auch zu einer objektiveren und für das eigene dichterische Schaffen weitaus produktiveren Auseinandersetzung mit der Antike. Schiller hat während der mehrjährigen Entstehungszeit des *Wallenstein* ein neues dramaturgisches Konzept der ‹tragischen Form› entwickelt, welches die Grundlage seiner gesamten klassischen Dramatik bildet.[41] Dieses tragische Modell hat er aber, wie seine Briefe aus dieser Zeit hinlänglich dokumentieren[42], in intensiver Auseinandersetzung mit der griechischen Tragödie und der *Poetik* des Aristoteles erarbeitet. Durch das Studium der antiken Tragödienpraxis und -theorie, durch welches er sich vor allem eine genaue und präzise Kenntnis tragischer Handlungsgesetze und -modelle erhoffte, hat Schillers Antikenrezeption eine ganz andere Qualität gewonnen: die antike Dichtung wird nicht mehr als Projektionsfläche moderner, subjektiver Ideale instrumentalisiert, Schiller versucht vielmehr, die antiken Tragödien von der jeweiligen «Eigenthümlichkeit des Falles»[43], d.h. von der besonderen dramatischen Handlung her und nicht aus allgemeinen metaphysischen Kategorien zu verstehen; ebenso will er die aristotelische *Poetik* von ihren eigenen, besonderen geschichtlichen Voraussetzungen und von der besonderen Absicht und Methode ihres Autors her begreifen[44] – ohne jedoch dabei «den unvertilgbaren Unterschied»[45] zwischen dem Vorstellungshorizont der Antike und dem eigenen, subjektiven Horizont modernen Denkens aus dem Blick zu ver-

---

[38] NA, Band 29, S. 183.
[39] Zwar ist der Herakles-Stoff als tradierter Mythos keine frei erfundene Fiktion, aber er wird von Schiller offensichtlich in derselben Weise behandelt.
[40] NA, Band 29, S. 183.
[41] Vgl. hierzu: Verf. (2004), S. 183–193; Hans-Jürgen Schings (1990).
[42] Vgl. v.a. Schillers Briefe an Goethe vom 4. 4. 1797, 5. 5. 1797, 7. 7. 1797, 2. 10. 1797, 24. 8. 1798, 18. 6. 1799 und an Körner vom 3. 6. 1797.
[43] NA, Band 29, S. 56 (Brief an Goethe vom 4. 4. 1797).
[44] Vgl. v.a. Schillers Brief an Goethe vom 5. 5. 1797.
[45] NA, Band 29, S. 82 (Brief an Körner vom 3. 6. 1797).

lieren. Das sein dichterisches Schaffen leitende «objective Verfahren» bringt Schiller dazu, auch die antike Dichtung objektiv, von ihrer besonderen geschichtlichen Erscheinung her verstehen zu wollen – wobei er ungeachtet seines Strebens nach Objektivität sich jederzeit der Unhintergehbarkeit seines subjektiven, modernen Standpunkts bewußt bleibt. Daher verkümmert sein Interesse an der Antike auch nicht zu einem bloß historischen, es kommt ihm vielmehr darauf an, die antike Vorstellungswelt mit seinem eigenen, modernen Denken zu konfrontieren, jene von diesem abzuheben, aber auch das durch die Auseinandersetzung mit der antiken Tragödie gewonnene Verständnis auf das eigene dichterische Schaffen produktiv anzuwenden.

Die Frucht dieser Begegnung mit der Antike zeigt uns die *Wallenstein*-Trilogie: Schiller gelingt es hier, durch die Weiterbildung antiker Formen – wie der gründlich studierten tragischen Analysis des *König Ödipus*[46] – ein Handlungsgefüge zu schaffen, das ihm die tragische Inszenierung der modernen Geschichte ermöglicht; durch die Interpretation antiker Denkbilder wie der Nemesisvorstellung vermag er neue Deutungsperspektiven auf die moderne Geschichte zu eröffnen.[47] Auf diese Weise findet Schiller zu einer neuen Form der Antikenrezeption, zu einer neuartigen Synthese von Antikem und Modernem, die ohne sein objektives Verfahren beim Studium der griechischen Tragödie undenkbar gewesen wäre. Antike verkümmert hier nicht zum Platzhalter moderner Ideale, sie wird vielmehr als Nährboden neuer dichterischer Gestaltungsmöglichkeiten, als Fluchtpunkt bereichernder Denkhorizonte entdeckt. Sie eröffnet Schiller Sichtweisen, in seinem dichterischen Schaffen die eigene Moderne, ihre Welt der Geschichte und Politik, in ihrer schrecklichen Tragik illusionslos zu erschließen und dem Zuschauer in erschütternder Weise vor Augen zu führen.

Literaturverzeichnis

BARONE, Paul: Schiller und die Tradition des Erhabenen. Berlin 2004.
EFFE, Bernd: Held und Literatur. Der Funktionswandel des Herakles-Mythos in der griechischen Literatur. In: Poetica 12, 1980, S. 145–166.
FRICK, Werner: Schiller und die Antike. In: Helmut Koopmann (Hrsg.): Schiller-Handbuch. Stuttgart 1998, S. 91–116.
GALINSKY, G. Karl: The Herakles Theme. The Adaptations of the Hero in Literature from Homer to the Twentieth Century. Oxford 1972.
HABEL, Reinhardt: Schiller und die Tradition des Herakles-Mythos. In: Terror und Spiel. Probleme der Mythenrezeption. Hrsg. von M. Fuhrmann. München 1961.
HINDERER, Walter: Das Reich der Schatten. In: Interpretationen. Gedichte von Friedrich Schiller. Hrsg. von N. Oellers. Stuttgart 1996, S. 123–148.
KOOPMANN, Helmut: Mythologische Reise zum Olymp. In: Gedichte und Interpretationen. Band 3: Klassik und Romantik. Hrsg. von Wulf Segebrecht. Stuttgart 1984. S. 83–98.
KRAY, Ralph u. a. (Hrsg.), Herakles/Herkules I: Metamorphosen des Heros in ihrer medialen Vielfalt. Basel/ Frankfurt a. M. 1994.
KURZ, Gerhard: Metapher, Allegorie, Symbol. Göttingen ^{4}1997.
MALHERBE, Abraham J.: Artikel «Herakles». In: Reallexikon für Antike und Christentum, Band 14, Stuttgart 1988, Sp. 559–583.

---

[46] Vgl. v. a. Schillers Brief an Goethe vom 2. 10. 1797.
[47] Vgl.: Verf. (2004), v. a. Kapitel III.3., IV.3 und IV.5.

OELLERS, Norbert: Friedrich Schiller. «Das Reich der Schatten» / «Das Ideal und das Leben». In: Louis Hay und Winfried Woesler (Hrsg.): Edition und Interpretation. Bern/ Frankfurt/ Las Vegas 1981, S. 44–52.

DERS.: «Herkules im Himmel» und «Orpheus in der Unterwelt». Zu zwei Gedichtplänen Schillers. In: ders.: Friedrich Schiller. Zur Modernität eines Klassikers. Hrsg. von Michael Hofmann. Frankfurt a. M./ Leipzig 1996, S. 192–208.

RIEDEL, Volker: Herakles-Bilder in der deutschen Literatur des 17. bis 20. Jahrhunderts. In: ders: Literarische Antikerezeption. Aufsätze und Vorträge. Jena 1996, S. 46–64.

SCHINGS, Hans-Jürgen: Das Haupt der Gorgone. Tragische Analysis und Politik in Schillers «Wallenstein». In: G. Buhr u. a. (Hrsg.): Das Subjekt der Dichtung. Festschrift für Gerhard Kaiser. Würzburg 1990, S. 283–307.

SÖRENSEN, Bengt Algot (Hrsg.), Allegorie und Symbol. Texte zur Theorie des dichterischen Bildes im 18. und frühen 19. Jahrhundert. Frankfurt a. M. 1972.

WERTHEIM, Ursula: «Der Menschheit Götterbild». Bemerkungen zur gesellschaftlichen und ästhetischen Funktion des Herakles-Bildes bei Schiller. In: Weimarer Beiträge 1959 (Sonderheft), S. 97–149.

GUNNAR HINDRICHS

Ein Wort des Äsop bei Hegel und bei Marx

I.

Im Randständigen verdichtet der Grundunterschied zweier Positionen sich bisweilen zur Deutlichkeit. Die Positionen, um die es geht, sind die Lehren von Hegel und von Marx, das Randständige ist ein Wort aus Äsops Fabel vom prahlerischen Fünfkämpfer (πένταθλος κομπλαστής).

> Der prahlerische Fünfkämpfer. – Ein Fünfkämpfer, der wegen seiner Schlappheit von seinen Mitbürgern verspottet wurde, reiste einmal ins Ausland und kehrte nach einiger Zeit wieder in die Vaterstadt zurück. Nun prahlte er mächtig: er habe in vielen Städten Hervorragendes geleistet, vor allem aber in Rhodos einen Sprung getan, wie ihn noch kein Olympionike vollführt habe. Bezeugen, sagte er, könnten das die Leute, die zugegen waren, wenn sie einmal hierherkämen. Da entgegnete einer der Umherstehenden: «Höre du, wenn das wahr ist, braucht es keine Zeugen. Denn hier ist Rhodos, und hier ist auch die Gelegenheit zum Sprung!»[1]

Hier ist Rhodos, und hier ist auch die Gelegenheit zum Sprung – αὐτοῦ ʽΡόδος καὶ πήδημα – hic Rhodus, hic salta: es ist das geflügelte Schlußwort, an dessen Behandlung der Unterschied zwischen Hegel und Marx plastisch werden wird. In der Fabel entlarvt es den Prahler, der nun zeigen muß, was er tatsächlich vermag. «Die Fabel zeigt: Bei Angelegenheiten, wo der Beweis leicht durch die Tat erbracht werden kann, ist jedes weitere Wort zuviel,» belehrt die später angehängte Erläuterung den Begriffsstutzigen in diesem Sinne. Der Prahler soll nicht reden, sondern springen; sein Tun erst wäre das Zeugnis seiner Worte. Die Stoßkraft des Schlußwortes ist somit klar: Die Fabel verlangt den Schritt vom behauptenden Wort zur beglaubigenden Tat an Ort und Stelle. Hegel und Marx indessen werden das Schlußwort umdeuten. Ihre jeweilige Lesart läßt es zur Trennlinie zweier Lehren werden.

II.

In der Fabel verlangt das Dictum den Schritt vom Wort zur Tat. *Hegels* Philosophie ist keine Philosophie der Tat. Sie ist eine Philosophie des Begriffs. Der Begriff aber kommt erst nach Beendigung der Tat zum Einsatz, indem er die vollzogene Tat begreift. Das meint Hegels berühmter Satz, die Eule der Minerva beginne ihren Flug erst mit der einbrechenden Dämmerung.[2] Nicht vor seinem Abend vermag das menschliche Tun durch das philosophische

---

[1] Corpus fabularum aesopicarum 33. – Übersetzung angelehnt an August Hausrath, Aesopische Fabeln, München 1940, S. 97.
[2] Georg Wilhelm Friedrich Hegel, Grundlinien der Philosophie des Rechts, Hamburg 1955, S. 17.

Denken erfaßt zu werden; nicht vor dem Abschluß einer Epoche historischer Taten kann der Gedanke dieser Epoche gebildet werden. Die Tat also muß getan sein, damit die Philosophie ihre Arbeit beginnen kann: eine Arbeit, die selber keine Tat, sondern das Durchdenken der Tat zu ihrem Begriff darstellt.

Und doch kommt an entscheidender Stelle, gerade im Zusammenhang des philosophischen Verzichts auf die Tat, das Wort aus der Fabel zur Geltung. Freilich wird es durch eine Kursivierung verwandelt. «*Hic* Rhodus, *hic* saltus», schreibt Hegel: *hier* ist Rhodos, *hier* ist der Sprung.[3] Die Kursivierung zeigt, daß es Hegel nicht um das Zeugnis der Tat für das Wort geht, daß es ihm vielmehr um das Hier und Jetzt des Sprunges zu tun ist. Um das Hier und Jetzt des Sprunges ist es ihm aber deshalb zu tun, weil er die Philosophie als die Erkenntnis dessen, was *ist*, und nicht dessen, was sein *soll*, zu behaupten sucht. Der Gegenstand des philosophischen Begriffs ist nicht die durch die Tat zu verwirklichende Zukunft; der Gegenstand des philosophischen Begriffs ist die durch die Tat bereits verwirklichte Gegenwart. Er stellt nicht die Zeit dar, die sein soll; er stellt die Zeit dar, die ist. Für diesen Zusammenhang zwischen Gegenwart und Philosophie läßt die Kursivierung das Wort aus der Fabel einstehen. Hegel: «Es ist ebenso töricht zu wähnen, irgendeine Philosophie gehe über ihre gegenwärtige Welt hinaus, als, ein Individuum überspringe seine Zeit, springe über Rhodus hinaus.» Der Sprung, der in der Fabel der Weg vom behauptenden Wort zur beglaubigenden Tat war, wird hiernach zu der geistigen Bewegung der Philosophie, die nicht über das, was ist, hinauszuspringen vermag. Die aber, die meinen, im Blick darauf, wie die Zukunft sein soll, über das, was ist, hinausspringen zu können, gleichen dem Prahler. Wie er reden sie über unwirkliche Zustände, als hätten sie sie in der Hand. Sie sind dasselbe wie der Fünfkämpfer – Schwadroneure. Wer hingegen nicht prahlt und schwadroniert, sucht die gegenwärtige Welt so, wie sie ist, zu begreifen.

Allerdings stellt nicht alles, was schlechthin und einfach so da ist, einen Gegenstand des philosophischen Begriffes dar. Gegenstand des philosophischen Begriffs ist vielmehr nur das Substantielle im Vergänglichen, ist das Wesentliche an dem, was sich ereignet. Diesem Ziel, das Wesentliche im Zufälligen zu erkennen und nicht sich in der Aufzählung alles möglichen Seienden zu verlieren, dient die Arbeit der Philosophie. Sie will das Vernünftige in dem Geschehen der Welt begreifen. In Hegels Worten: Philosophie strebt danach, «die Vernunft als die Rose im Kreuze der Gegenwart zu erkennen.» Das Sinnbild für den Gegenstand des philosophischen Denkens ist die Lutherrose. Ihre um den Stamm des Kreuzes gewachsene Blüte gleicht der im Gekräusel des Zufälligen wachsenden Vernunft, die der philosophische Begriff zu erfassen strebt. Mit dem Rückgriff auf die Lutherrose vollzieht Hegel aber zugleich seinen letzten Rückgriff auf das Wort aus Äsops Fabel. Er macht sich nämlich den Gleichklang von Ῥόδος und – ῥόδον zunutze und ändert, einige Zeilen nach dem ersten Zitat, das äsopische Wort ab. Es lautet nun: «*Hier* ist die Rose, *hier* tanze.» Der Sinn der Veränderung ist nach dem Gesagten klar. Die Betonung des Hier und Jetzt, die die Kursivierung vornahm, muß einhergehen mit der Betonung des Substantiellen in der Gegenwart, das die Rose in deren Kreuz darstellt. Ῥόδος muß zu ῥόδον werden. Das Dictum, das in der Fabel vom Wort zur Tat drängte, hat sich somit in ein Dictum von der Vernunft im Bestehenden verwandelt. Es stellt nicht der leeren Behauptung die Tat an Ort und Stelle gegenüber, sondern verdeutlicht die Vernunft des begrifflichen Denkens und die Vernunft der begriffenen Wirklichkeit.

---

[3] Ibidem, S. 16. – Auch die folgenden Zitate finden sich an dieser Stelle.

Das Wort aus Äsops Fabel unterstreicht demnach einen anderen berühmten Satz Hegels: «Was vernünftig ist, ist wirklich; und was wirklich ist, ist vernünftig.»[4] Der Tanz, den der philosophische Begriff vollführt, um die Rose im Kreuz der Gegenwart zu erkennen, besteht in dem Nachvollzug der Gleichung von philosophischer Vernunft und wesentlicher Wirklichkeit. Aufschlußreich genug, daß die Nachschrift zu Hegels Vorlesung über die Philosophie des Rechts von 1819/20, die den berühmten Satz in einer Variante überliefert, welche die Gleichung abmildert: «Was vernünftig ist, *wird* wirklich, und das Wirkliche *wird* vernünftig»,[5] – daß jene Nachschrift den Bezug auf das Wort der Fabel nicht enthält.

III.

Der Verzicht auf die Tat, der Hegels Philosophie zu eigen ist, stellte einen der wichtigsten Angriffspunkte der Junghegelianer dar. Diese stießen sich an Hegels Begriff der Geschichte. Er sei unvollständig, weil er in seiner Beschränkung auf die Gegenwart und die in ihr abgeschlossene Vergangenheit die Dimension der Zukunft ausklammere. So lautete der Vorwurf, und die Forderung erhob sich, «die Erkenntnis des Wesens der *Zukunft* für die Speculation zu vindicieren».[6] Die Dimension der Zukunft aber ist nicht das, was ist. Sie ist das, was noch nicht ist, mithin das, was erst noch durch die Tat herbeigeführt werden muß. Um die Zukunft für das philosophische Denken zu vindizieren, hat daher die Philosophie sich mit der Tat zu verheiraten. Moses Heß schrieb aus diesem Grunde gegen Hegel eine «Philosophie der That».[7]

Auch der Junghegelianer, der am entschiedensten mit seinen Mitstreitern brechen wird, lebt aus der Wendung zur Tat. Die Diagnose, die *Karl Marx* der Philosophie im Zuge seiner Auseinandersetzung mit Hegel stellt: daß man die Philosophie nicht verwirklichen könne, ohne sie aufzuheben,[8] bedeutet gar nichts anderes als die Diagnose dessen, daß die Philosophie nur dann wirklichkeitsgesättigt zu sein vermag, wenn sie den Übergang vom Begriff zur Tat vollzieht. Freilich gilt nach Marx auch das Umgekehrte: Man kann die Philosophie nicht aufheben, ohne sie zu verwirklichen.[9] Daher vollzieht nicht jede Tat die Aufhebung der Philosophie. Sofern sie unter das Niveau des philosophischen Begriffes abfällt, kann sie als dessen Aufhebung, im dreifachen Hegelschen Sinne von tollere, conservare und elevare, nicht gelten. Doch wenn der philosophische Begriff seinerseits meint, er könne sich mit der Wirklichkeit des Begriffenen gleichsetzen, wenn er sich also, mit Hegel zu sprechen, als der «machthabende Begriff»[10] mißversteht, dann verfehlt er das eigentümliche Verhältnis von Was und Daß. Die Vernunft in der Wirklichkeit – die Rose im Kreuz der Gegenwart – ist

---

[4] Ibidem, S. 14.
[5] Georg Wilhelm Friedrich Hegel, Philosophie des Rechts. Die Vorlesung von 1819/20 in einer Nachschrift, Frankfurt am Main 1983, S. 51. – Hervorhebungen von mir.
[6] August von Cieszkowski, Prolegomena zur Historiosophie, Berlin 1838, S. 8.
[7] Moses Heß, Die europäische Triarchie, Leipzig 1841, S. 24 ff.
[8] Karl Marx, Zur Kritik der Hegelschen Rechtsphilosophie. Einleitung, in: Marx-Engels-Gesamtausgabe (MEGA) I/2, Berlin 1982, S. 170–183, hier: S. 176.
[9] Ibidem. – Eine Vorform dieser Erwägungen findet sich in der Anmerkung über die Realisierung der Philosophie und den Streit der nachhegelschen Parteien, die Marx seiner Dissertation über die Differenz der demokritischen und epikureischen Naturphilosophie beifügt. Siehe MEGA I/1, Berlin 1975, S. 67 ff.
[10] Georg Wilhelm Friedrich Hegel, Wissenschaft der Logik II, Hamburg 1932, S. 410.

von der Vernunft des philosophischen Begriffes verschieden. Der Begriff kann zwar die Rose erkennen, aber er hat daher noch nicht die Wirklichkeit der Rose bedingt. Ihre Wirklichkeit, das heißt die Wirklichkeit der Vernunft im menschlichen Tun, muß erst noch durch einen Überstieg über den Begriff herbeigeführt werden. Dieser Überstieg freilich kann sich, angesichts der tatsächlichen Unvernunft des Bestehenden im Deutschland des Vormärzes, nur als dessen vernünftige Umwälzung vollziehen. Kurz: die Verwirklichung der Philosophie geschieht als revolutionäre Tat.

An dieser frühen Einsicht in die Not des philosophischen Denkens hat Marx zeitlebens, auch nach seiner Abrechnung mit den Junghegelianern in der «Heiligen Familie» und der «Deutschen Ideologie», festgehalten. Sein Gedanke lautet: Eine Philosophie, die sich auf die Erkenntnis des Hier und Jetzt beschränkt, bleibt selber unverwirklicht; erst der Schritt vom Hier und Jetzt zu dem, was noch nicht ist, was durch die revolutionäre Tat aber herbeigeführt wird, vermag die Verwirklichung der Philosophie zu gewähren. Diese antihegelsche Überlegung verdeutlicht Marx indessen mit dem – Wort des Äsop. Er verwendet es an einer Stelle des «18. Brumaire», im Zusammenhang allgemeiner Erwägungen über die Natur proletarischer Revolutionen. Man könnte vermuten, daß Marx hier die einfache Kehrtwende zurück vollzöge: zu der in der Fabel erhobenen Forderung, die Rede müsse durch die Tat beglaubigt werden. Allein der Zugriff geschieht subtiler. Marx fügt der Hegelschen doppelten Lesart des Wortes eine dritte Schicht hinzu. Auch er schreibt: «Hic Rhodus, hic salta! Hier ist die Rose, hier tanze!» Der Bezug auf Hegels Lesart von Ῥόδος als ῥόδον ist offenkundig, obwohl Marx an keiner Stelle auf Hegel verweist. Doch im Zusammenhang des Textes verändert der Sinn des Wortes sich abermals grundlegend. Denn bei Marx sind es die Verhältnisse selbst, die jenes Wort den Menschen entgegenrufen.

> Proletarische Revolutionen [...] kritisieren beständig sich selbst, unterbrechen sich fortwährend in ihrem eignen Lauf, kommen auf das scheinbar Vollbrachte zurück, um es wieder von Neuem anzufangen, verhöhnen grausam-gründlich die Halbheiten ihrer ersten Versuche, scheinen ihren Gegner nur niederzuwerfen, damit er neue Kräfte aus der Erde sauge und sich riesenhafter ihnen gegenüber wieder aufrichte, schrecken stets von Neuem zurück vor der unbestimmten Ungeheuerlichkeit ihrer eignen Zwecke, bis die Situation geschaffen ist, die jede Umkehr unmöglich macht, und die Verhältnis selbst rufen:
> Hic Rhodus, hic salta!
> Hier ist die Rose, hier tanze![11]

Der Zusammenhang zeigt, daß Marx die zwei Sätze des Dictums neu aufeinander bezieht. Der erste Satz, «Hier ist die Rose», bedeutet, gleichklingend zu Hegels Lesart, den Fingerzeig auf das Vernünftige, das in den Verhältnissen der Gegenwart enthalten ist. Bei Marx aber ist das Vernünftige im Wirklichen nur keimhaft enthalten. Die Rose im Kreuz der Gegenwart, zu der Hegel Rhodos gemacht hatte, ist nun das Vernünftige, was noch nicht verwirklicht ist. Zu seiner Verwirklichung muß der Tanz erst noch gewagt werden. Das ist der Grund für den zweiten Satz des Dictums: «Hic salta!» Es ist in der Tat eine Aufforderung zum Tanz, freilich nun zu einem sehr besonderem. «Hier tanze!» wird zum Aufruf zur Revolution, um die Rose zu brechen. Die «versteinerten Verhältnisse zum Tanzen zwingen»[12] war das Anliegen, das Marx seit seinen frühen Schriften verfocht. Dieser Tanz verbindet sich nun mit der äsopischen Redewendung. Die Verhältnisse rufen «Hic Rhodus, hic

---

[11] Karl Marx, Der 18. Brumaire des Louis Napoleon, in: MEGA I/11, Berlin 1985, S. 96–189, hier: S. 102.
[12] Karl Marx, Zur Kritik der Hegelschen Rechtsphilosophie, op. cit., S. 173.

salta!», weil sie die Schwelle zur Verwirklichung der Vernunft darstellen, die durch den Tanz der Revolution vollzogen werden muß.

So verwandelt Marx das Wort aus Äsops Fabel in das Wort der revolutionären Praxis. Auch bei ihm läuft es nicht auf die Forderung hinaus, den Worten nun das Zeugnis der Tat folgen zu lassen, sondern stellt ein Dictum über das Verhältnis der Vernunft zur Wirklichkeit dar. Dieses Verhältnis besteht jedoch nicht in der begrifflichen Erfassung des Hier und Jetzt. Es besteht in dessen revolutionärer Veränderung. An Ort und Stelle springen heißt Marx zufolge: Ort und Stelle umkrempeln, und zwar so, daß Rhodos, die Rose der Vernunft, endlich seine Wirklichkeit erlange.

IV.

In dem Wort aus der Fabel des Äsop ist der Ausgang der klassischen deutschen Philosophie und der revolutionäre Bruch im Denken des neunzehnten Jahrhunderts en miniature zu erkennen.[13] Hegel wie Marx anerkennen ein Denken nur dann, wenn es gesättigt von Wirklichkeit ist. Beide wollen daher die Vernunft des philosophischen Begriffes mit der Vernunft des außerbegrifflichen Daseins zusammenschließen. Doch während Hegel den Zusammenschluß in der begrifflichen Erfassung der Gegenwart und der in ihr enthaltenen Vergangenheit liegen sieht, besteht Marx auf dem Überstieg über das Denken zur zukunftbezogenen Praxis. Erst die revolutionäre Tat vermag die Vernunft des außerbegrifflichen Daseins herbeizuführen; erst der Weg von der Theorie zur umwälzenden Praxis kann jenen Zusammenschluß vollbringen.

Das Wort aus Äsops Fabel wird dadurch zu dem Brennpunkt, in dem der Unterschied zwischen Hegel und Marx aufleuchtet. Die allgemeine Moral, daß prahlerische Worte durch die Tat an Ort und Stelle zu beglaubigen seien, wird in eine Aussage über die Verwirklichung der Vernunft umgewandelt: Hegel wie Marx lesen Ῥόδος als die Rose im Kreuz der Gegenwart. Doch den Sprung versteht Hegel als die Bewegung des philosophischen Begriffes im Hier und Jetzt und Marx als dessen Revolution. Dieser Unterschied ist der Unterschied zwischen spekulativer Interpretation und aufhebender Veränderung. «Die Philosophen haben die Welt nur verschieden *interpretiert*, es kömmt drauf an, sie zu *verändern*», verkündet die elfte Feuerbachthese. An der ungleichen Auslegung des äsopischen Wortes trennen sich die in ihr benannten Wege. Die Marginalie steht im Zentrum.

---

[13] Die Wendung «Ausgang der klassischen deutschen Philosophie» stammt von Friedrich Engels, die Wendung «revolutionärer Bruch im Denken des neunzehnten Jahrhunderts» von Karl Löwith.

EUGEN BRAUN

«Kultur-» und «Fachmenschentum»
Altertumswissenschaftliche Marginalien zu Max Weber als Erzieher*

Jakob Braun (1915–2000) zum Gedächtnis

Die Auseinandersetzung mit dem Werk Max Webers ist in den letzten Jahren neben der Sachdiskussion der verschiedenen Einzelfächer (die im Fall der deutschen Altertumswissenschaft nach Alfred Heuß' grundlegendem Aufsatz[1] besonders von Jürgen Deininger, Christian Meier und Wilfried Nippel belebt wurde) durch das eindrucksvolle Ringen um die wissenschaftssystematische Einordnung gekennzeichnet. Vor allem Wilhelm Hennis hat mit entschiedenem Protest gegen die von soziologischer Seite vorgenommene Vereinnahmung Webers als Gründervaters ihres Faches[2] die Notwendigkeit einer geistesgeschichtlich ausgerichteten Sicht auf das Werk betont, dessen universalgeschichtliche Analysen als (letzter) großer Beitrag zu einer von Platon begründeten politischen Philosophie angesehen werden können.[3] Ein Vergleich des neuzeitlichen Wirklichkeitswissenschaftlers, dessen Einschätzung des Kapitalismus als der «schicksalvollsten Macht unseres modernen Lebens» (RS I 4) im düster-illusionslosen Menetekel von den «'Fachmenschen ohne Geist'», «'Genußmenschen ohne Herz'» (RS I 204) kulminiert,[4] mit dem Vater der abendländischen Metaphysik mag zwar hinsichtlich ihrer theoretisch-philosophischen Auffassungen befremdlich erscheinen;[5] neben der letztlich ethischen Wendung eines auf das Er-

---

* Der vorliegende Aufsatz, den ich (mit Ausnahme von wenigen bibliographischen Ergänzungen) 2001 geschrieben habe, war ursprünglich ein Beitrag für einen von Dr. Werner J. Schneider (Heidelberg/Berlin) geplanten Sammelband zum Thema ‹Schulwesen und Bildungsstrategien seit der Antike› (Arbeitstitel).
[1] Max Webers Bedeutung für die Geschichte des griechisch-römischen Altertums, HZ 201 (1965) 529–556. Zu den folgenden abgekürzten Literaturhinweisen siehe den bibliographischen Anhang.
[2] Siehe dazu auch Tenbruck (1988) 371 Anm. 17.
[3] Hennis (1987) 97; ders. (1996) 73, 100. Llano (1997) 13: «Es ist davon auszugehen, daß Webers Denken heute die gleiche Rolle spielt, welche die Philosophie (...) in der Zeit eines Sokrates, eines Platon (...) in bezug auf Gesellschaft und Kultur gespielt hat».
[4] Nach Mommsen (1985) 269f. spricht aus dem eigentlich (worauf Weber selbst hinweist) dem Gebiet der Wert- und Glaubensurteile zugehörenden (bis heute nicht entschlüsselten) Zitat zwar die Befürchtung, «daß die moderne Welt nach dem historischen Vorbild der Spätantike irgendwann einmal den Erstickungstod erleiden könne», doch habe es eher die Qualität einer ‹selfdenying prophecy›, mit der «Gegenkräfte mobilisiert werden (sollten), die jenen Trends gerade Einhalt gebieten.» Siehe auch ders. (1986) 60f.
[5] Es sei nur die zentrale Passage des programmatischen Objektivitäts-Aufsatzes (WL 170f.) zitiert: «Die Sozialwissenschaft, die *wir* treiben wollen, ist eine *Wirklichkeitswissenschaft*. Wir wollen die uns umgebende Wirklichkeit des Lebens, in welches wir hineingestellt sind, *in ihrer Eigenart* verstehen – den Zusammenhang und die Kultur*bedeutung* ihrer einzelnen Erscheinungen in ihrer heutigen Gestaltung einerseits, die Gründe ihres geschichtlichen So-und-nicht-anders-Gewordenseins andererseits.» Zur antimetaphysischen Abgrenzung (in geschichtsphilosophischem Zusammenhang) vgl. WL 195, wo Weber davor warnt, «daß man gar die «Ideen» als eine hinter der Flucht der Erscheinungen stehende «eigentliche» Wirklichkeit, als reale «Kräfte» hypostasiert, die sich in der Geschichte auswirkten.» Zur ‹empirischen› Strenge Webers, «der in der Soziologie die Metaphysik auch in jeder verkappten Gestalt ablehnte», siehe die eindrucksvolle Darstel-

kennen von Gemeinschaftshandeln gerichteten Denkens[6] ist er jedoch vor allem in einer Hinsicht angemessen und fruchtbar, in der des erzieherischen Impetus, der hinter dem Werk steht.[7] Im folgenden soll auch die diesbezügliche platonische Wahlverwandtschaft[8] Webers etwas genauer beleuchtet werden, wie sie vereinzelt in dem 1917 gehaltenen Vortrag *Wissenschaft als Beruf* aufscheint. Ferner wird den altertumswissenschaftlichen Anteilen überhaupt nachgespürt, welche in Webers Sicht auf Wissenschaft allgemein eingeflossen sind. Ein Vergleich mit diesbezüglichen altertumswissenschaftlichen Positionen des 19. und

---

lung bei Jaspers (1932) 48 ff. (das Zitat ebd. 55), Rossi (1986) 31. Warum bei Weber «trotz aller Nüchternheit der kritischen Einstellung ein Metaphysisches wirksam (blieb)» und seine «historisch-kritische Arbeit am Ende in ihr Gegenteil: metaphysische Sinngebung (umschlug)», zeigt Wolf (1930/1972) (die Zitate ebd. 16 f.).

[6] Zu Weber siehe Wolf (1930/1972) 14.

[7] Was Stenzel (1928) 87 über Platon schreibt («und so ist an der Tatsache nicht zu deuteln, daß Platon als den eigentlichen Sinn seines Lebens die Besserung der menschlichen Gemeinschaft angesehen hat, nicht die theoretische Forschung über die Prinzipien der Ethik, nicht das mystische Gottsuchen in der einzelnen Seele, sondern die tätige Einwirkung nach der in strenger Wahrheitsforschung erkannten Idee auf die Umwelt, auf den eigenen Staat und auf den, zu dem die ‹Tyche› – wie er selbst sich ausdrückt – ihn in Beziehung setzen sollte»), läßt sich, folgt man Hennis (1996) 98 («so vergreift man sich nicht, wenn man Webers Werk zu verstehen sucht als Beitrag zur Geschichte der Erziehung des Menschengeschlechts»), abgewandelt auch auf Weber übertragen. Besonders deutlich wird die ‹erzieherische› Verwandtschaft durch einen Vergleich von Pl. Gorg. 513 e (wonach eine politische Tätigkeit nicht an der ἡδονή des Volkes ausgerichtet sein darf, sondern am Ziel, die Bürger ‹besser zu machen›) mit einer Stelle aus Webers Korreferat vor dem 5. Evang.-soz. Kongreß vom 16. Mai 1894: «Wir wollen, soweit es in unserer Macht steht, die äußeren Verhältnisse so gestalten, nicht: daß die Menschen sich wohl fühlen, sondern daß unter der Not des unvermeidlichen Existenzkampfes das beste in ihnen, die Eigenschaften, – physische und seelische – welche wir der Nation erhalten möchten, bewahrt bleiben» (MWG I/ 4–1, 340 f.). Nach Hennis (1987) 87 Anm. 78 ist dies «der zentrale Gedanke des Politikwissenschaftlers Weber, von dem aus die üblichen Kategorisierungen (Imperialist, Nationalist, Machtstaatstheoretiker, Dezionist) sich gelinde gesagt problematisch ausnehmen.»

[8] Eine andere (ebenfalls antike) mag nicht nur für die Würdigung der scheinbar «kalte(n) Objektivität» (Jaspers [1932] 74) des empirischen Soziologen ungleich wichtiger sein, die mit Thukydides. (Aufschluß hierüber dürfen wir von Wilhelm Hennis erwarten.) Daß Thukydides nicht nur hinsichtlich der methodischen Strenge der historischen Analyse, sondern auch in seiner Rolle als Politiker und politischer Ratgeber für Weber ein (bislang unerkanntes) Vorbild gewesen ist, muß angesichts der Tatsache, daß er auch für einen Eduard Meyer Maßstab historischer Forschung und Identifikationsfigur bei politischen Äußerungen gewesen ist, so unwahrscheinlich nicht erscheinen. Weber kann in diesem Zusammenhang auch wichtige Anregungen aus der Thukydidesdarstellung Jacob Burckhardts gewonnen haben, dem der griechische Historiker vor allem wegen der (fortschrittlichen) Methode «der Subsumption der Ereignisse oder Phänomene unter allgemeine Gesamtbeobachtungen» als «Vater des kulturhistorischen Urteils» galt, hinter den «die Welt nun einmal nicht zurückdarf» (Burckhardt [1898–1902] III 414). Wenn Burckhardt (ebd. 416 f.) über den griechischen Historiker schreibt: «Dafür wird mit Recht seine große *sachliche* Durchsichtigkeit gerühmt, derengleichen für uns wegen der Trennung zwischen populärem Wissen und bestimmten Fachstudien und wegen der komplizierten Einrichtungen des modernen Lebens kaum mehr zu erreichen ist», so ist Weber vielleicht einer der letzten, denen dies dennoch gelungen ist. Die Wahlverwandtschaft mit Thukydides hätte Weber mit Nietzsche gemeinsam, siehe KSA 6, 156 (*Götzendämmerung*): «Thukydides und, vielleicht, der principe Macchiavell's sind mir selber am meisten verwandt durch den unbedingten Willen, sich Nichts vorzumachen und die Vernunft in der *Realität* zu sehn – *nicht* in der «Vernunft», noch weniger in der «Moral» ... Von der jämmerlichen Schönfärberei der Griechen in's Ideal, die der «klassisch gebildete» Jüngling als Lohn für seine Gymnasial-Dressur davonträgt, kurirt Nichts so gründlich als Thukydides. (...) In ihm kommt die *Sophisten-Cultur*, will sagen die *Realisten-Cultur*, zu ihrem vollendeten Ausdruck: diese unschätzbare Bewegung inmitten des eben allerwärts losbrechenden Moral- und Ideal-Schwindels der sokratischen Schulen. (...) Thukydides als die grosse Summe, die letzte Offenbarung jener starken, strengen harten Thatsächlichkeit, die dem älteren Hellenen im Instinkte lag. Der *Muth* vor der Realität unterscheidet zuletzt solche Naturen wie Thukydides und Plato: Plato ist ein Feigling vor der Realität – *folglich* flüchtet er in's Ideal; Thukydides hat *sich* in der Gewalt – folglich behält er auch die Dinge in der Gewalt ...»

beginnenden 20. Jahrhunderts mag zum Verständnis seiner Haltung beitragen. Zuvor sollen jedoch – nicht zuletzt vor dem Hintergrund einer bildungspolitischen Diskussion seiner Zeit – Webers Ausführungen über «diejenigen Standpunkte, welche gegenüber der Kultur des Altertums prinzipiell möglich sind» (WL 264), vorgestellt werden, zu denen er sich 1906 anläßlich seiner geschichtstheoretischen Auseinandersetzung mit Eduard Meyer veranlaßt sah. Wenn Weber hier zuletzt auf eine Betrachtungsweise hinweist, für die «der Kulturgehalt der Antike als Erkenntnismittel zur Bildung von generellen »Typen«» (WL 265) dient, so stimmt dies mit derjenigen überein, die er selbst auch bei seinen Ausführungen zur Soziologie der Erziehung angewandt hat. Die hier entworfene Erziehungstypologie soll zu Beginn rekapituliert und ihr antiker ‹Kulturgehalt› etwas näher in den Blick genommen werden. Es zeigt sich, daß der von Weber für die Moderne als kennzeichnend ausgewiesene Gegensatz zwischen Kultur- und Fachmenschentum auch am Ende des fünften Jahrhunderts v. Chr. (wenn auch weniger stark und anders ponderiert) das Bildungsdenken in Griechenland (mit)bestimmt hat. Wie sich insbesondere Friedrich Nietzsche und Jacob Burckhardt bei der Beschreibung dieses Sachverhalts zur Bildungssituation der eigenen Zeit geäußert haben, soll ebenfalls vergleichend zur Sprache kommen.

I

«(...) der wissenschaftliche Mensch und der gebildete Mensch gehören zwei verschiedenen Sphären an, die hier und da sich in *einem* Individuum berühren, nie aber mit einander zusammenfallen.»

F. Nietzsche, *Über die Zukunft unserer Bildungsanstalten* (KSA 1, 683)

Den Begriff der Erziehung verwendet Weber in zweifachem Zusammenhang: einmal in einem weiten, auf die erzieherische Wirkung von gesellschaftlichen «Ordnungen und Mächten» bezogen,[9] dann in einem engeren, bei dem die zwischenmenschliche, auch im eigentlichen Sinn pädagogische Beeinflussung vor allem hinsichtlich verschiedener Erziehungszwecke untersucht wird. In ersterem ist der Begriff für Webers eigentliches Erkenntnisziel einer «empirischen Erfassung menschlicher »Gesinnungen«»[10] und ihrer Auswirkung auf die Lebensführung von kaum zu unterschätzender Bedeutung und nimmt (oft unausgesprochen) einen breiten Raum ein, in letzterem konzentriert sich das vorwiegend soziologische Interesse[11] auf die komprimierte Darstellung einer Erziehungstypologie.

---

[9] Hennis (1996) 98: «Die «gesellschaftlichen Ordnungen und Mächte» im eigentlichen Titel von «Wirtschaft und Gesellschaft» sind Erziehungsmächte, als Erziehungsmächte interessieren sie Weber, wie Presse, Vereine, Fabrikarbeit, Hochschulen, Parteien, Verfassungsformen und was sonst diesem Mann alles unter die Augen kommt.» Eine vergleichbare Verwendung des Erziehungsbegriffs findet sich bei Burckhardt I 76: «Die Polis hat ferner eine erzieherische Kraft; sie ist nicht nur ‹die beste Amme, die früher euch als Knaben, welche spielten auf dem weichen Grund, treu hegte und pflegte und keine Last der Wärterin versäumte›, sondern sie erzieht den Bürger sein Leben lang.» Zur moralischen Ausrichtung dieser Poliserziehung Stepper (1997) 24 ff.
[10] Hennis (1996) 43, ders. (1987) 109 f.
[11] Auch dieses hat letztlich – mag Weber hier auch von einer Untersuchung der (pädagogisch-psychologischen) Erziehungsmittel absehen – seinen «einzig verständlichen Bezugspunkt »in der Seele des Einzelnen«» (Hennis [1996] 60 mit Bezug auf Webers *verstehende Soziologie* überhaupt). Auch die Untersuchung der Gerechtigkeit in Platons *Staat* nimmt ihren Ausgang von der Einzelseele.

Zunächst sei auf die 1905 veröffentlichte, Webers weltweite Anerkennung begründende Abhandlung *Die Protestantische Ethik und der «Geist» des Kapitalismus* verwiesen. Bei der Untersuchung der Frage, welchen Einfluß die vom Calvinismus bestimmte Lebensführung eines asketischen Puritanismus auf die Herausbildung einer kapitalistischen Berufs- und Wirtschaftsgesinnung ausgeübt hat, wird die festgestellte Haltungsänderung als Ergebnis eines «lang andauernden Erziehungsprozesses» (RS I 46) ausgewiesen. Wenn Weber am Ende der Schrift auf die geistige Verengung des modernen Berufsmenschen hinweist, die in deutlichem Gegensatz zu einem ehemals «vollen und schönen Menschentum»[12] steht, deutet dies bereits auf die spätere Erziehungstypologie (mit der Fachausbildung als einem Extrem) hin. Die hier in ihrer historischen Genese als Ergebnis eines Erziehungsprozesses diagnostizierte Problematik des neuzeitlichen Berufsmenschentums bildet nicht nur den zeitgeschichtlichen Endpunkt, sondern (wie man vermuten kann) auch einen motivationalen Ausgangspunkt für die systematische Vertiefung des modernen Erziehungs- und Bildungsbegriffs in den zwischen 1911 und 1914 verfaßten Einzelsoziologien zu *Wirtschaft und Gesellschaft*, wo Weber insbesondere auf den Zusammenhang von (bürokratischer) Herrschaftsform und Erziehung eingeht (WuG 576f.). Diese (noch über weitere Stellen in WuG verstreuten) Ausführungen und die bereits erwähnte Erziehungstypologie, die Weber in der erstmals 1916 veröffentlichten Konfuzianismus-Studie der Abhandlungen zur *Wirtschaftsethik der Weltreligionen* eher en passant anführt, um sich über das Wesen der altchinesischen Bildung Klarheit zu verschaffen, auf die er sich aber auch später bezieht, seien zunächst kurz skizziert.

Erziehung und Bildung sind demnach in ihren verschiedenen Ausprägungen zunächst auf die ihnen zugrundeliegende feudale, theokratische, patrimoniale, demokratische, in je unterschiedlichem Grad charismatisch oder bürokratisch geprägte Herrschaftsform bezogen.[13] Ihre Beziehung ist auch dergestalt, daß «Erziehung überall die wichtigste Angriffsfläche für die Beeinflussung der Kultur durch die Herrschaftsstruktur (bietet)» (WuG 639). Von besonderer Bedeutung für ihre Herausbildung (und soziologische Beschreibung) ist neben dem Gesichtspunkt des sozialen Prestiges die Kategorie des Standes, nicht zuletzt vor dem Hintergrund, daß «Bildungs- und Geschmackskultur-Schranken» als «die innerlichsten und unübersteigbarsten aller ständischen Unterschiede» gelten müssen[14]

---

[12] RS I 203: «Der Gedanke, daß die moderne Berufsarbeit ein *asketisches* Gepräge trage, ist ja auch nicht neu. Daß die Beschränkung auf Facharbeit, mit dem Verzicht auf die faustische Allseitigkeit des Menschentums, welchen sie bedingt, in der heutigen Welt Voraussetzung wertvollen Handelns überhaupt ist, daß also «Tat» und «Entsagung» einander heute unabwendbar bedingen: dies asketische Grundmotiv des bürgerlichen Lebensstils – wenn er eben Stil und nicht Stillosigkeit sein will – hat auf der Höhe seiner Lebensweisheit, in den «Wanderjahren» und in dem Lebensabschluß, den er seinem Faust gab, auch *Goethe* uns lehren wollen. Für ihn bedeutete diese Erkenntnis einen entsagenden Abschied von einer Zeit vollen und schönen Menschentums, welche im Verlauf unserer Kulturentwicklung ebensowenig sich wiederholen wird, wie die Zeit der Hochblüte Athens im Altertum. Der Puritaner *wollte* Berufsmensch sein, – wir *müssen* es sein.» Vermutlich bezieht sich Weber bei dem Verweis auf die «Hochblüte Athens» auch auf die «Berufsfreiheit» und «Berufsüberlegenheit» der Griechen, von der «die deutschen Hellenisten des 18. Jahrhunderts (...) mächtig berührt» wurden (Harder [1949/1962] 25).
[13] Diese allgemeine Formulierung wird der Darstellung eher gerecht als die bei Llano (1997) 301: «Jede Herrschaft wird durch eine charakteristische Erziehung bedingt.» In WuG 576 geht es im Gegenteil um die Auswirkungen der Herrschaftsform auf Erziehung und Bildung.
[14] Zum Zusammenhang zwischen der «Richtung der *Erziehung* und der Art der *Stände*bildung» siehe auch WuG 155. Ferner RS I 409: Die gleichermaßen von einem Kulturideal bestimmte Pädagogik fällt beim japanischen Kriegerstand anders aus als bei der Priesterschicht. WuG 577f.: Auch bei der bürokratischen

(RS I 569). Als Mittel rational einsetzbar, zielt Erziehung auf bestimmte Zwecke, deren «äußerste[n] historische[n] Gegenpole» die «Erweckung von Charisma (Heldenqualitäten oder magische Gaben) einerseits, – Vermittlung von spezialistischer Fachschulung andererseits» (RS I 408) sind. Zwischen diesen nie ganz rein vorkommenden «radikalsten Gegensätzen (...) stehen alle jene Erziehungstypen mitten inne, welche eine bestimmte Art einer, sei es weltlichen oder geistlichen, in jedem Fall aber: einer ständischen *Lebensführung* dem Zögling *ankultivieren* wollen» (ebd.). Auf diese erste Vorstellung der Erziehungstypen folgen kurze inhaltliche Erläuterungen, die nicht zuletzt wegen ihrer Prägnanz im Zusammenhang zitiert seien (im Anschluß werden weitere diesbezügliche Stellen angeführt):

> «Die charismatische Zucht der alten magischen Askese und die Heldenproben, welche Zauberer und Kriegshelden mit dem Knaben vornahmen, wollten dem Novizen zu einer im animistischen Sinne «neuen Seele»: zu einer Wiedergeburt also, verhelfen; in unserer Sprache ausgedrückt: eine Fähigkeit, die als rein persönliche Gnadengabe galt, nur *wecken* und erproben. Denn ein Charisma kann man nicht lehren oder anerziehen. Es ist im Keim da oder wird durch ein magisches Wiedergeburtswunder eingeflößt, – sonst ist es unerreichbar. Die Facherziehung will die Zöglinge zu praktischer Brauchbarkeit für Verwaltungszwecke: – im Betrieb einer Behörde, eines Kontors, einer Werkstatt, eines wissenschaftlichen oder industriellen Laboratoriums, eines disziplinierten Heeres, – *abrichten*[15]. Das kann man, sei es auch in verschiedenem Grade, prinzipiell mit einem jeden vornehmen. Die Kultivationspädagogik schließlich will einen, je nach dem Kulturideal der maßgebenden Schicht verschieden gearteten, «Kulturmenschen», das heißt hier: einen Menschen von bestimmter innerer und äußerer Lebensführung, *erziehen*[16]. Auch das kann prinzipiell mit jedem geschehen.» (RS I 408 f.)

Über «Wesen und Wirkung» des (wertfrei zu verstehenden) Begriffs Charisma überhaupt handelt WuG 654 ff. Zur charismatischen Befähigung als Gegenstand einer «Erweckungserziehung» siehe ferner WuG 260, 279, 677 ff. Grundlage dieses «ältesten überall verbreiteten magischen Erziehungssystems» ist «die Annahme, daß das Heldentum auf Charisma

---

Herrschaftsform geht die Fachausbildung der Beamten mit einer ‹ständischen› Differenzierung einher. WuG 610: Die ständische Exklusivität der chinesischen Beamten (ebenso wie der nicht angestellten Literaten, vgl. RS I 417 f.) gründet auf dem sozialen Prestige einer in zahlreichen Examina nachgewiesenen literarischen (!) Kulturqualifikation, während in der modernen «bürokratisierten» Gesellschaft «die ständische Schichtung» auf dem Ansehen von (Fach-)Bildungspatenten beruht. WuG 639: Zum spezifischen Erziehungssystem des Ritterstandes in Feudalgesellschaften. WuG 652: Zur ständischen *Gesinnungs*erziehung überhaupt. Besonders prägnant ist die diesbezügliche Analyse aus dem Jahr 1917 in der Schrift *Wahlrecht und Demokratie in Deutschland* (GPS 279): «Unterschiede der «Bildung» sind heute, gegenüber dem *klassen*bildenden Element der Besitz- und ökonomischen Funktionsgliederung, zweifellos der wichtigste eigentliche *stände*bildende Unterschied. Wesentlich kraft des sozialen Prestiges der Bildung behauptet sich der moderne Offizier vor der Front, der moderne Beamte innerhalb der politischen Gemeinschaft. Unterschiede der «Bildung» sind heute – man mag das noch so sehr bedauern – eine der allerstärksten rein innerlich wirkenden sozialen Schranken. Vor allem in Deutschland, wo fast die sämtlichen privilegierten Stellungen innerhalb und außerhalb des Staatsdienstes nicht nur eine Qualifikation von Fachwissen, sondern außerdem von «allgemeiner *Bildung*» geknüpft und das ganze Schul- und Hochschulsystem in deren Dienst gestellt ist. Alle unsere Examensdiplome verbriefen auch und vor allem diesen *ständisch* wichtigen Besitz.»

[15] Zur Formulierung siehe unten S. 151.
[16] Hennis (1996) 82 erkennt in dem Umstand, daß «Weber keinen Versuch unternommen hat, die pädagogischen *Mittel* [*wecken, abrichten, erziehen*] so in eine typologische Reihe zu bringen, wie er dies für die drei Zwecke versucht hatte», «ein Zeugnis der Klugheit eines wirklich politischen, «praktischen» Denkers, der weiß, daß die Umstände, unter denen der Mensch handelt, sich nicht so systematisieren lassen wie die Zwecke.»

beruhe» (WuG 677). Auch in anderem (als dem militärischen) Zusammenhang kann die charismatische Erziehung (etwa in der ‹Ausbildung› zum Medizinmann, Regenmacher, Exorzist, Priester, Rechtskundigen, die stets «irgendwelche fachbildungsmäßigen Bestandteile [in sich schließt]») zu einer «formell staatlichen oder kirchlichen Institution werden» (ebd.), auch einer «zunehmende(n) Monopolisierung durch die Wohlhabenden» (wie in Indonesien) unterliegen (WuG 679). In religiösem Zusammenhang (etwa bei der priesterlichen Erziehung) kann sie sich vom «ältesten rein charismatischen Stadium hinweg zur literarischen Bildung» (Buchreligion) entwickeln (WuG 280). Die «mit steigender Differenzierung der Berufe und Erweiterung des Fachwissens» an «rationaler Qualität» zunehmende (Geheim-)‹Lehre› der charismatischen Erziehung entwickelt sich in Sonderfällen schließlich dahin, daß etwa «als caput mortuum der alten asketischen Mittel zur Weckung und Erprobung charismatischer Fähigkeit die bekannten pennalistischen Erscheinungen des Kasernen- und Studentenlebens innerhalb einer wesentlich fachmäßigen Abrichtung übrig bleiben» (WuG 677).

Mit seinem ‹Berufs›-Ideal steht das Fachmenschentum am Ende eines mit der Bürokratisierung der modernen Gesellschaft zunehmenden Rationalisierungsprozesses und als solches im Gegensatz zu Lebensformen in feudal und charismatisch bestimmten Herrschaftsstrukturen (WuG 651ff., 677). Die «Bürokratisierung der Verwaltung» und der «Bedarf nach fachgeschulten Technikern, Kommis usw.» trägt die Fachschulung «aus ihrer (in Europa) hauptsächlichen Brutstätte: Deutschland (...) in die ganze Welt» (WuG 577). Sie hat den Erwerb von Bildungspatenten zum Ziel. Freilich ist «das Verlangen nach der Einführung von geregelten Bildungsgängen und Fachprüfungen» «nicht Ausdruck eines ‹Bildungsdranges›», diese sind vielmehr nötig, um die Stellenvergabe zu regulieren (ebd). Die mit (empirisch erworbenem) Wissen nachgewiesene Fachqualifikation, die «in der Bürokratie in stetem Wachsen» ist, wird von den führenden Vertretern (Minister, Staatspräsident) der durch sie geprägten modernen Gesellschaft nicht verlangt, die deshalb Beamte «nur im *formalen*, nicht im *materialen* Sinne sind» (WuG 127). Die Facherziehung findet sich freilich auch in «vorbürokratischen oder halbbürokratischen Epochen». Ihr «regelmäßiger erster geschichtlicher Standort sind *präbendal* organisierte» (d.h. geistliche und weltliche «Pfründe» vergebende) «Herrschaften» (WuG 577). Auch in die charismatische Erziehung oder in die an einem Kulturideal orientierte etwa des chinesischen Patrimonialismus (WuG 610) fließt sie ein. Freilich «mußte (es) dem konfuzianisch gebildeten Amtsanwärter (...) fast unmöglich sein, in einer Fachbildung europäischen Gepräges etwas anderes als Abrichtung zum schmutzigsten Banausentum zu sehen» (RS I 449), war doch für ihn «der *Fachmensch* (...) auch durch seinen sozialutilitaristischen Wert *nicht* zu wirklich positiver Würde zu erheben» (RS I 532).

Zwischen charismatischer und fachlicher Erziehung steht in der Typologie die zuletzt genannte Kultivationspädagogik, deren Ziel nicht der «Fachmensch», sondern der «kultivierte Mensch» ist (WuG 578). Diese vor allem bei feudalen, theokratischen und patrimonialen Herrschaftsstrukturen vorkommende Erziehungsform orientiert sich an einem inhaltlich je verschieden ritterlich, literarisch, asketisch, gymnastisch-musisch ausgerichteten Bildungsideal, das (nicht nur auf England bezogen) mit dem Begriff ‹Gentleman› umschrieben werden kann. Zu beachten ist, daß der Ausdruck ‹kultiviert› bei der Beschreibung dieser Erziehungsform «gänzlich wertfrei und nur in dem Sinne gebraucht (wird): daß eine Qualität der Lebensführung, die als «kultiviert» *galt*, Ziel der Erziehung war, nicht aber spezialisierte Fachschulung» (WuG 578). Die mit der Erziehung einhergehende «Qualifikation der Herrenschicht als solcher beruhte auf einem Mehr an ‹Kulturqualität› (in dem durchaus wandelbaren wertfreien Sinn ...) nicht von Fachwissen» (ebd.). Die auf die «Umgestaltung der äußeren und inneren Lebensführung gerichteten Arten der Bildung» in der «Kultivationspädagogik (bewahren) die ursprünglichen irrationalen Mittel der charismatischen Erziehung nur in Resten» (WuG 677). Sehr eindrucksvoll hat Weber die ‹Kulturqualifikation› der (als Beamte tätigen!) chinesischen Literaten beschrieben, die «im Sinne einer allgemeinen Bildung, von einer ähnlichen, aber noch spezifischeren Art (ist), als etwa die überkommene okzidentale *humanistische* Bildungsqualifikation, welche bei uns, bis vor kurzem fast ausschließlich, den Eintritt in die Laufbahn zu den mit Befehlsgewalt in der bürgerlichen und militärischen Verwaltung ausgerüsteten Aemtern vermittelte und die dazu heranzuschulenden Zöglinge zugleich auch als *sozial* zum Stande der «Gebildeten» gehörig abstempelte. Nur ist bei uns – darin liegt der sehr wichtige Unterschied des Okzidents gegen China – neben und zum Teil an Stelle dieser ständischen Bildungsqualifikation die rationale *Fach*abrichtung getreten» (RS I 409).

Die formal und inhaltlich (wie stets) sehr dichte Beschreibung des modernen Fachmenschentums in seinen feinsten (bildungs-)soziologischen Bedingtheiten und Auswirkungen (auch im Zusammenhang mit der skizzierten Erziehungstypologie) in WuG 576ff. schließt Weber mit einem Satz ab, der in der heutigen bildungspolitischen Diskussion kaum mehr Geltung besitzt:

> «Hinter allen Erörterungen der Gegenwart um die Grundlagen des Bildungswesens steckt an irgendeiner entscheidenden Stelle der durch das unaufhaltsame Umsichgreifen der Bürokratisierung aller öffentlichen und privaten Herrschaftsbeziehungen und durch die stets zunehmende Bedeutung des Fachwissens bedingte, in alle intimsten Kulturfragen eingehende Kampf des ‹Fachmenschen›-Typus gegen das alte ‹Kulturmenschentum›. –» (WuG 578)

Im vergangenen Jahrhundert hat dieser Kampf einen deutlichen Ausdruck nicht zuletzt in der schon seit 1890 geführten Auseinandersetzung um die Stellung des humanistischen Gymnasiums in Preußen gefunden, zu der sich Weber mehrfach äußert.[17] Während sonst durchaus auch bildungspolitische Erwägungen seine Stellungnahme beeinflußt haben können, hat die werturteilsfreie wissenschaftliche Analyse hier das Ziel, sich rational vertretbarer Standpunkte zu vergewissern,[18] und kann auch deshalb, trotz ihrer Zeitgebundenheit, als ein bildungstheoretisches κτῆμα ἐς ἀεί gelten.

Wie hat Weber nun den erziehungssoziologischen ‹Kulturgehalt der Antike› interpretiert und in die beschriebene Typologie eingeordnet bzw. bei deren Herausbildung fruchtbar gemacht? Seine kurzen verstreuten Anmerkungen hierzu beschränken sich fast ausschließlich auf die griechische Kulturgeschichte und reichen bis zur klassischen Zeit. Von grundlegen-

---

[17] Siehe dazu unten S. 164f.
[18] Denn nach Weber «(kann) es niemals Aufgabe einer Erfahrungswissenschaft sein, bindende Normen und Ideale zu ermitteln, um daraus für die Praxis Rezepte ableiten zu können» (WL 149). In diesem Sinn ist wohl auch Hennis (1996) 99 zu verstehen, wenn er Webers «eigentliches Thema» in die Frage kleidet: «Gibt es noch einen *intellektuell verantwortbaren* Weg [Kursive E. B.], die Menschen innerlich zu erwecken, oder erschöpfen sich die Möglichkeiten zur Erziehung in der Abrichtung zu praktischer Brauchbarkeit für Verwaltungszwecke «im Betrieb, einer Behörde, eines Kontors, einer Werkstatt, eines wissenschaftlichen oder industriellen Laboratoriums, eines disziplinierten Heeres» oder traditional kompensiert – soweit diese Kräfte einer Tradition noch wirken –, zur «Ankultivierung einer bestimmten Art ständischer, gebildeter Lebensführung».»

der Bedeutung für Webers Interpretation der griechischen Erziehungs- und Bildungsformen ist, unabhängig von einer genauen lokalen Differenzierung, seine Sicht auf die antike Polis als eine «*Kriegerzunft*» (WuG 809). Diese nicht nur den Halbkommunismus (WuG 767) Spartas prägende, stets latent militärische Ausrichtung des Polislebens[19] hat in einem grundlegenden Sinn eine Erziehung zum Krieger zur Folge, welche in unterschiedlichem Grad durch musische Elemente ergänzt wird. Die historische Entwicklungslinie reicht von der sich an einem spezifischen Ehrbegriff orientierenden, immerhin durch das Spiel (WuG 651) aufgelockerten ritterlichen Erziehung in den feudalen bzw. gentilcharismatisch geprägten Polisformen der vorklassischen Zeit bis hin zu dem noch stärker musisch-gymnastisch bestimmten Ideal «in der Demagogenherrschaft der hellenischen sogenannten Demokratie»[20] (WuG 578), welche die Erziehung zum kultivierten καλοσκἀγαθός zum Ziel hatte, doch ist auch hier die militärische Grundausrichtung bestimmend[21]. Wesentlich für die griechische Erziehung und Bildung allgemein ist schließlich das «Fehlen eines spezifisch priesterlichen Erziehungssystems überhaupt» (WuG 679).[22]

Typologisch ist die militärische Ausbildung in Teilen der charismatischen Erziehung zuzuordnen. Im Fall der sogenannten Ephebie ist diese auch staatlich organisiert.[23]

---

[19] «Ueberall aber waren nach dem Sturz der Geschlechter die Bürgerhopliten die ausschlaggebende Klasse der Vollbürger. (...) Auch die nicht spartanischen hellenischen Städte hatten den Charakter eines chronischen Kriegslagers in irgendeinem Grade ausgeprägt» (WuG 809). Diese Sicht auf die Polis, in der die «Bürgerschaft in jeder Hinsicht nach Belieben mit dem Einzelnen (schaltete)», ist mit der Burckhardts verwandt, zu ihr siehe Stepper (1997) 27f., 75. Zu einem diesbezüglichen Einfluß Ed. Meyers auf Weber siehe Deininger (1990) 137. Zur Kritik an Weber siehe Meier (1988) 19: «Die antiken Bürgerschaften waren primär nicht Kriegerzünfte, sondern Grundbesitzerverbände.»

[20] Zu ihrem «charakteristischen charismatischen Einschlag» unter Perikles siehe WuG 665. Zum überraschenden Umstand, daß Weber «die griechische *polis* schließlich dem Begriff der charismatischen Herrschaft unterordnete», und zu einer weiterführenden Sachdiskussion siehe Finley (1986) 95ff. (mit dem Kommentar Toru Yuges ebd. 107f.). Zu der sich an einer «ritterlichen Lebensform» orientierenden musisch-gymnastischen Erziehung als «Mittel[n] der Selbstverklärung und der Entwicklung und Erhaltung des Nimbus der Herrenschicht gegenüber den Beherrschten» im Feudalsystem siehe WuG 639f., dazu Llano (1997) 304f. Die Nähe zu Burckhardt ist in diesem Zusammenhang deutlich in der Darstellung des «das ganze Leben beherrschende(n) ‹Agón›», der «naturgemäß aus dem ritterlichen Ehrbegriff und der militärischen Schulung der Jugend auf den Übungsplätzen (entstand)» (WuG 767). Siehe ferner WuG 814: «Der Agón, das Produkt des individuellen Ritterkampfes und der Verklärung des ritterlichen Kriegsheldentums war Quelle der entscheidensten Züge der hellenischen Erziehung.» Vgl. dazu Burckhardt (1898-1902) IV 115f.: «Erst, als das Athletisch-Agonale und das Musisch-Agonale das griechische Leben vollständig durchdrang, wird auch die Erziehung sich völlig darauf eingerichtet haben.»

[21] «In Indien, im Judentum, Christentum und Islam war der literarische Charakter der Bildung Folge davon, daß sie ganz in die Hände der literarisch gebildeten Brahmanen und Rabbinen oder der berufsmäßig literarisch geschulten Geistlichen und Mönche von Buchreligionen geraten war. Der hellenische vornehme Gebildete dagegen blieb in erster Linie Ephebe und Hoplit, solange die Bildung hellenisch – und nicht «hellenistisch» – war. Mit jener Wirkung, die in nichts deutlicher als etwa in der Konversation des Symposion hervortritt: daß sein Sokrates im Felde nie, nach unserer studentischen Terminologie, «gekniffen hat», ist Platon ersichtlich reichlich so wichtig wie alles andere, was er den Alkibiades sagen läßt» (RS I 410 mit Hinweis auf Pl. Smp. 219d-221c). Mit «Ephebe» bezieht sich Weber auf die militärische Ausbildung in der sog. Ephebie, siehe dazu Anm. 23.

[22] Zu den Gründen RS I 565: «Von den großen Systemen der Pädagogik haben nur der Konfuzianismus und die mittelländische Antike, der erstere durch die Macht seiner Staatsbureaukratie, der letztere umgekehrt durch das absolute Fehlen bureaukratischer Verwaltung, sich dieser Macht der Priesterschaft zu entziehen gewußt und damit auch die Priesterreligion ausgeschaltet.»

[23] Bei dem häufigeren Hinweis auf das für die «Heldenaskesenerprobung» und «Jünglingsweihe» wichtige «Männerhaus», die «älteste[n] Form der militärischen Berufsorganisation» (WuG 136, siehe ferner ebd.

Die (anders als in China) nicht intellektuell-literarisch, sondern gymnastisch-musisch ausgerichtete Erziehung zur kultivierten Persönlichkeit (καλοσκάγαθός) ist eine historisch singuläre Ausprägung der Kultivationspädagogik. Das in der Moderne durch Fachqualifikation gewonnene soziale Prestige wird in der griechischen Antike in diesem Zusammenhang (wie in China) durch ein «Mehr an ‹Kulturqualität›» erreicht, wobei gleichwohl das «kriegerische, theologische, juristische Fachkönnen (...) eingehend gepflegt (wurde)»; freilich bilden «im hellenischen wie im mittelalterlichen wie im chinesischen Bildungsgang (...) ganz andere als fachmäßig ‹nützliche› Erziehungselemente den Schwerpunkt» (WuG 578).

Mag in Webers erziehungssoziologischer Sicht auf die griechische Kulturgeschichte die vom musisch-gymnastischen Bildungsideal bestimmte Kultivationspädagogik zu Recht im Mittelpunkt stehen, so fällt doch auf, daß er die fachbezogen-intellektuelle Erziehung nicht eigens in den Blick nimmt.[24] In WuG 578 ist dies darin begründet, daß die Erziehungsformen und die durch sie angestrebten Ziele vor allem hinsichtlich ihres sozialen Prestiges betrachtet werden und hier in der Tat die Facherziehung und die aus ihr hervorgehenden Berufe, welche niemals großes gesellschaftliches Ansehen besaßen,[25] nicht gewürdigt zu werden brauchten. Auch vor dem Hintergrund der Herrschaftsstruktur Griechenlands erscheint die bildungssoziologische Konzentration auf die musisch-gymnastische Kultivationspädagogik plausibel, pflegt doch die Erziehung vor allem dort, «wo die Herrschaftsstruktur ‹präbendal› organisiert ist [wie in China, E.B.], (...) den Charakter der intellektualistisch-literarischen ‹Bildung› anzunehmen, also in der Art ihres Betriebs dem bürokratischen Ideal der Beibringung von ‹Fachwissen› innerlich nahe verwandt zu sein» (WuG 640). Daß auch in Griechenland eine ‹intellektualistische Fachschulung› für die ‹Bildung› von Bedeutung und ihr Verhältnis zur Kultivationserziehung nicht immer streng abgegrenzt und spannungsfrei gewesen ist, zeigt eine nähere Betrachtung des griechischen Bildungsdenkens im letzten Drittel des fünften Jahrhunderts v. Chr. Hier kann man (vor allem in Athen) das Bestreben[26] erkennen, das alte Kalokagathieideal durch eine geistig-intellektuelle Ausbildung zu erweitern und so auf eine neue Grundlage zu stellen, welche auch den politischen Veränderungen Rechnung trägt. Dieser Prozeß läßt sich weder in sachlicher Hinsicht noch in seiner sozialen Bedingtheit genau beschreiben.[27]

153, 181, 223, bes. 678, 769, 684 ff.), bezieht sich Weber wohl auf Heinrich Schurtz, Altersklassen und Männerbünde, 1902. Zur «Ephebie als militärische(r) und gesellschaftliche(r) Einrichtung» siehe Burckhardt (1996) 26 ff., Christes (1988) 61 f., Vidal-Naquet (1989) 105–122.

[24] Zur «Fachausbildung» in den Philosophenschulen siehe die kurze Bemerkung in RS I 415, wo Weber allerdings einen Zusammenhang mit der «Erziehung hellenischer Gentlemen (kaloikagathoi)» herstellt. Universalhistorische Beobachtungen zur (in Griechenland oft homoerotisch geprägten) «Pietätsbeziehung» zwischen Lehrer und Schüler im Rahmen eines sozialethischen Unterrichts finden sich im Kapitel «Prophet und Lehrer» im religionssoziologischen Abschnitt von WuG 271 f.

[25] Vgl. dazu Burckhardt (1898–1902) IV 119: «Aristoteles (Pol. VI,1, VIII 2 f.) verbietet (...) in der Erziehung nicht nur das eigentlich Banausische, die schwere körperliche Arbeit, sondern findet sogar, die *artes liberales* seien nur mäßig zu pflegen, man sei der Einseitigkeit verfallen, wenn man sich zu sehr darauf verlege, sie vollkommen zu beherrschen.» Jaeger II 25 weist darauf hin, daß «selbst im Zeitalter des Triumphs der Fachwissenschaft (...) dieser Grundzug der alten Adelskultur immer wieder durch(schlägt).» Sieher ferner Kühnert (1961) 71, Dihle (1986) 190 (mit Hinweis auf Arist. EN 7, 1177 a 12 ff.).

[26] Zum folgenden siehe Wilamowitz (1918) 56 ff., Stenzel (1928) 46 ff., Jaeger I 364 ff., Marrou (1948/1976) 101 f., Tenbruck (1976), Graeser (1993) 14 ff.

[27] Siehe dazu R. Meister, Die Entstehung der höheren Allgemeinbildung in der Antike, (1956) 24 ff.; W. Nestle, Die Begründung der Jugendbildung durch die Griechen, (1927) 47 ff., E. Hoffmann, Der Erziehungsgedanke der klassischen griechischen Philosophie, (1930) 104 f.; (alle Beiträge in: Johann [1976]),

Doch hat jedenfalls die auch durch eine zunehmende Rationalisierung des gesamten Lebens[28] bedingte Herausbildung verschiedener Einzelwissenschaften zu einem steigenden Interesse vor allem der ‹gebildeten› Schichten[29] an der von den Sophisten propagierten fachwissenschaftlichen Erziehung geführt und den alleinigen Geltungsanspruch des musisch-gymnastischen Bildungsideals (zumindest zeitweilig) in Frage gestellt. Der in diesem Zusammenhang festzustellenden Tendenz einer Zersplitterung des Unterrichts hin zur Polymathie ist, wie es scheint, vor allem Protagoras entgegengetreten,[30] der (weil er die gesellschaftliche Notwendigkeit eines neuen umfassenden Bildungsideals erkannte?) die Facherziehung einer auf den Erwerb von sozialen und politischen Kompetenzen überhaupt ausgerichteten Ausbildung unterordnete. Wie problematisch das Verhältnis von (wissenschaftlicher) Facherziehung und Allgemeinbildung in ihrer inneren Verknüpfung gleichwohl gewesen ist, läßt sich an einer Stelle des platonischen «Protagoras» ersehen, wo Sokrates den Unterricht beim berühmten Sophisten mit demjenigen beim Grammatik-, Kithara- und Sportlehrer vergleicht und als Kriterium einer Bewertung seine Bedeutung für die Allgemeinbildung herausstellt. Der junge Hippokrates soll bei Protagoras studieren, nicht um Sophist, d. h. Fachspezialist, zu werden (ἐπὶ τέχνῃ), sondern um sich zu bilden (ἐπὶ παιδείᾳ).[31]

---

ferner Kühnert (1961) 42 ff. Tenbruck (1976) untersucht in seiner in der soziologischen Tradition Webers stehenden Studie nicht nur die gesellschaftlichen Auswirkungen der Sophistik, sondern geht vor allem auch der Frage nach ihrer wissenssoziologischen Bedeutung nach («4. Die Sophistik als Beginn der Wissenschaft.»).

[28] Jaeger I 370, vgl. Tenbruck (1976) 65 Anm. 9. Weber weist in anderem Zusammenhang (WuG 238: Kap. IV «Entstehung ethnischen Gemeinsamkeitsglaubens») freilich auf den «im ganzen geringen Grad der Rationalisierung des hellenischen Gemeinschaftslebens überhaupt» hin. Einwände dagegen auch bei Meier (1988) 23. Der Einfluß Webers auf Jaeger (Hinweise zu dessen soziologischen Interessen bei Tenbruck [1976] 57) wird nicht nur an dieser Stelle deutlich. Insbesondere die Bemerkungen zur universalhistorischen Geschichtsbetrachtung in der Einleitung von *Paideia* lassen auf eine Auseinandersetzung mit ihm schließen. In unserem Zusammenhang sei auch auf *Humanismus und Jugendbildung* (Humanistische Reden, Berlin/Leipzig 1937) verwiesen, wo die von den Griechen begründete Kultur identisch ist mit «Erziehung zum Menschen (...) nicht als Berufswesen, als nutzbares Glied einer Zweckgemeinschaft, wie für die soziale Pädagogik unserer Zeit, sondern rein als Mensch. Die griechische Erziehung ist darin schlechthin einzigartig, daß sie alle Rücksicht auf Beruf und praktische Nutzbarkeit ausschaltet (...) und daß sie einzig und allein den Menschen zu bilden gebietet» (zitiert nach Preuße [1988] 145). Stenzel (1928) 84 zufolge ist es «bis in späte Zeiten des Griechentums (...) die schmerzlichste Entscheidung für einen Jüngling, statt der Paideia den ‹Beruf› wählen zu müssen.» Zu «Werner Jaegers Problemgeschichte der griechischen «Paideia»» siehe jetzt Mehring (1999), ferner Gumbrecht (2002) 265.

[29] Tenbruck (1976) 60.

[30] Wilamowitz (1918) 56: «Da hat ein Mann durchgegriffen.»

[31] Zu dieser als einem locus classicus des antiken Bildungsdenkens oft zitierten Stelle (312b) siehe Jaeger I 380, Marrou (1948/1976) 123, Kühnert (1961) 10, 43 f. Zur (hellenistischen) Verhältnisbestimmung von Philosophie als *ars vitae* und den (auch im Rahmen der ἐγκύκλιος παιδεία) als propädeutisch aufgefaßten Fachwissenschaften ausführlich Dihle (1986), der den Wechsel der Berufsbezeichnung bei Eratosthenes (φιλόλογος statt φιλόσοφος) in der Emanzipation der Einzelwissenschaften begründet sieht, wonach «gelehrte Tätigkeit unabhängig von ihrem Nutzen für den Wissenschafler selbst oder seine Mitmenschen auch wie die Philosophie sinngebender Lebens- und Berufsinhalt sein könne, dass also der βίος θεωρητικός unter den Bedingungen der neuen Zeit des Hellenismus nicht ein Privileg des professionellen Philosophen sei, sondern sich auch im Dasein des Gelehrten und Forschers erfülle» (208). Für die Beantwortung der Frage: «Wie geben wir der Wissenschaft, die sich aus dem Ganzen der Erziehung und Bildung nun einmal losgelöst hat und selbständig geworden ist, ihre erzieliche Bedeutung, ihre bildende Kraft zurück, oder wie ordnen wir sie sinnvoll in das Ganze der Jugendbildung ein, ohne sie in ihrem eigentlichen Wesen zu beeinträchtigen» (Stenzel [1928] 108), immer noch hilfreich und von zeitloser Aktualität (trotz einer sehr beschränkten Sicht auf Nietzsche): Meyer (1907).

Nicht nur das Bildungsdenken der Zeit ist durch die Betonung einer fachlichen Spezialisierung herausgefordert worden. Wie sehr diese auch auf das literarisch-philosophische Schaffen eingewirkt hat, zeigt das Beispiel Platons, dessen Werk maßgeblich von der zeitgenössischen Techne-Diskussion beeinflußt ist.[32] Inhaltlich hat dies etwa im «Staat» einen sehr speziellen Ausdruck darin gefunden, daß der Philosophenkönig eine langwierige Fachausbildung durchlaufen muß (521 c ff.).[32a] Daß die Facherziehung, obwohl «die Frage nach der ‹Technizität› in allen wichtigen antiken Berufs- und Bildungsdisziplinen eine Rolle spielte»,[33] letztlich doch nicht die Bedeutung[33a] im öffentlichen Leben gehabt hat, die sie in der Moderne besitzt, mag außer im geringeren sozialen Prestige des Fachspezialisten in der verschiedenen Wirtschaftsform und dem Fehlen einer bürokratischen Herrschaftsstruktur (welche Fachkräfte erfordert) begründet sein.

Die von Weber im Rahmen universalgeschichtlich ausgerichteter Untersuchungen aufgezeigte unumkehrbare[34] innere Problematik des modernen Fachmenschentums findet sich bereits bei Nietzsche im engeren Zusammenhang der (geistes-)wissenschaftlichen Fachausbildung beschrieben. Seine Kritik, bei der er «mit feinem Gespür» von «seinem Nahbereich, dem philologischen Wissenschaftsbetrieb»[35], ausgeht, richtet sich gegen die Übermacht des Historismus und die lebensfeindliche Indienstnahme der ‹Auszubildenden› in der ‹Fabrik der allgemeinen Utilitäten›. Der Einfluß auf Weber wird nicht zuletzt in der Wortwahl deutlich:

«(...) man triumphirt darüber, dass jetzt ‹die Wissenschaft anfange über das Leben zu herrschen›: möglich, dass man das erreicht; aber gewiss ist ein derartig beherrschtes Leben nicht viel werth, weil es viel weniger *Leben* ist und viel weniger Leben für die Zukunft verbürgt, als das ehemals nicht durch das Wissen, sondern durch Instincte und kräftige Wahnbilder beherrschte Leben. Aber es soll auch gar nicht (...) das Zeitalter der fertig und reif gewordenen, der harmonischen Persönlichkeiten sein, sondern das der gemeinsamen möglichst nutzbaren Arbeit. Das heisst eben doch nur: *die Menschen sollen zu den Zwecken der Zeit abgerichtet werden*, um so zeitig als möglich mit Hand anzulegen; sie sollen in der Fabrik der allgemeinen Utilitäten arbeiten, bevor sie reif sind, ja damit sie gar nicht mehr reif werden – weil dies ein Luxus wäre, der ‹dem Arbeitsmarkte› eine Menge von Kraft entziehen würde.» (KSA I 299, *Vom Nutzen und Nachtheil der Historie für das Leben*, zweite Kursive E.B.)

Die von Weber als Kampf der Fachausbildung mit der alten Kultivationspädagogik beschriebene Bildungssituation ist auch in Jacob Burckhardts *Griechischer Kulturgeschichte* angedeutet. Bei der Erklärung des von ihm für das gesellschaftliche Leben der griechischen Antike als wesentlich angesehenen agonalen Prinzips beschreibt Burckhardt dessen Aus-

---

[32] Eine zusammenfassende Darstellung ihrer Geschichte überhaupt gibt Nesselrath (1985) 123 ff.
[32a] Siehe dazu Kühnert (1961) 72, 112 ff., zu Platons «Hochschätzung der Zahlenwissenschaften Geometrie, Arithmetik, Astronomie und Musiktheorie», die «den Menschen von der verwirrenden Welt der Sinne ablenken und auf die Dialektik, die kognitive Annäherung an die Intelligibilia, vorbereiten können», Dihle (1986) 195, 211 f., 227 (das Zitat ebd. 193).
[33] Nesselrath a.a.O. 125.
[33a] Zur Entwicklung in hellenistischer Zeit Marrou (1948/1976) 363 f.: «Der Geschichtschreiber stellt mit Überraschung fest, daß, die Medizin ausgenommen, keine Fachdisziplin (die der Ausübung eines bestimmten Berufs entspricht) (...) Gegenstand eines regelmäßigen Studienplans gewesen ist.»
[34] Vgl. Hennis (1987) 91: «In den Orientstudien zeigte er [Weber, E.B.] eine völlig andere Welt, eine zutiefst menschliche Welt. Nur wiederum: es gab kein Zurück.»
[35] Safranski (2000) 120.

wirkungen auf alle Lebensbereiche, auch den der Erziehung, die ganz auf das musisch-gymnastische Ideal hin ausgerichtet ist. Im Zusammenhang mit dem Hinweis auf die historische Einmaligkeit dieser Lebensform («Es entstand eine Existenz, wie sie auf Erden weder vorher noch nachher noch anderswo vorgekommen ist.»[36]) kommt er auch auf die Gegenwart zu sprechen. Als Hauptunterschied zwischen Antike und Moderne stellt er zunächst die Differenz (in Grad und Form) der öffentlichen Anteilnahme am Agon bzw. Wettbewerb heraus, der in Griechenland «immer eine ganze Bevölkerung zum Zeugen hat, während heute (...) ein entweder kaufendes, resp. Eintrittsgeld zahlendes oder nicht kaufendes und wegbleibendes Publikum entscheidet.» Während in Hellas zeitlebens «die Sehnsucht nach Ruhm» den Agon prägt, ist der so motivierte Wettbewerb in der Gegenwart nur bei «einigen höchst Ehrgeizigen» in der Schule (wo «freilich ein gewöhnlich geringer Grad von Ehrgeiz besteht») anzutreffen, an welche Stelle im späteren Leben die «Geschäftskonkurrenz» tritt. Die materielle Notwendigkeit bestimmt nicht nur die nachschulische Existenz, ihr muß auch die Erziehung Tribut zollen, die nicht mehr auf die Verwirklichung eines Kulturideals zielt, sondern ‹vielseitiges Wissen› vermitteln muß:

> «Der jetzige Mensch sucht viel eher eine Stellung in der Welt als plötzliche glänzende Anerkennung zu gewinnen, und er weiß wohl, warum er den Erfolg mehr auf der materiellen Seite sucht; denn das Leben ist pressant geworden.[37] Was aber die Erziehung betrifft, so ist an Stelle der fast ganz auf künftiges Können hin gerichteten griechischen Paideusis die heutige auf «gründliches und dennoch vielseitiges» Wissen abzielende höhere Schulbildung getreten.»[38]

Wenn Burckhardt (im Abschnitt über die Bewertung der Arbeit in der griechischen Antike) auf die innere Einheit der im Kalokagathieideal angestrebten Lebensform hinweist (die dem «vollen und schönen Menschentum» Goethes bei Weber verwandt ist), so spricht daraus

---

[36] Vgl. damit WuG 810: «Auf Markt und Gymnasium verbringt der Bürger den Hauptteil seiner Zeit. Seine persönliche Inanspruchnahme: durch Ekklesia, Geschworenendienst, Ratsdienst und Amtsdienst im Turnus, vor allem aber durch Feldzüge: jahrzehntelang Sommer für Sommer, war in Athen gerade in der klassischen Zeit eine solche, wie sie bei differenzierter Kultur weder vorher noch nachher in der Geschichte erhört ist.» Die agonale Beanspruchung des Bürgers bei Burckhard ist hier durch die der Politik und des Krieges ersetzt.

[37] Burckhardt zeigt hier eine gewisse Nähe zu Nietzsche, dessen Vorträge *Über die Zukunft unserer Bildungsanstalten* er gehört hatte, vgl. KSA 1, 715: «Jede Erziehung aber, welche an das Ende ihrer Laufbahn ein Amt oder einen Brodgewinn in Aussicht stellt, ist keine Erziehung zur Bildung, wie wir sie verstehen, sondern nur eine Anweisung, auf welchem Wege man im Kampfe um das Dasein sein Subjekt rette und schütze. Freilich ist eine solche Anweisung für die allermeisten Menschen von erster und nächster Wichtigkeit: und je schwieriger der Kampf ist, um so mehr muß der junge Mensch lernen, um so angespannter muß er seine Kräfte regen.»

[38] Alle Zitate Burckhardt (1898–1902) IV 116. Der topische Charakter dieser ‹Kritik› wird deutlich, wenn man die Bemerkung liest, die Wilamowitz zwei Jahrzehnte später im Kapitel «Jugenderziehung» seines Platon-Buches im Zusammenhang mit der Darstellung des Protagoras macht: «Wie vielen redet nicht heute dieser Protagoras aus der Seele, und der Staat ist ja auch auf dem besten Wege, die Schule zur Trägerin der sophistischen Vielwisserei zu machen, zur Schule der entsprechenden Gesinnungstüchtigkeit auch» (Wilamowitz [1918] 59). Eine Gesinnungserziehung ist nach dem Sieg des Kapitalismus freilich nach Weber nicht mehr nötig: «Indem die Askese die Welt umzubauen und in der Welt sich auszuwirken unternahm, gewannen die äußeren Güter dieser Welt zunehmende und schließlich unentrinnbare Macht über den Menschen, wie niemals zuvor in der Geschichte. Heute ist ihr Geist – ob endgültig, wer weiß es? – aus diesem Gehäuse entwichen. Der siegreiche Kapitalismus jedenfalls bedarf, seit er auf mechanischer Grundlage ruht, dieser Stütze nicht mehr» (RS I 203 f.).

freilich keine rückwärtsgewandete Idealisierung, stellt er doch im selben Zusammenhang die Angemessenheit einer solchen Lebensform durchaus kritisch in Frage und weist mit Sinn für die Wirklichkeit darauf hin, daß «wir als Nachwelt (...) uns doch einigen von jenen Einseitigen [gemeint sind die Fachspezialisten der bildenden Kunst, Musik, Literatur, E.B.] mehr verpflichtet (fühlen) als denen, die sich vor lauter harmonischer Kalokagathie gar nicht mehr zu lassen wußten, meist aber in der konkreten Polis, wie sie seit dem Peloponnesischen Kriege war, kaum mehr die Stelle fanden, um ihre ‹Trefflichkeit› zur Geltung zu bringen» (ebd. 129). Trotz aller Kritik[39] ist das ganzheitliche Lebensideal der Griechen für Burckhardt gleichwohl ein latenter Bezugspunkt auch der Reflexion auf die Gegenwart, wie aus (beiläufigen) Vergleichen deutlich wird: «Offenbar sollen alle Eigenschaften eine Harmonie bilden und keine vorherrschen; der Grieche will, wenn er irgend kann, ein Ganzes sein und wird dies, wenn er sich ganz der Öffentlichkeit und der Gymnastik und edlen Kultur hingibt (wozu heute, wenn es einem gelingen soll, unerhörte Anstalten und Glücksfälle nötig sind)» (ebd. 119).[40] Von einer durchaus (ironisch?-)kritischen Sicht auf die ‹wissenschaftliche› Lebensform zeugt in diesem Zusammenhang auch, daß sich Burckhardt beim Hinweis auf die antike Einschätzung der Spezialisten als ‹Banausen› (welche der von Weber geschilderten altchinesischen sehr verwandt ist) die (wiederum in Klammern gesetzte) Feststellung nicht verkneifen kann: «(Alle heutigen Gelehrten hätten damals Banausen geheißen, und die jetzigen Spezialisten ganz besonders.)» (ebd. 119 Anm. 224). Von Webers späterem Empfinden für die innere Problematik des modernen Fachmenschentums[41] ist dies allerdings weit entfernt.

Auch sonst stellt Burckhardt (en passant) feinsinnige vergleichende Beobachtungen zu antiker und moderner ‹Bildung› an, die, obschon sehr kurz, in ihrer Differenziertheit denen Webers nicht nachstehen und dessen universalhistorische Ausführungen und die

---

[39] Vgl. ferner ebd. 119: «Es fragt sich hierbei nur, wie weit die menschliche Natur die Verwirklichung solcher Ideale erträgt. Darüber, daß sie eine Menge von *falschen Bürgern* hatten, welche so banausisch als möglich nach den Vorteilen der Polis angelten, sind den Griechen auch später die Augen nicht aufgegangen.»

[40] In *Die Kultur der Renaissance in Italien* (Stuttgart ¹⁰1978, 129 f.) beschreibt Burckhardt («Die Vollendung der Persönlichkeit») das vielseitige Kultivationsideal im Italien des 15. Jahrhunderts, das auch die praktische Lebensführung mit einbezieht: «Der Humanist seinerseits wird zur größten Vielseitigkeit aufgefordert, indem sein philologisches Wissen lange nicht bloß wie heute der objektiven Kenntnis des klassischen Weltalters, sondern einer täglichen Anwendung auf das wirkliche Leben dienen muß. Neben seinen plinianischen Studien z. B. sammelt er ein Museum von Naturalien; (...) als Übersetzer plautinischer Komödien wird er wohl auch der Regisseur bei den Aufführungen.» Diese Vielseitigen werden noch von einigen «wahrhaft Allseitige(n)» übertroffen, besonders von Leon Battista Alberti, dessen umfassende Bildung auch in einem tiefen Naturempfinden zum Ausdruck kommt: «Beim Anblick prächtiger Bäume und Erntefelder mußte er weinen; schöne, würdevolle Greise verehrte er als eine ‹Wonne der Natur› und konnte sie nicht genug betrachten; auch Tiere von vollkommener Bildung genossen sein Wohlwollen, weil sie von der Natur besonders begnadigt seien; mehr als einmal, wenn er krank war, hat ihn der Anblick einer schönen Gegend gesund gemacht.»

[41] Zur «Herausarbeitung eines Stranges in der Geschichte des modernen Typus Mensch, der gelernt hat, sein Alltagsleben, sein Berufsleben insbesondere diszipliniert und methodisch zu führen, um damit – ohne es zu wollen – dem modernen Fach- und Berufsmenschentum den Weg zu bahnen», in der ‹Protestantischen Ethik› siehe Hennis (1987) 177. Ebd. 98: «Die Problematik der modernen, entzaubert – rationalisiert – disziplinierten Lebensweise ist Weber am *Kapitalismus* deutlich geworden.» Zur spezifischen Lebensführungsproblematik des modernen Intellektuellen siehe besonders WuG 307 f. Zur Notwendigkeit der Spezialisierung in der Wissenschaft unten S. 169.

Erziehungstypologie in Teilen, wenn auch nicht explizit formuliert, vorwegnehmen.[42] Abschließend sei eine Stelle aus dem Kapitel «Der koloniale und agonale Mensch» des vierten Buches der *Griechischen Kulturgeschichte* zitiert (137 f.) (die wohl auch über den bildungstheoretischen Kontext hinaus für Weber von Bedeutung gewesen ist):

> «Man liebte den Reichtum zu allen Zeiten, und brünstig, aber doch nicht so, daß man sich, um ihn zu gewinnen, leicht zum Erwerb entschlossen hätte, sobald derselbe mit irgendeiner unedel scheinenden Anstrengung verbunden war. Den Wert des Lebens suchte man, wenigstens der Anschauung, wenn auch nicht der Tat nach, im siegreichen Wettstreit irgendeiner (nur nicht der industriellen) Art mit andern.[43] Auch heute haben ja diejenigen Tätigkeiten gewisse Schranken, die sich ein sogenannter «Gebildeter», ja einer, der auch nur in einer Sekundarschule gewesen ist, gefallen läßt: Steinklopfer und dergleichen will ein solcher nie werden. Allein diese Schranken sind unendlich weiter gezogen; Manipulationen selbst sehr derber Art schließen nicht von der «Bildung» aus, welche gewissermaßen die damalige Kalokagathie vertritt, und künstlerische Tätigkeit adelt in der neuern Zeit vollends die leibliche Aktion, die damit verbunden ist. – Damals aber sagte noch Sokrates, in dessen Kreise sich die philosophische Kalokagathie der adligen substituiert hatte, die Muße (ἀργία) sei die Schwester der Freiheit.»

II

Waren griechische Erziehung und Bildung für Weber im Zusammenhang mit der Herausarbeitung einer Erziehungstypologie zunächst vor allem ein Gegenstand universalgeschichtlicher Betrachtung, so rückte die Antike (in einem umfassenden Sinn) auch vor dem Hintergrund zeitgenössischen Bildungsdenkens in seinen Blick. Der Zusammenhang, in

---

[42] Daß sich Weber von ihnen zumindest inspirieren ließ, kann man vermuten. Eine genaue Kenntnis des Werkes darf man nach GSW 283 voraussetzen: «*Burckhardts* posthum ediertes Kollegheft über «Griechische Kulturgeschichte» ignoriert die gesamte moderne Forschung und die monumentalen Quellen; die Benutzung ihrer trotzdem natürlich vielfach höchst geistvollen *Gesichtspunkte* ist daher im einzelnen durchweg nur mit Vorsicht möglich, das direkt Ökonomische übrigens wenig berücksichtigt (vgl. aber über die Bedeutung des Werkes – gegen v. Wilamowitz – die Ausführungen *C. Neumanns* in der «Hist. Zeitschrift», *Kaersts* in der Vorrede zu seinem «Hellenismus»).» Zu Webers Burckhardt-Rezeption siehe ferner Hennis (1987) 52, 189.

[43] Während bei Burckhardt die agonale Beanspruchung des Bürgers die Entfaltung eines kapitalistischen Wettbewerbs nicht zuläßt, ist es bei Weber vor allem diejenige durch den Krieg (vgl. oben Anm. 36): «Ein solcher Demos konnte unmöglich primär in der Richtung des befriedeten *ökonomischen* Erwerbs und eines *rationalen* Wirtschaftsbetriebes orientiert sein» (WuG 810). Ansonsten aber sieht Weber (mit sarkastischem Unterton) eine direkte Beziehung zwischen modernem Kapitalismus und ‹agonalen Leidenschaften›: «Auf dem Gebiet seiner höchsten Entfesselung, in den Vereinigten Staaten, neigt das seines religiös-ethischen Sinnes entkleidete Erwerbsstreben heute dazu, sich mit rein agonalen Leidenschaften zu assoziieren, die ihm nicht selten geradezu den Charakter des Sports aufprägen» (RS I 204). Vgl. dazu bereits Nietzsche KSA 3, 155 (*Morgenröthe*): «Man sieht jetzt mehrfach die Cultur einer Gesellschaft im Entstehen, für welche das *Handeltreiben* ebenso sehr der Seele ist, als der persönliche Wettkampf es für die älteren Griechen und als der Krieg, Sieg und Recht es für die Römer waren.» Zum Motiv der (religiösen) Wertschätzung der Arbeit in Webers Protestantismus-Studie vgl. ferner Burckhardt (1898–1902) IV 117: «Das Wesentliche für die Wertschätzung der Arbeit sind vielmehr die Zeit und die Umstände, unter denen sich bei einer Nation die Ideale des Daseins ausbilden. Dasjenige des jetzigen Europas stammt vorherrschend vom Bürgertum des Mittelalters her, welches allgemach dem Adel nicht nur an Reichtum überlegen, sondern auch an Bildung – freilich einer anderen als der des Adels – gleichwertig wurde. Die Griechen aber hatten das Phantasiebild ihrer heroischen Zeit, d. h. einer Welt ohne Nutzen, und wurden dasselbe nie los.»

dem dies geschah, war freilich kein im engeren Sinn bildungstheoretischer und soll deswegen kurz erläutert werden.[44]

In einer Stellungnahme zu Eduard Meyers 1902 erschienener Schrift *Zur Theorie und Methodik der Geschichte* hatte Weber 1906 im ersten Teil seiner «Kritischen Studien auf dem Gebiet der kulturwissenschaftlichen Logik» nachgewiesen, daß Meyer[45] den Begriff des Historischen unscharf verwendet und nicht klar zwischen der Wertbeziehung des Historikers zu seinem Objekt und der Kausalanalyse der historischen Tatsachen getrennt hatte (WL 261). Ein zweiter Haupteinwand bezog sich darauf, daß Meyer als Gegenstand der Geschichtswissenschaft nur das kausal Wirksame gelten lassen wollte.[45a] Weber zeigt dagegen, daß es auch andere Gesichtspunkte der historischen Forschung gibt, die sich auf die Eigenart des Gegenstandes (unabhängig von seiner kausalen Wirkung auf die Gegenwart) beziehen und wichtige Erkenntnismittel liefern können. Auch die Herstellung von Wertbeziehungen ist ein bedeutsamer Aspekt. Weber erläutert dies u. a. an Meyers ureigenem Forschungsgegenstand, der klassischen Antike, und verteidigt in diesem Zusammenhang auch die von diesem am Ende seiner Schrift kritisierte «philologische Methode», der es Meyer zufolge nicht um die Erhellung geschichtlichen Werdens, sondern um die Vergegenwärtigung vergangener Zustände geht[46] (WL 247). Nach Weber ist die philologische Methode nicht nur «durch die sprachlichen Voraussetzungen der Materialbeherrschung praktisch herbeigeführt», sondern auch durch die «"Bedeutung"» bedingt, «welche die Kultur des klassischen Altertums bisher für unsere eigene Geistesschulung gehabt hat» (WL 264). Deutlich hebt er auch im folgenden auf die je unterschiedliche Kulturbedeutsamkeit[46a] des Gegenstandes als Movens der Forschung ab, wenn er «diejenigen Standpunkte, welche gegenüber der Kultur des Altertums prinzipiell möglich sind, in radikaler und deshalb auch rein theoretischer Fassung zu formulieren» versucht (WL 264). Das Thema der Erziehung bzw. Bildung rückt nun insofern ins Blickfeld, als in allen Standpunkten die Frage nach dem Bildungswert der Antike berührt wird.

Bei der ersten Auffassung ist der Erziehungsgedanke von zentraler Bedeutung. Mit der «Vorstellung von» der «absoluten Wertgeltung der antiken Kultur», wie sie «im Humanismus, dann etwa bei Winckelmann und schließlich in allen Spielarten des sogenannten »Klassizismus"» zu beobachten ist, ist die Überzeugung verbunden, daß «antike Kulturbestandteile (...) wenigstens virtuelle Bestandteile «der» Kultur schlechthin» sind, «nicht weil sie «kausal» in E.M.s Sinn gewirkt *haben*, sondern weil sie in ihrer absoluten Wertgeltung kausal, auf unsere Erziehung, wirken *sollen*. Daher ist die antike Kultur[47] in erster Linie Objekt der Interpretation in usum scholarum, zur Erziehung der eigenen Nation zum Kulturvolk: Die «Philologie», in ihrem umfassenden Begriff, als «Erkenntnis des Er-

---

[44] Zum folgenden siehe Deininger (1990) 145 ff., Näf (1990) 296 ff., Tenbruck (1988) 349 ff.
[45] «Für Weber war Ed. Meyer nicht nur einer der maßgebenden Historiker des Altertums, sondern einer der Hauptvertreter der zeitgenössischen Historie überhaupt.» (Deininger [1990] 132)
[45a] Meyer (1902/1910) 41 ff.
[46] Meyer (1902/1910) 64 f.
[46a] Zum Begriff der «Kulturbedeutung» siehe die Ausführungen im Objektivitäts-Aufsatz WL 175 ff; ebd. 177: «Wir erstreben die Erkenntnis einer historischen, d. h. einer in ihrer *Eigenart bedeutungsvollen*, Erscheinung.»
[47] Zu ihrer absoluten Wertgeltung vgl. J. W. v. Goethe, *Maximen und Reflexionen*, Nr. 763, Hamburger Ausgabe 12, 505: «Chinesische, indische, ägyptische Altertümer sind immer nur Kuriositäten; es ist sehr wohlgetan, sich und die Welt damit bekannt zu machen; zu sittlicher und ästhetischer Bildung aber werden sie uns wenig fruchten.» Diesen Standpunkt vertritt auch Werner Jaeger in der Einleitung seiner *Paideia*.

kannten», erkennt im Altertum etwas prinzipiell Ueberhistorisches, zeitlos Geltendes» (WL 264).

Diesem klassizistischen Standpunkt, für den die Antike Maßstab der Erziehung ist, steht ein «andere(r), moderne(r) (...) radikal» entgegen, bei dem der ästhetische Genuß Weniger für die Rezeption kennzeichnend ist. Dieser Auffassung zufolge «(steht uns) die Kultur des Altertums in ihrer wahren Eigenart (...) so unendlich fern, daß es ganz sinnlos ist, den «Vielzuvielen» einen Einblick in ihr wahres «Wesen» geben zu wollen: sie ist ein sublimes Objekt der Wertung für die Wenigen, die in eine für immer dahingegangene, in keinem wesentlichen Punkte jemals wiederholbare, höchste Form des Menschentums sich versenken, sie gewissermaßen «künstlerisch genießen» wollen.» In einer Anmerkung dazu heißt es: «Dies dürfte wohl die «esoterische» Lehre von U. v. Wilamowitz sein, gegen den sich ja E.M.s Angriff in erster Linie richtet» (WL 264).

Nicht nur wegen des zuletzt genannten Hinweises seien, bevor der dritte Standpunkt vorgestellt wird, zunächst einige philologiegeschichtliche Erläuterungen gegeben. (Der hier eigentlich zu verfolgende Erziehungsgedanke und das Thema des Bildungswertes der Antike müssen dabei keineswegs in den Hintergrund treten.)

Wenn Weber die philologische Entsprechung zur zeitlos-idealischen Sicht auf die Antike als «Erkenntnis des Erkannten» beschreibt, so bezieht er sich auf den Philologiebegriff August Boeckhs.[48] Daß es ihm lediglich auf das abstrakte Schlagwort ankommt, mit dem die überhistorische Sichtweise verdeutlicht werden soll, kann man daraus schließen, daß Boeckh in der Philologiegeschichte eigentlich die Wende zum Historismus einleitet.[49] Weber bezieht sich hier insofern auch auf Meyer, als dieser am Ende seiner Schrift der historischen Betrachtung der Vergangenheit die philologische gegenüberstellt, «welche von den ihrem Wesen nach *zeitlosen* Beziehungen «historischer» Objekte: ihrer Wertgeltung, ausgeht und diese «verstehen» lehrt» (WL 247). Meyers Äußerungen zielen vor allem auf Wilamowitz,[50] den Weber freilich als Vertreter des zweiten Standpunktes anführt. Dies verwundert auch insofern, als Webers Ausführungen eher auf den Geistesaristokratismus Nietzsches zuzutreffen scheinen, dessen elitäre Auffassung vom Bildungswert der Antike in den 1872 gehaltenen Vorträgen *Über die Zukunft unserer Bildungsanstalten* besonders deutlich zum Ausdruck kommt.[51]

---

[48] Dieser hielt von 1809 bis 1866 in Berlin Vorlesungen über *Encyclopädie und Methodologie der philologischen Wissenschaften*, die 1877 unter diesem Titel von E. Bratuschek in Leipzig herausgegeben wurden. Zum Schlagwort ‹Erkenntnis des Erkannten› siehe ebd. 11f., 55.

[49] Siehe Reinhardt (1941/1960) 340, 349; zum umfassenden Philologiebegriff Boeckhs in diesem Zusammenhang Horstmann (1989) 112, wonach dieser «damit nicht eine Einzeldisziplin heutigen Verständnisses, (...) sondern – in der Gleichsetzung mit «Geschichte» – historische Geisteswissenschaft schlechthin (meint): Ihr Gegenstandsbereich ist nicht der einer geisteswissenschaftlichen Spezialdisziplin, sondern die gesamte geschichtliche Welt des Geistes, das «geschichtlich Producirte», d.h. alles, was – in jenem weiteren Sinne – «verstanden» werden kann.»

[50] Meyer (1902/1910) 65. Siehe Calder III (1990) 68f., zu Meyer selbst die ebd. zitierte Charakterisierung Werner Jaegers: «Eduard Meyer war zwar kein Humanist, der der eigenen Zeit die idealen Geisteswerte der Vergangenheit in Kunst und Philosophie als höchste Maßstäbe vorhält. Er war ganz historischer Realist, und die Quellen lesen, das hieß für ihn: rücksichtslos die geistige Form, in der die Geschichte überliefert ist, wie eine Maske abstreifen und sie in die Realität des noch gärenden Lebensvorgangs zurückübersetzen.»

[51] Siehe z. B. KSA 1, 687: «Das Gefühl für das Klassisch-Hellenische ist nämlich ein so seltenes Resultat des angestrengtesten Bildungskampfes und der künstlerischen Begabung, daß nur durch ein grobes Mißverständnis das Gymnasium bereits den Anspruch erheben kann, dies Gefühl zu wecken.» KSA 1, 700: «Alle die Menschen, die in einem glänzenden Moment der Erleuchtung sich einmal von der Singularität und Unnahbarkeit des hellenischen Alterthums überzeugten und mit mühsamem Kampfe vor sich selbst diese

Wie Nietzsche hat Wilamowitz eine scharfe Abkehr von den klassizistischen Idealen vollzogen,[52] doch lassen sein stark vom Historismus geprägtes Bemühen, antike Lebenswirklichkeit zu vergegenwärtigen,[53] und das damit zusammenhängende öffentliche Wirken[54] kaum den Schluß auf eine elitäre Versenkung in die höchste Form des Menschentums zu (wenn auch der allgemeinen Vermittlung antiker Kultur ein außergewöhnlich tiefes Einfühlen vorausgegangen sein wird). Es wäre hilfreich zu wissen, worauf sich Weber, der die

---

Ueberzeugung vertheidigt haben, alle diese wissen, wie der Zugang zu diesen Erleuchtungen niemals Vielen offen stehn wird, und halten es für eine absurde, ja unwürdige Manier, daß Jemand mit den Griechen gleichsam von Berufs wegen, zum Zwecke des Broderwerbs, wie mit einem alltäglichen Handwerkzeuge verkehrt und ohne Scheu und mit Handwerkerhänden an diesen Heiligthümern herumtastet.» Safranski (2000) 66: «Wer das Wohlergehen der größtmöglichen Zahl im Auge hat, denkt moralisch; wer die Aufgipfelung in gelungenen Gestalten, die *Verzückungsspitze*, zum Sinn der Kultur erklärt, denkt ästhetisch. Nietzsche entscheidet sich für die ästhetische Denkweise.» In der als fünfte *Unzeitgemäße Betrachtung* geplanten Schrift *Wir Philologen* (zu «Entstehung, Situation und Thema» siehe Cancik/Cancik-Lindemaier [2002]) wollte Nietzsche darlegen, «daß die bedeutende Rolle» der Altphilologie «im Erziehungswesen sich einer falschen Auffassung der Antike verdankt und daß (sie) daran sogar wider bessere Einsicht festhält, um ihre Machtstellung im Erziehungswesen behaupten zu können» (Safranski [2000] 141). Siehe etwa KSA 8,21: «Zu beweisen: A) das Missverhältnis zwischen Philologen und den Alten. B) die Unfähigkeit der Philologen, mit Hülfe der Alten zu *erziehen*.» Zu Nietzsches geistesaristokratischen Vorstellungen («Berufung einer mehrjährigen pädagogischen Bruderschaft») siehe Cancik/Cancik-Lindemaier (2002) 99 Anm. 11, 106, 111. Zu Weber siehe MWG I/17, 79: «Wissenschaftliche Schulung aber, wie wir sie nach der Tradition der deutschen Universitäten an diesen betreiben sollen, ist eine *geistesaristokratische* Angelegenheit, das sollten wir uns nicht verhehlen», dazu Gumbrecht (2002) 259. Zum gleichwohl vorhandenen Unterschied zwischen Nietzsches und Webers Aristokratismus siehe Schluchter (1996) 165, dem zufolge letzterem «die Arroganz gegenüber Nietzsches ‹Herde›, gegenüber seinen ‹Viel-zu-Vielen› (fehlt), weil Weber weder Nietzsches naturalistischen Monismus noch seine Degradation des Anderen zum Mittel oder gar seinen Antiinstitutionalismus teilte.»

[52] Reinhardt (1941/1960) 346 («Mit dem Ideal des Klassizismus allerdings wird furchtbar aufgeräumt») zitiert in diesem Zusammenhang aus Wilamowitz' *Griechischem Lesebuch*: «unsere Knaben haben ein Anrecht auf die Wahrheit.» Siehe ferner Canfora (1985) 638, Preuße (1988) 48f., zu Nietzsche auch Safranski (2000) 140.

[53] Hentschke/Muhlack (1972) 102: «Realismus und Aktualisierung – der Alltag des antiken Menschen und dieser Mensch als ‹Mensch wie du und ich› – sind die hervorstechendsten Merkmale aller großen Interpretationen Wilamowitz'.» Vgl. jedoch Jaeger (1960) 219: «Zwei Seelen rangen in seiner Brust unaufhörlich miteinander: der Historiker, der nichts anderes wissen will als was gewesen ist, und der Humanist und Philologe, der anbeten und verkünden muß, was groß und ewig ist.» Zu Wilamowitz' schulpolitischen Vorstellungen Matthiessen (1990) 40: «Der Unterricht sollte darum in den Griechen nicht länger das exemplarische Menschentum schlechthin, die reinste Verkörperung der Idee der Humanität vorführen, sondern eine geschichtlich bedeutende Kultur. Das Fach Griechisch sollte ein historisches Fach sein mit der Aufgabe, eine möglichst umfassende Kenntnis einer exemplarischen Kultur zu vermitteln. Diese Kultur sollte nicht mehr als klassisch, unerreichbar vollendet und allein nachahmenswert, gesehen werden, einerseits historisch bedingt, also auch mit Schwächen behaftet, und grundsätzlich ohne Vorzugsstellung gegenüber anderen Epochen, aber andererseits von höchster Bedeutung für die eigene Kultur.»

[54] Zu den Hörern seiner Vorträge gehörten nicht nur «Bildungshungrige der Arbeiterklasse, die eigentlich für die Sozialdemokratie zu schade» waren (Wilamowitz [1928] 252), sondern auch (Haus-)Frauen, siehe ebd. 225f.: «Öffentliche Vorlesungen hatte ich zu allen Zeiten nicht selten gehalten. (...) Diese Vorträge waren im Ganzen gleicher Art wie ich sie später im Victoria-Lyzeum in Berlin gehalten habe. Schade, daß sie abgekommen sind, seit die Frauen in der Universität allgemein zugelassen sind, denn für die Hausfrauen ist damit nicht gesorgt, gesetzt, sie könnten hingehen. Vor ihnen und für sie ernsthaft von so hohen Dingen reden zu dürfen, wie der Hellenist sie ihnen nahebringen kann, ist schön und lohnend. Da spricht man aus, was man vor gemischtem Publikum oder halbreifem zurückhält. Freilich war im Viktoria-Lyzeum der Unfug, daß Backfische hingeschleppt wurden, um zu gähnen und Pralinés zu lutschen, nachher blasiert zu schwatzen.» Zu Wilamowitz' Engagement auf der Schulkonferenz 1900 siehe Preuße (1988) 43ff.

Hauptwerke Wilamowitz' kannte, bei der Charakterisierung ‹esoterisch› (aus der doch wohl hervorgeht, daß ihm das exoterische Wirken des Philologen bekannt war) genau bezieht. Ob die so bezeichnete Haltung in der «Privatvorlesung» zum Ausdruck kam, in der Wilamowitz, wie man vermuten kann, vor allem «Philologie für die Philologen»[55] trieb? Möglicherweise wirkt hier bei Weber auch der Eindruck nach, den Wilamowitz durch seine 1892 in Göttingen gehaltene Prorektoratsrede hinterließ, in der er die Philologie scharf vom gewöhnlichen Schulbetrieb abgrenzte.[56]

War bei der ersten Auffassung antiker Kultur der Erziehungsgedanke in Form einer umfassenden Vermittlung zeitlos gültiger Kulturnormen, in der zweiten die ästhetische Wertschätzung Weniger für die Art der Rezeption bestimmend, so «kommt» bei der dritten «die altertumskundliche Behandlung einer wissenschaftlichen Interessenrichtung entgegen, welcher der Quellenschatz des Altertums in erster Linie ein ungewöhnlich reichhaltiges ethnographisches Material für die Gewinnung allgemeiner Begriffe, Analogien und Entwicklungsregeln, für die Vorgeschichte nicht nur unserer, sondern «jeder» Kultur darbietet.» Weber weist in diesem Zusammenhang auf «die Entwicklung der vergleichenden Religionskunde» hin, «deren heutiger Aufschwung ohne Ausbeutung der Antike mit Hilfe streng philologischer Schulung unmöglich gewesen wäre.» Daß bei dieser Auffassung ein im Gegensatz zu den beiden anderen wertfreies Erkenntnisinteresse für die ‹altertumskundliche Behandlung› des Stoffes leitend ist, kann man daraus schließen, daß «die Antike (...) hier insofern in Betracht kommt, als ihr Kulturgehalt zur Bildung von generellen «Typen» geeignet ist» (WL 265).

Bei den Ausführungen zu möglichen Standpunkten der antiken Kultur gegenüber sind für Weber wahrscheinlich nicht nur wissenschaftstheoretische Gründe maßgebend gewesen. Daß seine Kritik an Eduard Meyer, bei der es ihm auch um den Nachweis ging, daß es neben der Erhellung des Historisch-Wirksamen andere wichtige Formen der Auseinandersetzung mit dem Forschungsgegenstand gibt, nicht zuletzt «als Stellungnahme zur seinerzeitigen Diskussion und anstehenden Entscheidung über die Rolle der Antike in der Gymnasialbildung» angesehen werden kann, legt insbesondere der Schluß der Schrift nahe, wo Weber den Historiker «davor bewahren wollte, dem gemeinsamen Gegner Hilfe bei der Abwertung der Antike in ihrem Bildungswert zu liefern»[57]:

---

[55] Siehe Hölscher (1965) 24 (der aus dem Vorwort zu Euripides, *Hippolytos* zitiert): «Zum Wichtigsten seiner Berliner Wirksamkeit gehören aber die (...) öffentlichen Vorlesungen. Seine ganze Philologie war ja Interpretation, das heißt aber für ihn zugleich: Vermittlung an die Nichtfachleute. ‹Die Philologie für die Philologen; das Hellenentum, das, was daran unsterblich ist, für jedermann, der kommen, sehen, erfassen will.›» (Die «Privatvorlesung» hielt Wilamowitz «aus Rücksicht auf die älteren Kollegen nachmittags», Wilamowitz [1928] 247.)

[56] «(...) mögen andere Disziplinen und Berufe schreien, daß sie nicht bestehen können, wenn nicht dies und das auf der Schule gelernt würde: um der Philologie willen, um unsertwillen, die wir sie lehren, oder gar um der Wissenschaft willen, mögen die beiden Sprachen, denen Europa seine Kultur verdankt, ruhig aus dem obligatorischen Jugendunterrichte verschwinden. Wie Deutschlands Zukunft dabei fahren wird, das frag ich nicht: die Philologie kann es ruhig wagen» (Wilamowitz [1892/1913] 102). Wilamowitz hat später «aufs dringlichste (...) vor der Überfüllung der Universitäten und der planlosen Vermehrung der Professoren gewarnt» (Hölscher [1965] 23 mit Hinweis auf Wilamowitz [1928] 299f.): «Heißt es schwarz sehen, wenn uns die Furcht ankommt, die Universitäten könnten auf einen ähnlichen Zustand herabsinken wie vor 1810? Erzeugt unser Volk wirklich so viele Talente? Es ist ein abschüssiger Weg (...). Wenn die Qualität sinkt, wohin soll es führen? Gebe Gott, daß ich ein Schwarzseher bin.»

[57] Tenbruck (1988) 352 Anm. 53. Worauf sich der Hinweis einer «anstehenden Entscheidung» bezieht, ist nicht klar.

«Allein wenn (...) E.M. ernstlich alles vom Standpunkt der Gegenwart aus historisch nicht mehr «Wirksame» aus der Geschichte des Altertums ausmerzen wollte, würde gerade er, in den Augen aller derjenigen, welche im Altertum *mehr* als nur eine historische «Ursache» suchen, seinen Gegnern recht geben. Und alle Freunde seines großen Werkes werden es erfreulich finden, daß er mit jenem Gedanken gar nicht Ernst machen *kann*, und hoffen, daß er nicht etwa einer irrtümlich formulierten These zuliebe auch nur den Versuch dazu unternimmt» (WL 265).

Spricht aus diesen Worten auch die allgemeine Überzeugung vom Bildungswert der Antike, so stellt sich doch die Frage, welcher der drei genannten Auffassungen Webers besonderes Interesse galt. Die Antwort ‹jeder› überrascht bei einem so vielseitigen Denker nicht. Daß er auch mit Hilfe des antiken Anschauungsmaterials allgemeine ‹Typen› gewann, zeigen nicht zuletzt seine Ausführungen zur Erziehungstypologie. Auch mag die im griechischen Altertum auszumachende «höchste Form des Menschentums» ein wichtiger Bezugspunkt wenn nicht des ästhetischen Genusses,[58] so doch seiner ‹Wissenschaft vom Menschen› gewesen sein.[59] Daß Weber schließlich auch den Bildungswert einer für die Herausbildung von Kultur überhaupt normgebenden Antike hochgehalten hat, geht aus seinem Plädoyer für den Erhalt des humanistischen Gymnasiums[60] aus dem Jahr 1919 hervor. In der sicher auch von politischem Kalkül bestimmten Stellungnahme weist er zu Beginn darauf hin, daß «mehr als je (...) heute, nach dem Sturz der überlieferten Gewalten, die gründliche Vertrautheit wenigstens der berufsmäßig zu leitenden Stellungen ausgebildeten Schichten mit der Gedankenwelt des klassischen Altertums Bedürfnis (ist).» Frei vom Pathos des vorwiegend auf die ethisch-moralische Erziehung ausgerichteten Schulhumanismus begründet er (wohl auch vor dem Hintergrund der politischen Situation) seine Behauptung zunächst mit einem Argument, das die Leistung der Antike für die Heraus-

---

[58] Ein solcher mag sich wohl bei den Ausführungen zur altgriechischen Musik in der Musik-Studie eingestellt haben, wo er etwa darauf hinweist, daß die klassische Zeit eine Melodik von höchstem «Raffinement» geschaffen habe, welches «der antiken Musikkultur das entscheidende Gepräge» gegeben habe und von keiner späteren Epoche der europäischen Kulturentwicklung erreicht worden sei. Siehe dazu ausführlich Braun (1992) 115f. (das Zitat ebd.), der auf weitere Stellen hinweist, wo Weber sich zum Verhältnis des «Raffinements» materieller und künstlerischer Bedürfnisse bei den Griechen äußert.

[59] Nach Hennis (1987) 43 Anm. 51 «(spricht) manches dafür, daß Webers Verhältnis zur Antike genau wie bei Machiavelli und Rousseau hierfür den Schlüssel abgibt, wie ja schließlich auch für Nietzsche. Daß sich die «kulturwissenschaftliche Arbeit» ihrer Verankerung an den letzten Wertideen nicht immer bewußt sein könne – und das sei gut so – hatte Weber ausdrücklich betont (WL S. 214). Der «Begriff» für seine letzte Idee ist eindeutig: die «höchste Form des Menschentums.»» Dies direkt aus unserer Stelle zu schließen, wie Hennis in seinem Zusatz «(z.B. WL S. 264)» tut, ist freilich kaum möglich.

[60] Als dessen Existenz nach der Novemberrevolution gefährdet schien, traten zahlreiche Gelehrte verschiedener Fächer (unter ihnen Adolf von Harnack, Friedrich Meinecke, Eduard Meyer, Ernst Troeltsch) für seinen Fortbestand ein: *Das Gymnasium und die neue Zeit. Fürsprachen und Forderungen für seine Erhaltung und seine Zukunft.* Leipzig und Berlin 1919 (die folgenden Zitate aus der Stellungnahme Webers ebd. 133f.). Zur allgemeinen Tendenz des Bandes siehe Preuße (1988) 107: «Der Antike wird sowohl eine Vermittlerrolle als auch eine Stabilisationsfunktion gegen das revolutionäre Neue zugewiesen: die politische Haltung der Gymnasialanhänger drückt sich in ihren Argumenten für das Gymnasium aus, ohne daß jedoch in den Beiträgen (...) vom Aufbau eines Feindbildes gesprochen werden kann.» Zu Webers ‹erzieherischer› Haltung allgemein in dieser Zeit siehe Hennis (1996) 82, der aus einem Brief an Friedrich Crusius vom 24.11.1918 zitiert: Vor allem seien jetzt Kulturprobleme zu bewältigen: «Also ganz massive Erziehungsfragen. Mittel: nur das amerikanische Klubwesen, *einerlei* zu welchem Zweck: Ansätze dazu finden sich bei der ‹Freideutschen Jugend›. Andere Mittel kenne ich nicht, da das Autoritäre – dem ich ganz vorurteilslos gegenüber stehe – jetzt völlig versagt, außer in Form der *Kirche.*»

bildung einer «von patriarchalen und traditionalistisch gebundenen politischen und hierarchischen Mächten freie(n) geistige(n) Kultur, wie sie der Okzident allein hervorgebracht hat», herausstellt. Für deren Existenz wurde bei Marathon und Salamis gekämpft,[61] sie wurde durch die «Machtentfaltung der Römer» gesichert. Bezeichnend für Webers eher theoretisches Interesse am Bildungswert der Antike ist, daß er als zweites Argument die Bedeutung ihrer heute noch wirksamen «Denkarbeit» als Grundlage für die Entwicklung «alles ‹voraussetzungslose(n)›[62] Denkens auf wissenschaftlichem und insbesondere auf politischem Gebiet» anführt. Erst danach folgt der Hinweis auf «die künstlerischen und literarischen Monumente antiker Kultur», die «zu unserer eigenen Vorgeschichte und ihre geistigen Träger zu unseren eigenen Ahnen» gehörten. Auch hier erleichtert der «intime Verkehr mit den literarischen Erzeugnissen der Antike in der Ursprache dem jungen Menschen» nicht zuletzt «die Präzision und Nachhaltigkeit des Denkens mehr (...), als ihm selbst irgendwie bewußt ist.»[63] Sehr bestimmt weist Weber darauf hin, daß humanistische Bildung über alle politischen und nationalen Schranken hinweg auf Menschen eingewirkt hat, und bezeichnet es als «banausisch, unwahr und (...) traurige(n) nationalistische(n) Kleinglauben, zu meinen, die nationale oder die demokratische oder die sozialistische Eigenart unserer Jugend sei gefährdet durch die intime Berührung mit ewigen Werten, nur deshalb, weil deren Schöpfung örtlich und zeitlich weit von uns entfernt vollbracht wurde.» Der Bezug auf den zeitlos-humanistischen Bildungswert der Antike wird bei allem Realismus hier insofern besonders deutlich, als Weber von «ewigen Werten» spricht. Daß sein Plädoyer für die Erhaltung des humanistischen Gymnasiums alles andere als weltfremd ist, geht auch daraus hervor, daß er durchaus die Notwendigkeit erkennt, «die Gattungen der Mittelschulen hinlänglich (zu) differenzieren, um anderen unabweisbaren und durchaus ebenbürtigen Bedürfnissen und der Gefahr der Halbheit und inneren Zersplitterung der Schüler Rechnung zu tragen.» Eine gewisse Nostalgie spricht gleichwohl aus dem Schlußappell, «endlich auch das humanistische Gymnasium wieder zu dem werden zu lassen, was es für Deutschland einstmals gewesen ist.»

---

[61] Weber folgt in dieser hohen Bewertung der Perserkriege Eduard Meyer, siehe dazu Rossi (1986) 36, Näf (1990) 149, Deininger (1990) 151.

[62] Zur Hervorhebung vgl. MWG I/17, 93 (*Wissenschaft als Beruf*): «Man pflegt heute häufig von ‹voraussetzungsloser› Wissenschaft zu sprechen.» Ebd. 106: «Keine Wissenschaft ist absolut voraussetzungslos, und keine kann für den, der diese Voraussetzungen ablehnt, ihren eigenen Wert begründen.» Morgenbrod weist im Kommentar zur ersten Stelle darauf hin, daß die «Formulierung (...) auf das berühmte Protestschreiben zurück(geht), das Theodor Mommsen anläßlich der im Jahre 1901 aus politischen Gründen erfolgten Oktroyierung des Historikers Martin Spahn auf eine ausschließlich Katholiken vorbehaltene Professur an der Universität Straßburg verfaßte. Darin bezeichnete er die ‹Voraussetzungslosigkeit aller wissenschaftlichen Forschung› als das ‹ideale Ziel› und den Konfessionalismus als einen ‹Todfeind des Universitätswesens›. Mommsen, Theodor, *Universitätsunterricht und Konfession*, in: ders., *Reden und Aufsätze*, 2. Aufl. Berlin 1905, S. 432–436.» Wenn Weber diesen Aspekt hier betont, gibt er zu verstehen: Das humanistische Gymnasium ist weltanschaulich neutral.

[63] Vgl. dazu RS I 410: Den Zweck des humanistischen Gymnasiums «(rechtfertigt man) heute meist praktisch: durch die formale Schulung an der Antike.» Dieses schon bei Boeckh (1877) 30f. diskutierte Argument besitzt auch für den sonst der Gymnasialbildung gegenüber sehr skeptisch eingestellten Nietzsche eine gewisse Attraktivität: «Wenn die lateinischen und griechischen Studien auch nicht im Stande sind, den Schüler für das ferne Alterthum zu entzünden, so erwacht doch wohl, bei der Methode, mit der sie betrieben werden, der wissenschaftliche Sinn, die Lust an strenger Kausalität der Erkenntniß, die Begier zum Finden und Erfinden: wie Viele mögen durch eine auf dem Gymnasium gefundene, mit jugendlichem Tasten erhaschte neue Lesart zu den Reizungen der Wissenschaft dauernd verführt worden sein!» (KSA 1,738)

III

> «(...) der Mensch ist nicht dazu da, um glücklich zu sein, sondern um
> die Rolle zu spielen, die ihm sein Dämon zugewiesen hat.»
>
> U. von Wilamowitz-Moellendorff, *Erinnerungen 1848–1914* [64a]

Nach der Novemberrevolution richteten sich Webers Hoffnungen bei der Bewältigung der Kulturprobleme, welche für ihn vor allem Erziehungsprobleme waren, u. a. auf die ‹Freideutsche Jugend›, deren Organisationsform auch seinen praktisch-erzieherischen Vorstellungen nahekam.[64] Vordringlichstes geistiges Erziehungsmittel schien ihm die «Ablehnung *aller* geistigen Narkotika jeder Art, von der Mystik angefangen bis zum ‹Expressionismus›»[65]. Diese Haltung wird auch in dem ein Jahr zuvor in München gehaltenen Vortrag *Wissenschaft als Beruf* deutlich, zu dem ihn der bayrische Landesverband des «Freistudentischen Bundes» im Rahmen einer Vortragsreihe *Geistige Arbeit als Beruf* eingeladen hatte.[66] Weber geht in dieser Rede «über die individuelle (...) Selbstbestimmung unter den Bedingungen der modernen Kultur»[67], einem «appellativ-pädagogischen Anruf von ungeheurer Wucht»[68], auch auf den Erziehungs- und Bildungswert der Universität und die Rolle der Professoren ein. Bei der Beschreibung des gegenwärtigen Standortes der Wissenschaft unter lebensphilosophischen Gesichtspunkten und der ihr zugrunde liegenden inneren Haltung bezieht er sich auch auf die griechische Antike und die Altertumswissenschaft. Im folgenden soll besonders auf den wissenschaftshistorischen Kontext dieser Bezugnahmen aufmerksam gemacht werden. Ferner wird dem ‹platonischen› Einfluß auf die erzieherische Haltung Webers nachgespürt und ein verdeckter Hinweis am Ende des Vortrags erklärt.[69]

Um Webers ‹antike› Ausführungen angemessen würdigen zu können, gilt es zu berücksichtigen, daß er mit ihnen möglicherweise auch auf die Kritik antwortet, die Alexander Schwab, ein Mitglied des Kreises der Freistudenten um Gustav Wyneken, am Berufsgedanken und der mit ihm verbundenen Erwerbstätigkeit als Selbstzweck übte.[70] Dieser bezog sich dabei auch auf das Ideal eines harmonischen Ausgleichs zwischen geistigen und leib-

---

[64a] Wilamowitz (1928) 48.
[64] Diese lehnten sich an das amerikanische Club-Wesen an und waren vom Gesichtspunkt der ‹Exklusivität› bestimmt (die auch an diejenige in Platons *Staat* erinnert). Siehe Anm. 60 und MWG I/17, 22 (wo als Adressat des von Hennis zitierten Briefes nicht *Friedrich*, sondern *Otto* Crusius genannt ist): «*nur* das amerikanische [Mittel]: ‹Club› – und *exklusive*, d. h. auf *Auslese* der Personen ruhende Verbände jeder Art schon in der Kindheit und Jugend, einerlei zu welchem Zweck – Ansätze dazu bei der ‹Freideutschen Jugend›.»
[65] Ebd.
[66] Siehe dazu ausführlich Mommsen/Schluchter/Morgenbrod in: MWG I/17, 23 ff.
[67] Ebd. 3.
[68] Hennis (1996) 98.
[69] Mommsen/Schluchter im Vorwort der MWG I/17, VIII: «Webers Ausführungen sind voll offener, vor allem aber versteckter Bezüge. Sie verweisen häufig auf das eigene Werk und auf einen Bildungshorizont, der nicht mehr der heutige ist.»
[70] Unter dem Pseudonym Franz-Xaver Schwab, siehe ders. (1917) 97: «Der Beruf ist der Kern unserer geistig gesellschaftlichen Situation. (Der Krieg ist heute das dominierende Ereignis, aber der Beruf ist der Kern.) Der Beruf ist Wirkung und wiederum Ursache der Entfremdung vom Geiste, er ist Symbol und Tatsache zugleich, er ist zugleich massenhaftestes und individuellstes Geschick, hingenommen als Selbstverständliches, in Wirklichkeit das untrügliche Kennzeichen gerade nur dieser westeuropäisch-bürgerlichen Welt.»

lichen Bedürfnissen bei den Griechen.[71] Seinem schwärmerischen Antikapitalismus erteilt Weber eine entschiedene Absage[72] und stellt überhaupt der Neigung zum Irrationalismus und Erlebniskult seine Auffassung vom ‹Beruf› des Wissenschaftlers als eines selbstkritischen Fachmenschen entgegen, dessen Tun gerade nicht von der Sehnsucht nach ‹Entgrenzung›, sondern von strenger Selbstbescheidung und asketischer Hingabe an eine Sache gekennzeichnet ist. Dabei ist in Webers Ausführungen eine gewisse Spannung spürbar, wenn er einerseits mit großer Bestimmtheit darauf hinweist, daß von der Wissenschaft auf die Frage, wie man leben soll, keine Antwort zu erwarten ist, und er andererseits dennoch (in lebensphilosophischer Hinsicht) nach ihrem Sinn[73] fragt und (indirekt) ihren persönlichkeitsbildenden Wert herausstellt.

Subjektive Voraussetzung und Rechtfertigung wissenschaftlicher Praxis ist für Weber zunächst das, «was man das ‹Erlebnis der Wissenschaft› nennen kann» (81). Er verdeutlicht dies mit dem Hinweis auf die ‹Egomanie› des Philologen, der sein Seelenheil vom Gelingen einer Konjektur abhängig macht:

> «Ohne diesen seltsamen, von jedem Draußenstehenden belächelten Rausch, diese Leidenschaft, dieses: ‹Jahrtausende mußten vergehen, ehe du ins Leben tratest, und andere Jahrtausende warten schweigend›: – darauf, ob dir diese Konjektur gelingt, hat einer den Beruf zur Wissenschaft *nicht* und tue etwas anderes. Denn nichts ist für den Menschen als Menschen etwas wert, was er nicht mit *Leidenschaft tun kann*.»[74] (81)

---

[71] Siehe dazu den editorischen Bericht in MWG I/17, 53. Der Hinweis ebd. 37 Anm. 141: «Daß Weber in ‹Wissenschaft als Beruf› auf das Griechentum eingeht, ist möglicherweise Schwabs rückwärts gewandter Utopie geschuldet und nicht, wie mitunter behauptet, Georg Lukács, der in seiner von Weber zum Druck vermittelten Theorie des Romans ja gleichfalls das bürgerliche Zeitalter als Zeitalter vollendeter Sündhaftigkeit mit der griechischen Welt kontrastiert», könnte den Schluß nahelegen, Weber hätte ohne die provozierenden Thesen Schwabs nicht auf die Antike Bezug genommen, was wohl angesichts der argumentativen Bedeutung der Bezugnahmen kaum zutrifft.

[72] Vgl. dazu Marianne Weber (1926) 610: «Schwärmerei, die aus dem Alltag harter Kämpfe in ein Jenseits der Stimmung flüchtet, macht ihn ungeduldig.»

[73] Zur «tolstoianische(n) Akzentuierung» der dahinterstehenden «‹Sinn›-Frage» überhaupt Hanke (2001) 217 f.

[74] Vgl. damit Gerhardt (1999) 71 (im Zusammenhang mit Ausführungen über «Wert und Sinn des Lebens» bei Nietzsche): «Was immer wir uns auch für Ziele setzen: ‹sinnvoll› sind nur solche, die wir auch vor Augen haben, die wir nicht nur begreifen, sondern auch erleben können. Lust und Leid müssen noch in den höchsten Zielen sein, wenn ein Lebenssinn darin liegen soll.» Im philologischen Kontext vgl. Wilamowitz (1892/1910) 109: «und keine Fakultät und keine Behörde, nur das eigene Herz kann ihm [dem Studenten, E.B.] das Zeugnis ausstellen: du bist ein Philologe». Von «Rausch (im Sinne von Platons «Mania»)» spricht Weber bei der Erklärung wissenschaftlicher «Eingebung» (83). Zur Faszination der Konjekturalkritik siehe auch Anm. 63. Gumbrecht (2002), der das Thema «Classics as a profession» (255) vor dem Hintergrund eines tiefen Pessimismus heutiger Klassischer Philologen bezüglich ihres Selbstverständnisses behandelt und sich auch mit Webers Vortrag auseinandersetzt, schlägt dessen «invitation to reconstruct the historical circumstances which, from case to case, made possible the great cultural achievements» (265), ebenso aus, wie er ethische und (national-)pädagogische Zielsetzungen (Wilamowitz, Jaeger) verwirft. Diltheys Erlebnis-Begriff modifizierend, stellt er in Anlehnung an Gadamer ein «concept of ‹lived experience›» vor, dessen Bildungserfolg sich einstellt «by confronting ourselves and our students with objects of a complexity that defies easy structuring, conceptualization, and interpretation – especially if such a confrontation happens under conditions of low time-pressure» (267). Zu letzterem siehe schon Nietzsche KSA 3, 17 (*Morgenröthe*): «Philologie nämlich ist jene ehrwürdige Kunst, welche von ihrem Verehrer vor Allem Eins heischt, bei Seite gehen, sich Zeit lassen, still werden, langsam werden –, als eine Goldschmiedekunst und -kennerschaft des *Wortes*, die lauter feine vorsichtige Arbeit abzuthun hat und Nichts erreicht, wenn sie es nicht lento geschieht. Gerade damit aber ist sie heute nöthiger als je, gerade dadurch zieht

Daß Weber, der im folgenden seine Ausführungen mit Hinweisen auf die unterschiedlichsten Fächer (von Astronomie bis Zoologie) verdeutlicht, zu Beginn diesen für ihn wesentlichen Gesichtspunkt wissenschaftlicher Praxis am Beispiel der (klassischen) Philologie demonstriert, kann man auch vor dem Hintergrund ihrer einstigen Stellung als Leitwissenschaft interpretieren (mag auch ihr Stern im Jahre 1917 bereits im Sinken begriffen sein). Weber führt das Bild des Philologen, der «die Fähigkeit besitzt, sich einmal sozusagen Scheuklappen anzuziehen und sich hineinzusteigern in die Vorstellung, daß das Schicksal seiner Seele davon abhängt, ob er diese, gerade diese Konjektur an dieser Stelle dieser Handschrift richtig macht» (81 f.), zu Beginn seiner Ausführungen über den «*inneren*» Beruf zur Wissenschaft noch im Zusammenhang mit der Notwendigkeit der wissenschaftlichen Spezialisierung an, denn «eine endgültige und tüchtige Leistung ist heute stets: eine spezialistische Leistung» (80).

Dieses Wesensmerkmal moderner Wissenschaft ist in seiner Entwicklung in der Altertumswissenschaft des neunzehnten Jahrhunderts keineswegs als unproblematisch empfunden worden. Nietzsche, der fragt «Was hat die griechische Partikellehre mit dem Sinn des Lebens zu thun?»[75], erkennt zwar die Unausweichlichkeit, sich als Wissenschaftler spezialisieren zu müssen, kritisiert dies jedoch vor dem Hintergrund seines aristokratischen Bildungsideals als «Abirrung», die als «edle Genügsamkeit» verbrämt werde: «Denn so in die Breite ausgedehnt ist jetzt das Studium der Wissenschaften, daß, wer, bei guten, wenngleich nicht extremen Anlagen, noch in ihnen etwas leisten will, ein ganz spezielles Fach betreiben wird, um alle übrigen dann aber unbekümmert bleibt.» Andererseits «bewundert man wohl gar diese enge Fachmäßigkeit unserer Gelehrten und ihre immer weitere Abirrung von der rechten Bildung als ein sittliches Phänomen: die ‹Treue im Kleinen›, die ‹Kärrnertreue› wird zum Prunkthema, die Unbildung jenseits des Fachs wird als Zeichen edler Genügsamkeit zur Schau getragen» (KSA 1, 669 f.).[76]

Auch Jacob Burckhardt scheint das eigene wissenschaftliche Tun nicht den ‹speziellen› Erfordernissen des Wissenschaftsbetriebes untergeordnet zu haben. So wendet er sich in seiner Vorlesung *Über das Studium der Geschichte*[77] gegen «positivistische ‹Schuttschlepperei›»[78] und historisches Spezialistentum und rät, dann ein Konvolut wieder weg zu legen, «wenn der Ertrag der aufgewandten Mühe nicht mehr der persönlichen Bildung dient, son-

---

sie und bezaubert sie uns am stärksten, mitten in einem Zeitalter der ‹Arbeit›, will sagen: der Hast, der unanständigen und schwitzenden Eilfertigkeit, das mit Allem gleich ‹fertig werden› will, auch mit jedem alten und neuen Buche: – sie selbst wird nicht so leicht irgend womit fertig, sie lehrt *gut* lesen, das heisst langsam, tief, rück- und vorsichtig, mit Hintergedanken, mit offen gelassenen Thüren, mit zarten Fingern und Augen lesen ...»

[75] KSA 8,32 (*Wir Philologen*). Der Frage voraus geht der Satz: «Man sehe nur, womit ein wissenschaftlicher Mensch sein Leben todt schlägt».

[76] Siehe auch KSA 7, 298: «Auf Verengerung der Bildung führt jetzt die Arbeitstheilung der Wissenschaft und die Fachschule hin. (...) Die Fabrik herrscht. Der Mensch wird Schraube», dazu Reschke (2000) 19, 49 («*Werteverfall durch Maschinenkultur*»), Cancik/Cancil-Lindemaier (2002) 105, ferner Safranski (2000) 120: «Man bildet die jungen Leute aus, um sie dem wissenschaftlichen *Arbeitsmarkte* zuzuführen, dort setzt man jeden an ein kleinteiliges Thema und Problemchen, das er tüchtig bearbeiten kann, das Ganze ist eine *wissenschaftliche Fabrik*; von den Produkten des Eifers weiß man nicht, wozu sie gut sein sollen, jedenfalls ernähren sie ihren Mann.» Gerhardt (1984/1988) 160 Anm. 12 macht darauf aufmerksam, daß «Nietzsches Kritik des arbeitsteiligen Verfahrens der Wissenschaft» bereits bei Schiller («Was heißt und zu welchem Ende studiert man Universalgeschichte» [1789]) «formuliert (ist)».

[77] Burckhardt (1982), bes. 248–253.

[78] Hardtwig (1985) 228.

dern sich verselbständigt und den Arbeitenden seinerseits unterwirft»[79]. Sein scheinbar ‹dilettantisches›, gleichwohl «asketisches Erkenntnisideal» ist keineswegs das «eines rückwärtsorientierten Zeitkritikers oder eines ästhetisierenden Bildungsmenschen. Vielmehr spricht sich darin völlig schlüssig jenes personale Verständnis von Gelehrsamkeit aus, das seit der Mitte des 19. Jahrhunderts im Wissenschaftsbetrieb der ‹geistigen Arbeit› allmählich unverständlich zu werden begann.»[80]

Der Haltung Nietzsches nicht unverwandt ist auch diejenige Theodor Mommsens (der bekanntlich, «sollte er einmal in die Grube fahren müssen», dem jungen Weber seinen «Speer» übergeben wollte[81]). So heißt es in der am Leibniztag der Akademie 1896 gehaltenen Rede:

> «Die Wissenschaft schreitet unaufhaltsam und gewaltig vorwärts; aber dem emporsteigenden Riesenbau gegenüber erscheint der einzelne Arbeiter immer kleiner und geringer. Wenn Leibnizens Akademie als Fortführerin seiner Arbeiten betrachtet werden darf, so können wir eines doch nicht verbergen und müssen uns damit abfinden, daß diese Fortführung, in ihrer Zersplitterung auf mehrere Klassen (...) ein Surrogat ist, unentbehrlich und wirksam, aber nicht unbedingt gesund und nicht unbedingt erfreulich (...). Wir klagen nicht und beklagen uns nicht; die Blume verblüht, die Frucht muß treiben. Aber die Besten von uns empfinden es, daß wir Fachmänner geworden sind.»[82]

Den hier anklingenden resignativen Pessimismus scheint Wilamowitz, für den das Verhältnis von Wissenschaft und Leben offenbar nie ein Problem war,[83] trotz «der kleinlichen Werkeltagsarbeit» angesichts «der Größe des Objekts», der «Majestät der Wissenschaft»[84], nicht gekannt zu haben oder, sich selbst bescheidend, offenbar in Organisationseifer umgeformt haben zu können:

> «Lachmann und die Philologie seiner Zeit waren allerdings noch des frohen Glaubens, daß der einzelne in ungeheurer Anstrengung das Unmögliche zwingen könnte. Sie waren wohl größere und glücklichere Gelehrte als wir Nachfahren; aber das Ziel hoffen wir sicherer zu erreichen, indem wir uns bescheiden, indem an die Stelle der übermenschlichen Einzelleistung die organisierte Arbeitsgemeinschaft tritt.»[85]

---

[79] Ebd. 226.
[80] Ebd. 226, 241.
[81] Marianne Weber (1926) 121.
[82] Zitiert nach Hölscher (1965) 20. Reinhardt (1941/1960) 343 verweist in diesem Zusammenhang auch auf die Festrede in der Akademie aus dem Jahr 1887: «Ob wir nicht an der Großheit der Entwicklung leiden, ob nicht das Fortschreiten der Wissenschaft die Unzulänglichkeit des Individuums immer schärfer hervortreten läßt, das sind schwer abzuweisende und noch schwerer zu verneinende Fragen.»
[83] Hölscher (1965) 16.
[84] Wilamowitz (1892/1913) 108.
[85] Wilamowitz (1928) 233. Zur Spezialisierung in der Wissenschaft äußert sich Wilamowitz auch in seinem kurzen Rückblick auf die deutsche Universitätsgeschichte (ebd. 299f.): «Die Gründung von 1810 geschah in platonisch-aristotelischem Geiste: droht uns nicht die Geistlosigkeit der spätantiken Rhetorik neben der nur das im Grunde tote Wissen der sieben freien Künste stand, das den Geist verliert, auch wenn Spezialisten im Einzelnen noch so große praktische Erfolge haben. Es ist geradezu spaßhaft, wenn dieselben Leute über das angebliche Versinken der Wissenschaft im *Spezialistentum* zetern, und dabei die Schaffung von neuen Spezialdisziplinen, z. B. der Geschichte der Sozialdemokratie, betreiben. Die Vermehrung der Professuren namentlich in der philosophischen Fakultät (...) ist ein unheimliches Symptom. Man muß um die Wissenschaft wirklich Bescheid wissen, muß selbst kein *Spezialist* sein, um auch einem solchen gerecht zu werden. Es geschieht denen, welche sich auf ein Spezialgebiet beschränken, schweres Unrecht, wenn sie darum alle Scheuklappen tragen sollen. Die Wissenschaft kann ja die Spezialisten gar nicht entbehren, ge-

Diese stellt sich freilich im Rückblick Karl Reinhardt so dar, daß «gegen Ende des 19. Jahrhunderts (…) die klassische Philologie mühselig (wurde), wie ein überorganisiertes, in sich selbst leerlaufendes Unternehmen. Was mit höchster Begeisterung begonnen worden war, das endete nicht bei den Stumpfen, sondern bei den Wachen, in Askese, Pflichterfüllung, ausharrendem Heroismus.»[86]

Ein weiteres von Weber genanntes Merkmal der Wissenschaft, das nicht nur für die Altertumswissenschaft(en) zutrifft, bezieht sich auf die Unendlichkeit des Fortschritts. Nachdem Weber darauf hingewiesen hat, daß im Bereich der Kunst wohl zeitlose Vollendung und Erfüllung möglich sind, fährt er fort:

> «Jeder von uns dagegen in der Wissenschaft weiß, daß das, was er gearbeitet hat, in 10, 20, 50 Jahren veraltet ist. Das ist das Schicksal, ja: das ist der *Sinn* der Arbeit der Wissenschaft, dem sie, in ganz spezifischem Sinne gegenüber allen anderen Kulturelementen, für die es sonst noch gilt, unterworfen und hingegeben ist: jede wissenschaftliche «Erfüllung» bedeutet neue «Fragen» und *will* «überboten» werden und veralten. Damit hat sich jeder abzufinden, der der Wissenschaft dienen will. (…) Prinzipiell geht dieser Fortschritt in das Unendliche.» (85)

Nietzsche gibt in einem kurzen Streiflicht auf die diesbezügliche Frage (KSA 8,31) eine abschlägige Antwort, begründet aber die ‹Unendlichkeit der Philologie› gleichsam zeitlos-humanistisch: «Die Philologie als Wissenschaft um das Alterthum hat natürlich keine ewige Dauer, ihr Stoff ist zu erschöpfen. Nicht zu erschöpfen ist die immer neue Accommodation jeder Zeit an das Alterthum, das sich daran Messen. Stellt man dem Philologen die Aufgabe, *seine* Zeit vermittelst des Alterthums besser zu verstehen, so ist seine Aufgabe eine ewige.»

August Boeckh, der von einem umfassenden Philologiebegriff ausgeht, folgert im Zusammenhang mit Reflexionen über die ‹unendliche Aufgabe der Philologie›:

> «Wenn wir nun aber das Wesen der Philologie ganz unbeschränkt in das Erkennen des Erkannten setzen, *so scheint dies in vollem Umfange etwas Unmögliches*; nach Aufhebung aller Schranken scheint die Ausführung des Begriffs unerreichbar für irgendeinen menschlichen Geist. Aber diese Beschränktheit in der Ausführung theilt die Philologie mit jeder einigermassen umfassenden Wissenschaft. (…) Gerade in der Unendlichkeit liegt das Wesen der Wissenschaft; nur wo der Stoff ein ganz beschränkter ist, und selbst da kaum, ist eine Erreichung möglich: wo die Unendlichkeit aufhört, ist die Wissenschaft zu Ende.»[87]

---

braucht deren vielmehr immer mehr. (…) Wer seine Kraft auf den einen Punkt konzentriert und eben dadurch die Wissenschaft fördert, weil es nur so geschehen kann, verdient sich für dieses Opfer den wärmsten Dank. Den Blick auf das Ganze wird er nicht verlieren, wenn ihm dafür auf der Universität die Augen geöffnet sind. Damit ist gesagt, daß der Universitätslehrer seinen Unterricht auf das Ganze richten muß, auch wenn er das Forschen immer nur am Einzelobjekte lehren kann. Entbehren kann freilich auch die Universität die Spezialisten nicht, aber sie sind an ihr Extraordinarien und sollten es bleiben.»

[86] Reinhardt (1941/1960) 342.

[87] Boeckh (1877) 15. Ebd. 86 («Theorie der Hermeneutik»): «Ausserdem ist aber jede individuelle Aeusserung durch eine *unendliche* Anzahl von Verhältnissen bedingt und es ist daher unmöglich, diese zur discursiven Klarheit zu bringen. (…) Wenn also die fremde Individualität nie vollständig verstanden werden kann, so kann die Aufgabe der Hermeneutik nur durch unendliche *Approximation*, d.h. durch allmähliche, Punkt für Punkt vorschreitende, aber nie vollendete Annäherung gelöst werden.» Eine gewisse Nähe zu Boecks Reflexionen zeigen insbesondere Webers Ausführungen im Objektivitäts-Aufsatz, wo er die Kulturbedeutsamkeit als notwendiges Auswahlkriterium für die Behandlung der unendlichen Fülle des Stoffes hervorhebt (WL 213).

Explizit auf die griechische Antike bezieht sich Weber nach der Erörterung des Problems «Was bedeutet die Wissenschaft als Beruf für den, der sich ihr hingibt» bei der Behandlung der Frage «Welches ist der *Beruf der Wissenschaft* innerhalb des Gesamtlebens der Menschheit? und welches ihr Wert?» (88). Ein eminent wichtiger Bezugspunkt – «Ungeheuer ist da nun der Gegensatz zwischen Vergangenheit und Gegenwart» (ebd.) – ist hierbei für ihn die Auffassung von Wissenschaft, wie sie im Höhlengleichnis von Platons *Staat* bildhaft umschrieben ist.[88] Die Wahrheit der Wissenschaft, dargestellt im Bild der Sonne, ist identisch mit dem wahren Sein, zu dem der Philosoph, hat er es einmal erkannt, auch die übrigen Menschen emporführt. Diese existentielle Bedeutung von Wissenschaft und die Lebendigkeit der Beziehung zu ihr sind dadurch möglich geworden, daß «damals zuerst der Sinn eines der großen Mittel allen wissenschaftlichen Erkennens bewußt gefunden war: des *Begriffs*.» Das an einer ewigen Wahrheit ausgerichtete Begriffsdenken, das den «Schülern des Sokrates» als «ungeheure(s) Erlebnis» «aufging», bietet nicht zuletzt Hilfe bei der Frage: «wie man im Leben, vor allem: als Staatsbürger, richtig handle. Denn auf diese Frage kam den durch und durch politisch denkenden Hellenen alles an. Deshalb trieb man Wissenschaft» (90). Weber stellt diesem ‹lebendigen› Empfinden von Wissenschaft in der griechischen Antike die Einschätzung der Wissenschaftspraxis seiner Zeit als Tantalosqualen gegenüber:

> «Heute ist die Empfindung gerade der Jugend wohl eher die umgekehrte. Die Gedankengebilde der Wissenschaft sind ein hinterweltliches Reich von künstlichen Abstraktionen, die mit ihren dürren Händen Blut und Saft des wirklichen Lebens einzufangen trachten, ohne es doch je zu erhaschen.[89] Hier im Leben aber, in dem, was für Platon das Schattenspiel an den Wänden der Höhle war, pulsiert die wirkliche Realität: das andere sind von ihr abgeleitete und leblose Gespenster und sonst nichts.» (89)

Mag Weber auch das platonische Wissenschaftsverständnis als «Weg zum wahren Sein» für illusionär (93) halten und den Gegensatz zwischen Vergangenheit und Gegenwart betonen, so steht er dennoch selbst insofern in der Tradition des griechischen Philosophen, als er sich gegen den Irrationalismus und den Erlebniskult der Jugend wendet.[90] Die diesbezügliche Nähe zu Platon zeigt sich auch in der Verwandtschaft eines Abschnittes von *Wissenschaft als Beruf* mit dem Einleitungsgespräch des *Protagoras*. Ob dabei eine bewußte (literarische) Anspielung vorliegt oder Weber, lediglich von der Gedankenführung zur entsprechenden Motivwahl veranlaßt, ganz ohne Absicht ‹sokratische› Assoziationen hervorruft, ist nicht sicher zu erweisen.

Nachdem er den Mißbrauch der akademischen Lehrtätigkeit zu politischen Zwecken bei

---

[88] Pl. R. 514a-517a. Webers zusammenfassende Darstellung aus dem Gedächtnis ist nicht ganz genau. An das Bild der Sonne (auch im Sonnengleichnis) erinnert die Metaphorik in WL 213 f.: «Das Licht, welches jene höchsten Wertideen spenden, fällt jeweilig auf einen stets wechselnden endlichen Teil des ungeheuren chaotischen Stromes von Geschehnissen, der sich durch die Zeit dahinwälzt.» Hinweise auf Webers Platon-Lektüre als junger Student bei Hennis (1996) 100. Die Einleitung «Wenn Sie sich erinnern an das wundervolle Bild zu Anfang des siebten Buches von Platons Politeia» – Weber kann dessen Kenntnis bei der überwiegend studentischen Hörerschaft offenbar voraussetzen – erinnert ihrerseits an längst vergangene Zeiten ...

[89] Zur Anspielung auf den Stammvater der Pelopiden, der in der Unterwelt im Wasser steht, aber dennoch die vorbeiziehenden Wogen nicht erhaschen und die Früchte der stets zurückschnellenden Bäume nicht erreichen kann, siehe Hom. Od. 11, 582 ff. Die Kenntnis des Bildes scheinen die Herausgeber von MWG I/17 (wie Weber) vorauszusetzen.

[90] Siehe unten S. 175 und Krech/Wagner (1994) 766 Anm. 10.

seinen Kollegen, dem Kriegsbefürworter Dietrich Schäfer und dem Pazifisten Friedrich Wilhelm Foerster, kritisiert und die Notwendigkeit eines werturteilsfreien Unterrichts betont hat, geht Weber noch einmal auf die Haltung der akademischen Jugend ein, die irrtümlich im Professor «einen Führer» in Lebensfragen und nicht einen «Lehrer» in Fachfragen suche. Den Unterschied zwischen beiden Begriffen erläutert er an der Einstellung des jungen Amerikaners, der zwar weniger lerne als der Deutsche, aber sehr genaue Vorstellungen von seinem Unterricht habe. Weber leitet sein Beispiel mit einem Hinweis auf das (deutsche) Examenswesen ein:

«Der amerikanische Knabe lernt unsagbar viel weniger als der unsrige. Er ist trotz unglaublich vielen Examinierens doch dem *Sinn* seines Schullebens nach noch nicht jener absolute Examensmensch geworden, wie es der deutsche ist. Denn die Bureaukratie, die das Examensdiplom als Eintrittsbillet ins Reich der Amtspfründen voraussetzt, ist dort erst in den Anfängen. Der junge Amerikaner hat vor nichts und niemand, vor keiner Tradition und keinem Amt Respekt, es sei denn vor der persönlich eigenen Leistung des Betreffenden: *das* nennt der Amerikaner «Demokratie». (...) Der Lehrer, der ihm gegenübersteht, von dem hat er die Vorstellung: er verkauft mir seine Kenntnisse und Methoden für meines Vaters Geld, ganz ebenso wie die Gemüsefrau meiner Mutter den Kohl. Damit fertig. Allerdings: wenn der Lehrer etwa ein football-Meister ist, dann ist er auf diesem Gebiet sein Führer. Ist er das (oder etwas Ähnliches auf anderem Sportgebiet) aber nicht, so ist er eben nur Lehrer und weiter nichts, und keinem amerikanischen jungen Manne wird es einfallen, sich von ihm «Weltanschauungen» oder maßgebliche Regeln für seine Lebensführung verkaufen zu lassen.» Nicht ohne Pathos fährt Weber fort: «Kommilitonen und Kommilitoninnen! Sie kommen mit diesen Ansprüchen an unsere Führerqualitäten in die Vorlesung zu uns und sagen sich vorher nicht: daß von hundert Professoren mindestens neunundneunzig[91] nicht nur keine football-Meister des Lebens, sondern überhaupt nicht «Führer» in Angelegenheiten der Lebensführung zu sein in Anspruch nehmen und nehmen dürfen.»[92] (101 f.)

Der hier sehr anschaulich dargestellte Unterschied zwischen werturteilsfreiem Fachunterricht und lebensphilosophischer Führung ist auch Gegenstand der Unterhaltung, die Sokrates zu Beginn des platonischen «Protagoras» mit dem jungen Hippokrates führt. Sokrates konfrontiert seinen ungestümen Gesprächspartner, der Schüler des berühmten Sophisten werden will, mit der Frage, ob er wisse, was er tue, wenn er seine Seele zur Behandlung an einen Sophisten ausliefere und ihm Geld dafür bezahle. Bei der gemeinsamen Erörterung der Frage, was eigentlich das ‹Fachgebiet› eines Sophisten sei, werden Vergleiche mit einer Reihe ‹gewöhnlicher› Berufe (vom Arzt bis zum Gymnastiklehrer) angestellt. Auch wird (der Weberschen Gemüsefrau vergleichbar) das Bild vom Sophisten als «Groß-

---

[91] Bei Nietzsche («Wir Philologen», KSA 8, 20) heißt es: «Ich meine, 99 von 100 Philologen *sollten* keine sein.»

[92] Vgl. damit Wilamowitz (1928) 292: «Aber auch wir Universitätslehrer wollen nicht nur διδασκαλία, sondern ψυχαγωγία treiben, und wenn wir das wollen, werden wir auch dem Seelenzustande und der Fassungskraft unserer Hörer Rechnung tragen. Will man das Pädagogik nennen (obgleich der Student kein Kind ist und seine Freiheit haben will), so treiben wir sie je nach unserer Individualität. Auf den Menschen kommt auch im Professor mehr an als auf den Gelehrten. Vorschriften allgemeinverbindlicher Art, papierne Paragraphen einer sog. Hochschulpädagogik werden für einen Professor, der sein Amt und seine Studenten lieb hat, immer Papier bleiben.» Bei aller Sachbezogenheit ist auch Webers Haltung als Lehrer, dem in München «inmitten seiner Schüler eine zweite Jugend geschenkt zu sein» schien, wohl von pädagogischem Eros geprägt gewesen, siehe Marianne Weber (1926) 674 ff. (das Zitat ebd. 675).

händler oder Krämer in Waren, von denen sich die Seele ernährt» (313c), gezeichnet. Was in der Einleitung des *Protagoras* als langsam sich in Vergleichen entwickelndes Aufklärungsgespräch dargestellt ist – Sokrates will den jungen Hippokrates dazu bringen, sich über die Art der Erziehung bei Protagoras Klarheit zu verschaffen –, ist bei Weber ebenfalls in sehr anschaulichen Bildern verdeutlicht, doch im Rahmen der Rede eindrucksvoll zum pädagogischen Appell zugespitzt und verdichtet.[93]

Wenn Weber den Studenten, die im Professor nicht den Fachlehrer sehen, sondern einen Führer in Lebensfragen suchen, mit der (zurechtweisenden) Forderung nach strenger Sachbezogenheit begegnet,[94] entspricht dies seiner (erziehungssoziologischen) Auffassung, daß die Wissenschaft auf der Universität, da sie Kulturmenschen alten Stils nicht mehr hervorbringen kann,[95] nur als Facherziehung möglich ist. Diese soll freilich auch der Selbstbesinnung dienen, indem sie die Urteilskraft schärft und so zu rationaler Klarheit bezüglich möglicher Wertstandpunkte verhilft. Webers Absage an lebensphilosophische Erwartungshaltungen und einen darauf ausgerichteten wissenschaftlichen Unterricht ist vor allem als Reaktion auf die weltanschaulich geprägte Lehrtätigkeit zeitgenössischer ‹Sophisten› zu verstehen. Seine darin enthaltene Antwort auf die Frage nach dem Erziehungswert der Universität überhaupt läßt sich historisch noch besser verstehen, wenn man sie mit der diesbezüglichen Auffassung Nietzsches vergleicht, wie sie im fünften seiner 1872 gehaltenen Vorträge *Über die Zukunft unserer Bildungsanstalten* zum Ausdruck kommt.

Hatte Nietzsche in Schopenhauer den Erzieher gefunden, der als Erwecker und Befreier «einer *jungen Seele* dabei hilft, *das Grundgesetz* des *eigentlichen Selbst* zu entdecken»,[96] so wurden seine Hoffnungen, vergleichbare Erfahrungen auf der Universität zu machen, offenbar enttäuscht. So schildert er die Haltung des Studenten, der trotz allem Enthusiasmus merkt, «daß er sich selbst nicht führen, sich selbst nicht helfen kann» und sich deshalb «hoffnungsarm in die Welt des Tages und der Tagesarbeit» begibt, wo er bei dem «Mangel eines Führers zur Bildung» freilich in «enger kleinlicher Fachmäßigkeit»[97] zu versinken droht. Während der junge Nietzsche noch Erwartungen gegenüber der Wissenschaft hegte, die über die Fachausbildung hinausgingen und, offenbar auch Elemente der charismatischen Erweckungserziehung einbeziehend, in einer höheren Form von Bildung mündeten, sind diese Vorstellungen für Weber aus historischen Gründen unmöglich, mag auch im Motiv der «Selbstbesinnung» der Gedanke der *persönlichen Bildung* (wie ihn auch Burckhardt vertrat, s. o.) noch mitschwingen:

«Daß Wissenschaft heute ein *fachlich* betriebener «Beruf» ist im Dienst der Selbstbesinnung und der Erkenntnis tatsächlicher Zusammenhänge, und nicht eine Heilsgüter und

---

[93] Hennis (1987) 195 weist in größerem Zusammenhang auf Webers Rolle als neuer Sokrates in der Sicht Karl Jaspers' hin. Zu Webers ablehnender Haltung gegenüber modernen ‹Sophisten› (etwa Gustav Wyneken) siehe Mommsen/Schluchter/Morgenbrod in MWGI/17, 24.
[94] Vgl. Marianne Weber (1926) 674: «Manche der jungen Männer, die nun als Seminarteilnehmer in nähere Berührung mit Weber kommen, sehen in ihm mehr als ihren Lehrer – obwohl er nichts anderes sein will. Sie verehren ihn heimlich wie die Inder ihren «Guru», jene Lehrer der Weisheit, von denen erwartet wird, daß sie zugleich Nothelfer, Berater, Seelsorger sind. Aber sie fühlen: nur durch sachliche Hingabe finden sie Zugang zu seiner Person, nur wo er sachlichen Eifer spürt, erregen sie sein Interesse.» Zu Weber als «Protagonist(en) einer Moral der Versachlichung» siehe Rehberg (1994) 641.
[95] Vgl. Mommsen/Schluchter, MWG I/17, 32.
[96] Safranski (2000) 38, die kursiven Zitate KSA 1, 340 (*Schopenhauer als Erzieher*).
[97] KSA 1, 744f.

Offenbarungen spendende Gnadengabe von Sehern, Propheten oder ein Bestandteil des Nachdenkens von Weisen und Philosophen über den Sinn der Welt –, das freilich ist eine unentrinnbare Gegebenheit unserer historischen Situation, aus der wir, wenn wir uns selbst treu bleiben, nicht herauskommen können.» (105)

Anders als Nietzsche, welcher der Wissenschaft (als lebensfeindlicher Macht) ablehnend gegenübersteht, hält Weber, obwohl auch er ihren Lebensführungsanspruch zurückweist, streng fachbezogen an ihr fest und bejaht sie vor allem deshalb, weil er dem (Nietzsche zufolge mit Sokrates beginnenden) Prozeß der Rationalisierung des Lebens gleichsam mit dessen eigenen Mitteln begegnen will[98] in der (‹heroisch› anmutenden) Überzeugung, «daß man auch vor diesem Teufel, wenn man mit ihm fertig werden will, nicht – die Flucht ergreifen darf, wie es heute so gern geschieht, sondern daß man seine Wege erst einmal zu Ende überschauen muß, um seine Macht und seine Schranken zu sehen» (105). Gerade auch vor diesem Hintergrund hält Weber die von Nietzsche kritisierte «Ameisenarbeit»[99] im Wissenschaftsbetrieb nicht nur für nötig, sondern in pädagogischer Hinsicht als heilsame Hingabe an eine Sache sogar für das Gebot der Stunde. Die darin zum Ausdruck kommende sich zu außergewöhnlichen Arbeitsleistungen aufschwingende Haltung[100] eines asketischen «Dienstes»[101] an der Wissenschaft stellt Weber der «gerade bei der Jugend sehr populäre(n) Einstellung» entgegen, die «sich in den Dienst einiger Götzen gestellt (hat), deren Kult wir heute an allen Straßenecken und in allen Zeitschriften sich breit machen finden. Jene Götzen sind: die «Persönlichkeit» und das «Erleben«» (84).

---

[98] Webers ‹Strategie› ähnelt einer Denkbewegung Nietzsches, der sich bei seiner Kritik des Historismus des «Gegengift(es)» der «Inversion» bedient: «man muß das Prinzip der Geschichte gegen die Geschichte kehren. Die Macht der Historie durch das historische Wissen brechen. Nietzsche findet dafür die einprägsame Formulierung: *die Historie m u s s das Problem der Historie selbst auflösen*» (Safranski [2000] 122 mit Hinweis auf KSA 1,306).

[99] KSA 8, 32: «So sehen wir auch hier, wie zahllose Menschen eigentlich nur als Vorbereitung eines wirklichen Menschen leben: z.B. die Philologen als Vorbereitung des Philosophen, der ihre Ameisenarbeit zu nutzen versteht, um über den *Werth des Lebens* eine Aussage zu machen. Freilich ist, wenn es keine *Leitung* gibt, der *grösste Theil* jener Ameisenarbeit einfach *Unsinn* und überflüssig.»

[100] Vgl. dazu etwa den Hinweis in MWG I/17, 82 Anm. 19 auf die «50000 Rechenexempel», die Weber «in 6 Wochen» (!) für seine Untersuchung *Zur Psychophysik der industriellen Arbeit* «eigenhändig» durchführt. Zum Philologen Weber vgl. im Zusammenhang mit seiner Arbeit an der Dissertation *Zur Geschichte der Handelsgesellschaften im Mittelalter* seine Äußerungen bei Marianne Weber (1926) 120: «Dazu mußte ich hunderte von italienischen und spanischen Statutensammlungen durchlesen und mir erst noch die beiden Sprachen (…) aneignen (…) und dann ist das Zeug meist in uralten schändlichen Dialekten geschrieben, so daß man sich wundert, daß die Menschen selbst das Kauderwelsch verstanden haben! Nun ich bin tüchtig zu tun und nehme mir dabei nicht viel, sondern wenig herausgekommen ist, so kann ich weniger dafür als die italienischen und spanischen Stadträte, die gerade *das* nicht in die Statuten gesetzt haben, was ich darin suchte.» Zum (philologischen) Wissenschaftsbetrieb der Zeit siehe Reinhardt (1941/60) 343: «Die Häupter an» seiner «Spitze hatten außer ihren Wissensglorien auch noch die Nimben der Unternehmen um sich, denen sie vorstanden. Kritische Keckheit, die sich unter der Jugend regte, wurde bald wieder gedämpft, indem aus überlegener Hand ihr «Lebensaufgaben» gereicht wurden, an denen sie sich «ihre Sporen verdiene». Wenn das fin de siècle gern als pessimistisch, überfeinert, matt, ästhetisierend, dekadent geschildert wird, so ist nicht zu vergessen, daß es nicht zuletzt in ihm auch eine Flucht gab – in die Leistung.» Zur Auffassung von «Wissenschaft als gesellschaftliche(r) Arbeit» im 19. Jahrhundert siehe Hardtwig (1985) 222f.

[101] Vgl. MWG I/17, 85: Die «innere Hingabe» hebt den wahren Wissenschaftler «zu der Würde der Sache» empor, «der er zu dienen vorgibt.» Ebd. 88: «Hat der «Fortschritt» als solcher einen erkennbaren, über das Technische hinausreichenden Sinn, so daß dadurch der Dienst an ihm ein sinnvoller Beruf würde?» Siehe dazu auch Anm. 103.

Es fällt auf, daß Weber hier mit keinem Wort auf Nietzsche eingeht,[102] vor dem als großem Verführer zum Erlebniskult zehn Jahre zuvor Eduard Meyer am Schluß seiner Rede «Humanistische und geschichtliche Bildung» eindringlich gewarnt hatte. In einer sehr verkürzten Sicht, die vor allem ‹schulhumanistisch› geprägt ist und der Zielsetzung Nietzsches nicht gerecht wird,[103] erscheint hier der Philosoph als derjenige, der die Menschen dazu gebracht hat, «sich in eine Vergötterung des eigenen Ichs [zu] versenken, in ein Grübeln über sich selbst, in ein Liebkosen ihrer Gedanken.» Der Weg, den Nietzsche weise, führe «nicht zur Erzeugung einer besseren Menschheit, sondern zum Niederreißen aller Kultur, zur Vernichtung alles Höchsten, was die Menschen und was ein Volk geschaffen hat.» Mit seiner Auffassung von geschichtlicher Bildung appelliert Meyer dagegen an den «sittlichen Willen des Menschen» und entlarvt (unter Bezug auf Plato) «die Erbärmlichkeit einer egoistischen Betrachtung des eigenen Ichs, die in selbstgefällige Beschaulichkeit versunken nichts kennt als sich selbst»[104].

Webers Haltung gegenüber einer solchen von Meyer überspitzt dargestellten Einstellung, die er selbst auch als «Sich-Wichtig-Nehmen»[105] nennt, zeigt sich besonders eindrucksvoll noch einmal am Ende seines Vortrags, wo er die Situation der Zeit, in der viele «auf neue Propheten und Heilande harren», mit der bei Jesaja 21,11–12 beschriebenen vergleicht, jedoch zur unspektakulären täglichen Arbeit aufruft:

---

[102] Er führt ihn lediglich einmal als Kronzeugen seiner Ablehnung neuzeitlicher Glücksvorstellungen an (die auch durch die Wissenschaft nicht eingelöst werden können): MWG I/17, 92.

[103] Meyer (1907) verkennt Nietzsches humanistischen Ansatz als egoistisch und selbstbezogen. Man vgl. dazu nur (im engeren Zusammenhang mit Nietzsches Wissenschaftskritik) KSA 8, 34: «es hilft nichts, wir müssen alles wieder für uns und nur für uns thun und z. B. die Wissenschaft an uns messen, mit der Frage: was ist *uns* die Wissenschaft? Nicht aber: was sind wir der Wissenschaft? Man macht sich wirklich das Leben zu leicht, wenn man sich so einfach historisch nimmt und in den Dienst stellt. «Das Heil deiner selbst geht über alles» soll man sich sagen: und es giebt keine Institution, welche du höher zu achten hättest als deine eigene Seele.» Anders als Meyer (und Wilamowitz) zeigt Weber ein tiefes Verständnis für den Ethiker Nietzsche und schätzt in ihm «den bedeutenden Moral- und Kulturwissenschaftler» (Hennis [1987] 173), der nicht mit seinen ‹Jüngern› ineinsgesetzt werden darf. Bei der Frage nach Webers Verhältnis zu Nietzsche sollte auch berücksichtigt werden, was Reschke (2000) 52 (ohne Bezug auf Weber) zur Wissenschaftskritik des Philosophen schreibt: «Alternative Wissenschaften, die sich dem umklammernden Zugriff der Massen-Werteskala (etwa der modernen ‹Soziologie›, E.B.) verweigern, sah Nietzsche in Versuchen, eine ‹Theorie der *Herrschaftsgebilde* statt: *Sociologie*› (KSA 12, 208) zu entwickeln, der es gelingen könnte, jenseits von Heuchelei und Verdrängung den wirklichen Mechanismen von Gesellschaft und Kultur auf die Spur zu kommen und ein Wertesystem zu begründen, das Machtinteressen bewußt artikuliert und reflektiert als Grundvoraussetzungen für jede zukünftige Kultur, um dem ‹*Stillstand im Niveau des Menschen*› (KSA 12, 462) eine Perspektive entgegenzustellen; gegen die ‹Verkleinerung und Anpassung der Menschen an eine spezialisierte Nützlichkeit›, wenn auch für eine begrenzte Zahl von Gesellschaftsmitgliedern, ein neues ‹Wozu› (ebd.) zu setzen, das die kulturzerstörerischen Potenzen der absehbaren sozialen Entwicklung, die Nietzsche für unabwendbar, aber für tödlich hielt, aufzufangen, zu neutralisieren in der Lage sei.» Nach Schluchter (1996) 163 f. ist Webers Verhältnis zu Nietzsche dagegen «bei äußeren Gemeinsamkeiten» durch «größte innere Differenz» gekennzeichnet», Weber «kein sozialwissenschaftlicher Nietzscheaner». Siehe ferner Gerhardt (1983/1988) 120 f., zu «Berührungspunkten des Wissenschaftsverständnisses von Weber und Nietzsche» auch Krech/Wagner (1994) 761 f.

[104] Meyer (1907) 38 f.

[105] In WL 540 etwa spricht er von der «Geschmacksentgleisung sich wichtig nehmender Literaten». Hennis (1987) 207 Anm. 31 zitiert aus einem Brief vom 25. 12. 1915 (an die Mutter): «(...) Erlösung von dem ewigen ‹Suchen› nach sich selbst, das doch nur der Ausdruck eines ‹Sichwichtignehmens› ist, wie es entsteht, wenn keine ernsten sachlichen Probleme den Menschen innerlich an sich binden.» Siehe ferner Mommsen/Schluchter in MWG I/17, 29.

> «Das Volk, dem das gesagt wurde, hat gefragt und geharrt durch weit mehr als zwei Jahrtausende, und wir kennen sein erschütterndes Schicksal. Daraus wollen wir die Lehre ziehen: daß es mit dem Sehnen und Harren allein nicht getan ist, und es anders machen: an unsere Arbeit gehen und der »Forderung des Tages«[106] gerecht werden – menschlich sowohl wie beruflich. Die aber ist schlicht und einfach, wenn jeder den Dämon findet und ihm gehorcht, der *seines* Lebens Fäden hält.» (111)

Die eindrucksvolle Nüchternheit dieses Aufrufs zur Selbstbescheidung in der täglichen Arbeit, dessen pädagogischer Gehalt sich auch in einem (positiven) Bezug auf Friedrich Nietzsche[107] zeigt, erscheint in ihrer strengen Sachbezogenheit auch der Wissenschaft selbst gegenüber (als einer spezifisch ‹gottfremden, pietätsfeindlichen› Macht) besonders deutlich, wenn man sie mit einen ‹Aufruf› von Wilamowitz aus dem Jahr 1892 vergleicht (dessen Einstellung der von Weber als längst vergangen angesehenen bei Platon nahe kommt):

> «Wenn der Philologe von seiner kleinlichen Werkeltagsarbeit das Auge aufschlägt zu der Majestät der Wissenschaft, dann wird ihm zu Mute wie in der heiligen Stille sternheller Nacht. Die Empfindung der Herrlichkeit und der Unendlichkeit und der Einheit des Allganzen zieht durch seine Seele. Demütig muß er sich sagen: «Du armselig Menschenkind, was bist du? Was kannst du?» Aber wenn tönend dann der junge Tag geboren wird, ruft der ihm zu: «Steh auf, du Menschenkind, steh auf und wirke, was dein Tag von dir verlangt, wozu Gott in deine Seele die lebendige Schaffenskraft gelegt hat: erwirb dir durch Arbeit einen Anteil am Ewigen und Unendlichen».»[108]

Dieses Bekenntnis des Platonikers Wilamowitz, «das sein Pathos aus den verschiedensten Elementen: aus Christlichem, Goethischem, Kantischem und Preußischem bezieht, erhebt sich zu einem geradezu religiösen Gefühl»[109], das Weber, dem ‹religiös Unmusikalischen›, in einer «gottfremden, prophetenlosen Zeit» (106) unmöglich ist. An die Stelle ‹religiöser› Erhebung tritt bei ihm (neben dem Kantisch-Goethischen[110] Pflichtgefühl) allenfalls die ‹Leidenschaft› wissenschaftlichen Forschens. Und dennoch endet *Wissenschaft als Beruf* in dem Schlußpassus

> «Das Volk, dem das gesagt wurde, hat gefragt und geharrt durch weit mehr als zwei Jahrtausende, und wir kennen sein erschütterndes Schicksal. Daraus wollen wir die Lehre ziehen: daß es mit dem Sehnen und Harren allein nicht getan ist, und es anders machen: an unsere Arbeit gehen und der «Forderung des Tages» gerecht werden – menschlich sowohl wie beruflich. Die aber ist schlicht und einfach, wenn jeder den Dämon findet und ihm gehorcht, der *seines* Lebens Fäden hält.» (111)

---

[106] Ein Goethe-Zitat, siehe den Kommentar in MWG I/17, 111, wo auf die «Betrachtungen im Sinne der Wanderer» aus *Wilhelm Meisters Wanderjahren* verwiesen ist: «Was aber ist deine Pflicht? Die Forderung des Tages.»

[107] Nach Hennis (1996) 97 Anm. 9 hat Weber hier das «Werde, der du bist!» im Sinn, über das Nietzsche in *Schopenhauer als Erzieher* Kap. 1 handelt: «Mit Nietzsche legt Weber also nicht nur auf den *individuellen* Werdegang, sondern auf den wörtlich verstandenen aktiven *Werdegang* wert, wenn er die alltägliche «Arbeit», die «Forderung des Tages», in deren Erfüllung «jeder den Dämon findet und ihm gehorcht, der *seines* Lebens Fäden hält», betont. (WL 613) – eine genuin pädagogische Aufforderung mit einem Persönlichkeitsideal, das sicher heute ganz und gar unzeitgemäß und weit entfernt ist vom introspektiv-narzisstischen Ich-Ideal unserer Tage.» (Zur ‹philologischen› Kritik dieser Interpretation siehe Anm. 113.)

[108] Wilamowitz (1892/1913) 108 f.

[109] Hölscher (1965) 21.

[110] Bei Wilamowitz bezieht sich das ‹Goethische› wohl auf pantheistische Vorstellungen.

mit einem – bisher nicht erkannten – ‹metaphysischen› Motiv. Inwiefern dieses allerdings ein (zugegeben irritierend) ‹weltanschauliches› Licht auf das darin aufscheinende Menschenbild wirft, hängt davon ab, ob man es eher als beiläufige literarische Anspielung oder als ernstgemeinten Hinweis interpretiert.

In dem in seiner äußeren Szenerie ebenso wie in seinem philosophischen Sinn nicht einfach zu beschreibenden Mythos des «Er» am Schluß von Platons *Politeia* wird über das Schicksal der menschlichen Seelen berichtet, die sich nach dem Tod einem Richterspruch stellen müssen und nach einer langen Wanderung ihren ‹Dämon›, d.h. ihren Lebenstyp wählen, nach dem sie wiederum auf der Erde leben:

> «So spricht Anankes Tochter, Jungfrau Lachesis: Eintägige Seelen, die Zeit ist gekommen! Beginne, was sterblich ist, von neuem den Kreislauf der Tode! Euch lost der Dämon nicht, den Dämon wählt ihr selbst. Wes Los das erste ist, wähle zuerst das Leben, dem er vereint sein wird nach der Notwendigkeit. Tugend ist herrenlos: werft sie weg oder achtet sie, so habt ihr danach ihrer weniger oder mehr. Die Schuld ist des Wählenden, Gott ist schuldlos.»[111]

Bei der Ankunft auf der Erde vergißt der Mensch, was sich ereignet hat, und glaubt, er sei ‹leer› in die Welt gekommen, obwohl ihm der Dämon als Träger seines Schicksals mitgegeben ist.

Enthält dieser Mythos vor allem die (nicht einfach zu entschlüsselnde) Antwort Platons auf die Frage nach der Verbindung von selbstverantwortlicher «Freiheit» und vorgegebener «Notwendigkeit» «bei der Entstehung und Ausbildung der menschlichen Individualität», die weiter «in eine höhere Einheit»[112] hinausweist, so kann man Weber hier wohl nur mit aller Vorsicht eine derart ‹weitreichende› Auslegung des Dämon-Begriffs unterstellen. Das zweifelsfrei jedoch von Platon (und nicht von Goethe[113]) angeregte Bild impliziert die An-

---

[111] Pl. R. 617 d–e. Die Übersetzung nach Karl Reinhardt (1960) 269. Siehe ferner Schubert (1995) 169 ff. Zu Wilamowitz' Annahme eines menschlichen Dämons (in der Nachfolge Platons) siehe ders. (1928) 48: «Jeder Mensch bringt in seiner Seele seinen Dämon mit; die enge Welt, in die er hineingeboren wird, wirkt sofort auf ihn ein, stärker oder schwächer, und auch die Kraft des Dämons ist verschieden. So geht es ein Leben lang, so daß viele Menschen Gattungswesen zu sein scheinen, ganz durch ihre Umwelt bestimmt. Eigentlich kommt es also in einer Kindheitsgeschichte auf das Verhalten des Dämons zu der Umwelt an.» Vor diesem Hintergrund vgl. ebd. 130 (über Nietzsche): «Er hat getan, wozu ich ihn aufforderte, hat Lehramt und Wissenschaft aufgegeben und ist Prophet geworden, für eine irreligiöse Religion und eine unphilosophische Philosophie. Dazu hat ihm sein Dämon das Recht gegeben; er hatte den Geist und die Kraft dazu. Ob ihm die Selbstvergötterung und die Blasphemien gegen Sokratik und Christentum den Sieg verleihen werden, lehre die Zukunft.» Auf Platons Mythos bezieht sich auch J. Hellman bei seinen (spekulativen) Ausführungen über «Charakter und Bestimmung» in «The Souls's Code», New York 1996 (dt. München 1998).

[112] Stenzel (1928) 181 f.

[113] Daß Weber hier nicht von «Urworte. Orphisch ΔAIMΩN Dämon» (Hamburger-Ausgabe 1, 359), wie die docti editores der Max-Weber-Gesamtausgabe annehmen, sondern vom griechischen Philosophen inspiriert ist, kann man auch daraus schließen, daß er die (ihm offenbar wichtige) Platon-Stelle (mit explizitem Hinweis auf den Autor) im Wertfreiheits-Aufsatz ‹zitiert›, wo es um die Begründung bewußter Lebensführung in letzten Wertideen und menschliche Selbstverantwortung geht: «Die aller menschlichen Bequemlichkeit unwillkommene, aber unvermeidliche Frucht vom Baum der Erkenntnis ist gar keine andere als eben die: (…) sehen zu müssen, daß jede einzelne wichtige Handlung und daß vollends das Leben als Ganzes, wenn es nicht wie ein Naturereignis dahingleiten, sondern bewußt geführt werden soll, eine Kette letzter Entscheidungen bedeutet, durch welche die Seele, wie bei Platon, ihr eigenes Schicksal: – den Sinn ihres Tuns und Seins heißt das – *wählt*» (WL 507 f.). Ein weiteres Argument dafür, daß sich Weber auf Platon bezieht, kann man aus der Charakterisierung des Dämons gewinnen, der ‹des Lebens Fäden hält›. Dieses Motiv, das sich so weder bei Platon noch bei Goethe findet, läßt sich erklären, wenn man eine Assoziation an die bei Platon genannte Lachesis annimmt. Mommsen/Schluchter tragen, von einem unzutreffenden Dä-

nahme eines Wesenskerns im Menschen, in dem alles (auch der innere Beruf zur Wissenschaft ...) von Beginn an enthalten ist. Wer mit diesem Wesenskern verbunden (und nicht auf «Erlebnis» und «Persönlichkeit» fixiert) ist, für den ist die «Forderung des Tages» «schlicht und einfach». Die in einem so verstandenen Dämon-Begriff enthaltene Auffassung von Identität und menschlichem Schicksal widerspricht psychologischen, biologischen und modern-‹soziologischen› Lehrmeinungen, wonach diese aus frühkindlichen Erfahrungen, der Vererbung oder der Umwelt herzuleiten sind. Der wissenschaftlich vor allem an Kulturproblemen interessierte Soziologe Weber hat sich zu diesen Fragen nur in Andeutungen geäußert.[114] Dem Grundsatz des Erziehers Weber, der er in Angelegenheiten der Lebensführung eigentlich gar nicht sein wollte,[115] entspricht das wirkungsvoll unkommentierte[116] Bild in seinem jede pädagogische Explikation vermeidenden Charakter (in Anlehnung an Nietzsche) sehr genau: «Werde, der *du* bist!»

Bibliographischer Anhang

BOECKH, August (1877): Encyclopädie und Methodologie der Philologischen Wissenschaften. Hrsg. v. E. Bratuschek, Leipzig.
BRAUN, Christoph (1992): Max Webers «Musiksoziologie», Heidelberg.
BURCKHARDT, Jacob (1898–1902): Griechische Kulturgeschichte. Nach dem Text der Erstausgabe durch J. Oeri. Mit Verbesserungen von F. Stähelin und S. Merian aus der kritischen Ausgabe 1930–1931. Unveränderter Nachdruck der Ausgabe Basel 1956–1957, München 1977, (Bd. I–IV).
BURCKHARDT, Jacob (1982): Der Text der ‹Weltgeschichtlichen Betrachtungen› auf Grund der Vorarbeiten von E. Ziegler nach den Handschriften hrsg. von P. Ganz, München.
BURCKHARDT, Leonhard A. (1996): Bürger und Soldaten, Aspekte der politischen und militärischen Rolle athenischer Bürger im Kriegswesen des 4. Jahrhunderts v. Chr., Stuttgart.
CALDER, William M. III (1990): «Credo gegen Credo; Arbeit gegen Arbeit; Anschauung gegen Anschauung» Ulrich von Wilamowitz-Moellendorff contra Eduard Meyer. In: Eduard Meyer. Leben und Leistung eines Universalhistorikers. Hrsg. v. W. M. Calder III; A. Demandt, Leiden, 41–73.
CANCIK, Hubert/CANCIK-LINDEMAIER, Hildegard (2002): ‹Das Gymnasium in der Knechtschaft des Staates›. Zu Entstehung, Situation und Thema von Friedrich Nietzsches «Wir Philologen». In: Disciplining Classics = Altertumswissenschaft als Beruf, ed. by G. W. Most, Göttingen, 97–113.

---

mon-Verständnis ausgehend, unnötig Gedanken zu «Geistesaristokratie» und «Elitismus» an den Text heran (was in einer historisch-kritischen *Edition* ebenso unverständlich wie bedauerlich ist) und verkennen bei ihrer Interpretation im übrigen auch die Logik der Satzstruktur, wenn sie schreiben: «Jeder kann seinen Dämon finden, jeder zur Persönlichkeit werden, jeder ein selbstbestimmtes Leben führen, wenn er nur in rückhaltloser Hingabe einer selbstgewählten überpersönlichen Sache dient» (MWG I/17, 43). Auch Hennis (siehe Anm. 107) muß die konditionale Satzlogik der Dämon-Stelle verändern, um mit ihr seine (freilich ungleich sinnvollere) Interpretation des Epilogos ‹verdeutlichen› zu können.

[114] Zu Webers impliziter Anthropologie und einer Kritik der diesbezüglichen «Interpretationsansätze (Tenbruck, Hennis, Lepsius)» siehe Rehberg (1994) 635 f. sowie den Exkurs «Das ‹Tierische› im Menschen» ebd. 628 f. Siehe ferner Hardtwig (1994), der Webers Kulturbegriff in der ‹Protestantischen Ethik› mit denjenigen in Burckhardts Renaissance-Buch vergleicht und darauf hinweist, daß Burckhardt (wie wohl auch Weber, der «seine grundlegenden Prämissen in dieser Richtung nicht weiter ausführt», ebd. 189) Kultur als Sublimierungsleistung der menschlichen Triebnatur (Machthunger, Besitzhunger, Sinnlichkeit) auffaßt.

[115] Siehe Anm. 94 und Hennis (1996) 97.

[116] Während Weber bei der Darstellung des Wertekampfes in der Moderne die ‹antike› Metaphorik eines Götterkampfes in aller Deutlichkeit ausmalt und expliziert (MWG I/17, 100 f.), verzichtet er hier am Ende auf eine weiterführende Erklärung nicht zuletzt um der rhetorischen Wirksamkeit willen.

CANFORA, Luciano (1985): Wilamowitz und die Schulreform: Das ‹griechische Lesebuch›. In: Wilamowitz nach 50 Jahren. Hrsg. v. W. M. Calder III, H. Flashar, Th. Lindken, Darmstadt, 632–648.
CHRISTES, Johannes (1988): Gesellschaft, Staat und Schule in der griechisch-römischen Antike. In: Sozialmassnahmen und Fürsorge. Zur Eigenart antiker Sozialpolitik. Hrsg. v. H. Kloft, Grazer Beiträge, Supplementband III, 55–74.
DEININGER, Jürgen (1990): Eduard Meyer und Max Weber. In: Eduard Meyer. Leben und Leistung eines Universalhistorikers. Hrsg. v. W. M. Calder III, A. Demandt, Leiden, 132–158.
DIHLE, Albrecht (1986): Philosophie – Fachwissenschaft – Allgemeinbildung. In: Aspects de la philosophie hellénistique. Entretiens Fondation Hardt 32, préparés et présidés par H. Flashar et O.Gigon, 185–231.
FINLEY, Moses I. (1986): Max Weber und der griechische Stadtstaat. In: Max Weber, der Historiker. Hrsg. v. J. Kocka, Göttingen, 90–107.
GERHARDT, Volker (1983/1988): Das «Princip des Gleichgewichts». Zum Verhältnis von Recht und Macht bei Nietzsche. In: ders.: Pathos und Distanz. Studien zur Philosophie Friedrich Nietzsches, Stuttgart, 98–132.
GERHARDT, Volker (1984/1988): Leben und Geschichte. Menschliches Handeln und historischer Sinn in Nietzsches zweiter «Unzeitgemäßer Betrachtung». In: ders.: Pathos und Distanz. Studien zur Philosophie Friedrich Nietzsches, Stuttgart, 133–162.
GERHARDT, Volker (1999): Friedrich Nietzsche; 3. Auflage, München.
GRAESER, Andreas (1993): Die Philosophie der Antike 2. Sophistik und Sokratik, Plato und Aristoteles. 2. Auflage, München.
GUMBRECHT, Hans Ulrich (2002): Live Your Experience – And Be Untimely! What «Classical Philology as a Profession» Could (Have) Become. In: Disciplining Classics = Altertumswissenschaft als Beruf, ed. By G. W. Most, Göttingen, 253–269.
HANKE, Edith (2001): Erlösungsreligionen. In: Max Webers ‹Religionssystematik›. Hrsg. v. H. G. Kippenberg, M. Riesebrodt, Tübingen, 209–226.
HARDER, Richard (1962/1949): Eigenart der Griechen, Eine kulturphysiognomische Skizze, Freiburg.
HARDTWIG, Wolfgang (1985): Jacob Burckhardt. Wissenschaft als gesellschaftliche Arbeit und als Askese. In: Geschichte und politisches Handeln. Studien zu europäischen Denkern der Neuzeit. Th. Schieder zum Gedächtnis. Hrsg. v. P. Alter, W. J. Mommsen, Th. Nipperdey, Stuttgart, 216–242.
HARDTWIG, Wolfgang (1994): Jacob Burckhardt und Max Weber. Zur Genese und Pathologie der modernen Welt. In: Umgang mit Jacob Burckhardt. Zwölf Studien. Hrsg. v. H. R. Guggisberg, Basel/München, 159–190.
HENNIS, Wilhelm (1987): Max Webers Fragestellung. Studien zur Biographie des Werks, Tübingen.
HENNIS, Wilhelm (1996): Max Webers Wissenschaft vom Menschen. Neue Studien zur Biographie des Werks, Tübingen.
HENTSCHKE, Ada/MUHLACK, Ulrich (1972): Einführung in die Geschichte der klassischen Philologie, Darmstadt.
HEUSS, Alfred (1965): Max Webers Bedeutung für die Geschichte des griechisch-römischen Altertums, HZ 201, 529–556.
HÖLSCHER, Uvo (1965): Die Chance des Unbehagens. Zur Situation der klassischen Studien, Göttingen.
HORSTMANN, Axel (1989): *«Allgemeine Hermeneutik»* und *«philologisches Organon»*. Zu August Boeckhs Theorie des Verstehens. In: Disiecta Membra. Studien. K. Gründer zum 60. Geburtstag. Basel, 108–122.
JAEGER, Werner (1954): Paideia. Die Formung des Griechischen Menschen. Erster Band, 3. Auflage Berlin 1954. Zweiter Band, 2. Auflage Berlin.

JASPERS, Karl (1932): Max Weber. Deutsches Wesen im politischen Denken, im Forschen und Philosophieren. Oldenburg i.O.
JOHANN, Horst-Theodor (Hrsg.) (1976): Erziehung und Bildung in der heidnischen und christlichen Antike, Darmstadt.
KRECH, Volkhard/WAGNER, Gerhard (1994): Wissenschaft als Dämon im Pantheon der Moderne. Eine Notiz zu Max Webers zeitdiagnostischer Verhältnisbestimmung von Wissenschaft und Religion. In: Max Webers Wissenschaftslehre. Interpretation und Kritik. Hrsg. v. G. Wagner, H. Zipprian, Frankfurt a. M., 755–779.
KÜHNERT, Friedmar (1961): Allgemeinbildung und Fachbildung in der Antike. Deutsche Akademie der Wissenschaften zu Berlin. Schriften der Sektion für Altertumswissenschaft, Berlin.
LLANO SÁNCHEZ, Rafael (1997): Max Webers Kulturphilosophie der Moderne. Eine Untersuchung des Berufsmenschentums, Berlin.
MARROU, Henri Irénée (1948/1977): Geschichte der Erziehung im klassischen Altertum. Übers. v. Ch. Beumann, hrsg. v. R. Harder, München.
MATTHIESEN, Kjeld (1990): Der Altphilologe Ulrich von Wilamowitz-Moellendorff. Bildungsgeschichte und Bildungspolitik. In: Intelligenz und Allgemeinbildung 1848–1918. Anneliese Mannzmann zum 65. Geburtstag. Münster, 25–52.
MEHRING, Reinhard (1999): Humanismus als «Politicum», Werner Jaegers Problemgeschichte der griechischen «Paideia», AuA VL, 111–128.
MEIER, Christian (1988): Max Weber und die Antike. In: Max Weber. Ein Symposion. Hrsg. v. J. Kocka, München, 11–17.
MEYER, Eduard (1902/1910): Zur Theorie und Methodik der Geschichte. In: ders.: Kleine Schriften zur Geschichtstheorie und zur wirtschaftlichen und politischen Geschichte des Altertums, Halle, 1–67.
MEYER, Eduard (1907): Humanistische und geschichtliche Bildung. Vortrag gehalten in der Vereinigung der Freunde des humanistischen Gymnasiums in Berlin und der Provinz Brandenburg am 27. November 1906, Berlin.
MOMMSEN, Wolfgang J. (1985): Max Weber. Persönliche Lebensführung und gesellschaftlicher Wandel in der Geschichte. In: Geschichte und politisches Handeln. Studien zu europäischen Denkern der Neuzeit. Th. Schieder zum Gedächtnis. Hrsg. v. P. Alter, W. J. Mommsen, Th. Nipperdey, Stuttgart, 261–281.
MOMMSEN, Wolfgang J. (1986): Max Webers Begriff der Universalgeschichte. In: Max Weber, der Historiker. Hrsg. v. J. Kocka, Göttingen, 51–72.
NÄF, Beat (1990): Eduard Meyers Geschichtstheorie. Entwicklung und zeitgenössische Reaktionen. In: Eduard Meyer. Leben und Leistung eines Universalhistorikers. Hrsg. v. W. M. Calder III, A. Demandt, Leiden, 285–310.
NESSELRATH, Heinz-Günther (1985): Lukians Parasitendialog, Berlin/New York.
NIETZSCHE, Friedrich: Kritische Studienausgabe (KSA). Hrsg. v. G. Colli und M. Montinari 1967ff., 2. Auflage, München 1988.
NIPPEL, Wilfried (1994): Vom Nutzen und Nachteil Max Webers für die Althistorie, AuA XL, 169–180.
PREUSSE, Ute (1988): Humanismus und Gesellschaft. Zur Geschichte des altsprachlichen Unterrichts in Deutschland von 1890 bis 1933, Frankfurt a. M.
REHBERG, Karl-Siegbert (1994): Kulturwissenschaft und Handlungsbegrifflichkeit. Anthropologische Überlegungen zum Zusammenhang von Handlung und Ordnung in der Soziologie Max Webers. In: Max Webers Wissenschaftslehre. Interpretation und Kritik. Hrsg. v. G. Wagner, H. Zipprian, Frankfurt a. M., 602–661.
REINHARDT, Karl (1941/1960): Die klassische Philologie und das Klassische. In: ders., Vermächtnis der Antike. Gesammelte Essays zur Philosophie und Geschichtsschreibung. Hrsg. v. C. Becker, Göttingen 1960, 334–360.
REINHARDT, Karl (1960): Platons Mythen. In: ders. Vermächtnis der Antike, Göttingen, 219–295.

RESCHKE, Renate (2000): Denkumbrüche bei Nietzsche. Zur anspornenden Verachtung der Zeit, Berlin.
ROSSI, Pietro (1986): Max Weber und die Methodologie der Geschichts- und Sozialwissenschaften. In: Max Weber, der Historiker. Hrsg. v. J. Kocka, Göttingen, 28-50.
SAFRANSKI, Rüdiger (2000): Nietzsche. Biographie seines Denkens, München/Wien.
SCHLUCHTER, Wolfgan (1996): Zeitgemäße Unzeitgemäße. Von Friedrich Nietzsche über Georg Simmel zu Max Weber. In: «Vom Nutzen und Nachteil der Historie für das Leben». Nietzsche und die Erinnerung in der Moderne. Hrsg. v. D. Borchmeyer, Frankfurt a. M.
SCHUBERT, Andreas (1995): Platon, Der Staat, Paderborn.
SCHWAB, Franz-Xaver (1917): Beruf und Jugend. Die weißen Blätter, 4. Jg., Heft 5, 97-113.
STENZEL, Julius (1928): Platon der Erzieher, Leipzig.
STEPPER, Ruth (1997): Leiden an der Geschichte. Ein zentrales Motiv in der *Griechischen Kulturgeschichte* Jacob Burckhardts und seine Bedeutung in der altertumswissenschaftlichen Geschichtsschreibung, Bodenheim.
TENBRUCK, Friedrich H. (1976): Zur Soziologie der Sophistik, Neue Hefte für Philosophie, 10, 51-77.
TENBRUCK, Friedrich H. (1988): Max Weber und Eduard Meyer. In: Max Weber und seine Zeitgenossen. Hrsg. v. W. J. Mommsen, W. Schwentker, Göttingen, 337-379.
VIDAL-NAQUET, Pierre (1989): Der Schwarze Jäger, Denkformen und Gesellschaftsformen in der griechischen Antike. Aus dem Französischen von A. Wittenburg, Frankfurt/New York.
WEBER, Marianne (1926): Max Weber. Ein Lebensbild, Tübingen.
WEBER, Max: Landarbeiterfrage, Nationalstaat und Volkswirtschaftspolitik: Schriften und Reden 1892-1899. Erster Halbband, hrsg. v. W. J. Mommsen in Zusammenarbeit mit R. Aldenhoff, Tübingen 1993 (MWG I/4-1).
WEBER, Max: Wissenschaft als Beruf 1917/1919. Politik als Beruf 1919. Hrsg. v. W. J. Mommsen u. W. Schluchter in Zusammenarbeit mit B. Morgenbrod, Tübingen 1992 (MWG I/17).
WEBER, Max: Gesammelte Aufsätze zur Religionssoziologie, 3 Bände, Tübingen, 1920. Bd. 1: 7., photomech. gedr. Aufl. 1978 (RS I-III).
WEBER, Max: Wirtschaft und Gesellschaft, Grundriß der verstehenden Soziologie, besorgt von J. Winckelmann, Tübingen: Mohr-Siebeck, 5., revidierte Auflage, Studienausgabe, 1980 (WuG).
WEBER, Max: Gesammelte Politische Schriften. Mit einem Geleitwort v. Th. Heuss, hrsg. v. J. Winckelmann, Tübingen, 4. Auflage 1980 (GPS).
WEBER, Max: Gesammelte Aufsätze zur Wissenschaftslehre. Hrsg. von J. Winckelmann, Tübingen, 5., erneut durchgesehene Auflage 1982 (WL).
WEBER, Max: Gesammelte Aufsätze zur Sozial- und Wirtschaftsgeschichte, Tübingen, 2. Auflage 1988 (GSW).
WILAMOWITZ (1892/1913): von Wilamowitz-Moellendorff, Ulrich, Philologie und Schulreform. In: ders., Reden und Vorträge, 3. Auflage, Berlin, 98-119.
WILAMOWITZ (1918): von Wilamowitz-Moellendorff, Ulrich, Platon. Sein Leben und seine Werke. 3. Auflage Berlin, Frankfurt a. M. 1948.
WILAMOWITZ (1928): von Wilamowitz-Moellendorf, Ulrich, Erinnerungen 1848-1914. 2. Auflage, Leipzig.
WOLF, Erik (1930/1972): Max Webers ethischer Kritizismus und das Problem der Metaphysik. In: ders., Rechtsphilosophische Studien. Ausgewählte Schriften Bd. 1. Hrsg. v. A. Höllerbach, Frankfurt a. M. 1972, 12-29.

JAN CÖLLN

Alexander der Große in Europa und Asien. Mythisierung von Geschichte und ihre Präsenz nach dem Ersten Weltkrieg[1]

Alexander der Große ist kein Mythos. Er ist Wirklichkeit gewesen. Eine atemberaubende, viele Völker mit sich reißende Wirklichkeit, die zumindest die damalige Welt, also Griechenland, Nord-Afrika, den Nahen Osten und Asien bis nach Indien verändert hat. Wie oft in der Geschichte der Antike geben davon kaum zeitgenössische Zeugnisse Bericht. Aber über den gesamten Bereich dieser Welt verstreut, erzählt man sich in der nachfolgenden Zeit von Alexander und seinen Eroberungen in Asien. Geschichtsschreiber der Griechen und Römer genauso wie arabische Enzyklopädisten, Erzähler in griechischer Sprache genauso wie in koptischer, syrischer, hebräischer und persischer Sprache zu allen Zeiten von dem ersten vorchristlichen Jahrhundert bis in die Spätantike, vom Frühmittelalter bis in die Frühe Neuzeit und vom 19. Jahrhundert, dem Zeitalter der historistischen Erneuerung der Geschichtswissenschaft, bis heute, wie zuletzt im Filmepos Oliver Stones aus dem Jahr 2004. Warum erzählt man sich aber immer wieder neu von dieser Geschichte? Warum tut man das nicht nur in Form wissenschaftlich fundierter Geschichtsschreibung, sondern auch in Romanen und Theaterstücken? Gegenstände der folgenden Untersuchungen sind deutschsprachige Darstellungen Alexanders seit Droysens Biographie von 1833 und die kulturellen Funktionen ihrer Einbindung in einen wirkungsmächtigen Diskurs nach dem Ersten Weltkrieg, der vom Antagonismus Europas und Asiens handelt. Es erweist sich, daß die behandelten Texte von Droysen, Nietzsche und Burckhardt sowie von Spengler, Bloch und Coudenhove-Kalergi (II.) ebenso wie die Bühnenstücke Arnolt Bronnens (1926) und Hans Baumanns (1941) (III.) von mythischen Denkformen geprägt sind. Daher werde ich im folgenden zunächst kurz der Frage nachgehen, was Mythisierung von Geschichte bedeutet und in welchen Erscheinungsformen man das Phänomen beschreiben kann. Ich beschränke mich dabei auf wenige konstitutive Elemente, die Cassirer und Blumenberg herausgearbeitet haben. Sie helfen, Mythos-Phänomene in Texten der Moderne, für die der Mythos keine religiöse oder dem Religiösen analoge Funktionen mehr hat, beschreibbar zu machen und zu deuten.

---

[1] Der folgende Text entspricht einem Vortrag, den ich im Rahmen der Ringvorlesung «Antike in der Moderne: Mythos und Mythologie» des Heinrich-Schliemann-Institutes für Altertumswissenschaften der Universität Rostock am 20. 12. 2005 gehalten habe. Die Vortragsfassung ist im wesentlichen beibehalten.

I. Was ist und wie funktioniert Mythisierung von Geschichte?

1.) Geschichte und Geschichtsschreibung

Vieles ließe sich über das Leben Alexanders des Großen (356 - 10. Juni 323) und seine historischen Kontexte sagen und seit dem 19. Jahrhundert haben viele Historiker die Quellen zum größten Teil aus sehr viel späterer Zeit, aus der griechisch-römischen Antike – Diodorus Siculus: Buch 17 (1. Jh. v. Chr.), Curtius Rufus (1. Jh. n. Chr.), Plutarch (um 100 n. Chr.), Arrian (2. Jh. n. Chr.) –, immer wieder ausgewertet und zu wissenschaftlich abgesicherten Geschichten gestaltet. Schon die antiken Historiker taten dies nicht aus rein antiquarischem Interesse: Der Erfahrungsschatz der Vergangenheit sollte aufbewahrt sein zum Nutzen von Gegenwart und Zukunft; Herrscher werden in Erzählungen zu negativen oder positiven Vorbildern gestaltet, damit Könige oder Gelehrte und solche, die es werden sollten, von ihren Geschichten lernen. Die Geschichten der Geschichtsschreibung sind auch heute noch – so wissenschaftlich sie auch immer sind – nicht die Geschichte selbst. Das, was Sie zur Wissenschaft macht, sind Methoden: Methoden der Nachprüfbarkeit, der Argumentationslogik und der Herstellung einer wenigstens hermeneutischen, also analytischen Deutungs-Wahrheit, die intersubjektiv nachvollziehbar zu machen ist.

2.) Mythos

Was dagegen zeichnet eine mythische Geschichte aus? Auch sie erklärt die Welt, wie insbesondere Cassirer und Blumenberg herausgearbeitet haben.[2] Ursprungsmythen oder ätiologische Mythen werden erzählt, um präsent zu machen, wie Leben entsteht. Zahlreiche Troja-Mythen führen vor Augen, in welchem Ausmaße Menschen Gewalt ausüben und was sie dazu befähigt resp. bewegt; ebenso beschreiben sie, warum Menschen diese Gewalt ertragen und wie sehr sie in der Lage dazu sind. Mythen erklären denjenigen, für die sie erzählt werden und von denen sie immer wieder wiederholt werden, ihre Welt.

Darin sind sich wissenschaftliche und mythische Geschichten durchaus ähnlich: Sie müssen wiederholt werden. Es reicht ebensowenig aus, nur einmal in einer wissenschaftlichen Monographie von Alexander zu erzählen, wie eine einzige Erzählung von Achill diesen zu einem Mythos machte. Blumenbergs berühmter Titel «Arbeit am Mythos» gilt zunächst einmal für alle Traditionen: Sie werden nur welche, wenn sie wiederholt, immer wieder erneuert, an wechselnde Bedürfnisse und kulturelle Kontexte angeglichen werden, damit sie ihr Publikum erreichen. Trotzdem ist die Wiederholung ein spezifisches Merkmal mythischer Denkform. Cassirer hat diesen Begriff anthropologisch und letztlich insbesondere semiotisch fundiert, da er eine spezifische Form der Wahrnehmung von Welt, d.h. Auslegung von Zeichen, zugrundelegt, die ein Mythos in wiederum spezifischer Art zum Ausdruck bringt, also selbst zum bedeutungstragenden Zeichen werden läßt.[3] So suchen

---

[2] Ernst Cassirer (2002a). Hans Blumenberg (1971), S. 11–66; ders. (1979). Vgl. dazu einführend Annette Simonis (²2001) und Dietmar Peil (²2001); Christoph Jamme (1991), S. 99–103 und 116–120.
[3] Cassirer, S. 35–86 und zur mythischen Zeitvorstellung S. 123–166. Vgl. Blumenberg (1979), S. 165–191.

Cassirer und in seiner Nachfolge Blumenberg das Mythische in den Ausdrucksformen seines kulturellen Funktionierens.[4] Die Wiederholung gehört im engeren Sinn zur Methode mythischen Denkens: Bedeutsamkeit – ein zentraler Begriff in Blumenbergs Mythentheorie[5] – im mythischen Sinne wird nicht argumentativ hergeleitet, sie stellt sich ein im auf Wiederholung angelegten Erzählprozeß der Geschichte. Sie ist nicht für jedermann im einzelnen ableitbar von logischen Erklärungsgrundsätzen, sondern sie wird gesetzt durch die Autorität der Geschichte selbst, die sie durch ihr Alter, ihre Ancienität und die ‹longe durée› ihrer kommunikativen Gültigkeit erhält. Erst wenn sich Handlungen, Ereignisse, Begebenheiten als Wiederholung von etwas darstellen, was schon einmal war, zeigt sich ihre mythische Bedeutsamkeit. «[E]s ist Wiederholung als Erfüllung der Verbindlichkeit der Sache selbst», formuliert Blumenberg.[6] Diese Wiederholung ist aber nie identisch mit dem Muster, dem es folgt. Und erst die erzählte Geschichte erweist, daß es sich um eine Wiederholung handelt, und erklärt, was es ist, dem z. B. ein Handelnder wie Alexander folgt. In Zeiten, in denen das mythische Denken präsenter war als heute, konnte auch Alexander selbst dieser Denkform folgen und sich als zweiter Achill, Herakles oder als Dionysos verstehen und seinen Untergebenen zu verstehen geben.

In dieser letzten Formulierung steckt ein weiterer wesentlicher Charakterzug mythischen Denkens: Es produziert Erklärungen und erzeugt Bedeutsamkeit, die kollektive Gültigkeit bekommen. Mythen tragen dazu bei, daß die Teilhaber einer Gesellschaft sich durch die Anerkennung der Autorität ihrer Mythen zu einer Gemeinschaft einen.[7] Aus diesem Grund brauchen Mythen Öffentlichkeit und sie brauchen Institutionen, in deren generationenüberdauernden Organisationsformen ihre Autorität immer wieder bestätigt und erneuert werden kann. Sie bannt den Schrecken[8] der Wirklichkeit des Neuen, das z. B. Alexander geschaffen hat, in das mythische Denken von der Wiederkehr des Immergleichen.

3.) Mythisierung von Geschichte

Wie kann es nun geschehen, daß die Geschichte der Geschichtsschreibung mit ihren wissenschaftlichen Denkformen übertragen wird in eine Geschichte mythischer Denkform? Wie wird aus der historischen Gestalt Alexander ein Mythos? Inwiefern und warum deutet mythische Denkform Alexander zu einer Erzählung von mythischer Bedeutsamkeit? Und welche Bedeutsamkeit könnte dies sein?
Eine erste Antwort gibt uns der Prediger Salomo, den ich aus der Lutherübersetzung von 1545 zitiere:

---

[4] Ernst Cassirer (2002b), S. 52–69. Blumenberg (1979), S. 40–67. Die Beispielanalysen in allen genannten Arbeiten von Cassirer und Blumenberg stützen sich auf zahlreiches ethnographisches Material; ihre Auswertungen orientieren sich stets an der Frage nach den kommunikativen Funktionen mythischen Erzählens.
[5] Blumenberg (1971), S. 26, 31, 35, 66; Blumenberg (1979), S. 68–126; hier bes. S. 76–78 und S. 86.
[6] Blumenberg (1971), S. 37.
[7] Vgl. dazu: Aleida und Jan Assmann (1998).
[8] Hier sieht bekanntlich Blumenberg in allen seinen Arbeiten zum Mythos die anthropologische, für jede Kommunikationsgemeinschaft zugrunde gelegte kollektivpsychologische Motivation für das Erzählen von Mythen.

Ein Geschlecht vergehet / das ander kompt / Die Erde bleibet aber ewiglich. Die Sonne gehet auff vnd gehet vnter / vnd leufft an jren Ort / das [= so daß] *sie wider herumb an den Ort* [gelangt,] *da er* [sc. sie] *anfieng.* [...] *Was ists das geschehen ist? Eben das hernach geschehen wird. Was ists das man gethan hat? Eben das man hernach wider thun wird / Vnd geschicht nichts newes vnter der Sonnen. Geschicht auch etwas dauon man sagen möcht / Sihe / das ist new? Denn es ist vor auch geschehen in vorigen zeiten / die vor vns gewesen sind.* (Pr [=Eccl.] I 4–6, 9–10)

Während Salomo Geschichte als ewigen Kreislauf der Natur beschreibt und diesen christlich auswertet als Beleg für die Eitelkeit der Welt, bedeutet der gleiche Grundgedanke in mythischer Denkform, daß Geschichte im mythischen Sinne immer erklärt werden kann als etwas, das schon einmal war. Es ordnet das Neue ein in eine bekannte Ordnung gesicherten Wissens. Geschichtsmythen versichern, Geschichte vollziehe sich stets in gleichbleibenden Rhythmen. Das gilt auch für die Mythisierung der Geschichte Alexanders des Großen.

II. Die Mythisierung der Geschichte von Alexander dem Großen

1.) Historistische Geschichtsschreibung: Droysen

Die Mythisierung Alexanders des Großen beginnt in der Neuzeit mit seiner ersten großen wissenschaftlichen Historisierung. Johann Gustav Droysen (1808–1884) hat mit seiner *Geschichte Alexanders des Großen* 1833 – also mit jungen 25 Jahren! – nicht nur ein epochemachendes Buch geschrieben, sondern auch die erste Würdigung und wissenschaftliche Beschäftigung mit Alexander vorgelegt, die unser Alexanderbild der Tendenz nach bis heute bestimmt. Die Aufklärungshistorie hatte sich mit dem diktatorischen Machthaber so gut wie überhaupt nicht beschäftigt. Das Griechenland von den Renaissance-Humanisten bis hin zu den Philhellenen der Klassik und Romantik ist vorwiegend das Griechenland Homers oder der perikleischen Klassik. Dann widmet man sich v.a. der römischen Antike, der hellenistischen Spätantike und dem antiken Christentum. Erst Droysen hat unsere Vorstellung geprägt, daß Alexanders Eroberungszug in den Orient das welthistorisch ‹notwendige› Bindeglied zwischen antikem Griechentum und dem christlich-römischen Abendland gewesen sei und die kulturhistorischen Traditionskanäle ausgehoben habe, auf denen griechische Bildung und das Christentum ins abendländische Europa geflossen sei.[9]

Hier kann ich nicht in eine ausführliche Würdigung dieser erstaunlichen Leistung eines 25-Jährigen eingehen. Droysen hat dieses frühe Meisterwerk später verbunden mit zwei weiteren Monographien zu einer dreibändigen Darstellung des Hellenismus, die die großen welthistorisch relevanten Konsequenzen von Alexanders Eroberungszug bei seinen direkten Nachfolgern und im «hellenistischen Staatensystem» bis 221 v. Chr. behandelt (1877/78 erstmals zur *Geschichte des Hellenismus* zusammengefügt). Eine Fortsetzung bis zu den Anfängen des Christentums war geplant. Dieses letzlich christlich-heilsgeschicht-

---

[9] Zur historiographiegeschichtlichen Einordnung von Droysen vgl. Jörn Rüsen (1971); zu seinem Alexander-Buch siehe Daniel Fulda (1996), S. 447–454, und v.a. Horst Walter Blanke (1991), S. 227–230, 276–279, 289–291; vgl. ders. (1988).

liche Rahmenkonzept[10] formuliert Droysen bereits im Vorwort seiner Alexander-Deutung von 1833:

> *Und wie an dem ersten Schöpfungstage Gott das Licht von der Finsternis schied, und aus Abend und Morgen der erste Tag ward, so hat der erste Tag der Geschichte die Völker aus Abend und Morgen zum ersten Male geschieden zu ewiger Feindschaft und dem ewigen Verlangen der Versöhnung; denn es ist das Leben des Geschaffenen, sich aufzuzehren und zurückzusinken in die alte friedliche Nacht des ungeschaffenen Anfangs; drum ringen die Völker aus Abend und Morgen den Kampf der Vernichtung; sie sehnen sich nach endlicher Ruhe. (11) Denselben Kampf wiederholen die Jahrhunderte unablässig [...]. (13)*[11]

Droysen faßt hier Abendland und Morgenland als schicksalshaften Antagonismus auf, der seit der Schöpfung den Gang der Geschichte bestimme. Die Suggestivkraft der Worte Abend und Morgen schafft die Analogie zur Vorstellung vom gottgegebenen Schöpfungskreislauf, der sich wie Nacht und Tag zwischen Abendland und Morgenland vollziehe. Die Worte von den «ringenden Völkern» und vom «Kampf» machen deutlich, daß es um Herrschaft geht. «Feindschaft» und «ewiges Verlangen nach Versöhnung» läßt sich so nur in Kategorien der Unterwerfung und Eroberung denken. Die biblische Überhöhung der Aussagen durch die sprachlichen Anleihen bei der Genesis, die Evidenz, die die Worte und Metaphern erzeugen, und der sentenzenhaft gnomische Gestus von Sätzen wie «denselben Kampf wiederholen die Jahrhunderte unablässig» erzeugen eine Bedeutsamkeit, die keiner *wissenschaftlichen* Argumentationslogik folgt, sondern *mythischem* Denken entspringt, das außerordentliche Wirklichkeit in eine sie übergreifende Ordnung bringt. Das Ziel dieser Passagen ist es, die folgende Geschichte Alexanders des Großen einzuordnen in eine geschichtsmythische Denkform, die die Gewißheit einer übergreifenden Ordnung historischer Erfahrung behauptet und damit Geschichte erfaßbar macht für diejenigen, für die diese übergreifende Ordnung, hier christliches Schöpfungs- und Geschichtsverständnis, eine Gültigkeit hat, die ‹man› nicht weiter zu hinterfragen braucht.

2.) Diskursivierung von Geschichtsschreibung durch den öffentlichen Stellenwert des Historismus: Burckhardt und Nietzsche

Droysen hat die Koordinaten für jede weitere Beschäftigung mit Alexander dem Großen festgeschrieben: Seine Taten beschreiben eine für den weiteren Verlauf der Weltgeschichte notwendige historische Phase; die Tat des großen Mannes von welthistorischer Bedeutung habe mythische Bedeutsamkeit, weil sie zum einen ein Magnetfeld der Weltgeschichte bestätigt, das sich zwischen den Polen Abendland und Morgenland gebildet habe, aber auch weil Alexander es für kurze Zeit außer Kraft gesetzt und damit Natur und Schicksal überwunden habe, ohne es freilich zu beseitigen.

---

[10] Auf den Zusammenhang zwischen Hegelianismus und christlicher Heilsgeschichte bei Droysen geht Günter Birtsch (1964), S. 227–236, hier bes. S. 228 ein. Vgl. auch die oben genannten Arbeiten von Blanke (1991) und Rüsen (1971).

[11] Ich zitiere aus folgender Ausgabe: Johann Gustav Droysen, Geschichte Alexanders des Großen. Nach dem Text der Erstausgabe 1833. Mit einem Nachwort von Jürgen Busche. Unter herausgeberischer Mitarbeit von Paul König, Zürich ²1986 (Manesse Bibliothek der Weltgeschichte).

Zwei für die weitere Denkgeschichte dieser Vorstellungen entscheidende Generatoren des Diskurses sind Nietzsche und Burckhardt. Sie nehmen Droysens Gedanken auf. Durch die ungeheure Wirkungsmächtigkeit beider Autoren resp. ihrer Schriften führen sie eine weitere Stufe der Öffentlichkeitswirksamkeit der beschriebenen geschichtsmythischen Denkform ein. Diese Phase des zu beschreibenden Diskurses läßt aus der bei Droysen zunächst noch individuellen Mythisierung der Geschichte Alexanders eine Tradition dieses Geschichtsmythos hervorgehen.

Friedrich Nietzsche formuliert es in seinen *Unzeitgemäßen Betrachtungen* (1873-76), im vierten Stück: *Richard Wagner in Bayreuth* so:

> *Die Hellenisierung der Welt und, diese zu ermöglichen, die Orientalisierung des Hellenischen – die Doppelaufgabe des großen Alexander – ist immer noch das letzte große Ereignis [in der Geschichte der Entwicklung der Kultur]; die alte Frage, ob eine fremde Kultur sich überhaupt übertragen lasse, immer noch das Problem, an dem die Neueren sich abmühen. Das rhythmische Spiel jener beiden Faktoren gegeneinander ist es, was namentlich den bisherigen Gang der Geschichte bestimmt hat.* (379)[12]

Die «Hellenisierung der Welt» ist Ergebnis der Eroberung des Orients, Asiens bis nach Indien. Die Orientalisierung des Hellenischen wird als Alexanders Aufgabe bezeichnet, offenbar eine Aufgabe, die ihm seine historische Bestimmung gestellt hat. Die Vorstellung kann sich auf zahlreiche Berichte beziehen, die mit positivem oder negativem Vorzeichen davon erzählen, wie Alexander seine Herrschaft in Asien dadurch zu sichern versuchte, daß er die Makedonen seines Heeres mit den adligen Frauen der unterworfenen Völker verheiratete und als Statthalter einsetzte. Teilweise soll er auch treue Perser mit dieser Aufgabe betraut haben. Schließlich berichten alle Alexanderhistoriker, daß er in Babylon wie ein orientalischer Fürst gewaltet haben soll und sich als Gott hat verehren lassen. Diese Vermischung der Kulturen wird ihm von griechischen und römischen Historikern als Entartung vorgeworfen. Droysen, Nietzsche und Burckhardt erkennen hier aus welthistorischer Sicht einen entscheidenden Faktor dafür, daß die spätere Orientalisierung der Antike nicht zum Untergang der hellenischen Bildungswelt geführt habe. Ebenfalls kehrt bei Nietzsche die mythische Denkform vom «rhythmischen Spiel» wieder, das den «Gang der Geschichte» bestimme. Nietzsche stellt dann neben dem Alexander, der durch seine Zerschlagung des gordischen Knotens den Rhythmus der Weltgeschichte zwischen den Polen Europa und Asien in einen neuen Takt gebracht habe, Richard Wagner. Er verknüpfe durch seine neuartigen Opern die in zahlreiche Fasern zersprungenen Enden beider Stränge wieder neu, weil seine darstellende Musik europäisch und orientalisch-dionysisch zugleich sei.

Der enge gedankliche Kontakt Burckhardts zu Nietzsche ist bekannt. Ich kann hier keinesfalls näher auf die epochale Leistung seiner *Griechischen Kulturgeschichte* (1880-1883/84 entstanden, veröffentlicht zuerst 1898-1902) eingehen.[13] Sie soll mir hier als Beleg für das Weiterleben und die Popularisierung des Diskurses dienen, da dieses dreibändige Werk so etwas wie das bildungsbürgerliche Handbuch zum antiken Griechenland mindestens für die erste Hälfte des 20. Jahrhunderts darstellt. Seine Aussagen zum Hellenismus sind geradezu topisch geworden:

---

[12] Friedrich Nietzsche, Unzeitgemäße Betrachtungen (1873-76). Viertes Stück: Richard Wagner in Bayreuth. Abschnitt 4, in: ders., Werke in drei Bänden, hg. v. Karl Schlechta, Bd. 1, München 1973.
[13] Ich zitiere aus folgender Ausgabe: Jacob Burckhardt, Griechische Kulturgeschichte. 3 Bde., mit einem Nachwort zusammengefaßt hg. v. Rudolf Marx, Stuttgart 1952 (Kröner Taschenausgabe, 58-60).

> [*Das Griechenvolk war*] *im Verlauf der Zeiten dazu bestimmt, alle Völker zuerst zu verstehen und dies Verständnis der Welt mitzuteilen, gewaltige Länder und Völker des Orients zu unterwerfen, seine Kultur zu einer Weltkultur zu machen, in welcher Asien und Rom zusammentrafen, durch den Hellenismus der große Sauerteig der alten Welt zu werden [...]*. (I 52)

Die Vermischung der Kulturen von Okzident und Orient und die geschichtsmythische Vorstellung der Vorbestimmtheit eines Volkes sind die entscheidenden Akzentuierungen dieses klassisch gewordenen Satzes. Sogar die Metapher des «Sauerteigs» geht zurück auf die bei Droysen beschriebene Vorstellung von Wiederholung: Ein solcher Teig gärt und gebiert immer neue ‹Kulturen› aus sich heraus. Die bildungsbürgerliche Komponente von Burckhardts *Griechischer Kulturgeschichte* wird durch das folgende Zitat überdeutlich, in dem nun auch Alexander ins «rhythmische Spiel» des «Gangs der Geschichte» kommt:

> *Aber die Griechen hatten ihre Bildung, welche allein fähig war, die ganze übrige Welt zu begreifen und auszudeuten [...]. Dieser Bildung und ihren beweglichen Trägern konnte nur eine große Hellenisierung der Welt den Weg zu anderen Nationen bahnen, und diese war nur durch einen großen Eroberer zu bewirken.* (III 261) [*Durch*] *eine Gewaltnatur [...] im riesigen Sinne, welthistorisch im höchsten Grade, das Schicksal von Griechenland, Orient und aller Nachwelt auf ihre Schultern* [*nehmend*], *dazu berufen [...], die Welt zu hellenisieren, selbst über seinen individuellen Willen hinaus:* Alexander der Große. (III 260)

Wie schon Droysen und vollends Nietzsche stellt auch Burckhardt den großen Einzelnen, der Geschichte ‹macht›, in den Fokus seiner Perspektivierung des weltgeschichtlichen Verlaufs.

> *Aber es ist eine Eigenschaft der großen Weltbezwinger, daß sie nicht sowohl direkt die Zukunft bewirken, als vielmehr die Welt auf eine neue Grundlage stellen, worauf dann Neues aller Art aufgebaut werden kann.* (III 274f.)

Das nächste Burckhardt-Zitat verdeutlicht, wie er als gewissenhafter hermeneutischer Historiker den Standpunkt seiner Geschichtsdeutung benennt. Freilich in einer Weise, die einen Allgemeingültigkeitsanspruch stellt:

> *Unser Gesamturteil wird wesentlich bestimmt durch die enorme Wünschbarkeit derjenigen Kontinuität der Weltkultur, welche ohne Alexander nicht würde gewonnen worden sein. Rom lernte das Griechentum eigentlich erst durch das Medium des kulturbeherrschenden Diadochentums hindurch recht kennen, und Rom liebte an Griechenland wesentlich die Kultur; diese wollte und mußte es übernehmen und retten. Ferner war ihm die Bewältigung der hellenisierten Ostländer unendlich viel leichter und lag ihm näher, als dies bei früherm Zustande der Fall gewesen wäre. Die römische Weltherrschaft gehörte aber, wie die makedonische, im höchsten Grade zu der Kette der Wünschbarkeiten, von welchen unser Urteil umstrickt ist. Und an beiden Weltherrschaften hängt die Möglichkeit der Verbreitung des Christentums.* (III 275)

Alexander wird geradezu zu einer geschichtsmetaphysischen Notwendigkeit für all das, was ihm, Burckhardt, und seiner bildungsbürgerlichen Leserschaft im 20. Jahrhundert «Wünschbarkeiten», Resultate der Geschichte sind, die er damit zu unabdingbaren Grundpfeilern der Wertekultur seiner Gegenwart erklärt. Da breite Bildungsschichten der deutschsprachigen Kommunikationsgemeinschaften in der ersten Hälfte des 20. Jahrhunderts diese Ansichten teilen, hat Burckhardt mit seinen Formulierungen auch mehr noch als Nietzsche einen hohen Gültigkeitswert bekommen. Seine Darstellung geht sogar so weit,

Alexander in seiner Funktion als Einender der Kulturen Europas und Asiens wie einen Christus beim Abendmahl darzustellen:

> *Enorm wichtig für die Hellenisierung war jedenfalls das Entgegenkommen, das Alexander den Persern bewies. Er wollte die Verschmelzung der Völker und Religionen und feierte diese symbolisch an jenem großen [...] Festmahl, welches deutlich eine große sakramentale Weihe für das Schicksal Asiens sein sollte. [...] Um ihn saßen die Makedonen [...,] die Perser, alsdann aber auch ausgezeichnete Leute der übrigen Nationen, und aus demselben Mischkruge spendeten er und die übrigen dieselben Spenden [...]. Und er betete dazu um alles Gute und um Eintracht und Gemeinschaft der Herrschaft für Hellenen und Perser [vgl. Arrian VII 11,8].* (III 277 f.)

Entscheidend für die weitere Kulturgeschichte der hier im Mittelpunkt stehenden geschichtsmythischen Denkform ist der Gebrauch, der von den bislang vorgestellten Grundgedanken im Zusammenhang mit der Katastrophe des Ersten Weltkrieges in einem breiten öffentlichen Diskurs über den vermeintlichen Gegensatz von Europa und Asien gemacht wurde.[14] Durch diese Öffentlichkeitswirksamkeit wird aus einem gelehrten Geschichtsmythos ein moderner Mythos mit kollektiver Bedeutsamkeit.

3.) Die Funktionalisierung des Europa-Asien-Mythos im Zusammenhang mit dem Ersten Weltkrieg: Spengler, Bloch und Coudenhove-Kalergi

Die Orientalisierung der Antike war zur Jahrhundertwende noch ein zentrales Paradigma für die Erneuerung der Kultur auch der Moderne, wie insbesondere die Arbeiten Hofmannsthals zeigen. Jakob Wassermann hat im Rahmen dieses Grundgedankens 1905 seinen Roman *Alexander in Babylon* veröffentlicht, der den welthistorischen Protagonisten letztlich zu einem Typus Christi und zugleich zu einem Typus des «Juden, im mythischen Sinne» konzipiert.[15] Daneben aber steht eine, ebenfalls aus dem 19. Jahrhundert herrührende Aufwertung der Nationalismen, die durch eine Übertragung von Darwins Evolutionstheorie auch zu einer Hypostasierung von ‹europäischen Rassen› führt. Wenn Geschichte evolutionistisch als ‹Survival of the Fittest› gedacht wird, kann die Orientalisierung des Abendlandes als existentielle Bedrohung angesehen werden. Mit diesem ‹Orient› werden dann das kommunistische Rußland oder das revolutionäre China, aber eben auch das Judentum als ‹asiatische› oder ‹gelbe Gefahr› für die Kultur des Abendlandes heraufbeschworen.[16] Diesen wirkungsmächtigen Diskurs haben dann die Nationalsozialisten für ihre Rassenideologeme aufgenommen.

Im folgenden möchte ich drei Texte beispielhaft anführen, die diesen Diskurs auf jeweils unterschiedliche Art und Weise funktionalisieren: Spenglers *Untergang des Abendlandes*

---

[14] Vgl. dazu Hermann Dorowin (1991). Er behandelt drei Schriften von Henri Massis, Ramiro de Maeztu und Leopold von Andrian. – Im Kontext dieses Diskurses gibt Alfred Baeumler Bachofens Studien über antikes Matriarchat unter dem berühmt gewordenen Titel *Der Mythus von Orient und Occident* (1926) heraus; dieser Text hat großen Einfluß auf zahlreiche Autoren der 20er bis 50er Jahre bekommen; vgl. dazu Yahya Elsaghe (2005).

[15] Vgl. dazu Jan Cölln (2004).

[16] Vielleicht ist auch die Assoziation des gelben Judensterns mit der ubiquitären Formel von der ‹gelben Gefahr› nicht abwegig: vgl. die aufeinanderfolgenden Kapitel «Café Europe» und «Der Stern» in Victor Klemperers *LTI. Notizbuch eines Philologen* (1947).

läßt sich in die nationalistische und bereits antisemitische Diskursformation einordnen, Ernst Blochs *Geist der Utopie* in eine letztlich religiöse und kulturmetaphysische Diskursformation, die die Errettung der europäischen Kultur durch die Kulturen Asiens sieht, und schließlich Coudenhove-Kalergis politische «Pan-Europa»-Ideologie, aus der die heutige Europäische Union erwachsen ist. Es kann wiederum nicht darum gehen, ausführliche, jeweilige Kontexte berücksichtigende Detailinterpretationen zu leisten. Die vielgelesenen Texte waren einflußreiche Archive und zugleich Generatoren der weiteren Öffentlichkeitswirksamkeit des Diskurses.

Bei Oswald Spengler, der ersichtlich an Droysens, Nietzsches und Burckhardts Vorstellungen von der ‹Gewaltnatur› des außerordentlichen einzelnen Menschen von welthistorischer Bedeutung anschließt, heißt es z.B.:

Ich lehre hier den Imperialismus, *als dessen Petrefakt Reiche wie das ägyptische, chinesische, römische, die indische Welt, die Welt des Islam noch Jahrhunderte und Jahrtausende stehen bleiben und aus einer Eroberfaust in die andere gehen können – tote Körper, amorphe, entseelte Menschenmassen, verbrauchter Stoff einer großen Geschichte –, als das typische Symbol des Ausgangs begreifen. Imperialismus ist reine Zivilisation. In dieser Erscheinungsform liegt unwiderruflich das Schicksal des Abendlandes. [...] Deshalb sehe ich in Cecil Rhodes den ersten Mann einer neuen Zeit. Er repräsentiert den politischen Stil einer ferneren, abendländischen, germanischen, insbesondere deutschen Zukunft. Sein Wort ‹Ausdehnung ist alles› enthält in dieser napoleonischen Fassung die eigentlichste Tendenz einer* jeden *ausgereiften Zivilisation.* (51)[17]

Die Bedeutung von Spenglers Text für die Nationalsozialisten liegt, wie an diesem Zitat überdeutlich, auch in der für ihn typischen synkretistischen, kaum argumentativ-diskutierenden Sprache der Gewaltverherrlichung.[18] «Imperialismus», gewaltsame «Ausdehnung» begreift er als Zivilisationshöhepunkt. Der Mensch ist als «Menschenmasse» nur «toter Körper», entscheidend für die Geschichte ist die «Eroberfaust». Der Brite Cecil Rhodes, der in Süd-Afrika ein Vermögen mit Diamantminen gemacht hat und sich mit Rhodesien einen eigenen Staat schuf, wird kurzerhand zum Beispiel für germanische, insbesondere deutsche Hegemonie.

Alexander figuriert in dieser Konzeption als «große welthistorische Person», die «mit der Gestaltungskraft ihres Privatschicksals» «d[em] Schicksal von Tausenden, ganzer Völker und Zeitalter» seine Form «einverleibt». «Es gehört zum Wesen aller Kulturen [...], daß sich das Notwendige in Gestalt einer großen Einzelperson [...] vollzieht.» (194) Allerdings ist ihm Alexander auch ein «Romantiker, an der Schwelle der Zivilisation», der sich «in der Rolle des Achills» «gefiel» (52) und «ein Schwärmer, der nie aufgewacht ist». Als Schwär-

---

[17] Ich zitiere aus folgender Ausgabe: Oswald Spengler, Der Untergang des Abendlandes. Umrisse einer Morphologie der Weltgeschichte (EA 2 Bde. 1918–21) ²1923, München 1981.
[18] Diese Sprache findet ihr Echo nicht zuletzt in: Alfred Rosenberg, *Der Mythus des 20. Jahrhunderts*, München 1930; 1937 führte die zweite Auflage zum 500 000. Exemplar, 1942 betrug die Gesamtauflage 1 060 000 Exemplare. Hier wird Alexanders Herrschaft als «nordisch-mazedonische [...] Pfropfkultur [...]» (München 1942, S. 152) verstanden, die sich auf die Dauer nicht gegen das «unterjochte Blut» (ebd.) habe durchsetzen können. Zu Rosenbergs Leitbegriffen gehört unter anderem das «nordische Abendland» (z.B. S. 293), zu dessen künftiger Weltherrschaft Alexander, Cäsar und Napoleon die geschichtsmythischen ‹Vorleistungen› erbracht hätten (vgl. z.B. S. 516). Zu Spengler und der Kritik von Rechts vgl. Stefan Breuer (2004). Auch Rosenberg widmet Spengler kritische Anmerkungen, die sich natürlich auf dessen Prognose des Untergangs beziehen.

merei versteht Spengler Alexanders Versuch der Vermischung der Kulturen von Osten und Westen (746). Das genau entspricht Spenglers Imperialismus-Ideologie nicht.

> *Der apollinische Mensch sah auf ein goldenes Zeitalter zurück; das enthob ihn des Nachdenkens über das Kommende. Der Sozialist – der sterbende Faust des zweiten Teils – ist der Mensch der historischen Sorge, des Künftigen […]. Der antike Geist mit seinen Orakeln und Vogelzeichen will die Zukunft nur* wissen, *der abendländische will sie* schaffen. *Das dritte Reich ist das germanische Ideal, ein ewiges Morgen, an das alle großen Menschen von Joachim von Floris bis Nietzsche und Ibsen […] ihr Leben knüpften. Alexanders Leben war ein wundervoller Rausch, ein Traum, in dem das homerische Zeitalter noch einmal heraufbeschworen wurde; Napoleons Leben war eine ungeheure Arbeit […] für die Zukunft überhaupt.* (465)

Spengler spielt hier Antike und modernes Abendland gegeneinander aus. Napoleon ist der bessere Alexander – Korse hin oder her. Seine «Arbeit» «für die Zukunft überhaupt», ist das Muster, das sich nicht auf das Abendland beschränkt, sondern ein ewiges Morgenland schafft: «Das dritte Reich ist das germanische Ideal». Geschichtsmythisch ist dieser Text aufgrund seiner Methode, die auf Herstellung von Bedeutsamkeit abzielt, die sprachlich erzeugt, synkretistisch konzipiert und von mythischen Denkstrukturen durchzogen ist, wie z. B. von der Vorstellung, daß sich Geschichte nach vermeintlichen Naturgesetzen, einer ‹Grammatik der Kulturmorphologie› erfülle: In diesem Sinne bleiben Abendland und Morgenland immerwährende Gegensätze. Die ‹Gewaltsnatur› seiner Sprache erzeugt zudem eine Evidenz, die erschlagen nicht wissenschaftlich überzeugen soll.

Spenglers Antipode ist Ernst Bloch. Sein *Geist der Utopie* leuchtet aus Asien. Nach *seiner* Kulturmorphologie liegt dort die Rettung des Abendlandes, das sich durch Technik, Leistungsgesellschaft und Beschleunigung in allen Teilbereichen kulturellen Lebens von seinen kulturellen Werten entfremdet habe. Seiner Moderne-Kritik bleibt aber «die Ahnung unserer verdeckten Kraft, unseres latenten Anfangs und *Morgenlands*, unseres gediegenen, endlich enthülsten, endlich allernächst herangerückten Besitzes.» (200)[19] Seine Utopie ist das «Morgenland» in Europas Kultur selbst. «Also gehen wir nach Osten» – heißt es dort weiter –, «stets schon hatte sich die Abwehr gegen ihn als nutzlos erwiesen. Die Griechen etwa kämpften gegen die Perser, es gelingt ihnen Marathon und Salamis, aber Alexander vermählt sich mit Roxane, entläßt die mazedonische Leibwache und stirbt in Babylon.» (200)

> *Stets ging derart – am Anfang wie erst recht am Ende, beim Zusammenbruch des bösen, harten, schmalen, frierend glaubenlosen Lebens europäischer Welt – der sittlich-geistige Weg, Hilfe zu holen, wieder östlich. Wie oft schon, wie gar sehr einleuchtend ist Europa vor dem Orient: dem zeitloseren, niemals untergehenden […] zur schwachen Halbinsel geworden, deren Schicksal es bleibt, Kontakte zu suchen, um nicht immer wieder in ihrer Kleinheit und rein denkerischen Haltung, religiösen Anämie zu erkalten. Trotzdem pflegt dem griechisch-europäischen Hochmut […] die Welt, die Geschichte des Orients […] nicht einmal in Umrissen bewußt zu sein. Aber Alexander lenkte bewußt nach Persien ein, zwanzigjährig, der jugendliche Mensch, ein seinen Träumen nachziehender Jüngling des Märchens, nicht nur so eitel und substanzlos jung wie vor ihm Alkibiades und nach ihm, in sehr viel reinerer Weise, etwa Otto III., sondern mit Gesichten und Zielen, Griechenland nach Asien hinüberzurichten und großen Logos in die Geschichte zu bringen, gewaltsam genug, den gleichgültigen Zufall*

---

[19] Ich zitiere aus folgender Ausgabe: Ernst Bloch, Geist der Utopie (EA: 1918), Berlin ²1923.

> *der sogenannten Weltregierung zu ihrem Logos zu zwingen. [...] Alexander, der erwählte Bundesfeldherr der Hellenen, hat Griechenland verlassen, um auf seine «Vorstufe» herabzusteigen, müde des ganzen künstlichen Okzidentalismus.* (201) *Was Alexander, der echteste Grieche, aufgab, hat nicht minder Michelangelo, haben Schelling und Schopenhauer aufgegeben, um durch Europa, der Tat und der Schärfe des Begriffs vertraut, den dunklen, allein substanzvollen Orient hell werden zu lassen. [...] Aber auch wir, erst recht wir, die späten westlichen Menschen, suchen weiter, kräftig und traumhaft zieht der Osten wieder über uns herauf. Auch unsere Seelen, siech und leer, gehen wieder nach dem tiefsten Orient, beschreiben ihren Alexanderzug, Zauber und Patriarchenluft zu kosten, nach dem heißen, mütterlichen, mit Gebeten an den Himmel geschlossenen Land.* (202)

Da ist sie wieder, die mythische Denkform von dem Gang der Geschichte als ewige Wiederholung, hier als immer neue Suche des abendländischen Geistes nach metaphysischer Erlösung in Asien. Wie bei Spengler äußert sich der Grundgedanke bei Bloch in einem Synkretismus, dem Alexander, Otto III., Michelangelo und Schopenhauer gleichermaßen Belege für die eine Grundüberlegung sein können. Bei der Beschäftigung mit dem *Geist der Utopie* wird allzu gerne im Hintergrund gelassen, daß auch Bloch die deutsche Kultur für besonders auserwählt hält: Das deutsche Denken sei «im Inwendigsten, Tiefsinnigsten Osten, ein nicht gegebener, aber erwählter Orient, der Osten als Traum, als Nordlicht, als Licht im Nebel». (202) Bloch hat aber noch eine argumentative Überraschung auf Lager: Israel bezeichnet er als «Bindeglied zwischen Hier und Dort», als «Apriori Europas und Asiens zugleich» (204). Damit knüpft er an Konzepte an, die Anfang des Jahrhunderts schon Jakob Wassermann formuliert hatte. Auch Theodor Lessing sieht die kulturelle Funktion des Juden in seiner Aufgabe als Mittler zwischen Europa und Asien.[20] Lessing gehört zu den wortmächtigsten Vertretern des Europa-Asien-Diskurses zur Zeit des Ersten Weltkrieges und der 20er Jahre.[21] Aber er hat sich gegenüber Spengler, Bloch und Coudenhove-Kalergi mit seinen Gedanken nicht auf dem öffentlichen Meinungsmarkt durchsetzen können. Die westliche Überbevölkerung in Europa und Amerika müsse notwendigerweise nach Asien, insbesondere Rußland streben, wo allein Europa und Asien, das auch bei ihm stets mit religiöser Gemeinschaft verbunden ist, eine «harmonische Auflösung» erfahren könnten.[22] Diese Position hat sich freilich zur Zeit der geschürten Kollektivangst vor dem russischen und chinesischen Kommunismus nicht durchsetzen können. Bloch entgeht also antisemitischen Ideologemen. Auch sein Christus ist ein «Stern» aus Asien, der der europäischen Welt «das wahre Menschenleben» gewiesen habe. Seitdem aber liegt für Bloch die Lösung nicht mehr im geographischen Osten, sondern auch die «Urprobleme Asiens [sind] in Europa, seinem Diener, seinem Aussprecher, seinem Geistesprimat, allein beendbar.» (205) Die Kultur des Christentums nennt er denn auch unheilschwanger «Apriori des

---

[20] Theodor Lessing, *Europa und Asien*, Berlin 1918 (Politische Aktions-Bibliothek), S. 78.
[21] Theodor Lessing, *Europa und Asien oder Der Mensch und das Wandellose. Sechs Bücher wider Geschichte und Zeit*, Hannover 1923. Das Buch enthält die erste Fassung der Schrift, die mit Kriegsausbruch im Winter 1914 entstand, aber erst 1916 erschien [Druck von mir nicht eingesehen], eine überarbeitete Auflage seines Buches *Die verfluchte Kultur. Gedanken über den Gegensatz von Leben und Geist*, München 1921, und eine Sammlung von Gedichten und Aphorismen. «Und wie der mazedonische Mann [= Alexander], der dem Paulus im Traume erscheint (Apostelgesch. 16. 9) so strecken wir die Hände hinaus, weit gegen Sonnenaufgang. Da leuchtet ein Stern: Asiens Stern.» (S. 45)
[22] Ebd., S. 385. Daher solle das Ziel deutscher Bildungspolitik auch nach Rußland führen: «Die Gemeinschaft des deutschen und russischen Geistes schafft ein neues Europa. Vielleicht eine neue Religion.» (S. 386) Lessings Ideal ist das «Übervölkische» (S. 387).

totalen Europa» (208), das das für ihn ideale geschichtsmythische Resultat einer Verschmelzung Asiens in die westliche Welt sei. Die Konsequenz eines solchen «totalen Europa» ist die Auflösung Asiens.

Diese letztlich kulturimperialistische Pointe der Blochschen Utopie hat Richard N. Coudenhove-Kalergi für seine Pan-Europa-Ideologie politisch konkretisiert. Die Erfahrung der Katastrophe des Ersten Weltkrieges und die Angst vor den kommunistischen Revolutionen in Rußland und China sind die Hauptmotive für das politische Gefühl der Notwendigkeit eines in sich geschlossenen Europa. Deutlich wird dies v. a. im Ausschluß Rußlands, das mit China umstandslos gleichgesetzt wird als die «asiatische» oder «gelbe Gefahr». Sein erster Pan-Europa-Kongress fand im Oktober 1926 in Wien statt. Seine Kampfschrift «Paneuropa» erschien 1923 zum ersten Mal und wurde 1926 neu verlegt. Das antike Mazedonien wird hier übrigens mit dem modernen Rußland gleichgesetzt (49) und Europa so mit dem hellenischen Griechenland der Klassik identifiziert. Alexander der Große wird daher in der Schrift *Kampf um Europa*[23] als Zwischenschritt zwischen Klassik und hellenistischer Welt übersprungen:

> *Diese Insel wuchs: aus Kreta wurde Hellas – aus Hellas die hellenistische Welt, deren politischer Abdruck das Imperium Romanum wurde. Dieses Europa starb in der Völkerwanderung, um im Zeichen germanischen Blutes und christlichen Glaubens verjüngt wiedergeboren zu werden. Ein neues Europa entstand und sprengte, nach einem Jahrtausend, seine engen Grenzen, um die Welt mit seiner Herrschaft und seinem Geiste zu überziehen. Aber die europäistische Weltkultur, die so entstand und im Zeichen des Auto, Kino und Radio steht, ist von wahrhaft europäischer Kultur ebenso weit entfernt wie einst der Hellenismus von Hellas, wie Rom und Alexandrien von Athen. Wie damals der Sieg und die Ausbreitung der griechischen Kultur Griechenlands – so droht heute Europa und seine Kultur zusammenzubrechen, während die Welt sich scheinbar europäisiert.* (54)

Auch für Coudenhove-Kalergi besteht das Hauptproblem Europas in der Entfremdung von seinen Werten, die sie aus der griechischen Klassik habe – eine Art moderne Variante der ‹translatio artium›, die durch die Technisierung und Beschleunigung der Kultur gestört sei. Harmlos ist auch diese Modernekritik nicht, da sie Christentum, antikes Bildungsgut und Germanentum als tragende Säulen eines starken Europas verabsolutiert:

> Die europäische Seele ist dreidimensional: Christlich *die Tiefe*, hellenisch *die Weite*, germanisch *die Höhe*.
> Christliche *Gefühle und Lehren durchdringen nicht nur die europäischen Christen, sondern auch die europäischen Juden und Freigeister.* (55)

Anders Denkende werden eingemeindet, insofern sie sich dem Christentum unterordnen lassen.

> Hellenischer *Geist lebt nicht nur in den Europäern mit humanistischer Bildung – sondern jeder Europäer hat wenigstens aus dritter oder vierter Hand griechischen Geist in sich aufgenommen.*
> Germanischer *Sinn lebt nicht nur unter den sogenannten germanischen Rassen Europas, sondern in allen Völkern, die aus der Völkerwanderung hervorgingen und die von den stammverwandten Kelten und Slaven ihren Ursprung herleiten.*
> [...]

---

[23] Ich zitiere aus folgender Ausgabe: Kampf um Europa, II. Band, Wien und Leipzig 1926.

Das Christentum gab Europa Tiefe, das Griechentum Form, das Germanentum Kraft. Aber alle diese Drei Dimensionen und Elemente begegnen sich in einem Punkte der europäischen Seele: der Freiheit. Denn die christliche Religion ist individualistisch, die griechische Kultur ist individualistisch, die germanische Rasse ist individualistisch. (55)

Ich möchte an dieser Stelle auf eine eingehende Analyse und Wertung dieser Positionen verzichten.[24] Die Zitate reichen aus, um eine kritiklose Berufung auf Coudenhove-Kalergi bei der Formulierung der Grundwerte einer wie auch immer aussehenden politischen Union Europas als höchst problematisch auszuweisen. Überhaupt macht der Diskursrahmen der Entstehung der Pan-Europa-Idee diese verdächtig: Spengler und etwas mehr noch Bloch haben Pate gestanden. Coudenhove-Kalergis Europa ist ein Kampfbegriff, der gegen die Kulturen Asiens mobilisiert. Sein Europa ist nicht auf die Verknüpfung des gordischen Knotens ausgerichtet und basiert auf einer zutiefst zweifelhaften Wertetrias.

III. Alexander der Große auf der Bühne der Weimarer Republik und im Nationalsozialismus: Arnolt Bronnen und Hans Baumann

Vor dem Hintergrund dieses wirkungsmächtigen Diskurses, der durch seine fast ubiquitäre Öffentlichkeit das kollektive Bewußtsein der Gesellschaft Deutschlands nach dem Ersten Weltkrieg mitbestimmt, entstehen auch fiktionale Texte, die Alexander den Großen zum erzählerischen (Klaus Mann) und zum dramatischen Gegenstand wählen (Bronnen und Baumann). Die Aufführung auf öffentlichen Bühnen ist immer schon verglichen worden mit Einspielung von Ritualen in der gebildeten Kulturgemeinschaft einer Gesellschaft, die dort ihre Mythen zur Selbstvergewisserung präsent werden läßt und damit immer wieder erlebbar macht. Gerade die Wiederholbarkeit solcher Inszenierungen, die gleichwohl nie identisch sind, machen ihren mythischen Wert im Sinne einer «Arbeit am Mythos» mit kollektiver Bedeutsamkeit aus. Jan Assmann hat dies jüngst am Beispiel der Aufführungsgeschichte von Mozarts «Zauberflöte» erneut demonstriert.[25] In diesem kulturellen Funktionszusammenhang stehen auch meine beiden ausgewählten Beispiele: Arnolt Bronnens *Ostpolzug* und Hans Baumanns *Alexander*.

1.) Arnolt Bronnen

Arnolt Bronnens Schauspiel *Ostpolzug*, ist im Berliner Rowohlt-Verlag 1926 veröffentlicht und im selben Jahr am 29. Januar im Staatlichen Schauspielhaus am Gendarmenmarkt zu Berlin uraufgeführt worden.[26] Dieses außerordentliche Stück hat eine nicht unbedeutende Vorgeschichte, die bei dem großen Bertolt Brecht beginnt, als er noch nicht gar so groß war:
Brecht hatte nämlich bereits ein Alexanderstück geplant in seiner Münchener Zeit, als er einer Aufführung von *Alexander der Große. Schauspiel*, gedruckt Leipzig 1917, beiwohnen konnte. Der Autor, Max Pulver, ein schweizer Expressionist, Autor von mehreren Dramen

---

[24] Eine Kurzbiographie und Darstellung seiner politischen Ideen leistet Vanessa Conze (2004).
[25] Jan Assmann (2005).
[26] Vgl. Hans Mayer (1977), hier S. 316–318. Die Zitate folgen der Erstausgabe.

und des Romans *Himmelpfortgasse* (1926) ist später der Begründer der wissenschaftlichen Graphologie in Zürich geworden, wo er auch den ersten Lehrstuhl für diese Wissenschaft erhielt. Im September 1917 schreibt Brecht an seinen Freund Caspar Neher: «Ich schreibe ein Theaterstück *Alexander und seine Soldaten*. Alexander der Große. Ohne Jamben. Und seine Soldaten ohne Kothurne. Ich will, daß es unsterblich wird.»[27] Die Prosa-Fassung ist Zeichen für den Gestus seiner Planungen: Die Soldaten kennen ihren Alexander nur dem Hören nach; langweilen sich am Hindukusch, weil sie nicht die Spur eines Sinnes für ihr Tun sehen. Alexander wird als verhaßter Diktator imaginiert, der nicht mal so genau wisse, wo eigentlich die Städte liegen, die er zu erobern plant.[28] Die einzigen erhaltenen Fragmente dieses leider nicht zustandegekommenen Projekts aber sind «frühestens aus den Jahren 1922/23» und «im Frühling oder Sommer 1924 entstanden»[29], also erst seit Brechts enger Zusammenarbeit mir Arnolt Bronnen. Zu dessen furiosen *Vatermord* – das Skandalstück wird 1922 uraufgeführt – hat Brecht die Regieanweisungen geschrieben. 1923 verfassen sie gemeinsam das Drehbuch zum Film *S.O.S. Insel der Tränen*. Der Bruch zwischen den beiden so gegensätzlichen, sich aber stark anziehenden Schriftstellern vollzieht sich erst 1929, als Bronnen sich endgültig zur nationalsozialistischen Ideologie bekennt, indem er gegen seinen jüdischen Vater gerichtlich seine ‹arische Herkunft› bestätigen läßt und eine rechte Skandalrede auf der Tagung *Dichtung und Rundfunk* in Kassel hält.[30] Im folgenden Jahr ist Bronnen einer der Anführer der Krawallmacher, die Thomas Manns *Deutsche Ansprache* im Berliner Beethovensaal stören. Das bringt ihm die Freundschaft Goebbels ein, die aber nur zwei Jahre währt, da Bronnen sich zwar ideologietreu verhält – davon zeugen sein Hörspiel *Mussolini* (1932) und sein «Gelöbnis treuester Gefolgschaft» für Hitler 1933 –, sich aber so zu einem Favoriten von Goebbels parteiinternem Widersacher Alfred Rosenberg macht. So wird Bronnen (1939/40) von Goebbels aus der Reichsschrifttumskammer ausgeschlossen und für politisch unzuverlässig erklärt. Trotz zeitweiliger Wiederaufnahme und seiner Tätigkeit als Verfasser von Propagandaschriften für das Auswärtige Amt wird das Publikationsverbot wiederholt und er während des Krieges 1943 und 1944 wegen Wehrkraftzersetzung inhaftiert. Das führte den ursprünglich enthusiastischen Rechten in die Widerstandsgruppen der Linken und Ende des Krieges in die KPÖ. Seit 1948 versucht Bronnen über Johannes R. Becher in der DDR Fuß zu fassen, wo er 1955 als Theater-, Film- und Fernsehkritiker bei der *Berliner Zeitung* aufgenommen wird und auch seine Kontakte zu Brecht wiederbeleben kann. Sein *Aisopos*-Roman erscheint und er avanciert schnell zum Autor des parteitreuen *Aufbau-Verlags*.

Nach diesem Exkurs über die ideologischen Verstrickungen des Autors und sein Weiterwirken in der Nachkriegszeit zurück in das Jahr 1926, zur Uraufführung des Stückes. Bron-

---

[27] Bertolt Brecht, *Alexander und seine Soldaten*, in: ders., Werke. Große komm. Berliner und Frankfurter Ausgabe, hg. v. Werner Hecht, Jan Knopf, Wener Mittenzwei und Klaus-Detlef Müller, Bd. 10, Berlin, Weimar und Frankfurt am Main 1997, S. 1085f.
[28] Ebd., S. 319f.
[29] Ebd., S. 1085. Reflexe finden sich in Brechts Lyrik, so in den 1935 entstandenen *Fragen eines lesenden Arbeiters*, die er im dritten Teil der *Svendborger Gedichte* 1939 veröffentlicht hat (Bertold Brecht, Gedichte 2: Sammlungen 1938–1956, hg. v. Jan Knopf, Berlin und Weimar, Frankfurt am Main 1988 [Werke. Große kommentierte Berliner und Frankfurter Ausgabe, 12], S. 29). Der lesende Arbeiter fragt illusionslos «Der junge Alexander eroberte Indien. / Er allein?» (V 15f.)
[30] Zu Bronnens Verwicklungen in der NS-Zeit vgl. Friedbert Aspetsberger (1998). Aspetsberger widmet dem «Ostpolzug» in seiner über 800 Seiten fassenden Biographie Bronnens nur wenig Raum: ders. (1995), S. 344–352.

nen hatte Jahr für Jahr mit neuen Theaterskandalen für Furore in der Hauptstadt gesorgt: 1922 *Vatermord*, 1924 *Die katalaunische Schlacht*, 1925 folgen seine Verherrlichung deutscher Freikorpsaktionen in Oberschlesien in *Rheinische Rebellen* und *Exzesse* – ein Stück, das seinen Titel zu Recht trägt. Es spielt in Bozen und Stralsund während der Währungskrise. Die Personen, Schieber und Schwindler, sind selbst Zeichen für die Entwertung jeglicher Werte, allerdings ohne moralische Abscheu: Slapstick-Komik steht neben Haßtiraden gegen Italiener und Antisemitismus. Der *Ostpolzug*[31] knüpft an manche Motive seiner früheren Theaterstücke an: Entwertung bisheriger «altväterlicher» Kulturwerte, die Vorstellung vom Primat des jungen Tatmenschen, dessen Gewaltnatur neue Welten öffne. Bronnen hat zu einem genialen Theatertrick gegriffen, um das Leben und die Geschichte des jugendlichen Helden und kalten Eroberers Alexander zum mythischen Muster für die junge Generation seiner Gegenwart zu gestalten: Es wechseln neun sprachlich durch Wortwiederholungen miteinander verschränkte Szenen – man kann fast sagen: Bilder – aus Alexanders Zug in den Osten mit solchen, die eine moderne Mount-Everest-Besteigung zum Thema haben. 1924 war gerade eine britische Himalaya-Expedition tragisch gescheitert. Der moderne Alexander trifft im Laufe des Stückes (66) auf einen Gedenkstein. Die Erstbesteigung glückte dem Neuseeländer Hillary erst am 29. Mai 1953. Auch der Protagonist aus der Gegenwart heißt Alexander und wird von demselben Schauspieler dargestellt. Es ist der einzige Schauspieler des Stückes, der monologisiert oder zu nur gedachten, aber nicht auf der Bühne präsenten Personen spricht. Die Rezensenten der Uraufführung waren sich bei der Bewertung des Stücks nicht einig, aber alle feierten die Regieleistung des Intendanten Leopold Jeßner, der ein bewundertes Bühnenbild von dem Architekten Walter Röhrig bauen ließ und in rasch aufeinander folgenden Schnitten alle technischen Mittel (Telephon, Autos als Requisiten auf der Bühne, Lautsprecher) von Theater und Kino (Leinwandprojektionen) eingesetzt hat. Beifall erntete gerade auch die engagierte Leistung des Schauspielers, nämlich Fritz Kortners, der mit diesem Erfolgsstück eine Gastspielreise durch das Deutsche Reich unternahm.[32]

Beide Alexander des Monodramas sind Gewaltmenschen ohne Gewissen, getrieben nur von einem Ziel: dem Ostpol. Der antike Alexander ist in der ersten Szene ein noch verängstigter Jugendlicher, der ohne große Rührung die Ermordung seines Vaters beobachtet – selbstverständlich ohne einzuschreiten. Am Schluß der Szene bewährt sich zum ersten Mal die Gewissenlosigkeit der Macht:

> *Dort, wo Licht war, sitzt mein Vater, mein Kopf, arm, zerschlagen, weiß, lehnt sich an ihn, er streicht über ihn, ich höre seine tiefe Stimme, mein Kind sagt er,*
> *Ich höre es, mein Kind, ich höre es, ein Stein, ein Felsen hört es, seine tiefe Stimme, mein Kind sagt er, mein Kind, jetzt, jetzt, mein Kind sagt er,*
> *Jetzt, – (16f.)*

Die Regieanweisung schaltet einen Lichtwechsel ein von dunkel zu hell, ein Todesschrei erfolgt, man hört Stimmen im Palast, Alexander hebt sein Schwert: «Jetzt bin ich König geworden.» (17) Dieser Amoralismus im Angesicht des Todes und Menschenleids setzt sich erbarmungslos fort. Dieser Alexander tötet jeden irgend bedrohlichen Schatten, egal wer es ist: Hauptsache er ist tot. In dem im Stück dargestellten Fall war es sein getreuer Kleitos,

---

[31] Zur Charakterisierung des Textes vgl. auch Michael Krüger (1989), S. 105–110.
[32] Günther Rühle (1988), S. 678–683.

den Alexander nach der historischen Überlieferung im Alkoholrausch während eines seiner cholerischen Zornesausbrüche getötet haben soll. Hier, in Bronnens Stück, wird dieser Mord noch viel weniger motiviert. Alexander tötet, weil er Alexander ist. Er weiß noch nicht einmal, daß derjenige, den er getötet hat, Kleitos ist. Verräter werden hingerichtet ohne Milde. Die Namen der Gemordeten kann er sich nicht merken und verwechselt seine verbliebenen Getreuen, als sein Heer schon längst wieder in die makedonische Heimat zurück will. Alexanders Lebensmaxime aber ist:

> *Das Lebendige lebt nur, solange es angreift,*
> *Taten geschehen nur auf Vormärschen,*
> *Und die Größe der Ereignisse beruht nur auf Unrast.*
> *Von Stunden lebend, die wir dem Schlafe entrissen,*
> *Mordet Umkehr uns alle. Rückmarsch zerlöst dieses Heer.*
> *Muskeln und Sehnen sind Produkte der Anspannung. Um nach Hause zu gehen, brauch man*
> *nur Knochen. Wenn ihr Skelette haben wollt, tut euren Willen. Wollt ihr Heere befehlen, tut*
> *den meinen.* (47 f.)

Dieser Amoralität entspricht auch der moderne Alexander, der in seiner ersten Szene «Der gordische Knoten» ebenfalls über Leichen geht: Er ist Kellner in einer türkischen Kneipe, wo ihn ein vermögender Himalaya-Reisender als ortskundigen Führer gewinnen will. Alexander greift allerdings erst zu, als dieser Reisende tot über einem Bierglas zusammensackt und seine volle Brieftasche auf dem Kneipentisch liegt. Es ist gerade der moderne Alexander, der vom «gordischen Knoten, der seinerzeit Asien aufrollte bis Babylon» (21), spricht. «[A]lle Wege der Welt und alle Möglichkeiten aus Hirn und Händen haben sich dicht verschlungen in einen chaotischen Knoten.» (22) Der gordische Knoten dieser Gegenwart ist das Chaos der Welt Mitte der 20er Jahre und dieser Knoten ist nicht, nicht mehr!, zerschlagen und stellt damit die Aufgabe des modernen Alexanders dar. Der unmotiviert sterbende Reisende hat ihn wieder zu sich selbst gebracht:

> *Ich habe den Namen Alexander, von irgendwoher,*
> *Ich habe ein Leben, Träume, Wünsche, von irgendwoher,*
> *Ich sehe meine Augen, meine Hände gelegentlich an,*
> *Vieles scheint mir bekannt, anderes springt mich plötzlich meinen Nacken an,*
> *Wild tobt der Kampf aus dem Dunkeln um mich und alle meine Siege dauern Momente.* (24)

Der moderne Alexander weiß von sich, nicht nur er selbst, sondern im mythischen Sinne auch noch der andere, der antike Alexander zu sein. Dies zu erfüllen, macht er sich auf zu seinem Ostpol, dem Mount Everest. Er mißbraucht dafür Geldmittel, Sachmittel und Menschen, die er in den Tod treibt, ohne sich darum zu scheren. In einer Szene «Der Sieg von Kabul» hält er seinen Financiers eine atemlose Rede, um sie weiter auszupressen. Auf einer «Autokolonne durch Nepal» beobachtet er ungerührt, wie Vorräte, Lastautos und Helfer von einer abschüssigen Gebirgsstraße in die Tiefe stürzen. Er stößt selbst kistenweise Vorräte von seinem Laster, um besser voranzukommen. Gegen die Naturgewalten hilft nur: «Die letzte Chance ist Bewußtsein.» (60)

In der folgenden siebten Szene «Die Shimsha-Gletscher Katastrophe» wird der Rhythmus des Stückes geändert, indem nicht der antike, sondern wieder der moderne Alexander gezeigt wird. Dieser Rhythmuswechsel leitet den Schluß des Dramas ein. In einer furios zu inszenierenden Szene, stürzt Alexander am Seil in die Tiefe, verliert seine Helfer, bleibt aber selbst am Leben:

*Wäre ich nicht [ohne Seil] abgestürzt? Ich meine, Sie zehn toten Herren da unten sollten sich
das überlegen,
Ehe Sie mit Vorwürfen kommen, die Sie nicht mehr retten,
Mich aber entschieden verbittern. Ich werde an diesem Seil,
Das ich einfach nicht losließ, während Sie es losließen, meine Herren Toten,
Mich langsam in die Höhe bewegen, trotz ihres Einspruches* (67).

Die Erfüllungsgehilfen seiner Bestimmung mögen zugrunde gehen; ihn treibt es weiter zu seinem Ziel: dem Gipfel. Der Szenenvergleich zwischen des antiken Alexanders Tod und des modernen Alexanders Schluß macht die Zielrichtung dieses Stückes überdeutlich. Während der antike Alexander vergeblich befiehlt, daß er lebe und am Ende eingestehen muß «ein armselige[r] Mann», ein «Haufen Fleisch», «ein Nichts» (75) zu sein, hält die Szenenüberschrift für den neuen Alexander – bei der Inszenierung auf die Bühne projiziert – den «Triumph der Möglichkeit» bereit. Damit ist er ganz im Sinne von Bronnens Lebenskampf gegen die alte Generation und ihren konservativen Traditionsbezug nicht nur eine bloße Wiederholung, sondern eine mythische Steigerung des Alten. Bronnens Traditionsverhalten – und nichs anderes ist ja Arbeit am Mythos – richtet sich auf die Wertsteigerung der modernen technischen Welt der jüngeren Generation durch ihren Triumph über das Vorgegebene, das er gleichwohl als mythisch gegeben akzeptiert. Erst auf der Grundlage dieser Akzeptanz kann die Leistung der jungen Generation als Triumph über das Vorangegangene wirkungsvoll konzipiert werden. Der moderne Alexander ist an seinem Ziel, fast ganz erfroren zwar, kaum noch in der Lage zu atmen, aber auf dem Gipfel, seinem Ostpol. Was tut er? Auf seinem Berg zückt er ein Buch wie einst Petrarca und übertrifft damit wieder ein für das humanistische Bildungsideal paradigmatisches Vorbild der Kultur der älteren Generation. Denn sein Buch ist nicht das Buch eines anderen aus der Vorvergangenheit, den er verherrlicht; es ist sein eigenes «Tourenbuch» (80), das er vollendet:

*Das ist der neunte Juni, in der Stunde
Meiner Geburt vor dreiunddreißig Jahren
Auf dem Gipfel des Mount Everest, 8840 Meter,
Mit meiner Nase noch einen Meter darüber.* (80)

Dieser Alexander triumphiert nicht nur über die schrecklichen Gewalten der Natur und ist zudem fest davon überzeugt, wieder zurückzukommen zu den Lebenden (80, 81). Er triumphiert über Alexander den Großen, der am 10. Juni 323 mit 33 Jahren starb. Aber er hat auch das Schicksal besiegt:

*Das war der Ostpol, das war die unbesiegbare Erde,
Hier, wo ich stehe, Religionen unter meinen Füßen,
Zwar im Sturm, zwar unsicher selbst der nächsten Minuten,
Aber doch etwas höher, als es mir bestimmt war,
Doch etwas weiter, doch etwas stärker, doch etwas ewiger* (80f.).

«Das war» Asien; es ist besiegt vom modernen Vertreter des Westens. Asiens Gläubigkeit, von der Bloch sich seine Utopie im Europa nach dem Ersten Weltkrieg verspricht, liegt unter den Füßen dieses doch eher spenglerischen Alexander. Bevor der Vorhang fällt, ruft er gegen den «schwarzen Himmel»:

So geschehen die Taten, die Ereignisse, langsam,
Manche Wünsche werden Jahrtausende alt,
Aber unaufhaltsam wachsen die Organe ins Unsichtbare hinein,
Und der Gewinn der Unsterblichkeit ist nahe. (81)

Mit dieser Schlußprophezeiung wendet sich Bronnen letztlich an sein Publikum, das die letzte Szene, wie es in der Regieanweisung (80) heißt, in der Perspektive Alexanders, also vom Gipfel nach unten, verfolgen, ja miterleben soll. Ihre Aufgabe ist es, was so nahe ist, endlich zu erfüllen, nach Tausenden von Jahren, nämlich Europa und Asien gewaltsam zusammenzuzwingen – auf welcher symbolischen Ebene auch immer. Denn soweit ist der zur nationalsozialistischen Ideologie neigende Bronnen noch nicht. Im Gegenteil ist die bloße militärische Eroberung des Ostens eine Tat der zu übertreffenden Alten. Auf jeden Fall aber war Bert Brecht im Irrtum, der meinte, daß der «Ostpolzug das bisher exponierteste Drama [sei], das das epische Theater aufzubauen versuchte.»[33] Denn es war ja gerade konstitutiv für dieses Konzept, daß neben der Aufhebung des aristotelischen Zeit-Konzepts für das Drama eine epische Distanz zu den handelnden Figuren hergestellt werden solle. Bronnen aber gibt Identifikationsangebote, die er gerade auch hinsichtlich ihrer Wertvorstellungen affirmiert.[34] Anders als Brecht, der in seinem Alexander-Drama das Soldatenheer, also das Kollektiv, in den Mittelpunkt stellen wollte, sind es hier nietzscheanische Gewaltsnaturen, ist es der Einzelne Tatmensch, dem das Kollektiv folgen soll – in diesem Monodrama zugespitzt auf einen einzigen Schauspieler.

2.) Hans Baumann

Was bei Bronnen noch eine symbolische Übersteigerung der menschlichen Natur über ein mythisch gegebenes Schicksal ist, wird bei dem knapp 20 Jahre später geborenen und damit einer noch jüngeren Generation angehörenden Hans Baumann wieder auf den Boden der militärischen Konkretheit zurückgeführt. Ich komme damit zu meinem zweiten Beispiel: Hans Baumanns *Alexander*, gedruckt Jena 1941.

Der ehemalige Volksschullehrer und Hitlerjugendführer Hans Baumann[35] wurde 1934 zur nationalsozialistischen Reichsjugendführung nach Berlin berufen, wo er in verschiedenen Institutionen tätig war. Baumann hat zahllose Liederbücher für die Hitlerjugend verfaßt – Titel wie *Macht keinen Lärm* (1933), *Unser Trommelbube. Neue Lieder in Wort und Weise* (1934) und *Horch auf, Kamerad* (1936) zeugen von ihrem Charakter. Berüchtigt ist das HJ- und SA-Lied *Es zittern die morschen Knochen*, das mit seinem Refrain «Wir werden weiter marschieren / Wenn alles in Scherben fällt, / denn heute da hört uns Deutschland / Und morgen die ganze Welt» ab etwa 1934 zum berühmtesten nationalsozialistischen Lied avancierte, das in allen Organisationen der Partei gesungen wurde. Im Zweiten Weltkrieg gab er im Auftrag des Oberkommandos der Wehrmacht das Soldatenliederbuch *Morgen marschieren wir* (1939) heraus. Auch seine weiteren Lieder- und Gedichtbücher verdeut-

---

[33] Zitiert nach Rühle (1988), S. 678; vgl. auch Krüger (1989), S. 110–112.
[34] Es handelt sich auch hier sowohl konzeptionell als auch in den konkreten Bildern und Handlungsorten des Stückes um «Verhaltenslehren der Kälte»: Helmut Lethen (1994); zu Bronnens wenig später veröffentlichtem Roman *O.S.* von 1929 vgl. ebd., S. 262–267.
[35] Reinhart Müller (2001).

lichen sein propagandistisches Profil: *Vaterland, wir kommen* (1941), *Dafür kämpfen wir* (1942). Seine Geschichtsbücher und Reden dienen denselben Zwecken: *Heldengedenktag 1940 im Schiller-Theater zu Berlin, Das Reich und der Osten. Ein Blick in die deutsche Geschichte* (1942), *Der Retter Europas. Zum 20. April 1942* – dem Geburtstag Hitlers.

Sein in fünfhebigen Jamben, Chorliedern und anderen Gestaltungsformen der griechischen Tragödie verfaßtes Alexanderdrama ist nicht das erste Theaterstück Baumanns. Auch in diesem Schaffensbereich zeigt sich sein nationalsozialistisches Profil: *Rüdiger von Bechelaren. Das Passauer Nibelungenspiel* ist 1939 aufgeführt worden und später folgen *Ermanerich* (1944) und *Der Kreterkönig* (1944). Hans Baumanns *Alexander* verbindet die pathetisch-klassizistische Antikerezeption des Nationalsozialismus und dessen Führerkult mit einer erneuten propagandistisch gemeinten Hinwendung an den Soldaten. Denn Baumann sucht sich als Gegenstand seines Stückes ausgerechnet den historisch durch Arrian, Plutarch und Curtius Rufus recht gut belegten Soldatenaufstand der Makedonen aus: Die Soldaten sind bereits auf dem Indienfeldzug und müde, sich immer weiter von ihrer Heimat zu entfernen und statt dessen immer weiter in den Osten vorzudringen, um in wilden Meeren zu ertrinken, in Wüsten zu verdursten oder gegen ‹Barbaren› zu kämpfen, die nichts besitzen, was sie haben wollten.[36] Doch die Leitfigur der Soldaten, der Makedone Nearch, spricht den Tenor des gesamten Stückes bereits im ersten Dialog aus: «Seit Alexander Makedonien lenkt, / ist seine Spur die mächtigere Heimat.» (8) Auf alle Bedenken eines Persers vor den Widrigkeiten der vor ihnen liegenden Wüste antwortet er: «vor ihm [Alexander] verstummt die feindliche Natur. / Er kam, zu lehren, was ein Mensch vermag.» (10) Alexander ist der Inbegriff eines gewaltigen Tatmenschen, der mächtiger ist als jede menschenfeindliche Natur. «Er lehrt die Völker Freiheit im Gehorsam» (12), schwärmt Nearch. Sogar der Perser verehrt seinen neuen König, denn seine «Liebe [gilt] dem, der Asien weckte.» (11) Der große Europäer, als der Alexander gilt, muß kommen und Asien erobern, damit es zu sich selbst kommt. Den makedonischen Soldaten, die als Chor pathetisch-wehmütige Heimat-Lieder singen, hält Nearch entgegen: «Laßt diesem Flecken Erde einen Frühling / erstehn durch den Gehorsam eurer Waffen! / Erschafft euch Heimat!» (17 f.) «Ahnt Makedonien in des Königs Antlitz» (19), «Heimat pflanzt er an entfernte Küsten.» (20) Erst in der zweiten Szene sieht man Alexander selbst, der eherne Sätze spricht: «Nicht für ein Land erobern wir die Erde, die wirre Welt gewinnen wir der Ordnung.» (24) «Uns steht der Tod im Weg, daß wir uns prüfen» und «mit unsern Waffen warben wir uns Freunde», «Die Tat versöhnt.» (25) Auf Verlustmeldungen seines Getreusten, Hephaistions, spricht er: «Die Wüste brach das Heer, das Meer die Flotte, / der König steht und wird sie neu erschaffen.» (27). Gewalt wird in einer Art Kriegerapotheose verherrlicht zu einem vermeintlich naturüberwindenden und durch Unterwerfung Gemeinschaft schaffenden Element, das in übernatürlicher Weise nur dem Führer ganz und gar zu Gebote steht.

In den nächsten Szenen sieht das Publikum Verrat übende Heeresführer und junge und alte Soldaten im Zwiespalt zwischen Gefolgschaft und Verrat auf der Bühne. Wie bei den antiken Historikern schafft Baumanns Alexander in wenigen strahlenden Auftritten Heeresführer strafende und gegenüber den Soldaten milde waltende Gerechtigkeit. In der vor-

---

[36] Diese Sujetwahl hat dazu geführt, daß Baumann eine kritische Haltung zum Krieg oder doch eine Position zugeschrieben wird, die Hitlers Verherrlichung zunehmend relativiere: vgl. z. B. Jay W. Baird (1990), bes. S. 168–170. Die hier vorliegende Analyse sieht dafür keinen Anlaß. Bairds Studie stellt aber die gründlichste Darstellung insbesondere der in der Öffentlichkeit präsenten nationalsozialistischen Literatur dar.

letzten Szene «vor dem Königspalast / Mitternacht» begegnet Alexander dann einem Chor von Verstorbenen und künftigen Toten, die die mythische Wiederkehr der Taten Alexanders in eine unbestimmte, aber immerwährende Zukunft aussprechen: «Wir sind die Heere, die dein Beispiel führt»; «[w]ir sind die Völker, die dein Ruf erweckt.» «Wir sind die Kommenden, die du erschaffst.» (144) «Ihr Werdenden, erfüllt, was ich begonnen!» (145), ruft Alexander ihnen entgegen und bestätigt damit die mythische Denkform von dem sich wiederholenden Rhythmus der Zeit: Geschichte vollziehe sich in der Wiederholung und Steigerung vorgegebener Muster. Die Geister der noch kommenden Geschlechter – natürlich ist in Baumanns Perspektive die Gegenwart des nationalsozialistischen Deutschlands gemeint – bestätigen diese Kultur der Gewalt: «Das Leid birgt Zukunft, Opfertod ist Saat.» «Unsterblichkeit erschafft die Mannestat.» (146) Alexanders letzte Worte in diesem Stück wiederholen diese Lehre von Gewaltsnaturen und Opferbereitschaft für eine Tat, die vermeintlich Ewigkeit schaffe:

> *Sie, die das Schicksal*
> *heitern Gesichts*
> *vor das Schwert*
> *ihrer Liebe bannen,*
> *führen das irrende*
> *Menschengeschlecht.*
> *[...]*
> *Leid ist die Morgen-*
> *gabe der Götter.*
> *Sie entbehren*
> *das glühende Glück,*
> *opfernd Verhängnis*
> *zu überwinden.*
> *Ewigkeit schafft*
> *nur der hoffende Mensch.* (148 f.)

In diesen Metren aus Goethes *Faust*, II. Teil, formuliert sich die Schicksalsgläubigkeit der nationalsozialistischen Ideologie ebenso, wie der Glaube, daß der opferbereite Tatmensch für die Ewigkeit schaffe. Damit endet auch das Stück, in dem Nearch, der zweite Held des Dramas, das letzte Wort hat: «Hier hat ein Mensch das Rettende getan. / Er brach den künftigen Geschlechtern Bahn, / daß sie es wagen, ewig zu beginnen.» Der treueste Soldat der Makedonen spricht mit Reimen wieder aus Goethes *Faust* den mythischen Grundgedanken nochmals aus. Welthistorische Taten – die Eroberung Asiens durch den Europäer – vollenden Geschichte; Taten, die immer wieder wiederholt werden müssen, um den Mythos zu erfüllen.

Trotz dieser Ideologietreue, kann man sich gut vorstellen, daß die Reichsdramaturgie unter Rainer Schlösser, der direkt Joseph Goebbels unterstellt war, Bedenken gegen die Aufführung des Stückes am 14. Juni 1941 im Preußischen Staatstheater Berlin hatte. Ein Soldatenaufstand in Kriegszeiten war trotz der Führerverherrlichung nicht populär. Die längst geplante, aber strengstens geheim zu haltenden Invasionspläne gegen Rußland warteten nur noch auf den Führerbefehl, der acht Tage später erfolgte. Doch es war niemand Geringeres als Gustaf Gründgens, der sich mit Feuer und Flamme für dieses Stück einsetzte, so daß er das Stück nicht nur inszenierte, sondern gleich selbst den Alexander-Part «wie eine griechische Statue» mit «geschlossene[r] Energie, Zucht, Bescheidenheit» gespielt hat.[37] Er soll über sieben Wochen lang mit Baumann die Uraufführung vorausgeplant haben, die unter Mitwirkung von Mathias Wiemann, Lina Karstens, Lola Müthel und Bernhard Minetti – also gleich mehreren Starschauspielern des Staatstheaters – ein großer Erfolg war: Gründgens soll etwa 25 Vorhänge Applaus bekommen haben.[38] Baumann wurde u. a. für dieses Stück zusammen mit Adolf Bartels in Hamburg der Dietrich-Eckart-Preis verliehen und am 1. September 1942 erhielt er das ‹Kriegsverdienstkreuz 2. Klasse ohne Schwerter›.[39]

Als dann acht Tage später der Rußlandfeldzug begann, habe Gründgens das Stück abgesetzt, «weil da Parallelen auftauchten, die mir stärker als das Stück zu sein schienen».[40] Ob Gründgens tatsächlich selbst das Stück abgesetzt hat oder auf Druck der Reichsdramaturgie, kann hier ohne weitere Quellen nicht erörtert werden. Wie seine überlieferte Aussage genau zu verstehen ist (als Kritik gegen das Stück, als politische Rücksicht oder als emphatische Bewertung des Rußlandfeldzuges), ebenfalls nicht. Doch wird an Baumanns Stück, an seiner Aufführung durch Gründgens und schließlich auch an den Gründen für die Absetzung vom Spielplan ersichtlich, daß Hitlers Rußlandfeldzug mit Alexanders Eroberungen Asiens parallel gesehen wird. Freilich bleibt es in nationalsozialistischer Sicht die Aufgabe, erfolgreicher, im Sinne Spenglers ‹napoleonischer› als Alexanders Nachfolger Napoleon selbst zu sein: Alexanders Ostreich zerfällt und er hat es gerade nicht kulturell oder gar rassistisch ausrotten, sondern er hat eine Vermischung der Kulturen des antiken Griechenlands mit den Kulturen der Perser und Inder erreichen wollen. In Hitlers Geschichtsideologie muß es das Germanische sein, das seinen Weltherrschaftsanspruch legitimiert und erst eigentlich unter Beweis stellt, wenn es den asiatischen Pol des Kontinents, seinen entscheidenden Machtfaktor, bezwingt. Der gordische Knoten, den dieser greuliche Wiedergänger eines mythisch verstandenen Alexander zerschlagen will, um seine Ideologie von einer germanischen Weltherrschaft zu bestätigen, liegt in der Sowjetunion Stalins. Alexander ist eine zu übertreffende historische Exempelfigur, die eine mythische Denkform bestätigt: Zwischen den antagonistischen Polen Europa und Asien bewegt sich die geschichtsträchtige Herrschaft über die Welt; eine Herrschaft, die stets auf Eroberung des gegnerischen Pols beruht.

Hans Baumanns Karriere war nicht zu Ende: Er nahm als Leutnant am Zweiten Weltkrieg teil, kam in russische Gefangenschaft, wo er sich vom Nationalsozialismus zu distanzieren begonnen haben soll, und hatte das Glück, 1945 freigelassen zu werden. Vielleicht dokumentiert sich in seinen zahlreichen Übersetzungen aus dem Russischen (Achmatova, weitere russische Lyrik und russische Kinderbücher) tatsächlich zumindest Reue gegenüber den Schandtaten des Hitlerreiches gegen Rußland. Denn eine öffentliche Kontroverse um sein Antike-Drama *Im Zeichen der Fische*, das in Unkenntnis über den anonym gebliebenen Autor 1959 von der Berliner Freien Volksbühne mit dem Gerhart-Hauptmann-Preis ausgezeichnet wurde, zeugt von seiner prekären Nachkriegsgesinnung:[41] Diocletians Massenmorde an christliche Rebellen werden von den Schergen mit Führergehorsam vollzogen. Die Täter werden obendrein entschuldigt damit, daß die Opfer den Täter «in die Enge getrieben» hätten. Trotzdem avanciert Baumann in der ehemaligen BRD zum prämierten

---

[37] So schrieb es der Dichter Hans Hömberg, in dessen «Kirschen für Rom» Gründgens am 5. 10. 1940 den Lukull spielte; zitiert nach Peter Michalzik (1999), S. 111.
[38] Baird (1990), S. 168.
[39] Boguslaw Drewniak (1983), S. 160.
[40] Michalzik (1999), S. 111.
[41] Vgl. dazu Marcel [Reich-Ranicki] (1962).

Jugendbuchautor, dessen Titel unzählbar sind: Bekannt sind auch heute noch *Der Sohn des Columbus* (1951), *Ich zog mit Hannibal* (1960), *Flügel für Ikaros* (1978) und natürlich *Der große Alexanderzug* (1967).[42] Ein Jugendbuch, das von einem Jungen erzählt, der den Alexanderzug nach Asien begleitet.[43]

IV. Epilog: Ende der Geschichte oder Mythen gehen immer weiter

Wie nahe es gelegen hat, Hitler als mythische Personifikation oder Steigerung Alexanders und Napoleons zu sehen, zeigt auch eine freilich kritisch distanzierende Erzählung von Arno Schmidt: *Alexander oder Was ist Wahrheit* ist bereits 1949 entstanden, aber erst 1953 veröffentlicht worden.[44]

Ein junger Grieche macht sich dort auf die Reise nach Babylon, um sein Idol Alexander den Großen zu sehen. Auf einem Schiff trifft er eine Theatergruppe und schließt sich ihnen an. Auch hier gibt es deutliche Anleihen bei Goethe, in diesem Fall freilich beim Theaterroman *Wilhelm Meisters Lehrjahre*. Die Erzählung ist im Stile Wielands in Form eines historisierenden Tagebuchs gefaßt und enthält die Tag für Tag voranschreitende Desillusionierung des anfangs für Alexander begeisterten Griechen, der damit implizit auch zur allegorischen Personifikation der Hitler verherrlichenden, aber entsetzlich ahnungslosen oder eben ahnungslos sein wollenden Nachkriegsdeutschen gerät. Solche Analogien werden in der konsequent historisierenden Erzählperspektive nie explizit. Aber sie stellen sich ein durch den desillusionierenden Gestus der wiedergegebenen Gespräche, die Punkt um Punkt der Alexanderbiographie von Alexanders Verhältnis zu Aristoteles, seiner Machtergreifung, seinen militärischen Erfolgen und Städtegründungen bis hin zu seinen Motiven des Handelns aufgreifen und auf ein Charakterbild der bloßen Selbstsucht reduzieren. In dieser Sicht hat ein skrupelloser Wahnsinniger gemordet, sinnlose Irrfahrten unternommen und Taten vollbracht, die am Ende folgenlos bleiben würden. Die Geschichten über Alexander seien pure Propaganda oder Märchen.[45] Am Ende in Babylon angekommen, erfährt er bald, daß Alexander gestorben ist.

Doch der Mythos ist damit nicht gestorben. Im Zusammenhang mit den neuen Ost-West-Konflikten der ehemaligen Alliierten schreibt der traditionsorientierte Ernst Jünger[46] wieder von den welthistorischen Polen, zwischen denen sich Geschichte bewege:

---

[42] Vgl. auch Peter Bamm, *Alexander oder Die Verwandlung der Welt*, Zürich 1965. Zu Baumanns Wechsel vom HJ-Dichter zum erfolgreichen Jugendbuchautor der BRD: Marcel Reich-Ranicki (1965), S. 63–69; Winfred Kaminski (1987), S. 165–184.

[43] Damit folgt Baumann Zdenko von Kraft, *Alexanderzug. Vom Menschen zum Mythos*, Berlin 1940. Der Sudeten-Deutsche hat zahlreiche historische Romane und Theaterstücke geschrieben. Er war seit 1936 Archivar des Richard-Wagner-Archivs in Bayreuth. Sein Alexanderroman ist aus der Perspektive eines Erzähler-Ichs geschrieben, das vom Rand des griechischen Reiches in der Zentrale der makedonischen Macht aufgenommen worden ist. Die Tendenz des Romans ist nicht durchweg positiv: die Orientalisierung Alexanders führt zu seiner Entartung.

[44] Arno Schmidt, Bargfelder Ausgabe, Werkgruppe 1: Romane, Erzählungen, Gedichte, Juvenilia, Bd. 1, Zürich 1987, S. 77–114.

[45] Vgl. bes. ebd., S. 98–100 und S. 108–113.

[46] Ernst Jünger, *Der gordische Knoten*, Frankfurt am Main 1953. Vgl. z. B. auch Franz Altheim, *Alexander und Asien. Geschichte eines geistigen Erbes*, Tübingen 1953, S. 3: «Alexander und Asien verbindet eine echte Polarität: geschieden und doch vereint, wesenhaft anders und doch mit allen Fasern einander zustrebend.»

> ‹Ost und West›: diese Begegnung im Weltgeschehen ist nicht nur ersten Ranges, sondern beansprucht einen Rang für sich. Sie gibt die geschichtliche Hauptrichtung, die Achse, die sich nach der Sonnenbahn bestimmt. Aufleuchtend mit dem frühesten Lichte, spinnen sich ihre Muster bis in unsere Tage fort. Die Völker treten mit stets neuer Spannung auf die alte Bühne und in die alte Handlung ein. (5)
> Wer den gordischen Knoten zu lösen wußte, dem war nach alter Weissagung die Weltherrschaft bestimmt. [...] Sie [Alexanders Tat] ist das Sinnbild aller großen Begegnungen zwischen Europa und Asien. In ihr erscheint ein geistiges Prinzip, das eine neue und kürzere Verfügung über Zeit und Raum zu treffen weiß. (10)
> Der gordische Knoten hat, wie alle großen Bilder, sein Stets-Gegenwärtiges. Als Sinnbild der Erdmacht und ihrer Fesseln wird er bei jeder Begegnung zwischen Europa und Asien vorgewiesen und muß immer wieder zertrennt werden. (13)

Jünger erklärt den Konflikt des kalten Krieges mit der geschichtsmythischen Denkform von der Notwendigkeit der Wiederkehr eines scheinbar für immer gültigen Antagonismus um «Weltherrschaft». In dieser Sichtweise gibt es für «die Völker» kein Entrinnen: Sie sind gezwungen, Alexander zu folgen, «die alte Bühne» wieder zu betreten und «die alte Handlung» von neuem zu vollziehen. Aber Alexander-Darstellungen in Roman- oder Theaterform kommen erst einmal nicht mehr zustande. Der große kriegerische Eroberer des Ostens hat im Nachkriegsdeutschland keine Konjunktur mehr. Auch neue Konzepte kommen nicht mehr zum Abschluß: Als Hans Erich Nossak 1956 Harold Nicolsons Alexander-Essay übersetzte,[47] plante er ein Theaterstück, in dem Alexanders Mutter Olympias «das Heilige im Unterschied zum Sittlichen darstellen» sollte. Er folgt damit der Tradition der Alexanderhistoriker und Droysens, die in Olympias eine so furiose wie furienhafte Muttergestalt sehen, die Alexander zum Asienbezwinger gemacht habe. Nossaks Stück sollte denn auch «vor dem Aufbruch nach Asien» symbolträchtig schließen.[48]

Erst unsere Gegenwart hat wieder Verwendung für geschichtsmythisch überhöhte Konstruktionen, in denen Europa gegen Asien, Orient oder den Osten – wie auch immer die Konzeptionen lauten – ausgespielt werden. Freilich ist auch Mythen-Destruktion am Werk, wie etwa bei Gisbert Haefs; seine zweibändige Alexanderbiographie erschien 1992/93.

Mythendestruktion, das ist der wissenschaftliche Grundtenor auch dieses Beitrages: Wozu es führt, daß Europa und Asien als mythischer Antagonismus gedacht wird, ist Gegenstand der vorstehenden Ausführungen. Daß dieser Gedanke keiner wissenschaftlich gültigen Denkform, sondern einer mythischen entspringt, ist eines der Erkenntnisinteressen der Analyse des Europa-Asien-Diskurses. Mythen zu schaffen, die Europa und Asien als unentwirrbar miteinander verflochten und zum Heile der Kultur der Menschheit sich immer wieder verknüpfend darstellen, möge die Aufgabe der Mythopoeten unserer Gegenwart sein, die diese nötig hätte. Denn es wäre ein Mißverständnis, wenn Mythende-

---

[47] Harold Nicolson, *Die Kunst der Biographie und andere Essays* (*The English Sense of Humour* [1956]), übers. v. Hans Erich Nossak, Frankfurt am Main 1958; darin S. 27–50 über Alexander. Der englische Schriftsteller von Biographien und einer Diplomatiegeschichte war von 1935 bis 1945 als Politiker der National Labour Party Mitglied des Unterhauses. Seine Alexanderdarstellung bemüht sich explizit um einen nichtmythischen Grundtenor. Er bestaunt die Taten Alexanders, aber vorherrschend ist das «Gefühl von etwas Geheimnisvollem»: «Wie konnte ein so verständiger Mann so sinnlose Dinge verüben?» (S. 50)

[48] Hans Erich Nossak, *Die Tagebücher. 1943–1977*, hg. v. Gabriele Söhling, mit einem Nachwort von Norbert Miller, Bd. 1, Frankfurt am Main 1997, S. 559 (Kommentar, Bd. 2, S. 137).

struktion ein Ende von Mythen bewirken könnte. Mythen, mythische Denkformen sind anthropologische Grundkonstanten, die sich in immer neuer «Arbeit am Mythos» fortschreibt. Mythen enden nicht, sie ruhen allenfalls im kulturellen Archiv, bis sich Gemeinschaften ihrer wieder bedienen.

Literaturverzeichnis

ASPETSBERGER, Friedbert, Bürokratie und Konkurrenzen – eine Möglichkeit des (literarischen) Überlebens? Zu Arnolt Bronnen während der NS-Herrschaft, in: Macht – Literatur – Krieg. Österreichische Literatur im Nationalsozialismus, hg. v. Uwe Baur u. a., Wien, Köln, Weimar 1998 (Fazit, 2), S. 202–226.

DERS., Arnolt Bronnen. Biographie, Wien u. a. 1995 (Literatur in der Geschichte, Geschichte in der Literatur, 34).

ASSMANN, Aleida und Jan, Art. Mythos, in: Handbuch religionswissenschaftlicher Grundbegriffe, hg. v. Hubert Cancik, Burkhard Gladigow und Karl-Heinz Kohl, Bd. 4, Stuttgart, Berlin, Köln 1998, S. 179–200.

ASSMANN, Jan, Die Zauberflöte. Oper und Mysterium, München 2005.

BLANKE, Horst Walter, Historiographie als Historik, Stuttgart und Bad Cannstatt 1991 (Fundamenta Historica, 3).

DERS., Die Kritik der Alexanderhistoriker bei Heyne, Heeren, Niebuhr und Droysen. Ein Fallstudie zur Entwicklung der historisch-philologischen Methode in der Aufklärung und im Historismus, in: Storia della Storiografia 13 (1988), S. 167–186.

BAIRD, Jay W., To die for Germany. Heroes in the Nazi Pantheon, Bloomington und Indianapolis 1990.

BLUMENBERG, Hans, Wirklichkeitsbegriff und Wirkungspotential des Mythos, in: Terror und Spiel, hg. v. Manfred Fuhrmann, München 1971 (Poetik und Hermeneutik, 4), S. 11–66.

DERS., Arbeit am Mythos, Frankfurt am Main 1979.

BIRTSCH, Günter, Die Nation als sittliche Idee. Der Nationalstaatsbegriff in Geschichtsschreibung und politischer Gedankenwelt Johann Gustav Droysens, Köln und Graz 1964 (Kölner historische Abhandlungen, 10).

BREUER, Stefan, Retter des Abendlandes. Spenglerkritik von rechts, in: Jahrbuch zur Kultur und Literatur der Weimarer Republik 9 (2004), S. 165–193.

CASSIRER, Ernst, Philosophie der symbolischen Formen. Zweiter Teil: Das mythische Denken, Text und Anm. bearb. v. Claus Rosenkranz, Hamburg 2002a (Ernst Cassirer, Gesammelte Werke. Hamburger Ausgabe, 12).

DERS., Vom Mythus des Staates, übers. v. Franz Stoessl, Nachdruck der Ausg. Zürich 1949, Hamburg 2002b.

CÖLLN, Jan, Alexander als Orientale. Zur Konstruktion eines Kulturtypus für die Moderne in Jakob Wassermanns *Alexander in Babylon* (1905), in: Literaturwissenschaftliches Jahrbuch 45 (2004), S. 199–214.

CONZE, Vanessa, Richard Coudenhove-Kalergi. Umstrittener Visionär Europas, Zürich 2004 (Persönlichkeit und Geschichte, 165).

DREWNIAK, Boguslaw, Das Theater im NS-Staat. Szenarium deutscher Zeitgeschichte 1933–1945, Düsseldorf 1983.

DOROWIN, Hermann, Retter des Abendlands. Kulturkritik im Vorfeld des europäischen Faschismus, Stuttgart 1991.

ELSAGHE, Yahya, *Der Mythus von Orient und Occident* in Thomas Manns *Doktor Faustus*, in: Wirkendes Wort 55 (2005), S. 427–443.

FULDA, Daniel, Wissenschaft aus Kunst. Die Entstehung der modernen deutschen Geschichtsschreibung 1760–1850, Berlin und New York 1996 (European Cultures, 7).

JAMME, Christoph, Einführung in die Philosophie des Mythos. Band 2: Neuzeit und Gegenwart, Darmstadt 1991.

KAMINSKI, Winfred, Heroische Innerlichkeit. Studien zur Jugendliteratur vor und nach 1945, Frankfurt am Main 1987 (Jugend und Medien, 14).

KRÜGER, Michael, Vom ordnenden Subjekt zur subjektmäßigen Ordnung. Studien zu Arnolt Bronnens Dramen, Frankfurt am Main u. a. 1989 (Studien zur Deutschen Literatur des 19. und 20. Jahrhunderts, 9).

LETHEN, Helmut, Verhaltenslehren der Kälte, Lebensversuche zwischen den Kriegen, Frankfurt am Main 1994.

MAYER, Hans, Nachwort, in: Arnolt Bronnen, Stücke. Vatermord / Die Exzesse / Ostpolzug / Gloriana / Die Kette Kolin, Kronberg / Ts. 1977, S. 307–322.

MICHALZIK, Peter, Gustaf Gründgens. Der Schauspieler und die Macht, Berlin 1999.

MÜLLER, Reinhart, Art. Hans Baumann, in: Deutsches Literatur-Lexikon. Das 20. Jahrhundert. Biographisch-bibliographisches Handbuch, begr. v. Wilhelm Kosch, fortgef. v. Carl Ludwig Lang, hg. v. Konrad Feilchenfeldt, Bd. 2, München 2001, Sp. 14–18.

PEIL, Dietmar, Art. Hans Blumenberg, in: Metzler Lexikon Literatur- und Kulturtheorie. Ansätze – Personen – Grundbegriffe, hg. v. Ansgar Nünning, 2. überarb. Aufl., Stuttgart und Weimar 2001, S. 66/67.

MARCEL [Reich-Ranicki], Hüben und Drüben. Hans Baumann, in: Die Zeit 1962; den Artikel erhält man im Internet unter: http://www.zeit.de/archiv/1962.

DERS., Literarisches Leben in Deutschland. Kommentare und Pamphlete, München 1965.

RÜHLE, Günther, Theater für die Republik im Spiegel der Kritik, Bd. 2: 1926–1933, Berlin: Henschelverlag Kunst und Gesellschaft 1988, S. 678–683.

RÜSEN, Jörn, Johann Gustav Droysen, in: Deutsche Historiker, Bd. 2, hg. v. Hans-Ulrich Wehler, Göttingen 1971.

SIMONIS, Annette, Art. Ernst Cassirer, in: Metzler Lexikon Literatur- und Kulturtheorie. Ansätze – Personen – Grundbegriffe, hg. v. Ansgar Nünning, 2. überarb. Aufl., Stuttgart und Weimar 2001, S. 79/80.

Milet
Ergebnisse der Ausgrabungen und Untersuchungen seit dem Jahr 1899
Begr. v. Theodor Wiegand.
Im Auftrag des Deutschen Archäologischen Instituts
Hrsg. v. Volkmar von Graeve
7 Bände

Band 1: Bauwerke in Milet, Teil 10
Berthold F. Weber
■ Die römischen Heroa von Milet
2005. XIV, 171 Seiten. 94 Abb. 48 Tafeln. 7 Faltkarten. 2 Beilagen. Leinen.
ISBN 978-3-11-016260-8   (ISBN10: 3-11-016260-1)

In diesem Band der Milet-Reihe werden die beiden innerhalb der Stadt Milet gelegenen kaiserzeitlichen Ehrengräber behandelt. Beide Bauwerke, das Heroon II, ein Grabbau in der Form eines Antentempels auf einem Podium, und das Heroon III, ein dominanter Gewölbebau in einem Peristylhof, werden mit analytischer Bauaufnahme, vollständigem Bauteilekatalog und wissenschaftlicher Rekonstruktion vorgelegt.

Band 3: Feldforschungen im Latmos, Teil 6
Anneliese Peschlow-Bindokat
■ Die karische Stadt Latmos
2005. XII, 62 Seiten. 11 Abb. 128 Tafeln. 1 zweifarb. Tafel. 1 Falttafel 4 Faltkarten. Leinen.
ISBN 978-3-11-018238-5   (ISBN10: 3-11-018238-6)

Mit diesem ersten Band einer Reihe siedlungskundlicher Arbeiten des Gebiets von Herakleia am Latmos legt die Autorin die Ergebnisse ihrer Feldforschung der karischen Stadt Latmos vor. Genau und detailliert werden die Befestigungen, die Innenbebauung, der Bezirk vor den Stadtmauern und die Nekropole von Latmos beschrieben. Zahlreiche Abbildungen, ein Katalog der Wohnanlagen sowie ein Aufsatz über die Münzen von Latmos ergänzen die Darstellung.

Wolfgang Gaitzsch
■ Eisenfunde aus Pergamon
Geräte, Werkzeuge und Waffen
2005. XIV, 225 Seiten. 30 Abb. 76 Tafeln. 1 Farbtafel. Leinen.
ISBN 978-3-11-018240-8   (ISBN10: 3-11-018240-8)
(Pergamenische Forschungen 14)

WDEG de Gruyter
Berlin · New York

Ioannis Vassis
■ Initia Carminum Byzantinorum
2005. LIV, 932 Seiten. Leinen.
ISBN 978-3-11-018543-0
(Supplementa Byzantina / Texte und Untersuchungen 8)

Dieses Nachschlagewerk listet alphabetisch die ersten Verse von rund 20.000 byzantinischen Gedichten auf: profanen wie religiösen, edierten wie ungedruckten, in der Hoch- wie in der Volkssprache seit Beginn des 4. bis zum Ende des 15. Jhs. Jedem Anfangsvers werden alle nötigen Informationen über Verfasser, Sujet, Ausgabeort und Umfang eines Gedichts beigegeben.

■ Eustathii Thessalonicensis De emendanda vita monachica
Hrsg. v. Karin Metzler

2006. VIII, 56*, 270 S. Leinen.
ISBN 978-3-11-018904-9
(Corpus Fontium Historiae Byzantinae. Series Berolinensis 45)

Die Schrift, in der der Erzbischof Eustathios von Thessalonike (ca. 1115–1195) mit den Mönchen seiner Diözese wegen ihrer Weltlichkeit ins Gericht geht, wird in einer neuen kritischen Edition vorgelegt und durch Prolegomena und Indices erschlossen; eine parallel gedruckte deutsche Übersetzung eröffnet auch Interessierten über das byzantinistische Fachpublikum hinaus den Zugang.

Karin Metzler
■ Eustathios von Thessalonike und das Mönchtum
Untersuchungen und Kommentar zur Schrift „De emendanda vita monachica"

2006. Ca. 630 Seiten. Leinen.
ISBN 978-3-11-018905-6
(Supplementa Byzantina 9)

Der Untersuchungsband analysiert den historischen, literarischen und theologischen Hintergrund der Schrift „De emendanda vita monachica" und geht in einem Stellenkommentar den Problemen nach, die der rhetorisch ausgefeilte und an Anspielungen überreiche Text stellt.

Beide Bände sind auch als Set erhältlich:
2006. ISBN 978-3-11-019070-0

de Gruyter
Berlin · New York